Without Parallel

The Pantheon
Asia Library
New Approaches to the
New Asia

No part of the world has changed so much in recent years as Asia, or awakened such intense American interest. But much of our scholarship, like much of our public understanding, is based on a previous era. The Asia Library has been launched to provide the needed information on the new Asia, and in so doing to develop both the new methods and the new sympathies needed to understand it. Our purpose is not only to publish new work but to experiment with a wide variety of approaches which will reflect these new realities and their perception by those in Asia and the West.

Our books aim at different levels and audiences, from the popular to the more scholarly, from high schools to the universities, from pictorial to documentary presentations. All books will be available in paperback.

Suggestions for additions to the Asia Library are welcome.

Without Parallel

The American-Korean Relationship Since 1945

EDITED BY

Frank Baldwin

PANTHEON BOOKS
A Division of Random House, New York

Bernard Wideman gratefully acknowledges Kim Chi-ha and Ronin Publications, Ltd., Japan, for permission to reprint Kim Chi-ha's poem "The Road to Seoul," which first appeared in *Ronin* no. 2 (March 1972).

Mr. Wideman would also like to thank Kim Chi-ha for permission to translate and use his poem "Groundless Rumor," which first appeared in the monthly *Sasanggye* (*The Realm of Ideas*) in March 1972.

A portion of "Political Economics of Factor Inputs in Korean Agriculture" by Bernard Wideman was first published in the January 1973 edition of *Korea Journal* (The Korean National Commission for UNESCO).

Library of Congress Cataloging in Publication Data

Baldwin, Frank.
Without Parallel: The American-Korean Relationship Since 1945.

(The Pantheon Asia Library)
Includes bibliographical references.
1. United States—Foreign relations—Korea—Addresses, essays, lectures. 2. Korea—Foreign relations—United States—Addresses, essays, lectures. 3. Korea—History—1945-   —Addresses, essays, lectures.
I. Title. E183.8K7B34   1974   327.73'0519   73-18718
ISBN 0-394-47546-1
ISBN 0-394-70642-0 (pbk.)

To the People of Korea

Contents

Without Parallel

Introduction
Frank Baldwin

I

America's three-decade intervention in Korea has shattered an ancient East Asian society. Millions were killed and wounded; millions more became refugees separated from their families and birthplaces. Twenty-nine years after World War II and twenty-one years after the Korean War, the Korean people and peninsula are still divided into two hostile regimes. The consequences to the United States have also been grave. America suffered casualties of 33,629 killed and 150,000 wounded in the Korean War and has spent tens of billions of dollars for the security and economic development of the Republic of Korea (R.O.K.). The belief that U.S. policies in Korea were a successful model for resisting communism in Asia led directly to the U.S. intervention in Vietnam. Ironically, although American troops were withdrawn from Vietnam when the Vietnam War ended in disaster, a U.S. expeditionary force remains in South Korea to "ensure stability in Northeast Asia," a hostage to strategies and ambitions of the cold war past.

American involvement in Korea occurred at a moment of singular renaissance for the Korean people. Japan's crushing defeat in 1945 meant political and cultural liberation for the Korean peninsula. It was a chance to re-establish the Korean nation after thirty-five years of harsh Japanese colonial rule, and to decisively break free of a millennium of pervasive Chinese influence into a new era of Korean cultural expression. Unlike many areas and peoples that came under foreign colonial rule in the nineteenth and early twentieth centuries, Korea was a unified country when it lost its independence to Japan in 1910. The Yi Dynasty had ruled since the late fourteenth century; a literati bureaucracy administered a highly centralized government which maintained effective control over a peasant agricultural society. A homogeneous population speaking a com-

3

mon language lived on a distinct geographical unit, the Korean peninsula, where they had lived for over a thousand years.

However, Korea lacked political sovereignty. The Korean Kingdom was a tributary state to China, whereby China provided military protection in return for ritual deference and assurance that Korea would not align with a power hostile to China. China intervened against the Japanese invasion of Korea in the late sixteenth century to keep the Korean flank of its border regions secure. During centuries of peace, however, China did not station troops on Korean soil or intrude into Korea's domestic affairs. Nevertheless, Chinese cultural influence was ubiquitous and dominant from the long, steady flow of Chinese ideas and civilization into the peninsula. Confucianism shaped Korean values and attitudes and was the core of Korea's philosophic tradition; Chinese modes of government were adopted; and written Chinese was the official language and the literati class's favored form of expression. In a very real sense, Korea lacked cultural autonomy, so powerful was the prestige of things Chinese. Beneath these Chinese patterns, of course, a native Korean culture—the Korean language with its precise *han'gŭl* writing system, religious forms sustained by animistic East Asian religious beliefs, and distinctive family and lineage systems—formed a strong undercurrent of indigenous tradition and culture.

In 1876 Japan, repeating the pattern of its own opening by the West, compelled Korea to sign the Kanghwa Treaty and to open diplomatic relations. Korea became formally independent but economic weakness and political disunity left the peninsula defenseless against predatory neighbors. China reasserted an interest in Korea in the 1880s, despite its own territorial losses and humiliations by the Western powers, in a move to regain lost grandeur—and to thwart Japan. But Japan ended Chinese pretensions in the Sino-Japanese War (1894–1895) and gained undisputed authority toward Korea by defeating Russia in the Russo-Japanese War (1904–1905). Korea lost control of its foreign relations in 1905 with the establishment of a Japanese protectorate, only thirty years after Japan had opened an "independent" Korea to the world. In 1910, after bitter and prolonged resistance by Korean insurgents, Korea was annexed to Japan and ceased to exist as a country. Korea became Chōsen, an integral part of the Japanese Empire, and until August 15, 1945, remained under a particularly intense colonial control compared to other colonial areas, like India and Indochina, which were far from their metropolitan centers.

Allied victory in World War II offered Koreans a chance to re-establish or create new Korean political, social, and cultural patterns free of foreign interference. Japan was in ashes, civil war raged in China, and the Soviet Union, although victorious, had been ravaged by the war and was most concerned with Eastern Europe. The new institutions would be shaped by the ideologies and social changes that had affected Korea since the late nineteenth century, including democracy, Christianity, socialism, and communism. The social injustice and severe political cleavages of Korean society meant that the new society almost certainly would be formed in the cauldron of revolutionary violence. But the new political and economic structures would erase the humiliation of foreign interference and a new generation of Koreans would become citizens of a politically and culturally sovereign nation. Or so it seemed to millions of Koreans in August 1945.

American involvement in Korea before 1945 was minimal. The slight American presence that began in the 1880s—diplomatic representation and missionary activity—was eroded by the 1905 protectorate and engulfed by annexation five years later. The insignificant U.S. economic interest was eclipsed by Japanese capital even before 1905. Political interest was so slight that requests by King Kojong in the 1880s for retired U.S. military officers to train a Korean army were lost in Washington and went unanswered for years. Korea never excited the imagination of Americans, as had China by its sheer size and cultural majesty or Japan with its restless energy, rapid progress, and military challenge to the West. President Theodore Roosevelt was ignorant of Korea in 1905 and his indifference was typical of Washington and the American public then and later. Too poor, too far away, conceded to be in Japan's sphere of influence and under tough Japanese control, Korea was beyond American reach and attention until 1945. Only a small, determined band of missionaries remained in Chōsen after 1910. Preaching a stiff, conservative brand of Christianity, they held on until severe repression from the 1930s on followed by impending war finally forced them out.

The American forces that landed at Inch'ŏn, Korea, in September 1945 were not a reassertion of old imperial interests, as was the case with England, France, and Holland in Southeast Asia, but were a harbinger of America's new role in postwar Asia.

II

America has been deeply involved in Korea since World War II. The U.S.-U.S.S.R. agreement in August 1945 on a temporary zonal division of the peninsula to accept the surrender of Japanese forces gave America a limited "temporary" responsibility for southern Korea. An American military government ruled the south directly until 1948 when the Republic of Korea was established under U.S. auspices. American military intervention in 1950 preserved South Korea; U.S. troops remained in the R.O.K. after the war, one infantry division positioned on the demilitarized zone until 1971 as part of the U.S. guarantee of South Korea's security. Since 1948 the United States has paid directly a large percentage of the R.O.K.'s annual budget and has trained, armed, and supplied its military forces. By 1973, U.S. military and economic aid amounted to approximately $11 billion.[1] On the international front, the United States championed the Republic of Korea at the United Nations and supported it diplomatically. In addition to this vast official involvement, American citizens have provided massive aid to South Korea through private and religious relief and assistance programs. *No other country has been significantly involved in South Korea since 1945.* (Japan's role has grown since the establishment of diplomatic relations between it and the Republic of Korea in 1965.)

The post–World War II involvement in Korea differs from areas where U.S. power was traditionally paramount. No United Fruit Company dabbled in Korean politics. The Korean peninsula lacked natural resources and market potential, and it was too politically unstable to attract American capital. This is not to suggest that there were *no* American economic interests in

Korea. The "national security institutions" were staffed by Wall Street lawyers with a keen interest in American economic supremacy. And the Pentagon Papers show the U.S. government's concern with keeping entree to Asian markets and resources and denying areas to communist control because market access might be curtailed. To the extent that there was an important American economic interest in Korea, it was at the rarefied level of a national objective rather than the vulgar, direct manipulation of an International Telephone and Telegraph.

Domestic ethnic politics also was not a factor in the U.S. involvement in the Korean peninsula. Korea was not Poland or Israel. In the late 1940s there were only a few thousand Americans of Korean descent (the number increased greatly in the 1960s due to changes in the immigration laws). Free from ethnic pressure politics, the Congress might have limited the U.S. involvement, but instead it passively and indifferently acquiesced to executive branch policies. The most striking instance was allowing President Harry S. Truman to go to war in Korea in June 1950 without a declaration of war by the Congress, as required by the Constitution. This fateful lapse contributed to the plunge into Vietnam a decade later.

The U.S. intervention in distant Korea was due to post–World War II strategic interests in Asia. Those interests were defined by the military/foreign affairs bureaucracy and the senior political leadership—presidents, secretaries of state, and their foreign policy advisers. Policy was made in the State Department and in the offices of the new "national security institutions" created after 1945: the office of the Secretary of Defense (OSD), the office of the Assistant Secretary of Defense for International Security Affairs (ISA), and the Central Intelligence Agency (CIA), with assistance from think tanks and academic centers.

Initially, the U.S. objective was to block the spread of Russian power and influence. But Korea was an inconvenient place to draw the line. The U.S.S.R. shared a common border and had historical security and economic interests in the Korean peninsula. The United States had excluded the U.S.S.R. from the occupation in Japan, and hoped to negotiate a favorable political settlement for the entire Korean peninsula but at least to keep the area south of the 38th parallel out of Soviet hands.

The Cold War confrontation developed immediately in Korea. Although U.S.-U.S.S.R. negotiations continued until 1947, American policy moved irrevocably toward the division of the peninsula into communist and non-communist halves as the only way to secure the southern area. As the rivalry between the U.S.S.R. and the United States deepened into the Cold War, Korea began to take on global significance. American leaders accepted a set of strategic and ideological premises that assumed conflict between the communists and the "Free World." American policy toward the Soviet Union was codified into a doctrine: communism was monolithic; any increase in territory controlled by communism weakened the West; the United States had to resist the spread of communism; appeasement in one area would only encourage communist subversion and attacks elsewhere.[2]

The original "temporary" involvement was transformed into a crucial responsibility to keep southern Korea non-communist as proof of America's "will" and the resolve of the entire "Free World." Korea was important because *everywhere* was important. U.S. leaders gradually appreciated the special hazards of Korea and the limitations on the use of American power there; the United States tried to reduce the risk of conflict with the Soviet Union by negotiations and political moves. But as long as keeping southern Korea non-communist was regarded as vital to U.S. survival, the possibility of being involved in a war was great.

The U.S. intervention in Korea to block the Soviet Union overlooked one factor: the Koreans. It must be emphasized that in addition to "containing" the U.S.S.R. (later China) in Korea, the United States intervened in a local *Korean* revolutionary situation. American power collided not with the Red Army but with the Korean revolution, Korean demands for social justice and rapid political change. The U.S.S.R. was initially quite cautious. It agreed to a temporary zonal division of the country, halted its forces at the 38th parallel, and accepted U.S. initiatives for a postwar trusteeship for Korea. But Bruce Cumings shows in his essay "American Policy and Korean Liberation" that the Koreans had formed a government before the Americans landed in September 1945 and were impatient to rule themselves without foreign interference.

Korea was in revolutionary turmoil due to the deprivation of the Korean masses during the colonial period, their demand for land and rice, the hatred of conservative collaborators, the determination to re-establish an independent Korea, and the collapse of authority and government. It is crucial to an understanding of these and later events, including the Korean civil war, to note that the revolutionary situation was *indigenous to Korea.* It followed from the hardships and injustices of thirty-five years of Japanese rule, and the Left's claim to power was earned in the resistance to Japan. The revolutionary situation was *not* brought in by the Red Army in the north or communist agents dispatched to the south in late 1945.

To achieve U.S. objectives vis-à-vis the Soviet Union, the American command first had to contend with the Left in the south. The U.S. military government wanted order, stability, and control. Whether the Korean demands for immediate self-government and reforms were communist-inspired or advocated by non-communist radicals and liberals, the U.S. command would not risk a potential challenge to its control. Furthermore, the presence of Russian troops above the 38th parallel and the cooperation of southern communists with the north led many U.S. officials to equate the Korean Left with the U.S.S.R.

It was not initially U.S. policy to create an Oriental despotism to hold the line against the Soviet Union. During the years of U.S. military rule, American officials looked for "reasonable men" to form a "democratic," stable government, men who undersood that a divided Korea, half under American influence, was a "reasoned" solution. For a time, Syngman Rhee was out of favor with the United States because he intransigently opposed efforts to negotiate with the U.S.S.R. But the search for a political compromise in the south failed. Nationalistic and revolutionary elements rejected American interference; they preferred a united Korea under a leftist government to a divided peninsula under alien authority.

The Koreans refused to be reasonable, complained Lt. Gen. John R. Hodge, the U.S. military commander in Korea. Hodge suggested that the United States withdraw and leave Korea to the "whirlwind," but Washington ruled that there could be no retreat. The United States had no alternative but, in Bruce Cumings's phrase, to begin "conscious planning for counterrevolution." The American command threw its support to a privileged conservative elite against the desperate peasantry. The U.S. military government financed and armed rightist forces, encouraged the police to eradicate dissent, and used U.S. Army units to suppress protests. By 1948 the Left had been destroyed, gone underground, or been driven north, and the way was clear to establish a separate anti-communist government in the south.

Earlier treatments of these events have emphasized American "blunders" of a technical nature: the absence of Korean linguists, the U.S. Army's initial treatment of Koreans as defeated enemies, and the delay in receiving instructions from Washington. This approach has conceded that American actions were counterrevolutionary but implied that it was all an accident. Cumings cuts through these ephemeral errors to the core of U.S. policy in Korea: a political decision to use American power to maintain an American presence on the Asian continent. Of course, this is not to say that there were not clumsy pre-imperium mistakes. American power in 1945–1946 was not as majestic as it became in the mid-1960s. The United States had been only partially and temporarily mobilized for war with Germany and Japan, and the huge draftee armies were being dismantled in 1945. More importantly, the United States lacked the infrastructure to support global ambitions. That would come only in the late 1940s and 1950s with the establishment of the Central Intelligence Agency, the Ford Foundation's multimillion-dollar support for anti-communist centers and programs, the creation of schools of international affairs and East Asian institutes at the famous universities, and the production of a legion of American Asian specialists to execute and rationalize American policies.

By 1947 the U.S position in Korea was at a dangerous impasse. Negotiations with the Soviet Union had again failed to reach a political solution to end zonal occupation and create a unified Korea. At the same time, the U.S. troops stationed in Korea were thought to be needed in Europe and American military leaders were apprehensive about defending southern Korea if the increased tension with the U.S.S.R. led to war. Some of the logistical considerations deemed unimportant in 1945 now loomed large in Pentagon thinking. Korea was very far away, at the end of a long supply line, and defensible only by the use of facilities in Japan. Furthermore, it was a liability without compensating strategic advantage; even General MacArthur's headquarters in Japan did not regard the peninsula as vital to the defense of Japan.

The intractable political situation in Korea and America's limited military capabilities led to basic policy decisions: to establish a separate government in south Korea, to obtain international support for the new government by involving the United Nations in Korea, and to reduce the cost and risk of direct U.S. involvement by disengagement behind a UN screen. Southern Koera was to be kept non-communist by imaginative *political* action.

The United States took the "Korean question" to the United Nations in September 1947 with the request that it supervise elections to form a "unified, democratic Korea." Since two years of direct negotiations with the Soviet Union in Korea had failed to bring agreement on peninsula-wide elections, the American move was actually intended to obtain a UN sanction for U.S.-sponsored elections in the south—the political division of Korea. The U.S. bloc in the UN approved the dispatch of a United Nations Temporary Commission on Korea (UNTCOK) to investigate the possibility of a "national election."

The actions of the UNTCOK in Korea from December 1947 to May 1948 were the UN's first fateful involvement. It would be difficult to overstate the importance of the commission's decisions or the degree to which they were subsequently misrepresented by the United States and South Korea. Denied entry into North Korea, the commission decided to observe the 1948 elections in southern Korea alone. By this single act the UNTCOK lent UN prestige to the division of Korea and to the Syngman Rhee government of the Republic of Korea which emerged from the elections. This was a highly controversial and political decision. The commission's authority was doubtful and it lacked the staff to make more than token observations. Even before the voting, the commission lost its slight chance for objectivity and independence by making compromises with the American military command. The UNTCOK had only nine observation groups to observe elections throughout South Korea. Neverthe-less, it reported that "the results of the ballot were a valid ex-pression of the free will of the electorate in those parts of Korea which were accessible to the Commission and in which the in-habitants constituted approximately two-thirds of the people of all Korea." [3] The United States and South Korea misrepresented the commission's extremely limited role and described the elec-tions as having been "sanctioned" or "supervised" by the UN. U.S. government documents routinely repeat the phrase "A re-public was consequently formed in South Korea in 1948 under the aegis of the United Nations." [4]

The United States completed the coup d'état in December 1948 by gaining a limited General Assembly resolution regard-ing South Korea which then turned magically into UN support for the republic. General Assembly Resolution 195 (III), De-cember 12, 1948, declared that

> there has been established a lawful government (the Govern-ment of the Republic of Korea) having effective control and jurisdiction over that part of Korea where the Temporary Commission was able to observe and consult and in which the great majority of the people of all Korea reside; that this Gov-ernment is based on elections which were a valid expression of the free will of the electorate of that part of Korea which were observed by the Temporary Commission; and *that this is the only such government in Korea.* [Emphasis added.]

During the debate on this resolution the United States con-ceded that the R.O.K. was not the only government in Korea. However, after passage the United States and the R.O.K. cited this resolution in support of South Korea's claim to be the only legitimate government in Korea, thus entitled to sole membership in the UN.[5]

The UN involvement in Korea in 1947–1948 was a great cold war victory for the United States. In June 1950 the United States, with the support of Secretary-General Trygve Lie and in the absence of the U.S.S.R. delegation, obtained UN sanction for the *prior* U.S. military intervention in Korea. The U.S. gov-ernment *led* the UN into the Korean War; the Truman admini-stration then claimed that it was *supporting* the United Nations by providing forces to fight in Korea! Utterly swept along by events and U.S. pressures, the UN agreed to the formation of a United Nations Command (UNC) in Korea in July 1950. That command had the moral prestige of the "world body," carried the UN flag, and had token troop contributions from some UN members. But it was actually an American command with UN elements for window dressing. From Douglas MacArthur on, the "UN Commander" was an American general who reported directly to the U.S. Joint Chiefs of Staff, not to the United Nations. The "UN Command" fiction was challenged only once: when General MacArthur's push toward Manchuria in the fall of 1950 dragged U.S. allies into a war with China. The "UN Command" was useful to the Truman administration because it internationalized and legitimized the American intervention.[6] The war was initially more palatable to the American public because of its high esteem for the UN.

Perhaps it was impossible for the UN to be neutral and universal in the midst of the intense ideological and political struggles of the postwar years. Communist countries matched the West in fighting for partisan advantage regardless of the UN Charter. Yet the degree to which the UN was politicized and manipulated for U.S. foreign policy objectives was extraordinary. Consider that China intervened in the war to protect its borders but, at U.S. insistence, was branded an "aggressor" and kept out of the UN for more than two decades. The North Koreans were fighting a civil war but they were also declared "aggressors," almost destroyed by the "UN Command," and excluded from all UN agencies until finally granted membership in the World Health Organization in May 1973, reportedly over U.S. objections (the United States had argued in earlier years that "disease knows no boundaries").

The Korean War erupted early on June 25, 1950, with a coordinated North Korean attack across the 38th parallel.[7] R.O.K. forces were driven back and U.S. military officers reported that a quick northern victory was imminent. U.S. leaders faced a clear choice: to withdraw the U.S. military advisory group and aid mission and permit a communist victory or to intervene militarily to keep South Korea non-communist.

President Harry S. Truman decided to intervene, and American policy-makers and academic specialists (often the same individuals, perhaps accounting for the similarity of viewpoint) have overwhelmingly judged that decision courageous and correct.[8] It might now well be argued that it would have been more courageous to resist the pro-intervention pressures and to have kept hands off Korea. However, it is more pertinent to ask *why* the United States intervened and what the intervention meant to *Korea*.

President Truman and Secretary of State Dean Acheson have explained at length in their memoirs and elsewhere that the United States intervened in Korea because the North Korean offensive was regarded as a *Soviet attack*. The official consensus in June 1950 was that North Korea was a satellite under direct Soviet control. Convinced that communism was monolithic, U.S. leaders apparently believed that the U.S.S.R. ordered the attack as a probe in its general challenge to the West. If the United States did not respond in Korea, the Soviet Union would be encouraged to attack in other trouble spots. According to this analysis, the United States had to strike back forcefully to keep South Korea non-communist and to deter Russian attacks elsewhere. Compared with this sense of fundamental mortal confrontation, the other reasons for U.S. military action in Korea, such as considerations of national prestige, the opportunity to mobilize the nation (see Robert Simmons on NSC-68), and domestic political advantages, were less important.

Since the United States intervened in Korea to "repulse Soviet expansion," the degree of Soviet influence on the start and conduct of the war becomes crucial. Robert Simmons has examined the Soviet role and concludes that it was minimal. The best evidence now available suggests that the Soviet Union did not order or compel North Korea to attack the South. On the contrary, it appears that North Korea took the initiative in conceiving and executing military action. Perhaps the most obscured aspect of the war is that the Koreans in the north, who were communists, wanted to unify the Korean peninsula. It was, after all, their country, from the Yalu River to Pusan.

It is true that the Soviet Union did not *prevent* the D.P.R.K. from attacking the south, which it *might* have been able to do. But that is far different from the assertion that the attack was conceived in Moscow as part of world communism's timetable to destroy the west.[9] At a minimum, the Truman administration erred in thinking it was "stopping" the Soviet Union when actually it was crushing the local North Korean communists (many of whom had been born and had lived in the south). This was an inevitable misjudgment rooted in American policy in Korea from the early months of the U.S. occupation in 1945. For almost five years the United States had contrived for prestige and strategic reasons to hold on to southern Korea by insisting that the communists in the north were merely puppets of the Soviet Union. U.S. authorities repeatedly declared that communism had come into Korea with the Red Army and was not an indigenous force, *although there had been a Korean Communist party since 1925 and two decades of extensive communist political activity and resistance to the Japanese.*

Simmons's article recalls the essential fact, rarely if ever mentioned in the extensive writing about the Korean War, that it was a *civil war* fought initially by communist and noncommunist Koreans to resolve the basic political issues remaining from Korea's liberation, an extension by conventional means of the guerrilla struggles in the south since 1945. Many of the northern elite were former revolutionary veterans of the guerrilla warfare against the Japanese in Manchuria and China in the 1930s and 1940s. Much of the southern leadership, particularly in political life, the police, and the army, had served the Japanese. The two Korean elites represented radically different social forces, ideologies, and ideals. That both were armed, supplied, and encouraged by outside powers as part of a larger ideological struggle did not change the intra-Korean nature of the war.

Whether Truman and Acheson "deterred" the Soviet Union from planned military moves against the "Free World" remains highly speculative, since the U.S.S.R.'s intention to make such attacks has not been established. A comprehensive review of the consequences of the Korean intervention is beyond the scope of these remarks but a partial negative listing would include the following: a very costly commitment to South Korea's security, reversal of the tentative policy of accommodation with the People's Republic of China and the subsequent twenty years of hostility to China, domestic mobilization and the creation of a garrison economy (Pentagon capitalism), and heightened anti-communist hysteria at home culminating in McCarthyism.

What would have happened in Korea if the United States had not intervened? The war would have been over in two or three weeks with total casualties of perhaps less than 50,000. Several million people opposed to communism would have come under communist rule and probably, but not certainly, there would have been reprisals. A single communist Korean state would have been established, the unity of a millennium restored, and national energies immediately directed to urgent economic and social reconstruction.

The United States intervention prolonged the war by more than three years, bringing an estimated 4.5 million Korean, Chinese, and American casualties. The United States attained its objective of keeping the southern half of the peninsula non-communist, but the Koreans remain divided almost three decades later.

III

The Korean War was a watershed for American involvement in Asia. It confirmed, reinforced, and sanctified cold war verities for U.S. leaders and strategists. Their assumptions had withstood the test of actual warfare in Asia. The major lessons of Korea for the military/foreign affairs elite included the following: U.S. action had stopped a communist military offensive; exposed non-communist territory could be held by vigorous military and political action; China and the U.S.S.R., despite bluster and fraternal rhetoric, would intervene directly only when their own territory was threatened; and a native army could be organized and perform reasonably well in combat—if screened and supported by U.S. forces. The national security managers learned from Korea to stand and fight: Asian communism could be contained by U.S. arms. The memoirs of America's Korean War generals stress this conviction. It is also apparent in the writings of upper-echelon national security bureaucrats like Townsend Hoopes and Chester Cooper. To such men Korea was a success for America's anti-communist strategy and it pointed the way to defeating a "similar" communist insurgency in Vietnam.[10]

The Korean War shifted the object of the containment policy in Asia from the Soviet Union to China. While the United States intervened in Korea ostensibly to stop Russian communism, by war's end the containment of China was the principal goal of American Far Eastern policy. Given an emotional and racial twist by the savage combat between U.S. and Chinese forces, an aspect missing in the hostility with the Soviet Union, this policy continued for two decades. All hope was lost for an understanding with the Chinese revolution as John Foster Dulles treated the leaders of China with the Calvinist contempt reserved for the truly damned and U.S. military men muttered that perhaps it was time to "nuke the Chinks." The United States ringed China with bases from Korea on the northeast rim to Pakistan in the far south. With bombers in the 1950s and missiles a decade later, America's atomic arsenal in Asia was targeted against China. A series of bilateral treaties was concluded with anti-communist countries and the multilateral Southeast Asia Treaty Organization (SEATO) was established in 1954 to "block communist expansion" into Southeast Asia. Almost unnoticed, the United States replaced the French in Vietnam, vowing to protect Indochina from "Chinese aggression."

South Korea's role in American Far Eastern strategy was transformed by the war, the policy of containing China, and the U.S. military buildup on the peninsula. Designated a "forward defense country" by the Pentagon, the Republic of Korea became a valued site for air bases and atomic weapons (politically sensitive in Japan). The R.O.K. army was expanded to more than 600,000 men (from about 100,000 before the war) and became a model for U.S. military advisers trying to organize a native army in South Vietnam. *The concept of the R.O.K. military as a reliable Asian army available for service in Southeast Asia* was born on February 5, 1954, when President Syngman Rhee offered a South Korean division to fight in Laos. The Joint Chiefs of Staff carefully considered the proposal, noting that "it would represent a concrete step in fostering unity of action by anti-communist Asiatic forces in countering Communist aggression in Asia, with immense psychological gain to the Free World." [11] But on March 1, 1954, they regretfully rejected the offer "at this time," partly because the world would see it as a "case of United States employment of hapless oriental puppets for the benefits of the white imperialists." [12] Slightly more than a decade later R.O.K. forces, secretly paid by the Defense Department, were fighting in Vietnam.

The U.S. commitment to South Korea changed dramatically during and after the Korean War. Before June 1950 the peninsula was regarded as a dangerous cul-de-sac; American troops had been removed and the United States had no formal obligation to defend the R.O.K. Secretary of State Acheson omitted South Korea from the U.S. defense perimeter outlined in his famous Press Club speech on January 12, 1950. After June 1950, however, the limited and uncertain commitment of U.S. assistance and prestige was replaced with almost total American involvement. South Korea's security was guaranteed by the 1954 Mutual Defense Treaty wherein the United States recognized that an attack on the Republic of Korea would be "dangerous to its own peace and safety" and declared that "it would act to meet the common danger." [13] As tangible evidence of the U.S. commitment, a residual force of 50,000–70,000 American troops—two infantry divisions plus supporting ground and air units, including nuclear weapons—was stationed in South Korea after the 1953 armistice. (This was reduced in 1970–1971 to 20,000–30,000 troops.) A powerful military advisory group supervised training of the R.O.K. military, certified their professional performance, and selected officers for advanced study in the United States. Military aid, barely squeezed from a reluctant Congress in early 1950, now flowed into South Korea in the form of new weapons, equipment, supplies, and direct budget subsidies to the R.O.K. government. The United States provided $5.5 billion in military aid from 1953 to 1972, compared with a paltry $11.7 million until 1952.[14]

The rationale for U.S. intervention in Korea also changed during and after the war. The 4.5 million casualties to keep South Korea non-communist had to be sanctioned by a higher value than "containment." Thus the Rhee regime became part of the "Free World," the "defense of freedom" became America's "burden" in Korea, and U.S. troops along the demilitarized zone were described as guarding "freedom's frontier." Pentagon and State Department officials dutifully marched to annual congressional hearings to recite a litany about "freedom in the Republic of Korea." The testimony of Howard B. Porter, then U.S. Ambassador to South Korea, before a subcommittee of the Senate Committee on Foreign Relations in February 1970 is typical.

> There has been a substantial evolution towards a working democracy. All of the formal institutions exist—a constitution, universal suffrage, an elected President and Assembly, political parties. There is also a vocal press which, like the National Assembly, has criticized and opposed the government on important issues.
>
> These institutions, in their present form, are young and still feeling their way. . . . The press is frequently in opposition. But even here the tone of editorials has changed noticeably in past years from one of shrill and automatic criticism to one of more responsible comment.
>
> But if the essence of democracy is that the public can choose its leaders, and that public opinion should influence their action after they are chosen, then these essentials do exist in Korea today. The government is admittedly very powerful. . . .[15]

"The tone of editorials has changed noticeably in past years" indeed. Mr. Porter neglected to mention that the change was due to increased R.O.K. Central Intelligence Agency (R.O.K. CIA) censorship and terror against the press. The remainder of his testimony, a pastiche of half-truths and prevarications, is most noteworthy for its utter contempt for the intelligence of the Foreign Relations Committee and the American public. When Porter testified, the Park regime was already a police state with but a few trappings—the "formal institutions" of constitutional government—to avoid foreign criticism. In 1972 the same Park government emasculated those "formal institutions." From October to December 1973, protests by students, journalists, and Christian leaders demanded an end to R.O.K. CIA surveillance and abolition of constitutional changes imposed in late 1972. The government responded with unprecedented harshness and warned that there would be no return to the pre-October 1972 constitution. Howard Porter, however, had long since been rewarded for his loyal recital before Congress by appointment as Under Secretary of State.

James Palais, in his essay for this collection, has systematically reviewed the political history of South Korea to show the evolution from Rhee's disorganized dictatorship to Park's technocratic authoritarianism. South Korea's first quarter-century had little that could honestly be called freedom and less recognizable as democracy. Those concepts existed mainly in the statements of State Department spokesmen and South Korean propagandists.

American economic and technical assistance was the only major external influence on South Korea's economic development until after the normalization of relations with Japan in 1965. Modest amounts of aid began with the arrival of U.S. forces in 1945, and an Economic Cooperation Administration (ECA) aid mission was operating in South Korea before the Korean War. When the U.S. commitment to the R.O.K. changed during the war, the State Department had the task of strengthening the economic sector (while the Defense Department supervised the military buildup). The objective was to guide South Korea toward a "self-supporting economy," a formidable goal since the southern half of the peninsula was an unnatural economic unit lacking resources and even adequate electric power. Aid advisers hoped to gradually reduce American assistance and enable South Korea to finance its own defense costs and economic growth. From the 1954 Nathan Plan to the First Five-Year Plan (FFYP) in 1963, American aid officials worked to stimulate economic growth. But the destruction and dislocation of the war, combined with Syngman Rhee's indifference to planning and economic matters, reduced economic aid to stop-gap, subsistence handouts designed more to keep South Korea's desperate population from starvation and subversion than to raise the Gross National Product.

The 1961 military coup brought to power men who not only supported economic planning but counted on an effective performance in the economic sphere to overcome popular antipathy to their usurpation. The FFYP faltered in 1963 but U.S. capitalism intervened massively. The authoritative study of economic planning in South Korea describes the new U.S. intervention as follows:

A number of foreign advisory groups were drawn into the planning work to help the still relatively inexperienced Korean planners. In 1964 the U.S. Agency for International Development contracted with Robert Nathan Associates to provide a second team of planning experts . . . to work with and for the Korean government . . . to help them prepare the Second Plan. . . . Also the United States AID Mission took a very active and direct interest in the Korean government's planning from 1965 onward and, *in direct contrast to the normal pattern of relationships, functioned as a planning advisory group.* The AID mission and the Nathan team brought a number of experts in various aspects of planning to Korea in 1965 and 1966, who further contributed to the formulation of the Second Plan. Finally several teams were brought in to develop programs for particular sectors. These included an AID-supported study of the power industry and a World Bank-supported study of transportation. Thus there was much more participation of foreigners in the preparation of materials for and the formulation of the Second Five-Year Plan than there had been in any of Korea's previous planning efforts except the original Nathan Plan.[16] [Emphasis added.]

This assistance, supplemented by billions of dollars in grants and loans, additional billions in payment for the R.O.K. troops sent to Vietnam, and other aid was an important contribution to South Korea's development. American economists, particularly former AID officials, have not been reticent in claiming credit for their role or expressing satisfaction at the Republic of Korea's economic performance.[17] Two independent observers, however, authors of essays in this book, are far less sanguine.

Gerhard Breidenstein observed the South Korean "economic miracle" for three years, 1968–1971, as a visiting professor at Yonsei University in Seoul. Bernie Wideman lived in South Korea in 1972–1973 as a Ph.D. candidate from the University of Washington doing research on his doctoral dissertation. These were boom years, the money poured in from the Vietnam War, and Seoul was transformed as new office buildings reached toward the sky. The R.O.K. government and the U.S. AID mission churned out impressive statistics showing that exports and the GNP were increasing rapidly. South Korea was being "developed."

Neither Wideman nor Breidenstein disputes the impressive increases in GNP and exports over the last several years; they certainly do not begrudge South Koreans the hard-earned recovery from the war and the increase in national wealth so arduously achieved. Both authors refuse, however, to equate increased GNP with economic well-being or to ignore the moral question of earning foreign exchange by mercenary military service in Vietnam. They have looked behind the meretricious statistics to see who has benefitted, who has suffered, and where this development model leads.

Breidenstein read the statistics but he also visited the slums, interviewed deracinated, bewildered industrial workers, and saw the warrenlike textile sweatshops in Seoul's P'yŏngwha market. He saw the exploitation of young girls condemned to stitch their eyes and lives away fifteen hours a day for a pittance. In theory, labor laws protected the workers, but the authorities and management were in collusion and the laws were ignored. Other aspects of South Korea's "miracle" raised profound doubts about the values behind the development model. While American observers professed great satisfaction at South Korea's "astounding growth," Breidenstein concluded that any meaningful social justice was impossible under capitalism.

Wideman went to the countryside to see for himself what was being done to the Korean peasantry in the name of a higher GNP. He found that government policies, compounded by pervasive corruption and bureaucratic arrogance, were driving farmers off their land and turning them into unskilled day laborers in urban slums. He wrote of his observations in the *Far Eastern Economic Review* and other publications until the South Korean government deported him in August 1973 because of these articles.

To be fair to American and South Korean economic planners, they apparently believe that the development model criticized by Breidenstein and Wideman will eventually lead to social justice. Professional economists tend to compartmentalize economic and political moral questions, confident that development must precede such political questions as the equitable distribution of wealth. They argue that the pie must be baked before there can be discussion of who gets how many slices.[18]

In South Korea, the planners have been preoccupied with the first stage of development, the creation of wealth and a modest surplus. Their strategy has been to support business in order to accelerate capital accumulation and increase exports, to maintain severe pressure against labor and farmers to keep wages and prices down, and to emphasize high exports to earn foreign exchange. According to development theory, a "turning point" will come when labor scarcity will raise wages and the R.O.K. government will have a surplus to use for social investment and welfare. At that stage, a more-or-less welfare state will be formed and income redistribution, through tax policy for example, will become feasible. The government will then check glaring injustices in the accumulation of wealth because it may be threatened by elements in the private sector and because extreme disparities in income are a source of popular unrest. It will mediate between competing forces in the interest of justice and stability.

Is this likely to happen in South Korea? Actually, this model of U.S. economic and political pluralism has not worked elsewhere, including the United States, and it is not the evolving pattern in the Republic of Korea. To claim economic rewards and decent treatment there must be organized political power, and this is nonexistent. First, labor cannot organize or demand anything; it does not form a militant countervailing force against business or the government. Secondly, the Park administration has systematically destroyed political opposition, so that other kinds of social and political demands—for education, health care—cannot be aggregated and articulated. A paternal or enlightened government might emulate Bismarck and respond to obvious social needs without prodding. But aside from the rarity and difficulty of such statesmanship, South Korea's development strategy is dependent upon foreign borrowing and foreign investment. Foreign interests are in South Korea because labor costs are low—one-sixth to one-eighth of Japan's, for example—and they will not approve of tax or welfare policies that reduce profits (recent data, however, reportedly indicate a modest increase in real wages for urban workers). In a mixed capitalist system, without pressure from below, the chances of Korean workers and farmers getting a fair share of the increased wealth appear remote. It is more probable that they will be caught in a police state vise, working long hours for low wages, while the profits go to foreign capitalists and a small ruling elite in South Korea.

During the South Korean euphoria of the Vietnam War years, it was querulous if not subversive to express any basic doubts about this development model. By 1973, however, the Park government's authoritarian rule, heavy national debts, and the threat of impending Japanese economic domination had brought a re-examination of basic priorities and policies by many people out of government. In May 1973 a group of Christian ministers in South Korea published a Theological Declaration which included the following:

> The present dictatorship is responsible for the economic system in Korea, in which the powerful dominate the poor. The people, poor urban workers and rural peasants, are victims of severe exploitation and social and economic injustice. So-called "economic development" in Korea turned out to be the conspiracy of a few rulers against the poor people, and a curse to our environment.[19]

The Korean War demonstrated to U.S. strategists that the peninsula could only be defended with Japanese cooperation. For Japan's part, its conservative rulers saw cooperation with the United States as both highly profitable and a way of keeping communism half a peninsula away from Kyushu. Thus, U.S. and Japanese leaders agreed on *the strategic integration of Japan and South Korea into a military/political unit against North Korea and China.* Herbert Bix's bold essay on the Japan-South Korea relationship and American objectives in Northeast Asia discusses the broad context of regional integration. Bix reviews the *de facto* utilization of Japan during the war—bases, supply depots, repair facilities, armaments purchases, and R and R whoring for U.S. troops fresh from combat in Korea. The 1951 peace treaty and the security treaty, which was termed a "troop-stationing treaty," guaranteed American use of Japanese facilities after the war's end. Japan is still the logistics area for U.S. forces in South Korea and a secure espionage base for diverse intelligence forays against North Korea and China. The highly publicized 1968 *Pueblo* and 1969 EC-121 incidents were preceded by thousands of clandestine operations and electronic surveillance missions launched from U.S. bases in Japan.

From the American perspective, the U.S.-Japan-R.O.K. arrangements worked reasonably well in the 1950s. However, opposition to rearmament in Japan and anti-Japan sentiment in South Korea precluded an active Japanese military involvement in the peninsula.

By the early 1960s, American interests required that this popular opposition be overcome and that Japan assume a greater role in Korea. The United States sought to reduce its expenditures and forces in Korea, to find a way out of the open-ended and highly expensive commitment. This required that Japan be directly involved in Korea, for the United States could safely withdraw only when Japan was prepared to support South Korea economically, diplomatically, and, if possible, militarily. In addition, the deteriorating military situation in Vietnam suggested that South Korean troops might be needed for military operations in Indochina. The R.O.K. would need Japanese political support before committing troops overseas.

The 1965 R.O.K.-Japan Treaty provided the framework for South Korean participation in Vietnam, Japanese economic expansion into the Republic of Korea, and the integration of Japan and South Korea into U.S. military strategy for Northeast Asia. In particular, Japan's establishment of relations with South Korea but not with North Korea (in January 1974, the Japanese government still has not recognized the D.P.R.K.) and the anti-D.P.R.K. provisions of the treaty threw Japan's support to the Republic of Korea and gave President Park Chung Hee room to maneuver regarding Vietnam.

The bitter opposition in South Korea to the establishment of relations with Japan is best understood in historical perspective. To America, the treaty was a start toward disengagement from the peninsula but to Koreans it evoked memories and fears of colonial domination. Korean hatred of Japan and the Japanese was thick enough to cut in the early post–World War II years. Some Koreans had collaborated and prospered under Japanese rule, but most had only grudgingly acquiesced, and other thousands were killed, injured, tortured, and imprisoned for resistance. Their families suffered—and waited for liberation and justice. But liberation, three years of U.S. rule, and the new republic under Syngman Rhee brought no justice. Although an impeccable nationalist and foe of Japanese rule himself, Rhee made his peace with pro-Japan Korean conservatives after 1945 in return for their political support. He protected his new-found allies but also used and encouraged anti-Japanese sentiment. Anticommunism and anti-Japanism were Rhee's foreign policy. He made emotional public speeches that recalled Japanese brutalities, vitriolically attacked Japan for profiting from the Korean War, seized Japanese fishing boats that crossed his provocative "Peace Line," and staged thousands of nationwide demonstrations against Japan.

U.S. officials watched Rhee's anti-Japanese "antics" with dismay. They mocked him for not using former Japanese Government-General buildings, criticized his "unreasonable intransigence," and advocated an accommodation with Japan. After all, the American argument ran, the United States had fought a bloody war against Japan but had concluded a peace settlement and was creating a new relationship. Koreans replied that the United States had defeated Japan and could dictate a peace treaty. In South Korea's case, Japanese leaders showed little contrition for the annexation of Korea. On the contrary, they often insisted that Koreans should be grateful to Japan for developing the peninsula. South Korea was not yet strong enough to negotiate equally with Japan. It needed time—time for tempers to cool, ugly memories to fade, Korean culture to reassert itself after decades of Japanese influence, and for the economy to become strong enough to withstand Japanese capital.

The 1960 student revolt removed Syngman Rhee and the official anti-Japan policy. The 1961 coup brought military leaders to power who understood certain basic realities of Northeast Asia in the early 1960s: the U.S. security guarantee and military aid were finite and only Japan could take over the American role; South Korea needed Japanese aid for its new Five-Year Plan and subsequent development; and potentially lucrative opportunities in Vietnam due to the expanding U.S. military involvement there could only be pursued with Japanese political support. As the United States began to negotiate seriously for R.O.K. troops to be sent to Vietnam in 1964, the Park government moved to crush popular opposition and establish relations with Japan.

Many Koreans charged in 1964–1965 that R.O.K. leaders concluded the treaty for personal financial gain, that they were selling out their country. Memory of the "national traitors," corrupt officials who cooperated with Japan at the turn of the century, was part of the opposition to the treaty, and this charge is still made by opponents of the Park administration. Others feared that despite the Park government's attempts to limit Japanese influence, it would not be able to protect South Korea from the economic and political consequences of an influx of Japanese capital.

The Park administration was vulnerable to the first charge because so many of its members had close ties to Japan; some, including President Park, had distinguished careers in the Japanese Imperial Army. The government tried to reassure the public that it could safeguard South Korea's national interests vis-à-vis Japan. Government spokesmen argued that many South Koreans were living in the past and lacked confidence in Japan, that the Republic of Korea was not the hapless Korean kingdom of 1905, and that it could derive benefits from Japanese aid and investment without slipping under neocolonial control. This remains the vital question.

In early 1973 Japan's investments in Korea exceeded America's, Japan's goods dominated South Korea's, and by 1974 the country was becoming increasingly dependent upon Japanese capital. Japanese business leaders spoke openly about integrating South Korea's economy into Japan's long-range economic plans. The South Korean role was to be a low-wage labor pool and the site of pollution-producing industries. Japanese attitudes toward Korea and Koreans, Japanese business practices in Southeast Asia, and the history of Japanese-Korean relations since the Meiji Restoration permit only a pessimistic estimate of Japan's objectives in South Korea. The ability, in fact the very will, of South Korean leaders to resist Japanese economic domination is now in doubt.

The integration of military interests in Northeast Asia is best illustrated by the U.S. utilization of South Korean troops in Vietnam. In November 1964 the Johnson administration launched a "More Flags" campaign as a prelude to the impending U.S. military intervention in Vietnam. While designed to elicit concrete support for the Republic of Vietnam (R.V.N.), *the "More Flags" campaign was directly aimed at the American people.* The administration apparently never expected militarily significant "allied" troop contributions and they were not forthcoming (except from South Korea). Rather, "More Flags" was intended to establish a pragmatic basis for U.S. intervention— the visible, committed presence of allies who would associate themselves with U.S. actions in Vietnam militarily, if only in a token way, and diplomatically.[20]

The Johnson administration's hopes for a broad international support were frustrated, however, and ended in failure. In the 1966 Senate Foreign Relations Committee hearings, administration spokesmen claimed that thirty-one nations were "aiding" the war effort. The committee rebutted this claim decisively, showing that "about half of these had contributed services or materials amounting to $26,000 or less over a two-year period." Townsend Hoopes concluded that "when compared to the U.S. field force of 510,000 men and a war expenditure approaching $2.5 billion per month, this did not exactly make the case that the United States was being supported in Vietnam by a panoply of ardent and determined allies." [21]

Only a few countries in Asia sent troops to Vietnam: Australia, New Zealand, the Philippines, Thailand, and the Republic of Korea. Of these, South Korea was the weakest economically and in the most dangerous military position, according to its oft-repeated fears of a North Korean attack. In fact, over 50,000 U.S. troops were stationed in South Korea in 1964 "to defend the republic." Nevertheless, South Korea provided massive military forces to fight in Vietnam. *From 1964 to 1973, approximately 312,000 South Korean troops were deployed to Vietnam,* overwhelmingly as infantry, since logistical support was provided by the United States. The troop deployments were made in four major increments as shown in the table on page 29.

In 1954 the U.S. Joint Chiefs of Staff had rejected the offer of South Korean troops to fight in Laos, but now in 1964 the almost two-decade investment in training and equipping the R.O.K. Army had proven sound. In fact, *the Pentagon's need*

South Korean Troop Deployments to Vietnam

Dispatched	Organization	Strength
1964–65	Med/Engr (DOVE)	2,128
1965	Tiger Div (–RCT) with/supt. forces and Marine brigade	18,904
1966	9th Div (+Regimental Combat Team and support forces)	23,865
1967	Marine battalion and other support forces	2,963
1969	Authorized increase C–46 crews	12
	Total	47,872

(SOURCE: U.S. Congress, Senate, United States Security Agreements Abroad, Committee on Foreign Relations, Subcommittee on *United States Security Agreements and Commitments Abroad*, 91st Cong., 2d sess., 1970, p. 1544. The figure of 47,872 troops was the official maximum number of South Korean troops deployed to Vietnam. However, as noted above, the annual rotation of troops at the end of their tours of duty raised the total number of South Korean troops dispatched to Vietnam to approximately 312,000.)

for an Asian army in reserve appears to have been a primary factor in U.S. policy toward Korea since 1950. The Pentagon now had the use of a political military force fighting not in direct defense of the Republic of Korea but overseas in a foreign civil war. South Korea's objectives included the following: to prolong the U.S. security commitment to Korea, to provide combat training and experience for its army, to express appreciation for U.S. assistance in the Korean War, and to obtain maximum financial benefits from the war. While the anti-communist indoctrination of South Koreans was an ideological motivation, *the secret payments for R.O.K. troops in Vietnam, including bonuses for individual soldiers, were the decisive factor in the deployment of the South Korean expeditionary force to Vietnam.*

Under the terms of the extraordinary Brown Memorandum of March 4, 1966, the United States agreed to pay virtually all the expenses of the R.O.K. forces for Vietnam, plus providing billions of dollars' worth of new military equipment, assistance to South Korean businessmen in Vietnam, and employment of South Korean civilian workers in Vietnam.[22] Nearly all aspects of official U.S.-South Korean involvement were interwoven with various forms of payments. It is estimated that the United States paid more than $10 billion for the South Korean troops, including $3.16 billion in military assistance since 1966.

The most controversial element of these secret financial transactions was the overseas allowances paid by the Pentagon to South Korean troops. Although the R.O.K. and U.S. governments repeatedly insisted that the R.O.K. troops dispatched to Vietnam were highly motivated volunteers who desired to serve their country and defend the "Free World," in fact, the United States had to pay them special bonuses. The economic significance of these payments may be seen in the contrast with the regular salary scale of the R.O.K. Army. The basic *monthly* salary of a private was $1.60 (as of July 1, 1969). The *daily* U.S.-paid overseas allowance for service in Vietnam was $1.25, the monthly total $37.50. The U.S. overseas allowance for an R.O.K. Army private was *more than twenty-three times his normal base pay.*[23]

Senator J. William Fulbright focused on these secret payments, concealed from Congress as well as the American public, during the 1970 Symington Subcommittee hearings. He concluded:

> It seems to me that the fact that we paid them on this basis is all the more inexcusable. I see no reason for doubling [sic] their salaries, if they figure they are not mercenary, if they are doing their duty under their national honor, if you want to call it that.[24]

The secret arrangements between the State Department/Department of Defense and the Park government were part of the attempt to convince Congress and the American people that other countries shared U.S. objectives in Vietnam and were willing to make sacrifices for collective security. It was in the domestic political interests of the Johnson administration and the financial/security interest of the Park government that the American public's perception of the true nature of the Vietnam War be delayed or prevented completely. The congressional investigation and disclosure of these secret agreements finally brought a reaction against U.S. utilization of South Korean and other foreign troops in Indochina.

IV

What of the other Korea? While stationed in the South in 1958–1959, I often looked across the demilitarized zone into North Korea and wondered if life was better there. Syngman Rhee was killing opponents and preparing to rig the 1960 election, and the republic was economically stagnant, the people desperate. Could life be more difficult in the North? Could communism be that bad? In 1974 these thoughts may seem naïve, even antediluvian. Many would dismiss them as an irrelevant interference, arguing that it is not for Americans to judge and that Koreans must decide whether they want socialism or another system. I have no disagreement with that criticism. Only those who live in a society, raise children, and struggle for a personal and national identity can properly determine their political and economic arrangements.

Nevertheless, it should be noted that American actions in Korea have often rested on the implicit assumption that, with all its failings, South Korea was preferable to the North as a *system*. The South had the *possibility* of developing into an open society, while the North did not, according to one common argument. The South allowed some civil and political rights, including public criticism of the government by the press and a political opposition. The absence of an official ideology permitted a limited pluralism including religious diversity (but not socialist or progressive views, which were proscribed). These features made South Korea significantly different from the North and worthy of patient support. By contrast, the apparently totalitarian controls and the personality cult of Kim Il Sung left even empathetic foreign observers puzzled and ambivalent about North Korea.

As originally conceived, this collection was to include at least three essays on North Korea. They were not intended to supply answers to the question "Which Korea do you prefer?" but rather to examine the stereotype of North Korea presented in the West. It was hoped that the essays would probe misconceptions about the D.P.R.K. and offer new perspectives on a country virtually unknown to Americans. However, several potential essays were lost when various attempts to visit North Korea failed to win acceptance by the D.P.R.K. North Korean studies in the United States unfortunately had nothing to offer this kind of essay collection. On the one hand, career anti-communists dominate the field; on the other, the independent, objective, Korean-born researcher could be certain of pressure from R.O.K. CIA, including pressure on relatives in South Korea. Self-censorship prevented unbiased or sympathetic research on North Korea. As European and Japanese writings were being surveyed for suitable material, it became apparent that the present essays had reached a length that precluded additional material without sacrificing completed work. Therefore, the effort to include new writing on North Korea was abandoned.

The story of North Korea remains to be written. It will differ from the crude depiction current in the United States as a result of a propaganda and slanted "scholarship." The paucity of reliable data and the inaccessibility of North Korea to even sympathetic visitors, to say nothing of academic researchers, make analysis extremely hazardous. Yet a few comments may not be out of order.

First, North Korea's economic development deserves greater attention. Those features of socialism that have raised the standard of living of the mass of the population in the North are often ignored by critics of the D.P.R.K. North Korea's achievements in the fields of education, medical care, guaranteed employment, and social welfare appear to be especially noteworthy. A comparison, for example, of the health services available to factory workers in North and South Korea should explain much about the values and performance of each system. The economic justice of North Korean socialism is perhaps the most significant contrast with the South.

Secondly, the moral condemnation and one-sided portrayal of North Korea as "aggressive" and "bellicose" was a cold war contrivance. Assuming that North Korea started the Korean

War, one man's "aggression" is another's patriotic duty to restore national unity. The appellation "aggressor" was a powerful *political* weapon used by the United States against North Korea (and also against the People's Republic of China) but it had no validity as a moral judgment.

Since the Korean War, the United States and South Korea have kept unremitting pressure on North Korea through subversion, espionage, propaganda, and military attacks. These adventures have been kept secret for the most part and are little known in America. North Korea has used the same tactics against the South but these have been reported in the Western press as provocations, proof of "aggressive intentions," and submitted to the U.N. as "evidence" of North Korea's "belligerency."

It appears that North Korean military and intelligence activities have, to a considerable extent, been defensive responses to U.S.-R.O.K. attempts to harm or destroy the D.P.R.K. There is substantial documentation for this assertion regarding North Korean actions along the demilitarized zone after 1965 and with the *Pueblo* and EC-121 incidents. A full understanding of North Korea's defense and foreign policies, including its relations with South Korea, must take into consideration these minatory pressures *against* the North. More attention to the Pentagon's clandestine operations against the D.P.R.K. and less moralistic name-calling would be a good *point d'appui* for American researchers.

Third, how is North Korean socialism and the cult of Kim Il Sung to be interpreted? The hope for an alternative to South Korea—a unified, socialist Korea—shared by many Koreans and Americans, always runs into this reality. What is the potential for freedom? Is not the obsessive adulation of Kim Il Sung both an oppressive manipulation of the masses and an authoritarian elitism inconsistent with socialist egalitarianism? These are questions for Koreans to resolve, of course. Yet raising them reminds us that neither North nor South Korea is necessarily *the* Korea of the future.

V

The evaluation of the U.S. involvement in Korea since 1945 must await the withdrawal of American forces and a political settlement between the Koreas. Yet an interim assessment may help to clarify the brutal dilemmas facing Americans and Koreans.

In 1945 Koreans would have worked out a new destiny if the U.S. and the Soviet Union had not intervened. That destiny almost certainly would have been a leftist, perhaps a communist, government. In 1950 Korea would have been unified under communism if the U.S. had not entered the civil war. In those five years after World War II unification could have been achieved at a relatively low cost in human life and social dislocation. Now, however, a terrible war has severed the peninsula, ideological lines have hardened, and two antithetical regimes armed with modern weapons threaten to cause horrible casualties rather than compromise. U.S. atomic weapons in South Korea are also ready to devastate parts of the peninsula "in order to save it." In short, American actions (and the U.S.S.R.'s to a lesser extent) have impeded Korean unity and escalated immeasurably the dangers and costs of unification.

Nevertheless, unification is no less imperative now than it was in 1945 or 1950. This is evident in another aspect of American policy: encouraging Japanese involvement in the peninsula as a prelude to U.S. withdrawal. A single Korean state controlling the entire peninsula would have the human and material resources to coexist with Japan and avoid economic domination. But a divided peninsula with two hostile regimes wasting their resources on armaments and political competition is at a terrible disadvantage vis-à-vis Japan.

The United States has succeeded in its minimum objective of keeping half of Korea non-communist and under American influence. *And the Pentagon has had access to R.O.K. bases, useful against China and the U.S.S.R., and was able to mobilize the ROKA for Vietnam.* However, détente with China and the Soviet Union and new weapons systems have reduced the strategic value of South Korea. The risk of being involved in another phase of the Korean civil war, the endless cost of providing weapons and military aid to South Korea and of keeping U.S. forces there, and the embarrassing dictatorial methods of the Park government all argue for an end to U.S. involvement. South Korea is now a marginal asset to the State Department and the Pentagon; perhaps it is even a liability, as it was in 1947–1949.

The U.S. intervention lingers on, though the "stable democratic government" American policy-makers dreamed of in 1945 still has not appeared. In January 1974 the Park government declared the third state of emergency in three years. Anyone even petitioning for constitutional reforms was subject to trial by a military court and up to fifteen years' imprisonment at hard labor. That in late 1973 thousands of South Koreans risked torture and prison to demand minimum civil liberties is partially attributable to the diffusion of American democratic values. Those values and the democratic movement in South Korea deserve vigorous support but they will *never* get it from the official U.S. involvement in the Republic of Korea. No democrats need apply to the U.S. embassy in Seoul.

The Icarian surge of U.S. power into Asia in 1945 is now ebbing. Perhaps in a Korea of less interest to the U.S. State and Defense Departments, Americans can find ways to relate to both the Korean revolution in the North and the democratic movement in the South. These essays describe a benighted three decades when that has not been possible in the hope of a future American-Korean amity without parallel.

Notes

1. This figure was computed from various materials provided by the U.S. State Department and the U.S. Embassy, Seoul, Republic of Korea.

2. See, for example, the list of cold war axioms in Graham T. Allison, "American Foreign Policy and Japan," in Henry Rosovsky, ed., *Discord in the Pacific, Challenges to the Japanese-American Alliance* (Washington, D.C., Columbia Books, 1972), pp. 7–46, and Lincoln

P. Bloomfield, "Foreign Policy for Disillusioned Liberals," *Foreign Policy*, No. 9 (1972–73), pp. 55–68. The American Friends Service Committee report, *Anatomy of Anti-Communism* (New York, Hill and Wang, 1969) is one of the earlier analyses (with a helpful bibliography).

3. Shiv Dayal, *India's Role in the Korean Question* (Delhi, S. Chand & Co., 1959), p. 54.

4. Harold R. Porter, Testimony, Hearings before Senate Subcommittee on United States Security Agreements Abroad, Committee on Foreign Relations, *United States Security Agreements and Commitments Abroad*, 91st Cong., 2d sess., 1970, p. 1703. (Hereafter cited as *Symington Subcommittee Hearings*.)

5. Dayal, *India's Role*, pp. 59–61.

6. By 1970 the other UN members had long since withdrawn from the "UN Command," except for token contingents, usually one or two individuals. The United States had no objection to this, since the illusion of a United Nations presence was enough to confer legitimacy and a legal justification for the U.S. forces. General Michaelis, the "UN Commander," said they "give a flavor of the United Nations to our command." Harold Porter added that "they are visible on parade occasions to the population . . ." (*Symington Subcommittee Hearings*, pp. 1655–56).

7. North Korea has claimed that it reacted to a prior attack by South Korea on the morning of June 25. However, the available historical evidence points inescapably to a full-scale invasion by the D.P.R.K. For a recent discussion of the issue, see Karunakar Gupta, "How Did the Korean War Begin?" *The China Quarterly*, No. 52 (Oct.–Dec. 1972), pp. 699–716, and Robert Simmons, Chong-sik Lee, W. E. Skillend, and Karunakar Gupta, "Comment," *The China Quarterly*, No. 54 (April–June 1973), pp. 354–68.

8. For a detailed review of the U.S. intervention in Korea, see Glenn Paige, *The Korean Decision* (New York, Free Press, 1968).

9. For unleavened cold war analysis, rocklike in its immunity to new evidence and interpretations, see Zbigniew Brzezinski, "How the Cold War was Played," *Foreign Affairs*, Vol. 51, No. 1 (Oct. 1972), pp. 181–209. Brzezinski rejects even the possibility that the North Koreans may have taken the initiative. He analyzes the Korean War strictly in terms of Soviet ambitions and concludes that it must have been a Russian plot to get China and the United States into a war against each other.

10. The "lessons of Korea" were most assiduously memorized by senior foreign policy advisers. In 1965 President Lyndon Johnson convened a group of senior advisers to discuss impending U.S. actions in Vietnam. The group included Dean Acheson, Clark Clifford, John J. McCloy, George Ball, and McGeorge Bundy. Ball presented his now famous 1964 memorandum critical of U.S. involvement. President Johnson polled the group, which unanimously rejected Ball's position and supported Johnson's policies.

"They were for bombing the be-Jesus out of them," one eyewitness recalls. The matter disposed of, the elder statesmen fell to reminiscing to the President about Korea. That had been a far stickier business, they seemed to feel, which most of them had lived through; and that had gone off all right in the end, and so would this nasty little war in Vietnam. "Stick to it Mr. President" was the burden of the Wise Men's advice. [Godfrey Hodgson, "The Establishment," *Foreign Policy*, No. 10 (Spring 1973), pp. 3–40.]

11. U.S. Department of Defense, *United States-Vietnam Relations, 1945–1967* (Washington, D.C., 1971), Vol. 9, pp. 259–61.

12. *Ibid.*, p. 262.

13. The text of the mutual defense treaty is in *Symington Subcommittee Hearings*, pp. 1716–17.

14. These figures were computed from data provided by the U.S. State Department and the U.S. Embassy, Seoul, Republic of Korea.

15. *Symington Subcommittee Hearings*, p. 1706.

16. David C. Cole and Young Woo Nam, "The Pattern and Significance of Economic Planning in Korea," in Irma Adelman, *Practical Approaches to Development Planning: Korea's Second Five-Year Plan* (Baltimore, Johns Hopkins Press, 1969), pp. 11–37.

17. The Adelman book cited above is one example. Another is David C. Cole and Princeton N. Lyman, *Korean Development: The Interplay of Politics and Economics* (Cambridge, Mass., Harvard University Press, 1971).

18. Some development economists regard advice on income distribution as "political," something they must not offer lest their positions as neutral experts be compromised. Having helped to create the South Korean "pie" and placed it in the hands of a small government-business elite, AID economists will now pack up their slide rules and go home. This is a case of raising the GNP and leaving with "honor." For example, Dwight H. Perkins has written:

> Some decline in the growth rate in such fast growers as South Korea and Taiwan might be desirable if brought about as the price of a modest redistribution of income through, say the promotion of more social welfare programs, but *that is an issue for these countries to decide for themselves*. (Emphasis

38   FRANK BALDWIN

added.) ["The United States and Japan in Asia," in Rosovsky, *Discord in the Pacific,* pp. 47–77.]
19. "Korean Christian Manifesto," *Christianity and Crisis,* July 9, 1973.
20. Chester Cooper, *The Last Crusade: The Full Story of U.S. Involvement in Vietnam from Roosevelt to Nixon* (London, MacGibbon & Kee, 1970), p. 266.
21. Townsend Hoopes, *The Limits of Intervention* (David McKay Co., 1969), p. 169.
22. The text is in *Symington Subcommittee Hearings,* pp. 1549–50.
23. *Ibid.,* p. 1572.
24. *Ibid.,* pp. 1567–68.

American Policy and Korean Liberation

Bruce Cumings

> The moment of Japan's final defeat will be the most
> momentous in Korean history, a moment which may
> not return for hundreds of years, when so much public
> good can be achieved without bloodshed, without dec-
> ades or centuries of conflict.[1]

Japanese rule ended in Korea on August 15, 1945, providing
a fleeting instant in Korea's long history when the entire social,
economic, and political order was thrown up in the air like so
many chips, a brief interregnum afforded few peoples to make
real choices about their political destiny. Koreans hoped and
planned to make these choices themselves; no people ever de-
served wholesale change more. But Koreans did not count on
their nation's once again becoming the object of rivalry between
expansionist world powers, this time the Soviet Union and the
United States. Nor did they expect an America that would see
in change, chaos, and in reaction, stability. In the south, the
forces of reaction triumphed. But this victory required years to
achieve and culminated in a major war.

It also required the presence of American power, because the
case for counterrevolution was so weak—or, the case for revolution so compelling. Japan had exploited Korea until the need
for total independence and thoroughgoing change was undeni-
able. The Japanese colonial authorities has fostered a tiny, para-
sitic Korean elite sustained only at Japanese sufferance. In 1945
the opponents of this old order were the repository of Korea's
hopes. For Koreans who saw in counterrevolution their hope of
survival, the situation was perilous. For an America needing

39

allies to stem the tide of revolution, the pickings were slim indeed.

This was the task the United States set for itself in Korea in the autumn of 1945: stem the tide. Build a bulwark. But a bulwark of what? To stop whom? In American eyes, it would be a bulwark of democratic, loyal Koreans against communism. Instead, it became a bulwark of discredited privilege against the Korean people. Still, it was three long years before General Douglas MacArthur could look on South Korea and call it "an impregnable bulwark against all dissident elements." [2] And still it leaked.

This article examines how the United States began building the bulwark.* The key to the process is not to be found in design but in execution. There was no grand design. American planners envisioned a Korea given in trust to the Great Powers until Koreans proved themselves ready for independence. The implementation of this conception faltered from the beginning on Korean opposition, Allied misgivings, and, most importantly, the plan's inability to guarantee American interests. A different policy replaced it, forged by American actions in Korea.

Policy was made in the field, although eventually approved at the highest levels. It was initiated within days of the American arrival in Korea and implemented for the most part within six months. This article deals primarily with those first few months, although it will be necessary to examine the background of American policy and the revolutionary Korean setting, as well as to describe briefly the consequences in later years.

1. 1943–45: TRUSTEESHIP AND OCCUPATION

American planners had relatively little to say about Korea prior to the Japanese surrender; no careful or systematic policy analysis exists in the available record. But Korea did figure prominently in the general context of American thinking regarding the

---

* I am grateful to Frank Baldwin and Herbert Bix for their comments on this article. However, responsibility for the conclusions, opinions, and other statements is solely mine.

postwar disposition of former colonial areas. The essential question was one of power and control: who would get the colonies? Their former masters? The victorious allies? The colonial people themselves? How could Great Power desires for a manageable world be squared with pledges made in the Atlantic Charter and elsewhere of independence and self-determination for the colonies? In an attempt to reconcile these questions, the United States proffered the idea of Great Power trusteeships: the colonies would be given to the powers in trust until such time as they were deemed ready to handle their own affairs. Multilateral international bodies would replace unilateral colonialism, and the colonies would be started on the road to independence, however slowly and gradually.

The idea foundered immediately, from the day it was first broached in international discussions in a meeting held March 27, 1943 between President Franklin D. Roosevelt and British Foreign Secretary Anthony Eden. Roosevelt mentioned Korea and Indochina as areas ripe for postwar trusteeships. Eden remarked that "the President was being very hard on the French, . . ." but accepted an American draft on trusteeships for further study.[3] After much prodding, Eden finally responded to the draft in August 1943, a response that spoke volumes for the British attitude. According to Secretary of State Cordell Hull's account: "To be perfectly frank, [Eden] had to say he did not like our draft very much. He said it was the word 'independence' that troubled him. He had to think of the British Empire system, which was built on the basis of Dominion and colonial status." [4] Eden thereby joined the issue, and British— not to mention French—opposition to trusteeships marked all subsequent wartime conferences. Indeed, right up to Japan's surrender the British frustrated attempts to work out Allied plans for trusteeship, as the records of the Yalta and Potsdam conferences show.[5] The Russians suggested on several occasions that independence should be the goal rather than tutelage, but they humored Roosevelt and gave the Americans the impression that they were agreed on a trusteeship for Korea at least. Yet there was no written agreement or substantial planning for a trusteeship for Korea prior to the Japanese surrender.[6]

The British and the French did not like the implications of

this idea for their colonial holdings, to be sure. Some have therefore drawn a picture of American trust, idealism, and charity
toward colonial peoples frustrated and confounded by selfish
European powers and the forward thrust of Soviet communism.
But the issue was a bit more complex than that. The Allies, the
British in particular, understood the functions of the trusteeship
idea in furthering American interests. Eden clearly stated the
British view in his memoirs: "[Roosevelt] hoped that former
colonial territories, once free of their masters, would become
politically and economically dependent upon the United States,
and had no fear that other powers might fill that role." [7]

The idea has a peculiarly American ring to it. The trusteeship
concept, later incorporated into the United Nations Charter,
reflected the triumph of Wilsonian idealism twenty years after its
seeming defeat at the hands of the isolationists.[8] A concert of
the Great Powers would forge a new international order under
the rule of law. Trust, cooperation, and harmony would become
the rule rather than the exception in relations between nations.
Specifically, Great Power agreement on the disposition of the
colonies would prevent conflict after the war. Trusteeships would
place a friendly demeanor on the interests of the powers and
end the colonial system of unilateral exploitation. The colonies
would be opened up; the old, debased, illiberal spheres of influence would disappear. A spirit of partnership would prevail.
The world's resources would be open to all, on an equal basis.
But there is the catch.

Unlike an earlier era of American involvement in Asia, a new
"open door" would not simply maintain an entry for a weak
America in a world of power politics. Now the United States
would emerge the most powerful nation in the world and could
well expect to dominate international arrangements of this sort.

Trust, cooperation, partnership: on American terms. Trusteeships would work if the Allies would cooperate. But the Allies
had good reasons to resist.

Some Americans clearly recognized the essential ambivalence
of the trusteeship concept. However idealistic it was in intent,
its design was to further American interests without recourse
to the use of force. Its high-flown rhetoric and broad applicabil-
ity obscured a determination of exactly where American inter-

ests were or were not involved, or where a recourse to force might or might not be necessary. As a catch-all device for securing needed American bases in the Pacific and for breaking up European colonial holdings, it was bound to encounter resistance. Secretary of War Henry Stimson put it well when he said that no Allied discussions of trusteeship

> . . . could usefully proceed without a consideration of the nature of the specific areas to be trusteed. Immediately the subject is introduced, the various powers would certainly consider the subject in the light of how it would affect the areas in which they are interested or which they covet.[9]

This is precisely what happened every time the issue appeared in wartime Allied discussions.

It was the smaller nations, however, who really upset the calculus of trusteeship and demonstrated its utter lack of realism. Forces existed in the colonies—in Indochina, Malaya, and Korea (to name a few)—that would try to determine their own fate and hoped to redirect and control their own resources. They had waited too long for Great Power benevolence; and the Koreans, in particular, had heard it all before from the Japanese.

When the well-known proviso "in due course" was inserted into the Cairo Declaration pledge of Korean independence (December 1, 1943),[10] Koreans immediately grasped the intent— that Koreans would not be ready to govern themselves at the end of the war—and took it as a judgment on specifically Korean disabilities and infirmities. For the next two years they filled their exile publications with self-justification.[11] But in fact Americans had no knowledge of postwar Korean potentialities. The Cairo pledge reflected the paternalistic, gradualist element of the trusteeship idea, which deemed no colonial people fit to run its own affairs without a period of tutelage.[12]

Roosevelt, in particular, justified this paternalism by reference on several occasions during the war to the Philippine example of (presumed) American benevolence. When he told Stalin about the Cairo discussions at the succeeding Teheran Conference, Roosevelt "referred to one of his favorite topics, which was the education of the peoples of the Far Eastern colonial areas . . . in the arts of self-government," and cited the American record in the Philippines.[13] Again in informal discussions with Stalin on February 8, 1945 at the Yalta Conference, Roosevelt said that Korea should have a trusteeship of twenty to thirty years, since the Philippines had required fifty years of tutelage. Stalin replied by saying the shorter the period of trusteeship, the better.[14]

Trusteeship was one path to the goal of extending and consolidating American power and influence. American planners were determined to create in Korea a government friendly and responsive to American interests. They preferred to go about this in an atmosphere of trust and cooperation, which fed the presumption of American innocence. But they were prepared to use force as a de facto means to the end. Trusteeship was the liberal alternative, occupation the assured method. Thus as early as March 1944 State Department planning envisioned American occupation of Korea and noted the importance for American postwar aims of American participation in whatever military operations took place in Korea: "The assumption by the United States of a major part in civil affairs and in international supervision of an interim government would be greatly facilitated by the participation of the United States in such military operations as take place in and around Korea." [15] This paper also raised the possibility of a military government in Korea; hopefully for a short period, but potentially for one of "considerable duration." The Soviets were expected to be "in occupation of considerable portions of Korea," but the occupation was not to be zonal: American occupation forces were to cooperate with the Soviets in administering Korea prior to the imposition of a trusteeship. But the emphasis in this analysis is on occupation first, trusteeship later, because State Department planners were suspicious of the Soviets. Another document dated two months later stated that if Soviet forces occupied Korea alone, "the United States might consider such a development as a threat to the future security of the Pacific." [16]

In an important study on Korea written for the Yalta Conference, State Department planners wrote:

It is the view of the Department that the problems of Korea are of such an international character that with the completion of military operations in Korea, (1) there should be, so far as practicable, Allied representation in the army of occupation and military government in Korea; (2) such representation should be by those countries which have a real interest in the future status of Korea, such as the United States, Great Britain, and China and the Soviet Union if it has entered the war in the Pacific; (3) the representation of other states should not be so large as to reduce the proportionate strength of the United States to a point where its effectiveness would be weakened.[17]

Again it was suggested that Korea should be administered "as a single unit and not as separate zones." But, and this is the key, American strength should be large enough to ensure "effectiveness"—the United States "should play a leading role in the occupation and military government." [18] In this and succeeding planning the desire for predominant American influence in Korea was as little concealed in the diplomatic language as was American distrust of Soviet plans for Korea. A paper for the Potsdam Conference said:

> It is possible that the Soviet Union will make strong demands that it have a leading part in the control of Korean affairs. If such demands required the establishment of an administrative authority in which powers other than the Soviet Union had only a nominal voice, it might be advisable to designate Korea as a trust area and to place it under the authority of the United Nations organization itself.[19]

This paragraph stated succinctly the essential problem, "control of Korean affairs," and laid out three means to the end: an administrative authority (occupation), trusteeship, and the use of the fledgling United Nations organization. The sequence elaborated was indeed followed from 1945 to 1948. The paper overlooked only one matter: where is the voice of the Korean nation?

The development of the war in the Pacific did not augur well for significant American participation in Korean affairs in the summer of 1945. The American military planned an invasion of the Japanese home islands (Kyushu) to commence around November 1, 1945, and only after the homeland was secured would attention turn to Korea. The record at Potsdam clearly shows the unanimity of American military planners on the need for

Soviet entry into the war against Japan. The Americans had a high opinion of the Japanese Kwantung army in Manchuria and thought that losses in an invasion of Korea would be greater than in a Kyushu invasion. They thought it better to leave Manchuria and Korea, and these losses, to the Soviet land armies.[20] So it seems likely that no agreement on postwar Korea was possible at Potsdam because the Soviets seemed at that point to have the upper hand. Any agreement would have had to account for this reality.[21] The Americans bided their time, waiting to see how the war developed.

2. INTO THE BREACH: THE 38TH PARALLEL

The United States dropped atomic bombs on Hiroshima and Nagasaki on August 6 and 9, Soviet forces quickly and unexpectedly engaged Japanese forces on the Asian mainland, and Japan collapsed. In the immediate aftermath of these events, Korea was divided at latitude 38° north into American and Soviet occupation zones.

The initial decision to draw a line at the 38th parallel was wholly an American action, taken during a night-long session of the State-War-Navy Coordinating Committee (SWNCC), August 10–11, 1945. Two colonels in the War Department, Charles H. Bonesteel and Dean Rusk, were told to retire to an adjoining room and come up with a proposal. They were given thirty minutes.[22] Dean Rusk writes that the 38th parallel was "further north than could be realistically reached . . . in the event of Soviet disagreement"; when the Soviets later agreed to the line, Rusk was "somewhat surprised." [23] Thus the selection of this line was an explicit test of Soviet intentions. It was a time for testing the Russians. Korea was a prime index of Soviet plans for Asia, just as Poland was for Europe. The test went rather well in Korea. Soviet forces entered Korea almost a full month before American forces. The whole peninsula was theirs for the taking. Yet they honored the 38th parallel.[24] American troops were able to occupy a portion of Korea that included its capital, two-thirds of its population, a good share of its industry, and the greater part of its agricultural capacity.

Stalin probably agreed to honor the American act of partition because he interpreted it as a strict, sphere-of-influence quid pro quo. The Russians and the Japanese had discussed dividing Korea at the 38th parallel in 1896 and 1903.[25] Stalin made explicit references in 1945 to recovering interests lost to the Japanese in the Russo-Japanese War (1904–1905).[26] The Soviets would have preferred a unified, friendly Korea, but a divided Korea would well serve the basic security interest of the Soviet state: assurance that the Korean peninsula would not provide the basis for an attack against Russia.[27]

But in acknowledging the Soviet interest in a divided Korea, one must also assess the American interest. Of course American planners argue that the partition was to have been only temporary, that it was couched in terms relating only to the acceptance of the Japanese surrender in Korea, that it is part of the familiar story of American innocence and Soviet betrayal.[28] Former Secretary of State Dean Acheson says those responsible for the decision should have known of previous Russian-Japanese attempts to divide Korea,[29] and some try to argue that it was a purely military decision, isolated from diplomatic and political considerations.[30] But these interpretations assume that the United States had no interests to advance and no previous plans to occupy Korea. In fact, Japan's collapse provided an opportunity to throw American forces into a country all but conceded to the Russians only a few days earlier at Potsdam. In the crunch the conflict between trust and force was quickly resolved: occupation was the only reliable method, so American troops were rushed into the breach.[31]

No sleight of hand can remove the decision on the 38th parallel from the continuum of American thinking on Korea since 1943. Although the decision was taken quickly and rashly in the harried days of mid-August, it was the logical outcome of past planning. The occupation of Korea, as we have seen, was linked to the postwar security of the Pacific in early 1944. A Korea wholly in Soviet hands was seen as a threat to that security. Relating the division "only" to the acceptance of the Japanese surrender obscured what was, in fact, the point: the developing power relationship in East Asia was contingent on who received the surrender, and where, on the principle that "military victory

would define local politics." [32] The American assumption was
that "the United States would emerge as the dominant power in
the Pacific and preeminent in the Far East." [33] In August 1945
only possession could assure dominance.

Given these considerations, it can be said that the partition
of Korea was permanent from the transmittal of the War Department's General Order No. 1 on August 15, communicating
to the Russians and the British the decision on the 38th parallel
(and in general the American definition of postwar Asian power
relationships). To expect any other outcome would be to ignore
the context of Great Power relations in which the division of
Korea occurred. Maybe American planners were not entirely
aware of the consequences of their decision. But to say that consciousness lagged behind actions, that full recognition would
only come later, is only to become aware of the process whereby
the Truman Doctrine enunciated in 1947 a justification for
actions taken worldwide in the several years preceding it.

3. THE KOREAN SETTING

Korea in August 1945 was a far cry from the Rooseveltian
image of contented natives awaiting the fruits of benevolent
tutelage. Korea's problems were severe and required remedies
quite beyond the reach of friendly homilies and gradualist reform. Many Koreans, far from needing guidance, had a clear
idea of what their country required: a thoroughgoing revolution
to extirpate the legacy of Japanese colonial rule.

The most important legacy was the land situation. Korean
land conditions on the eve of liberation cannot be described with
complete accuracy; comprehensive studies are few and the obstacles to understanding many. However, available studies paint
a virtually unrelieved picture of poverty, oppression, and deg-
radation in agriculture in general, and in land relations in particular.[34] In 1945 Korea was still an overwhelmingly agrarian
nation with upwards of 75 percent of the population engaged
directly or indirectly in agricultural production.[35] A substantial
Japanese and Korean landlord class controlled most of the land.
From 1910 to 1918 the Japanese conducted a comprehensive

land survey to classify, register, and clarify the ownership of Korean land. A registration law was promulgated which allowed some Koreans, primarily those of the former *yangban* ruling and bureaucratic class, to establish title to lands, while peasants, through ignorance of the law and purposeful misinformation, were often dispossessed.[36] In this way, some Korean scholars maintain, the *yangban* class was transformed into a new landlord class.[37] The registration law enabled the Japanese to gain title to much Korean land (especially land formerly titled to the old Korean government). The Japanese Oriental Development Company and individual Japanese landlords took title to the better land, but a distinct Korean landlord class remained throughout the colonial period. This class, which differed hardly at all from the Japanese in its relation to tenant farmers, maintained its holdings through collaboration, the Japanese price for such privilege.

Concentration of land ownership increased throughout the colonial period, creating a tenancy situation with "few parallels in the world." [38] When part-owners are included in the statistics, nearly four out of every five farmers were tenants.[39] In southern Korea, where the major part of agricultural production was centered, the tenancy rate has been put as high as 94 percent.[40] Rents were sometimes 80 to 90 percent of the crop in the south, while averaging about 50 percent across the peninsula. This may be compared with the rate in Japan of about 35 percent of the crop at the time and with the worst tenancy areas in China, which had similar rental rates.[41] All the misery usually associated with such land relations was present in Korea: widespread debt and accompanying usury; constant renegotiation of leases to the detriment of the tenant; various forms of labor required sans compensation; utter insecurity for the farming family; and "extreme poverty [that] can hardly be imagined by the outsider." [42] Hoon K. Lee and Andrew Grajdanzev, both moderate scholars, were in agreement that the land situation was hopeless without radical change.[43]

The lot of the Korean peasant had never been very good, however, and such objectively wretched conditions do not of themselves necessarily lead to social and political action. What is additionally necessary, it seems, is (1) a sense of relative deprivation; (2) a perceived chance for real change; and (3) organized politics which can appeal to and direct discontent. The first two categories relate to the development of political consciousness, a murky problem which cannot be gone into here. But it is a reasonable hypothesis that the intense direct mobilization of Koreans during the war years, combined with a more subtle process of social mobilization reflecting the increasing industrialization of the peninsula (an incipient working class, increases in literacy, urbanization, mass communications and the like), had a direct relation to the extraordinary levels of political participation manifested in Korea when the lid came off on Liberation Day.[44]

From 1937 to 1945 the Japanese authorities attempted to organize nearly every aspect of Korean life to serve the war effort. The National Mobilization Law passed in Japan was extended to Korea.[45] Japanese authorities established a policy of "Japanese-Korean Unity," (*naisen ittai*) to obtain total Korean loyalty to Japan. Koreans were prohibited from speaking their own language, forced to take Japanese names, and forced to participate in Shintō worship and other Japanese cultural peculiarities. Hundreds of thousands of Koreans were sent to Japan as laborers; estimates place the total figure at 2.5 million by 1945.[46] The Japanese began drafting Koreans in 1942, and most able-bodied men and young people were compelled to labor in work gangs serving the war effort. The authorities organized numerous "patriotic" and "anti-communist" groups to penetrate Korean society at every level.[47]

These mobilization policies had two main effects. First, the Japanese confronted Koreans with political choices: join the group, fight the war, hate Japan's enemies—or resist and pay the price. The tolerance of sullen compliance grew smaller as the necessity to serve Japan actively was pressed. Such prodding and coercion made many Koreans hate the Japanese all the more, to be sure, but it may also have heightened political awareness and stimulated Koreans to think of political participation and power for themselves.

The second effect of such policies was to identify the enemies of Japan with communism. Underground insurgents, whom the Japanese called communists, were the last resistance to Japan within Korea. Japanese authorities blamed communists for the numerous landlord-tenant disputes of the 1930s.[48] Communists, Chinese and Korean, led the anti-Japanese resistance in Manchuria and China proper. Thus anti-communism was a dominant motif of Japanese propaganda, and many of the newly organized groups were expressly anti-communist.[49] The largest such organization was the Korean Anti-Communist Association (*Chōsen bōkyō kyōkai*) established in 1938, with branches in every province. However, "Anti-Communist associations were organized even in villages, factories, and companies; and cultural and religious organizations were required to establish anti-Communist cells." [50] Christian groups in particular were urged to denounce communism.[51] Leftism became almost synonymous with opposition to Japan. Communist resistance took on a nationalistic, patriotic aura. This identification lasted long after Japan's defeat. It made the Korean masses highly sympathetic to the Left throughout the liberation period (1945–48).

Neither abject poverty nor social and political mobilization in Korea would have led to political action without political organization. A final factor necessary to understand the preliberation setting is thus the Korean insurgency itself.[52] Koreans opposed Japanese control from the beginning, at first by widespread guerrilla activities before annexation, and then in 1919 in the massive March First Independence Movement.[53] This movement marks the beginning of the Korean nationalist movement and the split between the Right and the Left that eventually manifested itself in a divided Korea.[54] It is crucial to understand that this split began in 1919/1920. After 1945 attempts were made to internationalize the schism and to identify the entire Left with the Soviet Union and its interests. Yet the Korean nationalist movement was divided from about 1920 between those who favored radical change and those who opposed it; and while international influences have been involved from time to time, they have always been peripheral to the prevailing Korean cleavage.[55]

An exile Korean Provisional Government (KPG) was organized in Shanghai in 1919. It was a temporary alignment of socialist-inclined nationalists, who advocated armed struggle against Japan, and moderate-to-conservative nationalists, who preferred peaceful means, particularly diplomatic approaches through Western powers. These leaders really worked together only until 1921; after that the KPG was "almost defunct." [56] Even at the time of its organization a large faction argued against the designation "government," as the essential requisites of people, territory, and sovereignty were lacking.[57] Left and Right soon went their own ways, and most sources agree that the Left was ascendant in the anti-Japanese struggle after 1925.

Korea had one of the oldest communist movements in Asia, a Korean Communist party predating the formation of the Chinese Communist party in 1921.[58] The Korean movement was splintered and factious and continually reorganized. By 1945 four distinct groups were identifiable: domestic communists within Korea; a Yenan faction with the Chinese communists; a Soviet faction within Russia; and a variety of partisan groups in Manchuria united in anti-Japanese warfare. Exact figures on these groups are not available, but the movement was effective enough to require constant surveillance by the Japanese police.[59] Korean communists, in their desire to liberate Korea, showed an incredible willingness time and again to offer their heads to the Japanese chopping block. It was an eclectic movement with little doctrinal originality and many fellow travelers of questionable communist authenticity, and it never succeeded in its primary goal of overthrowing Japanese rule in Korea.[60] But by 1945 it had certainly earned the right to participate in determining the future of an independent Korea.

The Korean Provisional Government, barely more than a name since 1921, was to some extent revived after Pearl Harbor; however, factional struggles continued within the small hierarchy throughout the war. The KPG had a small military force under its command in China, estimated at less than 1,000 in 1944.[61] This force did not wage partisan warfare against Japan, but remained behind the lines in Chungking. Despite the KPG's general weakness and a complete lack of ties with the home Korean population, its supporters urged the U.S. government to recognize it as the sovereign government of Korea. An aging political exile in the United States, Syngman Rhee, was the prime mover in this effort, meeting and corresponding with various officials in Washington throughout the war. He described himself as the official representative of the KPG in the United States, although his relations with KPG leaders in China had long been stormy, and his association with the KPG tenuous at best.[62]

4. AUGUST 1945: REVOLUTION AND REACTION

Emperor Hirohito's August 15 surrender declaration brought spontaneous, emotional celebrations that made Liberation Day the most important day in the lives of an entire generation of Koreans. It was the ultimate deliverance from a hated foreign rule. Most, however, thought it was just the beginning of a new era in Korean history: a general social liberation, a revolution, would follow. For the next three years demands for land distribution, labor reforms and unions, political participation and power, national independence and self-determination dominated political discourse. Liberation was not just a day, but defined an entire period of great flux. It would prove difficult to put a lid on. A liberated Korea would make a lousy bulwark.

Koreans within Korea in August 1945 expected to handle their own affairs. On Liberation Day they began organizing their own national government. A Committee for the Preparation of Korean Independence (CPKI) was formed through the leadership of Lyuh Woon-hyung, and under its auspices local People's Committees quickly spread throughout the country. On September 6 local committee representatives and national leaders met in Seoul and organized a national group called the Korean People's Republic (KPR). For a brief moment Korea was unified under a Korean organization that, while imperfect, demonstrated Korean fitness for self-determination. We will briefly examine the origins and nature of the KPR.[63]

For months, as the war went badly, the Japanese had been worried at the prospect of being caught in a liberated Korea. They had good reason to fear Korean reprisals. When the surrender was only a few days away, accordingly, Japanese authorities began making approaches to Koreans about an interim administration to preserve law and order and allow the Japanese to leave Korea unscathed. They met several times with Song Chin-u, former editor of the *Tonga ilbo* (East Asia daily), a

Korean newspaper shut down in 1940. But Song did not want to assume such responsibilities.[64]

The Japanese turned to Lyuh Woon-hyung. Lyuh was a man of the moderate Left with great prestige among Koreans owing to his long record of opposition to Japanese rule; he also was a man of considerable charisma, perhaps the best orator among Korean leaders.[65] Lyuh agreed to organize an administration, after the Japanese accepted five demands. The demands went far beyond what the Japanese had hoped for, but they had few choices left.[66]

Lyuh and his supporters proceeded to organize the CPKI. On August 16, in accordance with one of Lyuh's demands, the Japanese released upwards of sixteen thousand political prisoners.[67] Many of these men became active in setting up People's Committees throughout the Korean peninsula. By the end of August, 145 committees were functioning. The composition of these organs was highly eclectic; a political vacuum existed in Korea and everyone was scrambling. Committee leaders and members covered the political spectrum from left to right. In some cases local landlords ran committees. It seems that only notorious collaborators were excluded. It is absurd to maintain that these groups were solely communist.[68] Perhaps the communist element was predisposed eventually to come out on top, because it was better organized (it usually is), and because it had greater prestige among the Korean masses. In addition, its program was made to order for land-hungry Korean peasants. But the communists did not control the People's Committees in 1945. These committees and the KPR represented a broad coalition of Korean leaders that may be traced in the fifty-five-man leadership roster announced on September 6, and one will look in vain for communist rhetoric in the detailed platform published shortly thereafter.[69]

The Korean People's Republic was short-lived in Seoul. The Japanese authorities turned against it when they found they could not control it, and when they learned that not Soviet but American forces would occupy southern Korea. U.S. forces meant much less chance of revolutionary confiscations, trials, and violence against Japanese.[70] The entrance of American forces was the prime factor in the KPR's demise, both because the Americans opposed it, and because American power provided conditions in which the Japanese and the native Korean Right could work against it.

The KPR organization in Seoul had its faults as well. It was quickly riven by factions and general disunity; some of this can be explained by Japanese and American pressure, but it is also true that its leaders had little experience with a political movement with strong roots in the countryside. They tended to think, incorrectly, that maneuvering in Seoul was the key to power.[71]

This did not mean the end of the People's Republic. In many parts of the south People's Committees continued to exercise authority well into 1946. American occupation forces were too short-handed to reach these areas for months.[72] The committees set down strong roots. A process of political participation began on August 15, directly related to Korean demands for land redistribution, labor reforms, and political power. The committees, moreover, were just one aspect of this phenomenon. Workers, farmers, students, women, and fishermen organized groups associated with the People's Republic, generally using the title *chohap* (roughly, association).[73] Few sectors of Korean society were left untouched. Unionization activities were particularly strong. The major labor union organized in these early days remained preeminent until the fall of 1946.[74] These various *chohap* were strong elements in committee power throughout Korea. To defeat this revolution, every local committee, union, and mass association would have to be excised one by one. It would take a long time.

Soviet actions in northern Korea sustained the committees and *chohap,* and the idea of a "people's republic," for years in the south. Soviet forces recognized the People's Committee apparatus organized north of the 38th parallel, turned over administrative authority to them on August 25, 1945, and worked with the committee structure through December 1945.[75]

The exact nature of Soviet policy in north Korea is not known. The Russians did not simply impose an alien puppet regime, nor did they relegate all authority to the People's Committees.[76] The Soviets seem to have come into Korea with few plans, but with a flexible policy and an obvious willingness to encourage the revolutionary activities of the committees. Indeed, the Soviets authorized expropriation and nationalization of Japanese property by the committees in late August. But they also wanted to exercise control, which they eventually did, not through a military government—Soviet forces never set one up—but through "inauspicious but firm" authority imposed from the top.[77] It was a brilliant political maneuver.

The Soviets successfully created the impression in the south that a government that had originated with the CPKI on August 15 was under Korean control in the north. This impression persisted until the official formation of the rival Korean governments in 1948 and had the most profound effect on south Korean attitudes. It sustained the Left in the south throughout the liberation period, despite severe repression.[78] It also encouraged moderates to believe that a unified Korean government was possible, even if one of the Left. North Korean newspapers reaching the south week after week announced far-reaching changes, revolutionary developments, all in the name of the People's Committees.[79] This was in sharp contrast to the lethargy, repression, and stagnation of the south. Leaders associated with the People's Republic in the south were emboldened to continue organizing activity long after the American command came out against the Left.

But if the Soviets stimulated some Koreans to continue their revolution, the Americans did the same for their opponents. The American Occupation stimulated a resurgence, or revivification, of the Korean Right. August 1945 was not a good month for Koreans who still had some measure of power, wealth, and influence. All Koreans, of course, welcomed the liberation, except perhaps for a tiny minority of Japanese sympathizers. But those who had benefitted from Japanese rule were highly apprehensive of the post-Japanese order. Would reprisals follow? Trials? Who would prevail?

All Koreans had had to make their peace with Japan by 1945. No effective resistance capable of threatening Japanese rule remained within the country. Some still did resist, of course, and they either paid the supreme penalty or wound up with indeterminate prison sentences. Others chose a middle path of sullen cooperation. Still others chose the path of least resistance and partook of Japanese benefits. Given the general poverty and the few positions of responsibility open to Koreans, this latter group was not large. However, again because of the general poverty, virtually anyone with wealth in 1945—even with a good education—was looked on by the masses as a collaborator, a pro-Japanese.[80]

In August 1945 wealthy and influential Koreans were faced with a popular movement to share the wealth and punish collaborators. In rural areas peasant radicalism led to the forcible dispossession of Japanese and Korean landlords. The CPKI controlled the national press, radio, and other communications facilities for a period of time [81] and railed against collaborators. Japanese and Koreans crossed the 38th parallel with tales of people's trials and dispossession in the north. How was privilege to be preserved in such a setting?

Koreans who had held high office, and especially those who had served in the Japanese police, dispersed and went into hiding.[82] Their privileges seemed gone for good. Some lesser collaborators and landlords succeeded in joining local People's Committees, and many wealthy Koreans contributed money to Lyuh Woonhyung's organization.[83] But by the end of August it was known that U.S. forces would occupy southern Korea. New opportunities presented themselves.

On August 28 a small group of leaders met and began talking about a party of the Right. On September 7, the day before American entry into Korea, they formed a preparatory committee to found the Korean Democratic party (*Han'guk minjudang*) (KDP), and on September 16 the party was officially established.[84] It became the pillar of the Right in the first few months after liberation and remained the strongest rightist party throughout the period from 1945 to 1948. Moderate and leftist sources viewed the KDP as a party of landlords, capitalists, and collaborators with Japan.[85] A large landlord element led by Kim Sŏng-su—generally identified as the *honam* group (meaning the two Chŏlla provinces of southern Korea)—was a mainstay of the party.[86] The KDP described itself as a party of "patriots, notables, and various circles of the intellectual stratum," [87] which probably contains a bit of truth as well as a good indication of its elitist values. The initial group included few true patriots, but it was not simply a party of landlords and collaborators. Also present were highly educated Koreans (some educated in the West), some Christians, business entrepreneurs, and various conservatives. They all had privileged positions which they hoped to preserve along with the structures and attitudes that made such positions possible. In short, the KDP represented the old order in a time of revolution.

The KDP expressed firm support for the Korean Provisional Government in Chungking, and bitterly condemned the Korean People's Republic. Besides this it had only the vaguest of political platforms, for the precise reason that in Korea in 1945 popularity was not won by urging the maintenance of landlordism, little or no punishment for collaborators, private ownership of industry, and the continuation in power of those Koreans who had authority under the Japanese.[88] In the revolutionary Korean context, the KDP represented a tenuous holding operation until the arrival of the American Occupation, whence came a new breath of life.

5. AMERICAN ENTRY: ENEMIES AND FRIENDS

> In general, the XXIV Corps had to do benevolently what more than half a million Japanese had done tyrannically.[89]

It was a strange fate that brought a onetime farm boy from Galconda, Illinois, to rule over fifteen million Koreans. John Reed Hodge, commander of the XXIV Corps of the United States Tenth Army, became Commanding General, U.S. Armed Forces in Korea (USAFIK), largely because in August 1945 his forces could be moved fastest to Korea.[90] These forces were quite ill-prepared for their task. They had almost no time for advanced planning. Many of their civil affairs officers had been trained for duty in Japan, and no one in the original entourage spoke fluent Korean. They had slim policy guidance from superiors in Tokyo and Washington.[91]

Many find in this lack of preparation the source of American failures in Korea. The failures have also been explained by the preference of military occupations for the status quo; necessary change is always sacrificed to the preservation of order and the dictates of military necessity.[92] But such interpretations ignore

the contradictions in already established policy between trusteeship and occupation, between ideal and real. They also suggest
that the American experience in Korea was unique, an anomaly,
a series of mistakes. But the Korean experience cannot be ab-
stracted from the general pattern of American actions in Asia in
1945 and since, a pattern of opposition to revolution and support for the old order. It is in the ensuing improvisation of the
American Occupation in Korea that this general pattern may be
seen in relief, in its pure form. The Occupation lacked not policy, but *workable* policy, policy that would prevent a revolution
contrary to American interests. So it improvised its own policy.
These basic considerations proved more important than the initial errors and fumbles of the American forces, much discussed
in other studies. The Occupation's brief fling with the Japanese
authorities, for instance, in which an attempt was made to use
the Government-General personnel and the Japanese police, had
little lasting significance. It only served as prologue to the more
prolonged attachment to the conservative elements in the Korean
political spectrum. Here was a romance that lasted, eventually
allowing these elements to prevail in south Korea. Americans
found new friends and in the process acquired new enemies.

The romance began immediately upon the arrival of the occupation forces, and stands out in the initial political reports of H.
Merrell Benninghoff, State Department political advisor to General Hodge, dated September 15, September 29, and October
10, 1945.[93] He began by describing the Korean situation:

> Southern Korea can best be described as a powder keg ready
> to explode at the application of a spark.

> There is great disappointment that immediate independence
> and sweeping out of the Japanese did not eventuate.

> [Those Koreans who] achieved high rank under the Japanese
> are considered pro-Japanese and are hated almost as much as
> their masters.

> It is believed that the removal of the Governor-General and
> the Director of the Police Bureau, both Japanese, accom-
> panied by wholesale replacements of (Japanese) police per-
> sonnel in the Seoul area will mollify irate Koreans even
> though the government itself is not strengthened thereby.

All [political] groups seem to have the common ideas of seiz-
ing Japanese property, ejecting the Japanese from Korea, and
achieving immediate independence. Beyond this they have few
ideas.

Korea is completely ripe for agitators.

Benninghoff alluded to the incipient romance between Americans and certain Korean friends:

> The most encouraging single factor in the political situation
> is the presence in Seoul of *several hundred conservatives*
> among the older and better educated Koreans. Although many
> of them have served with the Japanese, that stigma ought
> eventually to disappear. Such persons favor the return of the
> "Provisional Government" and although they may not consti-
> tute a majority they are probably the largest single group
> (emphasis added).

This is a remarkably frank admission of the process at work in
September 1945 whereby the American command found willing
friends in the Korean Democratic party and its sympathizers
who hoped to perpetuate a wholly discredited elite. So great was
that attraction that Benninghoff was willing within the space of
one paragraph to transform "several hundred conservatives"
into "the largest single group," a classic Freudian wish-fulfill-
ment. In reality it was the largest single group that Americans
could count on. The other group, the "agitators," the "Communists," just would not do:

> Communists advocate the seizure *now* of Japanese property
> and may be a threat to law and order. It is probable that well-
> trained agitators are attempting to bring about chaos in our
> area so as to cause the Koreans to repudiate the United States
> in favor of Soviet "freedom" and control (Benninghoff's
> italics).

Careful readers will note that Benninghoff transformed the legitimate demand of *all* Korean political groups for Japanese property into a demand of the "Communists."

Benninghoff complained of a lack of policy guidance from
Washington and quoted General Hodge's wish for "high-powered
officers . . . who are experienced in governmental affairs and
who know orientals." He ended his first report by suggesting a

new policy: "[Hodge asks] that consideration be given to returning the Chungking Government in exile to Korea as a provisional
government under Allied sponsorship to act as figureheads during occupation and until Korean people stabilize to where there
can be an election." It is likely, of course, that Benninghoff knew
nothing about this "government" in Chungking; he did know
that the Korean Democratic party advocated its return, so it
could not be all bad.

Two weeks later Benninghoff's thinking had evolved. He now
could identify "two distinct groups":

> There is the so-called democratic or conservative group. . . .
> [Its members include] many of the professional and educated
> leaders who were educated in the U.S. or in American mis-
> sionary institutions in Korea . . . they demonstrate a desire to
> follow the western democracies, and they almost unanimously
> desire the early return of Dr. Syngman Rhee and the "Pro-
> visional Government" at Chungking.

The largest element in this group was the Korean Democratic
party, which "consists of well-educated business and professional
men as well as community leaders."

The other group was the "radical" element; its main strength
lay in the People's Republic: "The radicals appear to be better
organized than their Democratic [sic] opponents . . . their pub-
licity material in the press has behind it a definite program and
probably trained direction." Benninghoff described Lyuh Woon-
hyung as "the guiding genius of the organization," but "the
people do not know how to judge him at present, however, because his political views have *apparently* changed from Christian * to Communist" (emphasis added). But in the next paragraph the qualifier is dropped; he became just "Yuh Woon
Hyung [sic], the Communist." Benninghoff then offered an interesting analysis of the People's Republic:

> [They] considered themselves the government, they released
> political prisoners, and assumed responsibilities for public
> safety, food distribution, and other governmental functions.
> This was perhaps the peak of power enjoyed by the Commit-
> tee [CPKI], which rapidly lost influence because of the disaf-

---

* "Christian" political views?

fection of the more conservative members following the ascendancy of the communist elements. Meanwhile the Japanese learned that the U.S. was to occupy southern Korea; they also realized that Yuh was not going to follow their dictates. They transformed the Committee into a Public Safety Committee in order to reduce its power, and added 3,000 Japanese soldiers to the police force of Seoul.

The less aggressive conservatives . . . [were] forced to organize for their own protection and in behalf of their anti-communist pro-democratic beliefs.

Benninghoff reported that the radicals were "vague as to the manner in which they will receive aid and guidance in rehabilitating their country." He then assured Washington that "The attitude of the American forces toward these political developments is one of aloofness as long as peace and order is maintained."

On October 10, Benninghoff wrote about the conservatives:

The Conservative [side] which is much less aggressive but which is believed to represent the thought of the majority of thinking Koreans are [sic] willing to cooperate with Mil Govt. Many of them have stated that they realize their country must pass through a period of tutelage, and that they would prefer to be under American rather than Soviet guidance.

He went on to urge the return of Syngman Rhee and other KPG leaders, but said that if Koreans in Yenan with Mao Tse-tung's forces wished to return, they should be told that "the Military Government finds it necessary for the time being to limit the number of Koreans who can return."

Within the space of three short weeks, Benninghoff managed to twist the Korean scene to fit his parameters, to make a democratic majority out of a handful of discredited plutocrats, and to make Soviet-controlled communists out of dedicated opponents of the defeated Japanese order. It was a wretched distortion, but the conservative group was "willing to cooperate," willing to sacrifice Korean independence for a period of tutelage —if *only* the Soviets were not part of it. These men had to be anointed, somehow legitimized: they became democrats.

Some will protest that the Occupation was ignorant of Korean conditions, that Americans were at the mercy of their interpreters. This was the burden of a cable from William Langdon, another State Department advisor in Seoul, responding to criticism of Occupation policies in Korea:

> As for favoring plutocracy in, and excluding popular left wingers from, Military Government, it is quite possible that at the beginning we may have picked out a disproportionate number of rich and conservative persons. But how were we to know who was who among unfamiliar people? For practical reasons we had to hire persons who spoke English, and it so happened that these persons and their friends came largely from moneyed classes because English had been a luxury among Koreans.[94]

This cable was for internal consumption; Langdon was protesting innocence to his superiors in Washington. He was, consciously or unconsciously, trying to deceive them. Lyuh Woonhyung, for instance, spoke English; his brother Lyuh Woon-hong was a graduate of Wooster College in Ohio. Yet the Occupation command would not receive Lyuh until early October.[95]

Readers may judge American "aloofness," as Benninghoff put it, by actions taken in September and October 1945. First, of course, was the decision to resuscitate the Korean element of the Japanese police force, to be described in detail below. Secondly, on October 5 the Occupation announced the formation of a Korean Advisory Council. The chairman was Kim Sŏng-su, a founder of the Korean Democratic party with landholdings of legendary proportions in North Chŏlla province. Nine of the council's eleven members were members of the KDP. The American military governor, however, described it as "the nucleus of democracy in Korea," composed of "men greater than politics and men above any groupings or outside interest." [96] An official welcoming ceremony for the American forces was held on October 20. Cho Pyŏng-ok, a founder of the KDP, and Kim Sŏng-su had earlier (September 27) been named managing director and vice-chairman, respectively, of the ceremony.[97] The occasion was an important public example of the degree of American-KDP camaraderie, and it also heralded the return of Syngman Rhee to Korea. At the welcoming ceremony, General Hodge secreted Rhee behind a screen and then "histrionically" presented him to the crowd, making American political sympathies all too obvious.[98]

More significant than these activities, however, were the Occupation's political and administrative appointments. The search for a separate force to counterpose to the People's Committees dominated the thinking of American policymakers in Korea. The Korean Democratic party seemed ideally suited, and therefore the Occupation opened up several crucial organs in the government bureaucracy to it. Ralf Dahrendorf has written:

> As a medium and instrument of domination, bureaucracy stands at the disposal of anyone who is called upon to control it. As a constant in political conflict it accompanies and supports whatever group is in power by administering its interests and directives dutifully and loyally.[99]

The American command proceeded to staff the Government-General (renamed Military Government) with members of the KDP or with Koreans who had served the Japanese. In lockstep fashion, it appointed: Cho Pyŏng-ok, director of the National Police; Chang T'aek-sang, chief of Seoul metropolitan police; Kim Yong-mu, chief justice of the Supreme Court; Yi In, chief prosecutor. Cho, Kim, and Yi were leaders of the small initial group that met August 28 to form the Korean Democratic party; Chang joined them on September 7.[100] These four men held their positions throughout the three years of the military government, and were largely free to act as they saw fit.[101] Moreover these men were simply the most powerful among the hundreds of KDP members and former servants of Japan who staffed the government at all levels. While the leaders of the People's Republic were still organizing in the provinces and calling for the transfer of power to the committee structure, the KDP and those it protected had, in the wink of an eye, achieved state power at the center.

These appointments utterly compromised American claims of neutrality, but they were functional for American aims. Men were needed who could be trusted to oppose the Left. The Occupation was quite willing to live with the results of these appointments, to defend and champion the actions of these men through 1948. As for the KDP leaders and their associates, they had no future if any government that advocated land redistribution and punishment of former collaborators succeeded the Occupation. They took it upon themselves to assure that such a consequence would not occur.

Syngman Rhee arrived in Korea on October 16 on one of General MacArthur's private planes, even though some individuals in the State Department had opposed his early return.[102] He quickly brought about a loose coalition of the Right under an organization called the Central Council of the Society for the Promotion of Korean Independence (SPKI).[103] The Korean Democratic party was the most powerful element within the SPKI, although Rhee himself never joined the KDP: he frowned on its collaborationist beginnings and its influence within the Occupation. However, Rhee could not ignore the KDP's new-found power, and KDP leaders needed Rhee to give them some legitimacy as patriots. It was a marriage of convenience.[104]

Some leftists initially participated in the SPKI. They knew Rhee only as a long-lost exile, and had great respect for him when he first returned. Furthermore, Rhee seemed to be a friend of the Americans, and the Left did not yet see itself as an enemy of the United States. But Rhee squelched these initial efforts at cooperation with his denunciation of the People's Republic in a radio broadcast of November 7, 1945. He quickly assumed an uncompromising position against any form of coalition or agreement with the Left, whether in northern or southern Korea. He became the earliest and most stubborn proponent of a separate government in the south. He would take half a loaf, on his terms.[105]

6. HALF A LOAF:
THE OCCUPATION MAKES POLICY

Within the Occupation a policy that implied a separate southern government was well under way by November 1945. It was developed because existing policy could not achieve the necessary results. The Occupation had come face-to-face with the contradictions inherent in American policy toward Korea since early 1944: trust, cooperation, true democratization—the higher posture—could not guarantee the American position in Korea. Korea was a bed of sand and the Occupation was sinking. Only force would work. The bulwark would have to be built from existing materials, whatever the cost. The new policy had four aspects: strengthening the alliance with the Right, including the proposal that it be used to establish a new Korean government; building up a reactionary police force; developing separate south Korean national defense forces; and suppressing the Left.

One interpretation of this policy-making might be that it was essentially unilateral, quite at odds with the wishes of superiors in Washington. Washington did oppose it for a while. Yet it was advocated by State Department advisors on the scene and by emissaries dispatched to Korea. It eventually became American policy in Korea, after two years of experimentation and attempts at negotiation, after Washington got trusteeship out of its system and saw the light. The Occupation could later have claimed that it was right from the start (no pun intended).

Washington transmitted a detailed, comprehensive statement of policy to Korea in mid-October.[106] This "initial directive" urged "the progressive elimination of all vestiges of Japanese control over Korean economic and political life." Such agencies as the police "will be progressively purged of undependable and undesirable elements, and in particular, of Japanese and Koreans who collaborated with the Japanese." This document authorized the Occupation to encourage democratic parties and to abolish "those whose activities are inconsistent" with the requirements and objectives of policy, but it expressly stated that "you will not extend official recognition to, nor utilize for political purposes, any self-styled Korean provisional government." Finally, the Occupation was ordered to establish the greatest possible uniformity in administrative practices with the Soviet forces in the north, so that unification would not later prove difficult.

It is quite obvious that such a policy was impossible to implement in mid-October 1945. No uniformity in administrative practice was possible. The Soviets had recognized and used the People's Committee structure in the north; the Americans were operating through the existing Japanese structures and using employees both in the government and the police who violated the strictures against former collaborators. Furthermore, the

Occupation had embraced an understanding of democracy that justified close relations with a conservative party of the old order, including many collaborators. Finally, the Occupation hoped to utilize the "self-styled Korean provisional government."

We have seen that as early as September 15 Benninghoff had reported General Hodge's suggestion that the KPG be used as "a provisional government under Allied sponsorship to act as figureheads during occupation." The acting political advisor to MacArthur in Japan, George Atcheson, pushed this idea again in mid-October, after a conversation with Hodge:

> We should commence to use some progressive, popular and respected leader, or small group, to act as a nucleus of an organization which in cooperation with and under the direction of our military government could develop into an executive and administrative governmental agency.[107]

He then suggested three names: Syngman Rhee, Kim Koo, and Kimm Kiu-sik, all KPG leaders. He acknowledged that such a proposal was "contrary to past American thinking," but "unless positive action is taken . . . our difficulties will increase rather than diminish, and the Communistic group set up and encouraged by the Soviets in northern Korea will manage to extend its influence into southern Korea."

The Director of the State Department Office of Far Eastern Affairs, John Carter Vincent, answered that he opposed using the KPG, but in saying so starkly revealed the essential conflict between hope and reality in American policy.[108] He agreed that "there is need for some kind of responsible Korean leadership to counter-balance the activities of the Communist elements" but:

> This Government has consistently advocated a policy that nothing be done by this Government or by the Commander in Korea to give any group, such as the Kim Koo group [KPG] . . . or any individual, such as Dr. Rhee, the impression that we were supporting such a group or individual as against any other Koreans.

But the American command could not afford to be neutral in revolutionary Korea; it just could not come up with both "responsible" and anti-communist leadership. It had to find allies where it could. Assistant Secretary of War John J. McCloy in a responding memorandum accurately criticized Vincent's cable:[109] it had avoided "the really pressing realities facing us in Korea." McCloy said that Hodge feared that "the Communists will seize by direct means the government in our area, . . . [which] would seriously prejudice our intention to permit the people of Korea freely to choose their own form of government." The best approach was to "build up on our own a reasonable and respected government or group of advisors . . . [which would] provide the basis for, at some later date, a really free and uncoerced election by the people." After describing alleged Soviet activities in north Korea, and identifying all Koreans on the Left with the Soviets, McCloy urged that Hodge be given discretion to handle the communists, and to "use as many exiled Koreans as he can" (presumably non-communist Korean exiles).*

McCloy clearly stated the contradictions in American policy toward Korea and agreed with the Occupation: Americans must build up a government on their own. The memorandum is also interesting for its assumptions, which echo American involvement in Asia since World War II. First, a choice for communism (as Americans define it) is ipso facto "unfree." Second, the leaders America sponsors must be "reasonable" men; they must not question the legitimacy of American power and interests. Third, the implication is that once a firm decision for anticommunist leadership is made, a process must ensue whereby this leadership is consolidated—that is, its opponents (who may or may not be communists) are hounded, suppressed, and refused participation in political power. After this process—and only after it—a basis exists for "a really free and uncoerced election." This is largely what happened in south Korea during the two years prior to the United Nations-"sponsored" elections in May 1948. Elections could never decide the fundamental questions about economic, political, and social structure that

---

* McCloy noted that Hodge had found Syngman Rhee helpful, and "was using him then in negotiations with the communist leaders," which must have pleased those leaders—undoubtedly he means the People's Republic leaders—no end.

divided Koreans in 1945–48. The structural basis had to be determined first, and that was a question of relative political power. Then the election could be held, after the crucial decisions had already been made.[110]

The American determination unilaterally to establish a government was most clearly stated in William Langdon's cable of November 20, 1945.[111] After saying that the trusteeship idea should be dropped and averring that the Kim Koo KPG group "has no rival for first government of liberated Korea," he outlined a new policy:

(1) The Commanding General directs Kim Koo to form a council in MG [Military Government] representative of the several political groups to study and prepare the form of government of Korea and to organize a Governing Commission. . . .

(2) The Governing Commission is integrated with MG (presently rapidly being built up as an all Korean organization).

(3) The Governing Commission succeeds MG as interim government, with Commanding General retaining power of veto and of appointing such American supervisors and advisors as he deems necessary.

(4) Three other powers concerned are requested to supply some supervisors and advisors in Governing Commission in place of American [advisors].

Lest there be any doubt of the implication of point four, Langdon added the following note:

Somewhere in the transition . . . negotiations to be signed with Russia for mutual withdrawal of troops and extension to Russian zone of Governing Commission's authority. Russia should be informed in advance of above plan and invited to further it by allowing persons in Russian zone nominated to Governing Commission *by council* to proceed to Seoul, but if Russian participation is not forthcoming plan should be carried out for Korea *south of 38th parallel* (emphasis added).

Langdon spoke of Korea as if it were Mexico, rather than a nation contiguous to Russia in which she had long had an interest. Then, belaboring the obvious, Langdon offered his view on the receptivity of such a government toward foreign interests, a

view that will interest those familiar with Korea's fate at the end
of the nineteenth century:

> The old native regime internally was feudal and corrupt but
> the record shows that it was the best disposed toward foreign
> interests of the three Far Eastern nations, protecting foreign
> lives and property and enterprises and respecting treaties and
> franchises. I am sure that we may count on at least as much
> from a native government evolved as above. . . .

In other words, Korea's postwar position was to be identical with
that of the old Yi Dynasty: prostrate. Langdon ended this remarkable document with a pointed reference to a recent Military
Government Ordinance authorizing an Office of the Director of
National Defense and a Bureau of Armed Forces, "which has
as aim, organizing, training, and equipping armed Korean military and naval forces."

Coming two short months after American forces arrived in
Korea, this proposal is shocking. But given the Korean context
in which a separate government was already being discussed by
conservative Koreans, and given an Occupation command which
thought war with the Soviets imminent,[112] it was understandable.
This policy was not only being implemented at the time of Langdon's proposal, as shown by the reference to national defense
forces, but it was the basis for later developments: the "Representative Democratic Council" under Syngman Rhee established
in February 1946, and the South Korean Interim Government
inaugurated in the fall of the same year.[113] The implication of
such a policy, of course, was that no cooperation was possible
with the Soviets and that Korea was already effectively and per-
manently divided.

Washington's response to Langdon's cable stated that it would
be "safer" to negotiate with the Soviets "before attempting to
introduce a new idea such as the governing commission concerning which the USSR has made no commitments." Trusteeship
was U.S. policy and was one necessary "to secure the elimination of the barrier of the 38° parallel." [114] Langdon quickly
answered that the United States should "bypass trusteeship." As
if he misunderstood the department's position, he said, "To meet
the Dep'ts [sic] wishes General Hodge will name the projected

council something less imposing than 'governing commission' and assign to it functions in scope to our zone." [115]

The Occupation was increasingly frustrated by its inability to render Korean affairs tractable. It was forced to take several critical steps to strengthen its hold on the south; the "governing commission" was one. General Hodge's remarkable report on the first three months of occupation, submitted December 19, 1945 to General MacArthur,[116] delineates the context of these actions:

> [There] is growing resentment against all Americans in the area including passive resistance. . . . Every day of drifting under this situation makes our position in Korea more untenable and decreases our waning popularity. . . . The word pro-American is being added to pro-Jap, national traitor, and Jap collaborator.

Hodge said that Koreans wanted independence immediately, but "by occidental standards Koreans are not ready for independence." He found that "the situation in the [sic] South Korea makes extremely fertile ground for the establishment of Communism."

> The approximate international influences and our occupation policies of insuring all freedom and maintaining property rights and order among liberated oriental people favor Communistic activities.

> Koreans well know that the Russians have a force locally of about 4 to 1 to Americans and with the usual oriental slant are willing to do homage and are doing homage to the man with the largest weapon. On the part of the masses there is an increasing tendency to look to Russia for the future.[117]

> In summary, the U.S. occupation of Korea . . . is surely drifting to the edge of a political-economic abyss from which it can never be retrieved with any credit to United States prestige in the Far East. Positive action on the international level or *the seizure of complete initiative* in South Korea by the U.S. in the very near future is absolutely essential to stop this drift (emphasis added).

He urged the abandonment of trusteeship and suggested that if no positive action followed, "both the U.S. and Russia withdraw forces from Korea simultaneously and leave Korea to its own devices and an inevitable internal upheaval for its own self-purification."

The Occupation chose to act in four basic areas: (1) inaugurating a south Korean defense force; (2) building up the national police, to effect "the seizure of complete initiative" in the south; (3) strengthening the alliance with rightist political groups; and (4) the inevitable obverse of the first three, suppressing the Left.

American officers initiated planning for a south Korean defense force six weeks after the Occupation began for the purpose of defending south Korea's borders and "quelling internal disturbances." [118] Ordinance No. 28, November 13, created the Office of the Director of National Defense, with jurisdiction over the Bureau of Police and "a new Bureau of Armed Forces comprising Army and Navy Departments." Hodge later stated, "I was very interested in establishing a Korean Army from the beginning of the Occupation . . . to get a head start for the future when we accomplished our mission of setting up a Korean Government. I met much opposition at higher levels." [119] The Joint Chiefs of Staff disapproved Ordinance No. 28 on January 9, 1946, saying that any action along such lines should be "deferred" pending "unsettled problems connected with international commitments." [120]

Still the plans went ahead. The "National Defense" designation was not dropped until June 1946, when this office became the Department of Internal Security, and the Bureau of the Armed Forces became the Bureau of Constabulary.[121] The names were changed, but the forms remained through 1948. Restrictions imposed at higher levels were often ignored, as the constabulary "might one day emerge as the Korean Army." [122]

Official sources describe the recruiting of officers: "The young Korean officers who were to command new companies were selected on the advice of Lee Hyung Koon, former colonel in the Japanese Army then serving as an 'advisor' to the Director of National Defense." [123] Lee was but one of a host of high-ranking Koreans in the Japanese military who populated the officers' ranks in the constabulary and later in the Republic of Korea Army. In early December 1945 the Americans selected sixty key officers to be trained in the English language (their Japanese no longer served them well). Twenty came from the Japanese army, twenty from the Japanese Kwantung army in Manchuria, and twenty from the anti-Japanese Kwangbok army associated with the KPG in Chungking. The latter group never achieved any influence within the constabulary because it had difficulty associating with officers widely viewed as pro-Japanese and because, according to the Americans in charge, it lacked rudimentary military training. But the other officers emerged dominant in the constabulary and the succeeding Republic of Korea Army.[124] It would be difficult to overestimate the significance of placing this key coercive apparatus in the hands of Korean officers who had served in the Japanese military.

The immediate purpose of such a force in late 1945 was the "quelling [of] internal disturbances." American officers found that "civil disorders and guerrilla-like activities by Communist elements offered opportunities for tactical training." [125] The constabulary became one of the two primary weapons used against the widespread disorders in south Korea during the next two years. The other primary weapon was the Korean National Police.

The tragedy of the liberation period is most fully revealed, and the depth of American responsibility most obvious, in the history of the national police. The SWNCC Basic Initial Directive of mid-October cited above called particular attention to rooting out collaborators in the police force, the most hated Japanese institution in Korea. Initial Supreme Command, Allied Powers (SCAP) reports stated that the police had been "thoroughly Japanized and efficiently utilized as an instrument of tyranny." [126] The Occupation was quickly thwarted in its attempt to use the Japanese police force, including its Japanese members, in September 1945. However, the Japanese structure—a highly centralized, arbitrary, self-contained national force—remained unchanged, and the Koreans who served in the Japanese force were re-employed on a wholesale basis. Lee Won-sul has estimated that 85 percent of the Koreans formerly employed in the Japanese police were back on the Korean police force by October 1945, and Cho Pyŏng-ok said that in 1948, 53 percent of the officers and 25 percent of the rank and file were former Japanese employees.[127] These figures included Koreans in Japanese employ who fled south after liberation, fearing reprisals in the north.[128]

The Occupation began training this police force on October 15, 1945 at the former Japanese Police Academy; for a time the uniforms, too, were Japanese. Far from making a mistake in employing this discredited Korean force, the Occupation recognized its use as the only really cohesive body that could be counted on to oppose the Left.[129] With the official inauguration of the U.S. Army Military Government in Korea (USAMGIK) in January 1946, and the increasing centralization of all decision making in Seoul, "all police in the country were integrated into a single machine, equipped with U.S. Army vehicles, Japanese Army rifles, bayonets and machine guns, and their own private telephone and radio network." [130] The stage was set for the bloody two-and-a-half-year drama in which the Korean National Police acted openly and continually as an instrument of the Right to control and suppress leftist and moderate political activity. Virtually all American accounts of the period are critical of the KNP. MacDonald noted that the police "were enthusiastic in subduing leftists," but tended to stand around "watching the fun" when rightists demonstrated. A. Wigfall Green, a top official in the Military Government Justice Department, said "the arrogance of the police, engendered by the Japanese, continued." [131] Many American officers tended to explain away police excesses as "the way Orientals do things," neglecting of course the American role in installing those particular "Orientals" with experience in an oppressive police force.[132] However, top American officials punctuated the actions of the KNP with the most hypocritical praise. In February 1946, for example, the military governor, General Archer L. Lerch, said:

> It is indeed refreshing to know that throughout Korea there stand 18,000 neat, clean, well-uniformed and well-trained policemen who have put politics aside to work for Korea.
>
> The wrongdoers of Korea are already learning that crime does not pay.
>
> You have built up a splendid police force which has operated in a thoroughly democratic manner without partiality and without political favoritism.[133]

Despite the police putting "politics aside," there were more political prisoners in Occupation jails by 1947 than at the end of Japanese rule, nearly all of them suspected leftists (even though rightist violence was a dominant characteristic of the period).[134] The Military Government did occasionally take action against police excesses. However, the usual pattern was to force a handful of resignations, issue pious statements full of democratic spirit, and do nothing about the basic police structure, the personnel who had been employed by the Japanese, and police methods which included the routine use of torture to gain confessions.[135]

The results of the Moscow Conference of Foreign Ministers were released on December 27, 1945. The Moscow provisions included a four-power trusteeship for Korea of up to five years, and a joint commission of the United States and the Soviet Union, "in order to assist the formation of a provisional Korean government * and with a view to the preliminary elaboration of the appropriate measures." [136] Publication of the accords in Korea caused an overnight furor. Nearly all Korean political parties opposed trusteeship initially. Trusteeship was translated as "trust rule" (*sint'ak t'ongch'i*), an acceptable translation but one with unfortunate connotations because of the Japanese use of similar legitimizing phrases. The widespread opposition aptly demonstrated the unreality of the trusteeship approach for Korea.

The Kim Koo KPG group, which had returned to Korea on November 23, seized the initiative and organized widespread work stoppages and demonstrations in opposition to trusteeship. Although the American command feared these demonstrations, it supported the anti-trusteeship forces. Hodge transmitted Kim's statement opposing trusteeship to the State Department and recommended that it be distributed to the other three powers.[137] He met with Korean groups and "interpreted" trusteeship to them, saying it could be bypassed if only they would give full support to American plans.[138] In giving support to rightist opposition to trusteeship, the Occupation helped turn the issue to their favor.

---

* Not to be confused with the Korean Provisional Government.

The trusteeship imbroglio was crucial to defining what the essential issue was in liberated Korea. If it was to be the nature of the social order under which Koreans lived, the Right was hopelessly compromised. But if it was to be control by the Soviets (through a trusteeship) versus independence, the Right could hope to restore its "patriotism" and some degree of legitimacy through opposition to trusteeship. Thus the rightists urged the Korean people to believe that the Soviet Union and communist sympathizers in the State Department were the only supporters of trusteeship—this despite the evidence that trusteeship had always been proposed by the American side and was so at Moscow.[139]

This activity seriously compromised attempts to implement the Moscow accords. Stalin felt it necessary to call in Ambassador Harriman on January 23 and complain:

> The US representatives [in Korea] were advocating that the decision to set up a trusteeship be abrogated; that meetings were being held in public at which demands were being expressed to this effect, and that articles had been carried by the Korean press which stated that only the USSR and not the US had insisted on a trusteeship. General Lerch, Chief of Civil Administration, was named as being specifically implicated with the above.[140]

No doubt exists that Koreans as a whole opposed any sort of trusteeship, as they had since the Cairo Declaration. From this opposition the Right was able for the first time to mobilize real support for its policies. It was a crucial opportunity, particularly for those identified as collaborators with Japan. They could oppose trusteeship and hope to establish their patriotism (although they had privately expressed support for American tutelage); at the same time they could blame trusteeship on the Soviets and perhaps prevent the emergence of any coalition government, thus safeguarding their own personal futures. In this effort these men found allies in the true rightist patriots like Syngman Rhee and Kim Koo.

The Left, in the face of this resurgence by the Right, switched to support of trusteeship in early January 1946. This has been interpreted as the result of an order from Moscow or P'yŏngyang, but more likely it resulted from domestic south Korean factors: rightist initiatives in opposing trusteeship, their continuous denunciations of Moscow and the Left, and the Right's support by American authorities. The Left gained the temporary and dubious advantage of being in agreement with official American and Soviet policy, an anomalous situation for the American command in Korea. But the Left lost popular support by endorsing an unworkable plan opposed by most Koreans.

General Hodge recognized that he had stepped beyond the bounds of his authority in supporting the opponents of official American policy and offered his resignation in late January.[141] When he was urged to stay on, he took the offensive and sent off a blistering message to the State Department. Hodge had the virtue of being able to state simply the requirements for maintaining American power in Korea, perhaps too simply for the sensibilities of some in Washington. Hodge's vision would eventually prevail, but the State Department lagged behind him.

> . . . the Department has paid little attention either to the information painstakingly sent in from those actually on the grounds as to the psychology of the Korean people or to the repeated urgent recommendations of the commander and State Department political advisors.
>
> I do not know who have been the experts on Korea who have advised and guided the State Department in their disregard of my recommendations. It may be the educated Koreans in the United States. It certainly has not been anyone who has seen and really knows Korea since the war. I hope that it can be impressed upon the Department that here we are not dealing with wealthy U.S. educated Koreans, but with early, [sic] poorly trained, and poorly educated Orientals strongly affected by 40 years of Jap control, who stubbornly and fanatically hold to what they like and dislike, who are definitely influenced by direct propaganda and with whom it is almost impossible to reason. We are opposed by a strongly organized, ruthless political machinery designed to appeal to the millions of this type.[142]

Acting Secretary of State Dean Acheson responded to Hodge's message by saying he failed to see the "pertinency" of Hodge's complaints that his "urgent recommendations" had not been acted upon. Acheson noted that Benninghoff and Langdon had been brought to Washington for consultations and were sent back to Korea to give Hodge firsthand information on the Department's views. Then Acheson, quite rightly, questioned Hodge's capacity for negotiating with the Russians in the Joint Commission meetings just opened in Seoul: "I confess myself somewhat perturbed by the attitude taken by General Hodge. . . . I should feel less concern as to the outcome if General Hodge were not so convinced of failure at the very outset of the discussions." [143]

7. SUPPRESSION OF THE LEFT

The inevitable result of the Occupation's policy-making was the suppression of the Left within south Korea, proving once again that intervention in favor of the status quo in a revolutionary situation is no more neutral or disinterested than active support for the forces of change. The Occupation could not pursue the policies discussed above and avoid opposition. It could not enroll the forces of the old order on its side and then proclaim neutrality. Regardless of its intentions, the Occupation was forced to begin the suppression of Koreans who actively sought change.

Some have claimed that Korea was a morass of conflicting factions, cliques, parties, and interests; that the Occupation could not have been expected to know quite what to do amid this chaos. The Occupation cultivated such an image. One can find various figures of fifty-four, or seventy-two, or ninety-five distinct political parties competing for power in the liberation period.[144] But these figures distort the Korean reality. A great many cliques and factions, often involving a handful of cronies and no more, were encouraged to register as full-fledged political parties under the Occupation's registration law. Yet the fundamental bifurcation was between Left and Right.[145] It was recognized as such by both sides and acted upon by the Occupation command. Theodore Lowi has written: "Issues that involve redistribution cut closer than any others along class lines and activate interests in what are roughly class terms. . . . In redistribution, there will never be more than two sides and the two sides are clear, stable, consistent." [146] No better proof of this statement exists than the record of liberated Korea. Left and Right were like two scorpions in a bottle, and the American role was to nourish one at the expense of the other.

The de facto policy followed by the Occupation and its Korean employees was to break up organizations oriented to the Left, create a vacuum, and encourage organizations of the Right to move in, with police and constabulary support.[147] The two most important objects of this policy were the People's Republic and the labor union associated with it, the National Council of Korean Labor Unions, better known by its shortened title, *Chŏnp'yŏng* (the full Korean title was *Chosŏn nodong chohap chŏn'guk p'yŏngŭi-hoe*). Yet it should be recognized that the policy was extended to all organizations of the Left.

The Occupation was hostile to the People's Republic from the day it entered Korea. Hodge refused to receive Lyuh Woonhyung until early October; he then showed his acceptance of rightist propaganda by asking Lyuh, "What connections have you with the Jap? How much money did you receive from the Jap?" [148] The first military governor, Maj. Gen. Archibald V. Arnold, issued a press statement on October 10 describing KPR claims to be the rightful government of Korea as "boyishness" by old men, "so foolish as to think they can take to themselves and exercise any of the legitimate functions of the Government of Korea." [149]

American officers thought they saw the hand of the Soviets in all KPR activities—and if it was not immediately obvious, they tried to find it. General Hodge cabled Washington on November 2 that he was "sure [the] most radical elements are Russian instigated but cannot get positive proof"; the entire activity "has the smell of being agitated by a well-trained group of outside experts." [150] Later that month General Hodge, alarmed at continuing KPR strength, sent the following assessment to Washington:

This political party is the most powerful Communist backed group in Korea and has some connections with Soviet politics. Included also [sic] considerable number of Leftists, not true Communists . . . [their claims to be a government] gained them many followers among the uneducated and laboring classes, and has fostered radical activities in the provinces under the guise of orders from the KPR.[151]

Hodge admitted that the KPR had offered "full support and aid" to the United States; however, they refused to drop the word "government" from their title, and thus he thought it essential to oppose the KPR publicly:

> This will constitute in effect a "declaration of war" upon the Communistic elements in Korea, and *may result in temporary disorders*. It will also bring charges of political discrimination in a "free" country, both by local pinko and by pinko press (emphasis added).

Hodge ended this summa by saying that if KPR activities continued, it "will greatly delay the time when Korea can be said to be ready for independence." General Hodge's public denunciation of the KPR came on December 12, 1945; its activities were "unlawful" from then on. Still, "the Conservatives thought the General's position was not firm enough." [152]

The KPR was still a threat to American plans. The Occupation was undermanned and just then reaching Korea's hinterlands. Well-established People's Committees were functioning as de facto governments. American forces were in several cases forced to operate temporarily through the committee structure. The problems this caused, and the solution it indicated, were stated by a former American officer in South Chŏlla province:

> Either the whole provincial government had to be turned over to the Republic or its control had to be broken. The conclusion finally reached was to use the Japanese framework of government and incumbent lesser officials as a basis, and to staff it with Korean key officials as rapidly as suitable leaders could be found.[153]

Rarely has a decision for counterrevolution been so baldly stated. Later on, as if the above statement of American responsibility were not relevant, as if elementary cause and effect did not apply, this officer commented that "the dead hand of Japanese ideology lay heavily upon Korean officials' thought processes—particularly on men who had served under the Japanese." [154]

In North Kyŏngsang province the committees were also

strong, controlling numerous towns when American units arrived in late September. The Americans at first retained Kim Tae-u as Governor (he had served under Japan); Kim "proceeded to change large numbers of *kun* and other local officials, removing Japanese and appointing Koreans. The resulting chaos, together with [Kim's] reputation for being pro-Japanese, made his retention seem undesirable." He was replaced on October 11 by an American political science Ph.D., Colonel Edwin A. Henn. Henn retained Kim as his advisor and gave him the predominant role in further personnel appointments, although "almost any Korean who could make himself understood in English was employed." [155] The Fortieth Division, which then had control of the Kyŏngsang provinces, developed a "standard operating procedure":

> A tactical unit occupying a community was to expel the former head of the local government, if he was a Japanese, but retain him as an advisor if necessary. Other Japanese were to be replaced by Koreans as soon as possible. If the head of the government was a Korean, he was to be retained until a suitable replacement could be found. If a political party [read People's Committee] had expelled the former officials and taken over the government, the officials put in by the party were to be arrested and suitable substitutes appointed. Former police officials were to be used, if they were available and suitable, and backed up if necessary by the [American] military. [156]

This pattern was followed in numberless communities—arrest the People's Committee leaders, reinstall Korean civil officials, recall the police from the hills. Even the police officers themselves could not believe the Americans were putting them back at their posts; on numerous occasions they had to be searched out in their hiding places and forcibly marched back to duty. And always, in dealing with the committees and the groups associated with them, force was the *ultima ratio*. Korean force, if sufficient; American force, if necessary. On any number of occasions in the first year of occupation American tactical units had to be called out to restore order. This first year drew to a close in the fall of 1946 with a general strike throughout Korea, followed by massive rioting in Taegu and throughout the Kyŏngsang provinces, resulting in fifty-three police deaths in Taegu alone, and untold thousands of rioters killed and imprisoned.[157]

This general strike was the excuse for breaking up the *Chŏnp'yŏng* union. *Chŏnp'yŏng* had succeeded in organizing units in numerous factories throughout Korea. An American Labor Department officer said:

> When the Japanese industrialists abandoned their plants, committees of workers were formed which assumed responsibility for plant operation and protection. These committees soon formed themselves into the All-Korea Council of Labor Unions commonly known as Chung Pyong [*sic*]. . . . For a short period Chung Pyong was in almost complete control of those plants which had been Japanese-owned.[158]

This union published a newspaper; in its pages can be traced the success of the union's organizing activity, as well as its essentially reformist character.[159] It remained the strongest union in south Korea until the fall of 1946.

The American command began to undermine this union in December 1945. First, the Occupation decided to vest all former Japanese properties in its own hands, to be held and managed until a Korean government was formed. The factories were taken from *Chŏnp'yŏng* hands and placed under the control of the Military Government. Second, Ordinance No. 34 of December 8, 1945 established labor mediation boards to settle labor disputes and prohibited strikes. An American officer described this action:

> Koreans appointed to these boards were in no instance industrial wage earners or their representatives. The personnel of the boards are for the most part business men, professional men, and employers . . . [Ordinance No. 34] consisted of a declaration to protect the right of labor to work under those terms specified by business and professional people. Korean labor had this "right" during the entire Japanese regime.[160]

This same officer later visited factories throughout the south and found "systematic suppression" of *Chŏnp'yŏng* leaders and activities.[161]

American forces did not participate directly in the suppression of this labor union until fall 1946, when in Taegu martial law was declared and American troops moved in in the wake of nationwide strikes and uprisings. Previously the Occupation had tolerated the activities of the General League of Korean Labor (*Taehan nodong ch'ong yŏnmaeng*) (*Noch'ong*), an organ for strikebreaking and violence against workers that eventually formed the basis of the official trade union under the Rhee regime.[162] Its origins reflect a familiar pattern:

> It was an appendage to a political party backed by large Korean landowners and others who managed to make not only their peace but their fortune under the Japanese. Its funds were supplied by factory managers, business men's groups and others whose primary concern was to block rather than foster the formation of real labor unions.[163]

Noch'ong attempted to crush *Chŏnp'yŏng* workers through intimidation, violence, and torture.[164] For those who might attribute such activities to American ignorance of Korean practices, let the American director of the Department of Transportation speak for American methods used against *Chŏnp'yŏng* in the fall of 1946:

> We went into that situation just like we would go into battle. We were out to break that thing up and we didn't have time to worry too much if a few innocent people got hurt. We set up concentration camps outside of town and held strikers there when the jails got too full. It was war. We recognized it as war. And that is the way we fought it.[165]

After such action *Noch'ong* "quickly installed itself in power in many plants." [166]

The fall 1946 strikes were the beginning of the widespread violence and unrest that characterized the years 1946–50 in south Korea. General Hodge thought his "declaration of war" on the Left in December 1945 might "result in temporary disorders," but he was sadly mistaken. The disorders eventually touched nearly every city and town south of the 38th parallel. Space permits only a brief examination of the first major insurrection, or what official sources called "The Quasi-Revolt of October 1946." [167]

On September 23, 1946 a railroad strike shut down transportation and quickly spread into a general strike. Worker demands were largely related to the scarcity and high price of rice. The Military Government released captured documents which were allegedly "Instructions from the North" to KPR people in the south urging a "struggle" on the anniversary of the original founding of the KPR, September 6, 1946.[168] Hodge seized on this to describe the strikers as "misled by radical agitators . . . those who make great promises of something for nothing"; here was proof positive that "the Korean people are not yet ready to handle their own affairs." [169]

The strike was beyond the reach of General Hodge's quaint homilies, however. At the end of September the Noch'ong was mobilized to break the strikes. Three thousand members, supplemented by three thousand more from rightist youth groups, attacked strikers at Seoul's Yongsan railroad yards; the battle resulted in three dead, sixty injured, and two thousand arrests (nearly all strikers).[170] Taegu erupted in riots shortly thereafter and led to what leftists called the "October Peasant Revolution." The Occupation declared martial law and moved in American tactical units. By October 7 police deaths in the Taegu area alone numbered fifty-three. Revenge against the hated police, a feature of most unrest during the liberation period, was often taken in the most brutal manner.[171] Rioting continued during October throughout North and South Kyŏngsang provinces.[172]

General Hodge and his advisors panicked amidst this insurrection and dispatched a top secret memorandum to General MacArthur on October 28, 1946 stating that "evidence is growing that Russians are planning an invasion of South Korea after gathering of rice crop this fall." [173] This message demonstrated just how far removed USAMGIK was from Korean realities and the effects of its decisions over the past year. Hodge recommended to his superiors that, among other things, the Occupation "build up a Rightist Youth Army to augment and assist occupation forces and the police and constabulary." [174] John Carter Vincent replied that "it seemed to me entirely inappropriate for us to organize a 'Rightist Youth Army' in Korea and that General Hodge might achieve the ends he desired by increasing the strength of the Korean police and constabulary." [175]

But General Hodge was not deterred. The Occupation granted 5 million wŏn to "General" Yi Pŏm-sŏk, a former Korean exile in China with close connections to the Kuomintang, to equip and establish training facilities for his Korean National Youth.[176] These "youths" (they usually ranged in age from twenty to thirty-five) engaged in political activity and violence in favor of the Right; the Korean National Youth quickly became the most powerful youth group and eventually made Yi second only to Syngman Rhee in power. It was widely criticized by both Americans and Koreans as being "fascist": its training center was "under the spiritual leadership of Dr. An Ho-sang, a graduate of Jena during the Nazi era, a student of Hegel, and an open admirer of Hitler's Jugend." [177]

The Occupation went to extreme lengths, to be sure, but they were not sufficient to quiet south Korea. Riots, strikes, and minor insurrections took place in 1947; the decision to hold separate United Nations elections in the south in 1948 led to open guerrilla warfare in the Chŏlla provinces and Cheju island, lasting until the outbreak of the Korean War in June 1950.

8. CONCLUSIONS

The first few months of the Occupation do not tell the whole story of south Korea's three years of American tutelage. It was not an unbroken string of ignominy and failure. In early 1946 the State Department urged the Occupation to moderate its ties to the Right and cultivate middle-of-the-road leadership. This led to a long, energetic, but abortive effort to forge a "third-force" coalition around Lyuh Woon-hyung and Kimm Kiu-sik. It ended when Lyuh was assassinated on July 19, 1947. But actions taken in the first months seem to have compromised any later efforts at conciliation and cooperation between Left and Right, or between the United States and the Soviet Union.

The course taken in the first few months made separate Korean governments inevitable. The United States gave power to men who could only lose it if popular demands for land redistribution, ousting of former collaborators, labor reform, and unionization were acted upon. Nor did the Occupation lift a finger to change the structures through which such men operated: the slightly modified former Government-General, the national police, and the constabulary. Instead it opened these structures to them and encouraged paramilitary groups that served as storm troopers of the Right. To expect the opponents of such men, whether in south or north Korea, to acquiesce in such arrangements was to ask them to sign their death warrants. Nor could the panacea of free elections legitimize such leadership or absolve Americans of responsibility.

The better course would have been to let Koreans reap the whirlwind in 1945, to, as General Hodge put it, "leave Korea to its own devices and an inevitable internal upheaval for its own self-purification." If American forces had been better prepared, had known more about Korea, had had sufficient personnel, would this have been done? Were Americans fooled into misperceiving circumstances in Korea and disarmed by elites who spoke their language? If, somehow, Korea had been occupied in the 1960s, task forces would have been set up, problems fed into computers, and grants lavished on social engineers. Would the result have been different? The evidence suggests otherwise. In a series of critical decisions on Korea from 1945 to 1948—the division at the 38th parallel, governing southern Korea through military occupation, holding separate elections in the south, supporting Syngman Rhee's regime—a similar pattern prevailed. In each case, when the crunch came, earlier hopes and considerations were thrown out and whatever was necessary to ensure American power in Korea was done. American opposition to real change and support for reaction in Korea was not an anomaly but a link in a pattern of intervention. As Gabriel Kolko has written, "To separate [such] events from a continuum, in the hope that decision-makers will apply reason in one case and not in others, is to do violence to the history of the great shifting and reintegration of the world system that occurred between 1943 and 1949." [178]

The United States opposed revolution in principle in Korea as elsewhere. This was the underlying assumption of all American thinking about Korea beginning in 1943. Korean independence and self-determination were invariably considered not on their merits but only as they affected American interests. Creating a responsive Korea was more important than self-determination. Trusteeship, despite the highly principled rhetoric surrounding it, was an artifice, an attempt to hide power while asserting it, to wield power but somehow deny it. It was abandoned when it no longer served its purpose and when American planners came to see that their interests coincided with those of the colonial powers against which trusteeship was directed. A State Department directive of May 13, 1947 made this perfectly clear:

> Key our position is our awareness that in respect developments affecting position Western democratic powers in southern Asia, we essentially in same boat as French, also as British and Dutch. We cannot conceive setbacks to long-range interests France which would not also be setbacks our own.[179]

American planners rationalized their departure from the precepts of self-determination by seeing the hand of Soviet power in all activities of the Left. In Korea this meant that no responsible American policymaker could suggest support of the People's Republic, and none ever did. It was the only way Korea could have been unified, but the fear of the Left put the issue beyond the pale. In a sense it can be said that the end sought by the United States—a friendly Korea—inevitably corrupted the means. The Koreans willing to serve this end were compromised old men; the United States could not prop them up and hope to prevent a revolution. Without a massive American presence, the opponents of such men could have cut through the fabric of their support like a knife through butter; only the use of elemental force allowed this discredited elite to prevail.

The United States had to live with the results of using such means, and it turned the Occupation into a nightmare. To explain it Americans had to make democrats of those Koreans who would cooperate and Soviet-controlled communists of those who would not. Thus, "Korea" became to Americans a fantastic construct, "an ideological battleground upon which our entire success in Asia may depend," and "the proving ground of civilization—the arena in which the fate of mankind is being contested." [180] These absurdities seem to be necessary to charge the American imagination, but they did great violence to the legitimate aspirations of Koreans who opposed such ethnocentric conceits.

Notes

1. Andrew Grajdanzev, *Modern Korea* (New York, Institute of Pacific Relations, 1944), p. 285.
2. This statement was in General MacArthur's speech at the inauguration ceremonies of the Republic of Korea, August 15, 1948. E. Grant Meade has described a policy briefing in October 1945 at MacArthur's Tokyo headquarters for civil affairs officers departing for Korea in which the impression was given that U.S. policy in Korea was "to form a bulwark against communism." See E. Grant Meade, *American Military Government in Korea* (New York, King's Crown Press, Columbia University, 1951), p. 52. Established against communism in Korea. Rather, the bulwark idea is descriptive of de facto policymaking which began immediately after the American entry into Korea.
3. Anthony Eden, *Memoirs: The Reckoning* (Boston, Mass., Houghton Mifflin Co., 1965), p. 438. Soon Sung Cho is quite wrong when he says Eden "agreed" on a trusteeship for Indochina and Korea at this meeting (Soon Sung Cho, *Korea in World Politics, 1940–1950* [Berkeley and Los Angeles, University of California Press, 1967], p. 16). Cho is apparently interpolating Cordell Hull's rendering of Eden's response: Hull wrote that "Eden indicated that he was favorably impressed with this proposal," in his *Memoirs* (New York: Macmillan Co., 1948), Vol. 2, p. 1596. But Eden says he did not like the trusteeship idea "when Roosevelt brought it up in Washington in 1943" (*The Reckoning*, p. 595), and Hull delineates Eden's opposition several months later at the Quebec Conference in August 1943. It is thus proper to conclude, as do the Pentagon Papers, that the trusteeship idea "foundered as early as March 1943." See *United States–Vietnam Relations 1945–1967*, U.S. Department of Defense (Washington, D.C., 1971), Vol. 1, p. A-2.
4. Hull, *Memoirs*, Vol. 2, p. 1237.
5. At Yalta British Prime Minister Winston Churchill "declared hotly" that "under no circumstances . . . would he ever consent to the fumbling fingers of forty or fifty nations prying into the life's

existence of the British Empire. As long as he was Prime Minister
. . . he would never yield one scrap of Britain's heritage." See Edward R. Stettinius, Jr., *Roosevelt and the Russians: The Yalta Conference,* ed. Walter Johnson (New York, Doubleday & Co., 1949),
p. 236. See substantiating account, Foreign Relations of the United
States Diplomatic Papers (hereafter referred to as FRUSDP), *The
Conferences of Malta and Yalta, 1945,* U.S. Department of State
(Washington, D.C., 1955), p. 844. At Potsdam Stalin specifically
asked that the Allies discuss trusteeship plans for Korea, but
Churchill obstructed further discussions by accusing Stalin of covet-
ing Libya and other Italian colonies under the ruse of trusteeship.
FRUSDP, *The Conference of Berlin, 1945,* U.S. Department of
State (Washington, D.C., 1960), Vol. 2, July 22, 1945 meeting,
pp. 252–56 and pp. 264–66 (hereafter cited as *Potsdam Papers*).
6. Stalin agreed verbally and informally to a trusteeship for Korea
in his talks with Roosevelt at Yalta, and in his May 1945 discussions
with President Harry S. Truman's advisor, Harry Hopkins. See *Conferences of Malta and Yalta,* p. 770, and the transcript of the Hop-
kins-Stalin talks of May 28, 1945 in *Potsdam Papers,* Vol. 1, p. 47.
Hopkins urged a four-power trusteeship for Korea; its duration
"might be twenty-five years; it might be less, but it would certainly
be five or ten." According to the American transcript, Stalin said
"he fully agreed with the desirability of a four-power trusteeship
for Korea," but the discussion ended there with no written agreements or further planning, as a subsequent top secret memorandum
on Korea noted (*Potsdam Papers,* Vol. 1, pp. 309–10).
7. Eden, *The Reckoning,* p. 593.
8. Gordon Levin, Jr., *Woodrow Wilson and World Politics* (London, Oxford University Press, 1968), p. 260.
9. Memorandum of January 23, 1945 in *Conferences of Malta and
Yalta,* pp. 78–81.
10. "The aforesaid three great powers, mindful of the enslavement
of the people of Korea, are determined that in due course Korea
shall become free and independent." Text in *Foreign Relations of
the United States (1945),* U.S. Department of State (Washington,
D.C., 1969), Vol. 6, p. 1098 (hereafter cited as *FRUS*). Hull
thought the passage on Korea in the Cairo Declaration was composed hastily and without proper consultations; he noted also that
it excluded the Soviets (*Memoirs,* Vol. 2, p. 1584). Japanese
Premier Hara Kei, in announcing Japan's "cultural policy" toward
Korea in the aftermath of the 1919 March First Independence

Movement, used a phrase that was also translated as "in due course": "It is the ultimate purpose of the Japanese Government in due course to treat Korea as in all respects on the same footing with Japan proper" (Hugh Heung-woo Cynn, *The Rebirth of Korea* [New York, The Abingdon Press, 1920], p. 169).

11. See for example *Korea Economic Digest* (New York, Economic Society, 1944–45); *Voice of Korea* (Washington, D.C., Korean Affairs Institute, 1943–45); Changsoon Kim, ed., *The Culture of Korea* (n.p., Korean-American Cultural Association, 1945–46), p. ix and *passim*. Korean writers compared Korea's more than one thousand years of self-rule and America's piddling one hundred and seventy years.

12. Secretary Hull at one point explained to Eden that the American view was not to give colonial peoples independence "tomorrow or next week," but

> . . . to offer them, at some time when they could prove they were capable of independence, the possibility of so conducting their political development that they might be able to hope for this achievement. I cited the example of the Philippines in that we had always held out independence to them as a possibility if and when they were able to assume the responsibilities that went with such status (*Memoirs,* Vol. 2, p. 1238).

13. Robert E. Sherwood, *Roosevelt and Hopkins: An Intimate History* (New York, Harper and Bros., 1948, 1950), p. 777. The Americans freely interpreted Allied reactions to trusteeship plans. Roosevelt later claimed that at Teheran Stalin agreed with him that "the Koreans are not yet capable of exercising and maintaining independent government and that they should be placed under a forty-year tutelage." See Foreign Relations of the United States Diplomatic Papers, *The Conferences at Cairo and Teheran, 1943,* U.S. Department of State (Washington, D.C., 1961) p. 864. But according to the Teheran records, Stalin said only that "it was right that Korea should be independent" (*ibid.,* p. 566). Roosevelt also thought that Chiang Kai-shek wanted a trusteeship over Korea (*ibid.,* p. 257), but again the Cairo record shows only that the Chinese urged Korean independence (*ibid.,* pp. 325, 389).

14. *Conferences of Malta and Yalta, 1945,* p. 770. This is from minutes of the meeting taken by Charles (Chip) Bohlen. Ambassador Harriman was also present and quoted Stalin as asking why a trusteeship was necessary if the Koreans could produce their own government, which Harriman thought meant a Soviet-style government. See Walter Millis, ed., *The Forrestal Diaries* (New York, The Viking Press, 1951), p. 56. But the Yalta record does not show this.

15. "Korea: Occupation and Military Government: Composition of Forces," March 29, 1944, in *FRUS* (1944), Vol. 5, pp. 1224–28.

16. *Ibid.,* pp. 1239–42.

17. "Briefing Book Paper," *Conferences of Malta and Yalta,* pp. 358–59. It is interesting that Great Britain should be assumed to have "a real interest" in Korea, but the Soviet Union, whose borders touch Korea, has such an interest only if it enters the war against Japan.

18. *Ibid.,* p. 359. The thinking and phraseology here is quite similar to an important State Department paper on Japan, "Japan: Occupation and Military Government" (*Potsdam Papers,* Vol. 1, pp. 933–35), in considering Soviet interests and the necessity for American supremacy in the occupation.

19. *Potsdam Papers,* Vol. 1, p. 313.

20. Joint Chiefs of Staff memo, June 18, 1945, *ibid.,* p. 905; see also "Briefing Book Paper," *ibid.,* pp. 924–26; also Herbert Feis, *The Atomic Bomb and the End of World War II* (Princeton, Princeton University Press, 1966), p. 8; also minutes of Tripartite Military Meeting at Potsdam, July 24, 1945 (*Potsdam Papers,* Vol. 2, pp. 351–52). On the American view that Soviet entry against Japan was entirely necessary, see Feis, *Atomic Bomb,* pp. 465–66; Gabriel Kolko, *The Politics of War: The World and United States Foreign Policy, 1943–1945* (New York, Random House, Vintage Books, 1968), pp. 204–208, 344, 365, 535, 554–56, 560–67.

21. Cho errs in stating that agreements limiting Soviet activity in Korea should have been reached at Potsdam (*Korea in World Politics,* pp. 37, 44, 52). Had an agreement been reached, it might have given the Soviets a free hand in all of Korea, instead of limiting their activities. That is probably why the Americans did not push for an agreement. Cho's study is generally excellent, but weakened by his adherence to what might be called the "fumbling" hypothesis, i.e., that American policy toward Korea in the 1940s may be explained in the following manner: "Lacking an informed, effective, or consistent policy, the result was frustration, fumbling, and finally a half-hearted commitment to Korean defense" (p. 7). However, the United States was never hamstrung by a lack of policy in Korea, but by the limits of its own power.

22. See J. Lawton Collins, *War in Peacetime: The History and Les-*

92   BRUCE CUMINGS

sons of Korea (Boston, Houghton Mifflin Co., 1969), pp. 25–26n.
23. Dean Rusk, *FRUS* (1945), Vol. 6, p. 1039.
24. The decision on the 38th parallel was included in *General Order Number I*, transmitted to the Allies on August 15. Stalin's response to it made no mention of Korea. *Stalin's Correspondence with Churchill, Attlee, Roosevelt and Truman, 1941–1945* (New York, E.P. Dutton & Co., 1958), first published in Moscow by the Ministry of Foreign Affairs, pp. 261–66.
25. Cho, *Korea in World Politics*, pp. 47–50, offers an excellent account of various attempts to divide Korea dating back to 1592.
26. For instance, on September 2, 1945 Stalin said, "the turning of the tables on Japan in Manchuria was something for which the older generation had awaited for the entire forty years since the Russo-Japanese War." Quoted in Max Beloff, *Soviet Policy in the Far East 1944–1951* (London, Oxford University Press, 1953), p. 246.
27. Soviet representatives to the first U.S.-Soviet Joint Commission in Seoul said in initial discussions on March 20, 1946: "The Soviet Union has a keen interest in Korea being a true democratic and independent country, friendly to the Soviet Union, so that in the future it will not become a base for an attack on the Soviet Union" (*FRUS* [1946], Vol. 8, p. 653).
28. Arthur Grey is frank about these protestations in "The Thirty-Eighth Parallel," *Foreign Affairs*, Vol. 29, No. 3 (April 1951), p. 486n:

> For some time after the Japanese surrender it was officially maintained in Washington that American troops entered Korea only to facilitate the surrender of Japanese troops, and indeed this was the nominal reason. During the year preceding the [June, 1950] Communist invasion, however, military spokesmen showed a willingness to explain the occupation as the "best" that could be done under the circumstances to prevent Russia from taking all of Korea.

29. Dean Acheson, *Present at the Creation: My Years in the State Department* (New York, New American Library, Signet Books, 1970), pp. 689–90. Acheson also admits that planners did not know this history when the parallel was again a point of issue during the 1951 Panmunjom negotiations—a startling admission. Acheson also credits Dean Rusk alone for the decision to draw a line at the 38th parallel.
30. Grey, "The Thirty-Eighth Parallel," p. 487: also Cho, *Korea in World Politics*, pp. 56–58.

31. Cho, *Korea in World Politics,* p. 58, suggests that the United States should have rushed troops to P'yŏngyang and Dairen in August. But the Americans were hard pressed just to get to Seoul; the Soviets could have easily occupied the whole peninsula. Some degree of moderation had to prevail on both sides.

32. Kolko, *Politics of War,* p. 140.

33. *Ibid.,* pp. 443–44.

34. Hoon K. Lee, *Land Utilization and Rural Economy in Korea* (Shanghai, Kelly & Walsh, Ltd., 1936) is the best work in English. Other good information on land conditions may be found in Andrew Grajdanzev, *Modern Korea;* in Takashi Hatada, *A History of Korea,* trans. and ed. by Warren Smith and Benjamin Hazard (Santa Barbara, Calif., American Bibliographical Center, 1969); and in *A Study of Land Tenure System in Korea* (Seoul, Korea Land Economics Research Center, 1966), a massive study with important data on Korean land relations.

35. Lee, *Land Utilization,* gives a figure of 80.8 percent in 1930 (p. 49), but that figure probably declined to about 75 percent owing to the increasing Japanese emphasis on industrialization from 1931–45.

36. *A Study of Land Tenure,* p. 44; Hatada, *History of Korea,* pp. 113–14.

37. *A Study of Land Tenure,* p. 44; see also Kim Yong-mo, "Social Background and Mobility of Landlords under Japanese Imperialism in Korea," *Journal of Social Sciences and Humanities* (Seoul, Korean Research Center), No. 31 (June 1971), pp. 87–109.

38. *A Study of Land Tenure,* pp. 45, 58; see also Hatada, *History of Korea,* p. 118.

39. Lee, *Land Utilization,* p. 159; see also W. Ladejinsky, "Chosen's Agriculture and its Problems," U.S. Department of Agriculture, (Washington, D.C., Office of Foreign Agriculture Relations, 1940), p. 111.

40. Hatada, *History of Korea,* p. 127.

41. Conditions in China before the 1949 revolution varied widely from area to area and statistics are often unreliable. Tawney gave the tenancy rate in the worst areas—the Canton delta and the Shanghai environs—as 85 percent and 95 percent, respectively. R. H. Tawney, *Land and Labor in China* (Boston, Beacon Paperback, 1966), first published London, 1932, p. 37.

42. Lee, *Land Utilization,* gives a figure of 20 to 40 percent of total tenant-worked land changing hands annually, an astounding figure made possible by a large supply of potential tenants (p. 163).

Even official Japanese sources admitted seasonal starvation and itinerancy (Hatada, *History of Korea,* pp. 126–27). Tawney's description of the extremes of tenant life in China corresponds to the norm in Korea. See Tawney, *Land and Labor in China,* p. 63.

43. Lee, *Land Utilization,* p. 280. Grajdanzev agreed and argued forcefully for redistribution of land without recompense to owners, and advocated preventive measures to prevent the Korean landlord class from dominating postwar Korea. See *Modern Korea,* concluding chapter.

44. See Karl W. Deutsch, "Social Mobilization and Political Development," *American Political Science Review,* Vol. 55 (September 1961), p. 494.

45. Hatada, *History of Korea,* p. 124.

46. Gregory Henderson, *Korea, The Politics of the Vortex* (Cambridge, Mass., Harvard University Press, 1968), p. 100. This figure includes voluntary immigrants as well; it is difficult to distinguish between those forced to go to Japan and those who went voluntarily, i.e., the latter may have left because of untenable economic circumstances within Korea.

47. Many of these groups are listed and described in *Ch'in-Il p'a kunsang* [The pro-Japanese groups] (Seoul, Samsaeng munhwa-sa, 1948), pp. 105–64.

48. In 1931, for example, there were 661 such disputes involving 10,282 persons. Many of these disputes were encouraged and organized by Communists and other resistance groups, but it is difficult to know what percentage were organized and what percentage were spontaneous (Hatada, *History of Korea,* p. 128).

49. *Ibid.,* p. 125.

50. *Ibid.*

51. For example, a statement of October 2, 1940 by the General Board of the Korean Methodist Church includes as part of the "Right Guidance of Thought" the aim to "extirpate cruel and irreligious communism," along with other passages urging Shinto shrine worship, and recitation of the Imperial Subject's Oath. In Robert T. Oliver, *Korea: Forgotten Nation* (Washington, D.C., Public Affairs Press, 1944), pp. 122–28. Grajdanzev cites "compulsory participation in the 'spiritual' mobilization of patriotic anti-communist organizations, which now have three million 'members'," in *Modern Korea,* pp. 69–70.

52. This subject is much too large to pursue in detail here. Those interested should consult Dae-Sook Suh, *The Korean Communist Movement, 1918–1948* (Princeton, Princeton University Press,

1967); and Chong-sik Lee, *The Politics of Korean Nationalism* (Berkeley and Los Angeles, University of California Press, 1963).
53. See Frank Baldwin, "The March 1 Movement: Korean Challenge and Japanese Response," unpublished Ph.D. dissertation, Columbia University, 1969.
54. See Chang Pok-sŏng, *Chosŏn kongsan-dang p'ajaeng-sa* [History of the factional struggles of the Korean Communist party] (Seoul, Taeryuk ch'ulp'an-sa, 1949), p. 11. It is true that many prominent Korean leftists remained in the south until 1948. But other leftists, not only those associated with Kim Il Sung, went to the north immediately in 1945, and by 1948 most of the leftists of all factions were in the north. The new North Korean government in 1948 represented not simply the imposition of one faction of the Left, but a coalition (see Suh, *Korean Communist Movement*, pp. 315–29). It remained a coalition until after the Korean War, when the Kim Il Sung faction, in the wake of recriminations over the war, began to dominate.
55. The Korean Communist party and the Korean Left in general had no effective relationship with the Soviet Union before World War II; the relationship between the Soviets and the Kim Il Sung faction may have been important during the war, but it is still shrouded in mystery. The numerous leftist publications in the south during the years 1945–48 that I have consulted give no indication of Soviet control of their content or ideological line.
56. Suh, *Korean Communist Movement*, p. 18; also Lee, *Politics of Korean Nationalism*, p. 136.
57. The comments of Lyuh Woon-hyung, who was part of this faction, are in *Yŏ Un-hyŏng sŏnsaeng e taehan p'an-gyŏlsŏ* [The judicial record of Yŏ Un-hyŏng] (Seoul, Kunsŏdang sŏjŏm, 1946), pp. 45–46. This study includes transcripts of Lyuh's interrogation by the Japanese thought police.
58. Suh, *Korean Communist Movement*, p. 15; a Communist faction under Yi Tong-hwi organized a Korean Communist party (*Koryŏ kongsan-dang*) "between January and May 1921."
59. The best treatment is in Suh, *Korean Communist Movement*, pp. 187–293, but he offers few figures on the numbers involved in each faction.
60. *Ibid.*, p. 251 and *passim*.
61. Lee, *Politics of Korean Nationalism*, pp. 223–24; *FRUS* (1944), Vol. 5, p. 1226.
62. Rhee's disputes with other KPG leaders went back to 1919; he was officially ousted from the KPG in 1925 for "usurping authority"

(Bong-youn Choy, *Korea: A History* [Rutland, Vt., Charles F. Tuttle & Co., 1971], p. 181; also Henderson, *Korea,* p. 86).

63. The Korean name of the CPKI was *Kŏn'guk chunbi ŭiwŏnhoe;* that of the KPR was *Chosŏn inmin kongwhaguk.* *Kŏn'guk* literally means "national construction," but "independence" renders the flavor better.

64. See *Han'guk minju-dang t'ŭkbo* [Korean Democratic party special news], December 19, 1945; also Ko Yŏng-hwan, *Kŭmil ŭi chŏnggaekdŭl* [Today's politicians] (Seoul, Tonga ilbo-sa, 1949), pp. 88–89. Right-wing Korean sources, such as the above, uniformly condemn the KPR. They charge that it was the source of Korea's division, that the KPR was pro-Japanese, and that it was a means whereby the Japanese could perpetuate their rule in Korea—an interpretation that would perhaps be most surprising to the Japanese themselves. Song's refusal to organize an administration or to cooperate with the KPR is attributed to his desire to await the return of the KPG. See Ko, *Kŭmil ŭi chŏnggaekdŭl,* pp. 88–91; in English, see Louise Yim, *My Forty Year Fight for Korea* (Seoul, International Culture Research Center, 1951), pp. 227–36. It is more likely that Song refused because he could have avoided the taint of collaboration had he agreed to the Japanese offer.

65. Lyuh was one of a number of Koreans with careers of remarkable involvement in the revolutionary tides of Asia. In the 1920s he had close ties with both the Kuomintang and the Chinese Communists and participated in the Northern Expedition; he claimed to have met Lenin and Trotsky in Moscow; he was arrested in 1929 by Japanese police and returned to Korea. In the 1930s he edited the *Chungang ilbo* [Central daily]. After liberation he was a tireless advocate of a Left-Right coalition. For his efforts he was beaten in September 1945, almost lynched in October 1946, had his house partially destroyed by a grenade in March 1947, and was finally shot dead within sight of a police box on July 19, 1947. His political views were a mixture of socialism, Christian ideals, and Wilsonian democracy. He told the Japanese police that he admired communist ideals, but had never joined the party; he remained "spiritually" a Christian and could not believe wholeheartedly in the materialist view of history. See *Yŏ Un-hyŏng p'an'gyŏlsŏ,* pp. 31, 37–39. Biographical materials in Korean include his brother's account, Yŏ Unhong, *Mongyang: Yŏ Un-hyŏng* (Mongyang was Yŏ's pen name) (Seoul, Ch'ŏngha-gak, 1967); Yi Man-gyu, *Yŏ Un-hyŏng t'ujaeng-sa* [A history of Yŏ Un-hyŏng's struggle] (Seoul, Ch'ongmun-gak, 1946): see also biographical sketch in Kim O-sŏng, *Chidoja kunsang*

[The leaders] (Seoul, Taesŏng ch'ulp'an-sa, 1946), Vol. 1, pp. 1–14.
66. The demands were to release all political and economic prisoners; to guarantee food provisions for three months; not to interfere
with the maintenance of law and order by Koreans or with CPKI
organizing activities; not to interfere with the organization of students, workers, and peasants. Chaemi Hanjok yŏnhap ŭiwŏnhoe,
Haebang Chosŏn [Liberated Korea] (Hawaii, Chaemi Hanjok yŏnhap ŭiwŏnhoe, 1948), p. 2.
67. This is my own estimate, based on information in *History of
the Occupation of Korea,* Headquarters, Far East Command (Tokyo, 1947, 1948), Pt. I, ch. 3, p. 7, unpublished ms. at Office of the
Chief of Military History, Washington, D.C. (hereafter cited as
HOK).
68. Lee Won-sul, "The Impact of United States Occupation Policy
on the Socio-political Structure of South Korea, 1945–1948," unpublished Ph.D. dissertation, Western Reserve University, 1961, argues that the CPKI was under communist control by the end of
August (see p. 62); but the published announcements and procla-
mations of the CPKI show no communist rhetoric through the fall
of 1945; CPKI materials of the time are easily distinguished from
the true communist publications of August–September 1945, such
as *Taechung* [The masses], and *Hyŏngmyŏng sinmun* [Revolution
news], published in Seoul, August–November, 1945. *Taechung* was
the organ of the Seoul branch of the Korean Communist party. I
examined Nos. 2–5, August 30, 1945 to September 8, 1945.
69. A translation is in Kyung-cho Chung, *Korea Tomorrow* (New
York, Macmillan Co., 1956), pp. 304–6. Among other things, this
proclamation demanded an eight-hour work day, child labor laws,
union organizing rights, a minimum wage, and women's equality—
reformist demands, although revolutionary in the Korean context.
They have yet to be implemented in South Korea.
70. See Lee Won-sul, "Impact of U.S. Occupation Policy", pp. 53–
54.
71. According to the communist newspaper *Hyŏngmyŏng sinmun*
(October 4, 1945), the KPR leaders in Seoul spent too much time
haggling amongst themselves and too little in building strong links
with the committees in the provinces; denigrated the importance of
mass participation in various decisions; and made decisions in a
"bourgeois, bureaucratic manner." Still, the paper urged communists to continue supporting the KPR, because it was staunchly opposed by "the landed bourgeoisie."
72. See Meade, *Military Government,* p. 63; also Donald S. Mc-

Donald, "Field Experience in Military Government: Cholla Namdo Province, 1945–1946," in Carl J. Friedrich et. al., *American Experiences in Military Government in World War II* (New York, Rinehart & Co., 1948), p. 365.

73. Meade, *Military Government*, p. 75.

74. The union was the *Chosŏn nodong chohap chŏn'guk p'yŏngŭihoe* [National Council of Korean Labor Unions], which will be discussed below. It was the only true labor union in Korea from August 1945 to the fall of 1946.

75. See Cho, *Korea in World Politics*, pp. 81–82; Suh, *Korean Communist Movement*, p. 315. Soviet sources stress the spontaneity of the People's Committees. See Max Beloff, *Soviet Policies*, p. 158.

76. Soviet and North Korean sources stress the latter interpretation; see Beloff, *Soviet Policies;* Donald Tewksbury, *Source Materials on Korean Politics and Ideologies* (New York, Institute of Pacific Relations, 1950), pp. 101–3 and 133–34, for laudatory comments on the People's Committees by Kim Il Sung and Pak Hŏn-yŏng. *North Korea: A Case Study in the Techniques of Takeover*, U.S. Department of State (Washington, D.C., 1961) is the official American study, and argues the former interpretation; it is, however, a weak study based on refugee and prisoner-of-war interviews and a sampling of North Korean documents, compiled by people who were not expert in Korean affairs.

77. This apt phrase is George McCune's, *Korea Today* (Cambridge, Mass., Harvard University Press, 1950), p. 45.

78. This, it seems to me, explains why the leftist leaders remained in the south until 1948—not because they misjudged the permanence of Korea's division and the impact of dual occupation (Suh, *Korean Communist Movement*, pp. 296–97), but because they thought the People's Republic had triumphed in the north, and that the Left still had the strength to prevail in the south.

79. The *P'yŏngyang minbo* [Pyongyang people's report] was available in the south. It announced with great fanfare such events as the fixing of tenancy rents on October 21, 1945, and the far-reaching land reform of March 7, 1946 (see issues of October 23, 1945 and March 8, 1945). South Korean newspapers, too, prominently featured such news from the north.

80. The problem of how one defines a collaborator is, of course, a difficult one and subject to varying interpretations. The point here is to describe mass attitudes as stated in numerous Korean newspapers and other publications of the time.

81. *Haebang Chosŏn*, p. 7; also Ko, *Kŭmil ŭi chŏnggaekdŭl*, p. 88.

82. *Haebang Chosŏn*, p. 7.

83. Ko, *Kŭmil ŭi chŏnggaekdŭl*, pp. 88–89.

84. See a history of the Korean Democratic party in *Han'guk minju-dang t'ŭkbo*, December 19, 1945; also Kim Chun-yŏn, *Han'guk minju-dang so-sa* [A short history of the Korean Democratic party] (Seoul, Han'guk minju-dang sŏnjŏn-bu, 1948), p. 8. Self-preservation is the first law of politics, and KDP leaders were quite frank in admitting that they sought comfort from the incoming American Occupation. Indeed, they said they did not begin organizing until assured that the Americans were coming. See Kim Chun-yŏn, *Tongnip nosŏn* [The path of independence] (Seoul, Hŭnghan chaedan, 1947), pp. 7, 13.

85. This was a common theme of most political analyses during the liberation period. For a scholarly concurrence, see Han T'aesu, *Han'guk chŏngdang-sa* [A history of Korean political parties] (Seoul: Sin t'aeyang-sa, 1961), p. 13. Fifty-five members of the KDP resigned on October 21, 1946, saying that KDP leaders " . . . insist on maintaining landownership which will do no good for a liberation of the people" (*Seoul Times*, October 22, 1946).

86. Henderson calls this "the Posŏng group," after the Posŏng School (later Korea University), which Kim founded (*Korea*, p. 114).

87. See *Han'guk minju-dang t'ukbo*, December 19, 1945, and Kim, *Han'guk minju-dang so-sa*, p. 16, for identical examples of this phrase.

88. The KDP advocated, in very general terms, "the prosperity of the masses," democracy (undefined), and anti-communism. Given the Korean setting, they had to advocate some measure of land reform; this evolved into a position of redistribution with compensation to the owners; yet in 1949 they continually opposed just such a mild reform. See *A Study of Land Tenure System in Korea*, pp. 76–79.

89. *HOK*, Pt. I, ch. 4, p. 46.

90. Lee, "Impact of U.S. Occupation Policy," pp. 65–66. Hodge was a highly decorated soldier, often called "the Patton of the Pacific" by war correspondents. (See his obituary in *The New York Times*, November 13, 1963.) Dwight MacDonald, in *Memoirs of a Revolutionist* (New York, Meridian Books, 1958) wrote that "Patton is my favorite general because he expresses so naively the real nature of World War II," (p. 99). The same could be said of Hodge with respect to the Cold War. He had a knack for brutal simplicity and always had his eye firmly fixed on doing whatever was necessary to maintain American power in Korea.

91. It is true that certain policy statements, such as the comprehensive SWNCC "Basic Initial Directive," did not reach Korea until mid-October. But the fundamental policies of demilitarization and democratization to be applied to Japan were well known to civil affairs officers accompanying General Hodge to Korea; a lack of policy guidance cannot explain Occupation policies in Korea in September and October.

92. A. Wigfall Green, *The Epic of Korea* (Washington, D.C., Public Affairs Press, 1950), p. 7.

93. In *FRUS* (1945), Vol. 6, pp. 1049–53, 1061–65, and 1070–71, respectively. Herbert Feis refers to Benninghoff's September 15 report as "a farsighted description and analysis of the situation" (*Atomic Bomb*, p. 166n).

94. *FRUS* (1945), Vol. 6, cable of November 26, 1945, pp. 1134–36. It is true, of course, that Koreans who could speak English used their capability to advantage. Indeed, since 1945 the highest calling for a Korean, in American eyes, has been fluency in English and a capacity to handle the symbols and constructs that excite Americans. It is this writer's experience that the further a Korean is from his origins, the more pleasing he is to Americans.

95. *Voice of Korea*, August 15, 1947.

96. *New York Times*, October 6, 1945. Benninghoff noted that the Korean response to this council had been less than overwhelming, "perhaps because of similar council under Japanese auspices (recently dissolved) was regarded as a gathering of collaborationists" (*FRUS* [1945], Vol. 6, p. 1069).

97. *Seoul Times*, September 27, 1945.

98. Green, *The Epic of Korea*, p. 72.

99. Ralf Dahrendorf, *Class and Class Conflict in Industrial Society* (Stanford, Stanford University Press, 1965), p. 300.

100. See *Han'guk minju-dang t'ukbo*, December 19, 1945, and Kim, *Han'guk minju-dang so-sa*, pp. 8, 16. Cho Pyŏng-ok's appointment as director of the police was timed to coincide with the October 20 welcoming ceremony; Chang T'aek-sang was chief translator at the same ceremony. Cho later claimed "a central role" in reorienting south Korea's political and social organizations from the Left to the Right in the years 1945–48. See Cho Pyŏng-ok, *Na ŭi hoegorok* [My recollections] (Seoul, Min'gyo-sa, 1959), pp. 147–50, 156–57. Cho ran for president of the Republic of Korea in 1960. Chang T'aek-sang was a British-educated scion of one of Korea's oldest and wealthiest landlord families. He became the first foreign minister of the Republic of Korea.

101. The latitude given these men is best exemplified in their daily involvement in the suppression of leftist activity from 1945 to 1948, as reported in the *Seoul Times, Voice of Korea,* and other newspapers during these years. No doubt they often went beyond the wishes of their American superiors; when the Occupation allied with the forces of reaction, it caught a tiger by the tail.

102. Henderson, *Korea,* p. 128.

103. The Korean title was *Taehan tongnip ch'oksŏng chungang hyŏpŭihoe.* I have translated the terms *Chosŏn, Taehan,* and *Han'guk* as "Korea," but it should be noted that Left and Right disagreed about what to call their country; the Right preferred *Taehan* and *Han'guk,* which had connotations linked to the old Yi Dynasty, while the Left preferred the more vernacular and popular term *Chosŏn.*

104. Stewart Meacham, "Korean Labor Report," Labor Department, U.S. Armed Forces in Korea (November 1947), pp. 34–35. Meacham was labor advisor to General Hodge. I am indebted to Gregory Henderson for bringing this report to my attention.

105. The separate government question was the most contentious issue of the liberation period; even in 1948 moderates like Kimm Kiu-sik and rightists like Kim Koo still stopped short of endorsing actions that would inevitably divide Korea. Both men refused to participate in the UN-"sponsored" elections of 1948 and instead went to P'yŏngyang for the famed unity conference. But Syngman Rhee recognized both the permanence of Korea's division and its uses for his own ambitions, and capitalized on it.

106. The full title of this document is "Basic Initial Directive to the Commander-in-Chief, U.S. Army Forces Pacific, for the Administration of Civil Affairs in Those Areas of Korea Occupied by U.S. Forces." It was prepared by SWNCC in August, but not transmitted to Korea until October 17 (*FRUS* [1945], Vol. 6, pp. 1073–91).

107. *Ibid.,* pp. 1091–92.

108. *Ibid.,* pp. 1113–14, memo of November 7, 1945.

109. *Ibid.,* pp. 1122–24. McCloy had visited Seoul and held several long conversations with Hodge.

110. In November 1947 an American officer said:

Any election held without first having police and land reform would be an election hopelessly marred by landlord intimidation of tenants, hooliganism by privately-organized terrorists, and police suppression of all campaign efforts as hostile to their partisan interests (Meacham, "Labor Report," pp. 31–32).

111. *FRUS* (1945), Vol. 6, pp. 1129–33.

112. Green, *Epic of Korea,* p. 53.

113. On the Representative Democratic Council as successor to the "governing commission," see *HOK,* Pt. II, ch. 2, pp. 81–85, 90–91; also Pt. II, ch. 4, pp. 149–50. American and Soviet policies had a curious parallelism. Beginning in late December, the Soviets and the north Koreans imposed central control on the People's Committee structure through a provisional Central People's Committee, chaired by Kim Il Sung. Additional research is necessary to determine whether the Soviets or the Americans acted first in inaugurating separate Korean administrations.

114. Secretary of State to Langdon, November 29, 1945, *FRUS* (1945) Vol. 6, pp. 1137–38.

115. *Ibid.,* pp. 1140–41.

116. *Ibid.,* pp. 1144–48.

117. American racism toward Koreans was a constant factor during the Occupation, and the use of the term "gook" was ubiquitous (*HOK,* Pt. II, ch. 1, p. 64). A former president of the Judicial Board of Review and judge advocate during the Occupation saw fit to begin his account of the period with the following:

> Korea, to some Americans, is a land of gooks. Everyone knows vaguely, but not specifically, what a gook is. Perhaps a gook is anyone other than a North American, but he is, more especially, an Oriental: a native of any of the South Pacific Islands, a Filipino, a Japanese, a Chinaman, or a Korean. Gook is sometimes used to belittle; but it is also used to express familiarity and even fondness. . . . Korea is a land of gooks; the Korean is a gook. He is incomprehensible because his thought processes are different . . . he belongs to another world. But just when we think that we can never understand the Korean, the light of comprehension shows in his dark eyes and in his ready smile and laughter, and we call him gook with foolish tenderness. . . . Almost unwittingly we find ourselves so fond of him that we want to shelter him from all harm (Green, *Epic of Korea,* p. 7).

118. The plan was initiated in a memo from Brig. Gen. Lawrence E. Shick, October 31, 1945. Shick was provost marshal of the Twenty-fourth Corps and the first Military Government director of the Korean National Police. See the account based on as yet unpublished materials in Robert K. Sawyer, *Military Advisors in Korea: KMAG in Peace and War*, ed. Walter G. Hermes (Washington, D.C., U.S. Department of the Army, Office of the Chief of Military History, 1962), pp. 9–26.

119. Letter quoted in *ibid.*, p. 21.

120. *FRUS* (1945), Vol. 6, p. 1157.

121. Sawyer, *KMAG in Peace and War*, pp. 20–21.

122. *Ibid.*, p. 24.

123. *Ibid.*, p. 15. "Lee Hyung Koon" here is probably Yi Ŭng-chun, colonel in the Japanese army and later the first R.O.K. Army chief of staff. It might also be Yi Hyŏng-gŭn, an officer of somewhat lesser importance. Yi Ŭngchun played a major role in selecting officers for the constabulary; he was recommended to the Americans by Cho Pyŏng-ok (*Na ŭi hoegorok*, p. 157).

124. Taehan min'guk kukbang-bu chŏnsa p'yŏnch'an uiwŏnhoe, *Han'guk chŏnjaeng-sa* [History of the Korean War], Vol. 1, "Haebang kwa kŏn'gun" [Liberation and establishment of the army] (Seoul, Taehan min'guk kukbang-bu, 1967), p. 258, 265. A complete account of the history of the constabulary is in this volume; it indicates that almost all the top officers in the constabulary and the R.O.K. Army had served in the Japanese military. (See esp. pp. 277–78.)

125. Sawyer, *KMAG in Peace and War*, p. 25. Sawyer says that the constabulary had no legal right to make arrests, but it "consistently ignored this lack of legal right, making arrests at will, and searching without warrants" (p. 26).

126. *Summation of Non-military Activities in Japan and Korea* (Tokyo, Supreme Command Allied Powers), No. 1, September–October 1945, p. 175 (hereafter *SCAP Summation*).

127. Lee Won-sul, "Impact of U.S. Occupation Policy," p. 93; Cho's figures were presented to the United Nations Temporary Commission on Korea in February 1948. See *First Part of the Report of the United Nations Temporary Commission on Korea*, v. 3, annex 9, p. 117, in United Nations General Assembly, *Official Records*, 3rd session, supplement no. 9 (A/575, Add. 2). Meacham, citing late 1946 USAMGIK figures, said 80 percent of police at the rank of captain or above had served the Japanese ("Labor Report," p. 31). Official Korean accounts freely admitted that the entire Korean element of

the Japanese police force was used as a basis for the south Korean police. See Sudo kwan'gu kyŏngch'al-ch'ŏng, *Haebang ihu sudo kyŏngch'al paldal-sa* [History of the development of the Seoul police after liberation] (Seoul, Sudo kwan'gu kyŏngch'al-ch'ŏng, 1947), p. 105.

128. A wholly new police force was created in north Korea, making suspect American protestations that Koreans formerly employed by Japan had to be used because other Koreans had no training. See *North Korea: A Case Study*, p. 6.

129. Mark Gayn quoted William Maglin, American director of the Korean National Police in the fall of 1946, as saying, "We felt that if [the Koreans] did a good job for the Japanese, they would do a good job for us" (Mark Gayn, *Japan Diary*, [New York, William Sloane Associates, 1948], p. 391).

130. McDonald, *American Experiences in Military Government*, p. 375.

131. *Ibid.*, p. 376; Green, *Epic of Korea*, p. 61. Readers may also find similar evidence in Henderson, *Korea;* McCune, *Korea Today;* and Meade, *Military Government*.

132. John C. Caldwell said that "many of the American police advisors . . . were themselves convinced through race prejudice, ignorance, and lack of education in national differences that the 'gooks' only understood force" (John C. Caldwell, *The Korea Story* [Chicago, Henry Regnery Co., 1952], p. 8). Caldwell was a civilian information specialist with the Occupation in 1948, and the former director of the USIS in China under the Marshall Mission.

133. *Seoul Times,* February 27, 1946.

134. Henderson says that there were 20,544 political prisoners in July 1947 as compared with 16,000 at the end of Japanese rule (*Korea*, p. 421n.); the *Seoul Times*, September 2, 1948, put the figure at 22,321 as of July 31, 1948.

135. See the *Seoul Times*, November 4 and 5, 1946, for such a pattern. Henderson, *Korea*, p. 144, details some of the police tortures.

136. The full text is in *FRUS* (1945), Vol. 6, pp. 1150–51.

137. Cable of December 30, 1945, in *ibid.*, p. 1154.

138. *Ibid.*, p. 1153.

139. Byrnes submitted an initial proposal on a trusteeship for Korea at the Moscow Conference; the Russians added to this proposal a plan for a Korean provisional government to function under the trust powers, and this draft was accepted (Harry S. Truman, *Years* *of Trial and Hope, 1946–1952* [New York, Doubleday and Co., 1956], p. 363).

140. *FRUS* (1946) Vol. 8, p. 622. Stalin was correct about Lerch. He was on the podium when Syngman Rhee's SPKI adopted a resolution blaming trusteeship on the Russians, and their "cohorts" in the State Department in Washington. The resolution also charged that those in the State Department urging trusteeship were the same people who refused recognition to the KPG during World War II, and were the same people then urging reforms on the Kuomintang in China. The resolution is in Yi Hyŏk, ed., *Aeguk ppira chŏnjip* [Collection of patriotic handbills] (Seoul, Choguk munhwa-sa, 1946), Vol. 1, pp. 32–37. When leftists in south Korea tried to publish the fact that the Americans urged a trusteeship at the Moscow discussions, the Occupation censored their publications (*HOK,* Pt. II, ch. 2, p. 53).

141. Hodge and his supporters also claimed they had received no policy directives until late January 1946 (*HOK,* Pt. II, ch. 2, p. 91).

142. *FRUS* (1946) Vol. 8, pp. 628–30.

143. *Ibid.,* pp. 654–56.

144. See for example Cho, *Korea in World Politics,* p. 73; Henderson cites the great number of "parties" as evidence of a supposed propensity of Korean society for fragmentation and atomization and ignores the fundamental class conflict of the liberation period (*Korea,* pp. 113–47). It is interesting to see how such scholarship filters down and comes to characterize a period. An otherwise sound book on the Cold War says that Koreans were "nearly politically illiterate . . . 54 different parties sought power" (Walter LaFeber, *America, Russia, and the Cold War, 1945–1966* [New York, John Wiley & Sons, 1967], p. 23).

145. Numerous sources cite this fundamental bifurcation. See for example George M. McCune, "Korea's Post-war Political Problems," Institute of Pacific Relations Secretariat Paper No. 2 (September 1947), p. 12. Both leftist and rightist newspapers often made the point. See the leftist *Kŭnyok chubo* [Korea weekly], November 3, 1945, and the rightist *Tongnip sinmun* [Independence news], November 11, 1945. The latter said "even a blind man groping in the dark can see there is only democracy and communism." Two books that argue the point (and which, incidentally, are evidence that Koreans were hardly "politically illiterate") are Yi Chaehun, *Minjok ŭishik kwa kyegup ŭishik* [National consciousness and class consciousness] (Seoul, Tongyang kongsa ch'ulp'an-sa, 1946), and Paek Nam-un, *Chosŏn minjok ŭi chillo* [The path of the Korean nation], (Seoul, Sin'gŏn-sa, 1946).

146. Lowi, quoted in Michel Oksenberg, "Policy Making Under Mao, 1949–1968: An Overview," in John M. H. Lindbeck, *China: Management of a Revolutionary Society* (Seattle, University of Washington Press, 1971), p. 113.

147. Even with such help, the Right never could forge viable political organizations outside of Seoul. Often they simply did not recognize the issue—why organize peasants? They will follow leadership like grass bending in the wind. Franz Schurmann has written that "nothing reveals the nakedness of a ruling class so starkly as its impotence in organization" (*Ideology and Organization in Communist China* [Berkeley and Los Angeles, University of California Press, 1968], p. xxxix).

148. See Lyuh Woon-hyung's last letter, written just before his assassination, in *Voice of Korea*, September 16, 1947. This was the only alleged "pro-Japanese" activity Hodge ever objected to.

149. *Seoul Times*, October 11, 1945, General Arnold's attempt to link KPR activities to immaturity and "boyishness" was extremely demeaning to the KPR leaders. Nothing an American said in 1945 hurt Koreans more than this attack, if one can judge by the frequency with which it was mentioned.

150. *FRUS* (1945), Vol. 6, p. 1106.

151. Cable of November 25, 1945, *ibid.*, pp. 1133–34.

152. *SCAP Summation*, No. 3, December 1945, p. 187.

153. McDonald, in *American Experiences in Military Government*, p. 368.

154. *Ibid.*, p. 372. McDonald's article is quite critical of various Military Government decisions, although not this one.

155. *HOK*, Pt. I, ch. 6, pp. 42, 52–53.

156. *Ibid.*, p. 61.

157. On the fall 1946 riots, see *HOK*, Pt. I, ch. 6; Naemubu ch'ian'-guk, *Taehan kyŏngch'al chŏn-sa* [Military history of the Korean police], (Seoul, Hŭng'guk yŏn'gu hyŏp-hoe, 1952), Vol. 1, pp. 50–57.

158. Meacham, "Labor Report," p. 10.

159. *Chŏn'guk nodongja shinmun* [National worker's newspaper], Nos. 1–15, November 1, 1945–April 19, 1946. Each number reported on widespread organizing activities throughout Korea. The union's demands were largely reformist, emphasizing an eight-hour work day, workmen's compensation, child labor laws, and the like. For an English-language account of this union, see an article by

Harold Zepelin, a former Military Government officer, in *Korean Independence,* April 10, 1946.
160. Meacham, "Labor Report," p. 11.
161. *Ibid.,* p. 22.
162. *Ibid.,* p. 28, called it "a sort of national company union"; see also McCune, *Korea Today,* p. 162.
163. Meacham, "Labor Report," p. 22.
164. The U.S. Army Counter-Intelligence Corps found several *Chŏnp'yŏng* workers castrated by *Noch'ong* thugs in April 1947 (*ibid.,* p. 26). This resulted in an Occupation order to dissolve *Noch'ong,* but it had little effect on the organization's activities. Meacham wrote that he did not know of "a single instance where any member of this organization was arrested and brought to trial for their beatings and murders until the April 1947 incident resulting in the dissolution order" (p. 26).
165. Quoted in *ibid.,* p. 24. Mark Gayn was in Korea during the fall 1946 uprisings; his account details similar American methods (*Japan Diary, passim*).
166. Meacham, "Labor Report," p. 25. Meacham says *Chŏnp'yŏng* was not totally ruined by this suppression campaign, but the effect was to turn it rapidly leftward.
167. *HOK,* Pt. I, ch. 6.
168. *Seoul Times,* September 24, 1946.
169. *Ibid.,* September 28, 1946.
170. *Ibid.,* September 30, 1946.
171. *Ibid.,* October 7 and 9, 1946.
172. *Ibid.,* issues for month of October 1946; see *HOK,* Pt. 1, ch. 6; also Gayn, *Japan Diary,* pp. 388–89, 418–21. Upon seeing an official chart of unrest throughout south Korea in October 1946, Gayn said, "It was a full-scale revolution, which must have involved hundreds of thousands, if not millions of people" (p. 388).
173. *FRUS* (1946), Vol. 8, p. 750.
174. *Ibid.,* p. 751.
175. *Ibid.,* p. 752. This statement is good evidence that State Department officers differed with the military over means, not ends. A "Rightist Youth Army" offended Vincent's sensibilities and his Wilsonian liberalism, but he did not question Hodge's ends.
176. Both American and Korean sources confirm this. See Richard Wilson, "Korean National Youth, Inc.," *School and Society,* July 30, 1949. Wilson noted innocently that Yi Pŏm-sŏk spent many years studying European youth movements (p. 135); Wilson did not mention Yi's admiration for the Hitler *Jugend.* Yi acknowledged receiv-

ing five million wŏn from the Occupation in his *Minjok kwa ch'ŏng-nyŏn* [Youth and the nation] (Seoul, Paegyŏng-sa, 1948), p. 76.

177. Henderson, *Korea*, p. 141.

178. Kolko, *Politics of War*, p. 9.

179. *U.S.-Vietnam Relations, 1945–1947*, Vol. 1, pp. 31–32.

180. An endless list of similar statements could be compiled. These two are from Edwin Pauley, quoted in Truman, *Years of Trial and Hope*, p. 365, and Green, *The Epic of Korea*, p. 7. Pauley went on to say that it is in Korea where "a test will be made of whether a democratic competitive system can be adopted to meet the challenge of a defeated feudalism or whether some other system, i.e., Communism will become stronger." Pauley's report to Truman was dated June 22, 1946.

The United Nations and Korea

Jon Halliday

SENATOR SYMINGTON. We go into this country splitting business. . . . First we split Germany. Then we split China. We stay with billions and billions of dollars and hundreds of thousands of people in the case of Germany, China we stay with billions of dollars and thousands of people. Then we split Korea, and stay there with billions of dollars and tens of thosuands of military, all at heavy cost to the American taxpayer. Then we split Vietnam. . . . Now we split Laos. . . . Do you know of any other country we plan to split pretty soon?

MR. PORTER [U.S. ambassador to South Korea]. No, sir.

SENATOR SYMINGTON. This has been quite an interesting policy, hasn't it, over the years? . . . Our allies don't do [this], nor do our possible enemies. We do it all over the world. . . .[1]

1. INTRODUCTION

The United Nations was not called in to concern itself with Korea by the people of Korea. It was mobilized by the United States to add the weight of what was alleged to be "world opinion" in support of America's policy. U.S. policy had as its maximum goal the establishment of an anti-communist reactionary regime throughout Korea; if this could not be accomplished, the United States would settle for a split Korea, with a reactionary regime in the southern part (geographically only half, but with two-thirds the total population).

It should be emphasized at once that in 1947, and right on through the war of 1950–53 and for many years thereafter, the United Nations was in no way a neutral or balanced organization. The United States had a solid and overwhelming majority on every single issue, regardless of its merits. In almost all cases it is comparatively uninteresting to try to follow the contortions and meanderings of the intrigues between the United States and its allies and satellites. Specific instances where the UN is not synonymous with the United States are noted below; otherwise, UN policy simply followed the line laid down by Washington, sometimes as an apparently independent echo from New York, other times abandoning even the simulated autonomy of an echo (as in the case of the Unified Command established in Korea in 1950).

The history of the division of Korea prior to the U.S. mobilization of the UN in 1947 is fairly well known and relatively uncontentious, inasmuch as there is little dispute over the actual events.

The central political fact about Korea in 1945 was that it was one single country with an unchallenged sense of national identity and a heroic left-wing revolutionary movement that had the support of the overwhelming majority of the population.[2] The ensuing technicalities of how the United States sabotaged the will of the majority of the Korean people must be seen against this basic background. By the time the first U.S. troops arrived in Korea in September 1945, a nation-wide government, the Korean People's Republic (KPR), was already in place.[3] The Soviet Union agreed to work with the KPR in the north; the United States refused to recognize it, reinstated the Japanese authorities, and went all out to destroy the KPR and its infrastructure. These actions, right at the start of the American occupation of the south, were designed to wreck the Left and prevent its ever being able to demonstrate its majority support. Since much of the subsequent disagreement, first between the U.S. and Soviet governments and later between the United States and its opponents in the UN, was over the representativeness of different organizations in Korea, these initial moves (refusal to recognize the majority, followed by attempts at its physical destruction) are of fundamental importance.

2. 1945–47: THE PRE-UN PHASE

The Korean question was taken up in some detail at the Moscow
Conference of Foreign Ministers in December 1945, the last
full-scale attempt at a general Soviet-American settlement in the
Far East, but Korea was not represented at the conference. The
conference's final declaration is a confused document, open to
multiple interpretation. Its main points are: (1) a provisional
democratic government should be set up as soon as possible;
(2) a Joint Commission (Soviet-U.S.) should also be instituted
"in order to assist the formation of a provisional Korean government"; (3) The Joint Commission should submit proposals "for
the working out of an agreement concerning a four-power trusteeship of Korea for a period of up to five years." [4]

Neither the Joint Commission nor the trusteeship ever functioned effectively. A provisional democratic government was
never established nation-wide. The fundamental reason for the
breakdown was America's tyrannical policy in the south. As far
as the future role of the UN is concerned, though, the main issue
was which parties and organizations would be allowed to take
part in the political process. Both the Russians and Americans
established discriminatory criteria. Most Western texts have
seized on an apparently restrictive legalistic interpretation by the
Soviet Union. In retrospect it can be said that the Soviet Union
chose bad ground on which to try to make what was essentially
a correct stand against the American counterrevolutionary
steamroller. The Moscow Agreement had specified that the Joint
Commission should "consult with the Korean democratic parties
and social organizations." The U.S. side sanctioned a maneuver
whereby thoroughly undemocratic movements in the south would
be in a position to swamp the genuinely democratic organizations in both south and north. To avoid this, the Russians tried
to limit consultation to those bodies which had backed the Moscow Agreement—which had been widely opposed by Left and
Right. A subsequent compromise whereby bodies which were
"truly democratic in their aims and methods" and would agree
to declarations to "uphold the aims of the Moscow Agreement"
also failed. After further failures to agree on who should be

consulted, how, and by whom, direct negotiations between the Soviet and American representatives finally broke down in late 1947.[5]

To summarize this first, pre-UN phase: the Americans had refused to recognize the genuinely democratic Korean People's Republic; they had gone all out to wreck the Left and foster the Right in the south. On this basis, they were maneuvering to force an unpopular right-wing regime on the whole of Korea. The Russians, who also did not represent the Korean people—although they came a lot nearer to protecting their interests than did the Americans—could do little to thwart the American plan except to consolidate their secure base in the north. The Russian argument that undemocratic organizations should have no place in the consultations for setting up a democratic government was essentially correct, but its specific justification (the criterion of support for the Moscow Agreement and a trusteeship) was a political error. The vast majority of the Korean people was against the Moscow Agreement and against the United States and the puppet regime it was trying to install in Seoul. It was unfortunate that the Russians, completely on the defensive, helped to obscure this situation. However, this inadequate performance by the Soviet Union should not be allowed to obscure the fact that the United States was not simply contravening the Moscow Agreement by promoting undemocratic organizations, but going directly against the wishes of the Korean people in attempting to set up a reactionary regime. In spite of their blunder over the Moscow Agreement, the Russians were far more willing to heed the opinions of the Korean people. But, of course, heeding the wishes of the people was precisely what American policy was designed to avoid.

3. THE UNITED STATES MOBILIZES THE UN: 1947–50

In September 1947, the United States, without advance warning, asked that Korea be put on the UN agenda. The U.S.S.R. attempted to block discussion of Korea in the UN, on the grounds that it fell under the Moscow Agreement and other international agreements. The most solid objection was based upon article 107 of the UN Charter, which stated that the UN had no competence in matters relating to action against the enemy in World War II. Even a number of Western delegates adopted a cautious attitude on these grounds.

As with most of the UN discussions over Korea, the vast mass of speeches and maneuvers can be ignored. The American resolution called for separate elections in the two zones of Korea, thus leaving two options: either to split Korea, or to steamroller the north with the larger southern population. The key point in all the U.S. proposals was to get a UN committee or commission into Korea to act as a buffer and screening mechanism between the Korean people and the UN.

The Russians and their friends did their best to stave this off. In the Joint Commission on September 26, 1947 the U.S.S.R. had proposed the full withdrawal of all foreign forces from Korea and an end to the trusteeship. In the debate on the U.S. proposals in the First Committee at the UN, Soviet delegate Andrei Gromyko reiterated this position; he also demanded that the UN hear the elected representatives of the Korean people. He repeated that the Moscow Agreement had established the criteria for excluding certain political groups from consultation, and that there was an agreed-upon procedure for deciding which groups could be heard by the Joint Commission (which the U.S.S.R. was still backing as preferable to the UN).[6] The Americans, with a built-in majority, stonewalled on both key issues: withdrawal of foreign forces from Korea and hearing representatives of the Korean people. A UN commission, they argued, was necessary to decide which Koreans were indeed representative— in other words, to ensure a screening mechanism, and prevent the voice of the Korean people from being heard. The Soviet proposals for rapid withdrawal of foreign forces, leaving the Koreans themselves to settle the questions of unification and independence, had had a warm welcome in Korea, and the Americans employed every form of deviousness to prevent the possibility of Korea's simply being allowed to establish its independence. This would inevitably have produced a solidly anti-imperialist government. It was also still far too dangerous to allow a representative spectrum of Korean opinion to speak at the UN, even to its pro-U.S. majority. The United Nations Temporary Commission on Korea (UNTCOK) was invented to form a wall between the Korean people and the UN.[7]

This "Temporary" Commission was made up of Australia, Canada, China (Kuomintang), El Salvador, France, India, the Philippines and Syria. The Ukraine was appointed but refused to participate.[8] The membership of UNTCOK was proposed by U.S. delegate John Foster Dulles without explanation. There seems never to have been any rationalization for the composition of the Commission. It was, of course, heavily weighted in favor of the American position. In addition, the UN Secretary-General, Trygve Lie of Norway, appointed a number of aides to the Commission: chief among these were Assistant Secretary-General, Victor Chi-Tsai Hoo (former vice chairman of foreign affairs in the Chinese Nationalist government) as his personal representative "to get work started in Korea," and Petrus J. Schmidt as principal secretary to the Commision.[9]

The Commission began work in south Korea in January 1948, but was in every way inadequate to its alleged task, quite apart from its heavy overall political bias. From the start the Commission was at a disadvantage in assessing the political situation in Korea. Trygve Lie notes that the Commission's offices and living quarters were under a twenty-four-hour guard by the U.S. Army.

> In addition, Korean guards were stationed at the same places. . . . They made it difficult for Koreans to gain access to the Commission. . . . In theory, the function of the guards was to ensure that visitors would enter unarmed or disarmed. In practice, however, the presence of the guards tended to discourage Korean visitors, who were fearful that the news of their attempts to gain admission would be transmitted to their political opponents. Objections were raised by the secretariat . . . and the authorities were reminded that . . . the guards . . . were not to serve as a political screening agency. A gradual improvement in this respect was noticeable.

In addition, Lie records that the Commission's mail was opened by the U.S. censor "at the beginning . . . once or twice." [10]

The tiny Commission—some thirty-five people in all, including

both delegates and secretariat—was thoroughly ignorant about
Korea. It relied heavily for information on the American military, and what information reached it from Koreans was largely
filtered through interpreters who held far-right views.[11] The
verbatim records of UNTCOK's hearings in Korea are both revealing and utterly damning, for the American administration
and for the Commission itself. The Commission repeatedly failed
to follow up the crucial areas—political prisoners, intimidation,
and police terror. American military and civilian officials were
allowed to evade all these issues. Brig. Gen. John Weckerling,
U.S. liaison officer with UNTCOK, the first witness before Sub-
committee One,[12] gave the Commission two examples to show
that south Korea was not, in his opinion, a police state: first,
the streets were dirty; second, a Korean had grabbed his seat
at a performance of *La Traviata*. Indeed, Weckerling and others
hardly bothered to conceal their contempt for both the Korean
people and the Commission; on the earlier "election" in the U.S.
zone, Weckerling simply declared, "We do not claim that the
one [election] we held here was an entirely democratic election
as that term is understood in the United States." [13] Weckerling
earlier suggested that the U.S. commander, General John R.
Hodge, would like the UN to ask for U.S. observers. The French
delegate interrupted, "You mean United Nations observers." [14]
Weckerling did not; he meant quite simply that the UN should
increase its already overwhelming reliance on the American military regime.

It was also of relevance that the Commission was turning up
in Korea well over two years after the start of the American
occupation. Those years had not been wasted by the United
States. A systematic campaign had already weakened the Left,
much of which was by now outlawed, imprisoned, dead, exiled
or tortured into silence. The infrastructure for future elections
had been built through this long campaign of terror, and in particular through the thoroughly rigged 1946 election, on which
some vivid testimony from an unimpeachable American source
survives.[15]

Moreover, the U.S. Army Military Government in Korea
(USAMGIK) was not above exercising a bit of persuasion on

the Commission. Hodge complained to the First Sub-Committee on March 3, 1948:

> Already rumours leaking out from the Commission are demoralizing the police and demoralizing many Koreans; they fear, as stated by some Koreans, that there is an effort by the Commission to build up the communists. . . . They [the Koreans] have had a lot of violent communist activity, and I can speak for most Koreans when I say they are fed up with it.
>
> Many of you gentlemen here think that I am cracked on the subject of communism. All I can say is: if you had lived here . . . [as] I have, . . . you would not believe in Santa Claus either.[16]

Hodge and the USAMGIK, of course, made it as difficult as possible for the Commission to consult whatever left-wing persons were still free to testify, or dared to appear (or, perhaps, even thought it was worthwhile). In its second report to the UN, the Commission recorded that it had "experienced considerable difficulty in making contact with the left-wing organizations, certain of whose representatives were found to be either in prison, under order of arrest or some form of police surveillance." [17]

Even so, simply on the basis of the evidence presented to it, mainly by the Right and what the Commission termed "moderates," UNTCOK decided that it should refer back to the UN central organization early in 1948. In the first place, as was always clear would happen, north Korea refused to allow UNTCOK to enter its territory. The Commission was therefore unable to carry out its "mandate" of observing nationwide elections. This item in a sense stands on its own, since all the members of the Commission who agreed to take part in its work were aware beforehand that they would not be allowed to enter north Korea. However, additional important factors emerged. Of all opinion heard in Korea, only the Syngman Rhee Right and the USAMGIK advocated separate elections in the south; even right-wing leaders such as Kim Koo and his Korean Independence party opposed holding separate elections. Thus, within south Korea alone, a solid majority was against holding a separate election.[18] In its turn, a majority of the Commission decided that the formation of a separate government in the south would not facilitate "the attainment of the national independence of Korea" and that on these grounds alone it could not fulfill the mandate of the General Assembly resolution.

The second key point was whether, if such separate elections were held in the south, they could possibly be free. In the words of the American pundit, Leland M. Goodrich, "A majority of them [the members of the Commission], after consultations with Korean leaders, were not convinced that such a free atmosphere existed at that time." [19] Again, the same solid majority of the Left, "moderates," and the non-Rhee Right unanimously stated that free elections in the south would be impossible.[20]

This second point, of course, came up only because the Commission was unwilling to take a resolute stand on the first principle: that it would be breaking its mandate (quite apart from sabotaging the wishes of the Korean people by being in Korea at all) if it complied with elections in the south alone. But it is worth recording here the minimal role of the Commission, particularly since this has become much distorted in later literature. The original resolution requiring that the occupation powers hold elections was subsequently changed to: "that elections be held," with the rest left open. During the hearings in Seoul, the Commission made it quite clear how limited its own role was: "We do not regard our functions in any sense as holding or supervising elections and setting up the machinery for that purpose." [21] Given the composition and political orientation of the Commission, this is not surprising, but it does serve to show the degree of abdication by the Commission. In Trygve Lie's words, "In practice, the Commission took the view that the actual conduct and detailed supervision of the election was a matter for the United States military authorities and the South Korean Interim Government and the election authorities constituted by them." [22]

It is not necessary to dwell at length on the conditions of police terror obtaining in south Korea at the time. The Commission repeatedly, but feebly, questioned the USAMGIK and south Korean officials about this and was repeatedly fobbed off with inaccurate information or led up the garden path.[23] The Commission had no machinery to conduct a thorough investigation of prison conditions, arrests of political opponents of the regime, false registrations and disenfranchisements—and, later, rigged voting. Related but fundamentally technical matters, such as the survival and continued use of Japanese legislation (and the resulting legal confusion), were similarly dealt with in a half-hearted manner.[24] This aspect can be summed up as follows: the Commission heard an overwhelming majority of the witnesses before it state flatly that a free election would be impossible in south Korea under present conditions; and the Commission failed lamentably to carry out any investigation into the whole area of police terror which could in any way invalidate the thus undisputed conclusion of the vast majority of the evidence presented to it. This conclusion is amply documented in the verbatim UNTCOK reports.

As noted above, when confronted with the actual situation in south Korea (which was much more important in changing the minds of members of the Commission than north Korea's ban on their entry), the majority of UNTCOK decided on February 9, 1948 to refer back to the United Nations, where the question was debated by the Interim Committee of the General Assembly.[25] The Interim Committee decided that UNTCOK should go ahead and observe the election "in such parts of Korea as are accessible to the Commission." Both Canada and Australia, allies of the United States and members of UNTCOK, voted against the Interim Committee resolution; another eleven countries abstained (this does not include the socialist countries, which were absent). The United States decision to push for a separate election in the south, and to mobilize its UN majority behind this policy, was widely understood to mean both a break with the Soviet Union and a definitive move to set up a separate anti-communist regime in Seoul.[26] It is probably fair to say that some of the uneasiness in the Interim Committee was due to tactical differences between imperialists and their friends, rather than to fundamental political contradictions.

Back in Korea, UNTCOK was severely shaken by the Interim Committee's decision.[27] The impression given by the UNTCOK report is that the Commission's decision to refer back to headquarters was basically a stalling maneuver to get itself off the hook. The real crisis in the Commission came when it was confronted with the Interim Committee resolution. The Commission first met on February 28, 1948, two days after the Interim Committee adopted its resolution; at the February 28 meeting both Canada and the chairman were absent. The members of the Commission present decided to issue a statement that UNTCOK would observe elections in such parts of Korea as were accessible to it. And two days later General Hodge announced that elections would be held on May 9 in accordance with the General Assembly Resolution "and under the observation of the United Nations Temporary Commission on Korea." [28] At the first formal meeting of the Commission, the Canadian representative challenged the regularity of the previous proceedings and the grounds for General Hodge's proclamation. After much dissension, the Commission adopted by a vote of 4–2–2 (four in favor, two against, and two abstentions) a resolution agreeing to observe the May election "provided the Commission has ascertained that the elections will be held in a free atmosphere wherein the democratic rights of freedom of speech, press, and assembly would be recognized and respected." [29] In effect, therefore, this was simply a cover for a climb down (admittedly on a split vote) from UNTCOK's earlier position. Australia opposed the resolution on the grounds that the vote would be unrepresentative even within south Korea alone, much less representative of the country as a whole. Canada declared that the Interim Committee ruling was both "unwise and unconstitutional." [30] While it is important to stress that only 50 percent of this Commission—whose membership had been unilaterally proposed by the United States and which was overwhelmingly pro-American —would go along with the Interim Committee decision, even in a qualified way, it must be repeated that no member of the Commission then or at any other time took anything remotely approaching a resolute stand in favor of the wishes and rights of the Korean people.

After this series of decisions, UNTCOK was left (partly by its own actions) in a completely passive position, to observe elections stage-managed by the USAMGIK and the Rhee political machine. A minimal set of criteria even for "observing" the election would have included the following: a check on the registration of voters; information on political prisoners and their treatment; information on the reasons for which citizens might be imprisoned or discriminated against; and checks on polling officials, voting procedures and vote counting. On every one of these criteria UNTCOK was woefully wanting; its observation could certainly not stand up in any court of law. On the issue of voter registration, Lie later wrote: "A number of incidents occurred in connexion with the registration for the election . . . . Usually, the Main Committee or the Commission took no further action, being satisfied with the explanations of the authorities." [31] In other words, UNTCOK did not "usually" bother to verify for itself actual *incidents* connected with voter registration. The result: considerably less than half of the 21 million inhabitants of the south were even given the right to vote at all.[32]

The Commission was equally incapable of checking on the vast number of violent acts committed by the police against opponents of Rhee. In any case, it had only thirty-five people to cover the entire country. As frequently noted, this was a risible number compared with any similar operation in the past (such as in Nicaragua or the Saar).[33] Of course, UNTCOK was not *checking* an election; it was simply observing, quite fragmentarily, a tiny part of the whole process. This procedure of presenting a minute part as though it were the whole, later masked in UN and Western documents, was to characterize much of the UN role in Korea.

Lie gives a clue to the original limitations on the Commission's information-gathering procedures. Apart from hearing a few political leaders and USAMGIK officials, "Other oral evidence was admitted when members of Sub-Committee 2 interviewed a [*sic*] village headman and ordinary people ('the man in the street') in the city of Seoul." [34] As regards the actual election, Lie notes that, "the Commission's methods of observation were largely determined by the very limited staff available for field observation (approximately 35 persons, including secretariat officers)." [35] Furthermore, "The records of the observation groups indicate that in gathering information they relied to a considerable extent on interviews with election committee officials, including United States Military Government officials." [36] This dependence on USAMGIK and Rhee officials was acute before, during, and after the May 10 election. "A considerable number of election complaints," wrote Lie, were received and submitted to the U.S. authorities; their comments were

> . . . in general accepted without further action by the Main Committee. In a few instances, where observer groups on the spot had taken an interest, the Commission made vigorous attempts to assist complainants *vis-à-vis* the election committees and other authorities. In certain cases, it was noted by the Committee that complaints had been investigated by the Korean authorities against whom those complaints had been made and the opinion of the United States authorities as to the adequacy of the investigation was requested. In general, however, no investigation, other than for the purpose of gathering information concerning a given complaint, was undertaken by the Commission or its agencies acting independently.[37]

Most of the UNTCOK observers were accompanied by U.S. military personnel while observing the elections. A few teams went without such escorts. "They [the teams without escorts] undoubtedly succeeded in creating a freer atmosphere for observing the election procedures." [38] In other words, according to the Secretary-General, the U.S. military presence was inimical to a free atmosphere (an atmosphere is either free or it is not).

On the basis of this paltry observation, the Commission gave its opinion (unanimously) that "the results of the ballot of 10 May 1948 were a valid expression of the free will of the electorate in those parts of Korea which were accessible to the Commission and in which the inhabitants constituted approximately two-thirds of the people of all Korea." [39] This opinion is worth little more than the paper it is written on and is based on less than hearsay: the UNTCOK groups actually paid short visits to a mere 2 percent of the polling centers in south Korea; [40] severe fraud was visible in several of the polling centers visited; those voting, according to official USAMGIK-Rhee figures, amounted to about one-third the population of south Korea,[41] and considerably less than one-quarter the total population of Korea. A final point needs to be noted: the Commission's report refers to "*those parts* of Korea . . . accessible to the Commission" (emphasis added). This is a curious formulation to apply to a unit of territory and may reflect a desire to qualify the meager observation of one polling center out of every fifty. In many later texts referring to the Commission's opinion, including the December 12, 1948 General Assembly resolution, this formulation becomes "that part of Korea . . . ," which effectively removes whatever revealing nuance there may have been in the original.

The subsequent history of the relationship between UNTCOK and Seoul is one of feeble surrender on the part of the Commission and ruthless extrusion by the USAMGIK and the Rhee regime. In spite of later disclaimers, the Commission effectively endorsed both the May 10 election and the installation of the Rhee government immediately afterwards. The Commission was aware that even on the basis of the unverified and certainly rigged election, the Rhee regime was by no means a majority one. Yet the Commission failed to take a single step to question the validity of the regime or to assist other members of the UN to understand the true situation by making available further information on the matter. The Commission withdrew to the tranquillity of Shanghai to write the first part of its report and was, consequently, almost totally out of touch with events in Seoul during the crucial weeks after the election.[42] The Commission, having falsified its own report by claiming to have observed the May 10 election, then abdicated responsibility completely by failing to check any of the subsequent stages—the convening of an assembly in Seoul that called itself the "National Assembly"; the "Constitution of the Republic of Korea" (July); the installation of Syngman Rhee as president of the Republic and the formation of a government (July–August 1948).[43] Washington and Seoul, having obtained what they most wanted—the stamp of legitimacy that came from the Commission's "observation" of the election—made little pretense of needing UNTCOK further. A number of UNTCOK members tried to challenge the post-election exploitation of UNTCOK by Seoul; but it must be stated that UNTCOK as a body failed miserably to dissociate itself adequately from Rhee's claims not just that the assembly was a "National Assembly" and the government a "national" one but, much more important, that UNTCOK endorsed these assertions.[44]

Nonetheless, the UN Secretariat did all it could to silence UNTCOK in the period between its endorsement of the May election and the General Assembly debate in December 1948. The Secretariat (i.e., the United States plus Lie) tried to prevent the Commission from attending the Assembly debate by refusing to pay their fares to Paris, where the General Assembly was meeting.[45]

The debate was crucial for the United States. It had to complete its coup of involving the UN in Korea by getting a General Assembly resolution endorsing the Seoul regime. The maximum U.S. position was to get the UN to designate the South Korean regime as the sole legitimate government in Korea, representing the majority of the Korean people—allowing this regime to present itself as the "national government." The minimum U.S. position was to obtain a resolution giving a measure of legitimacy to the "Republic of Korea" and ensuring continued UN involvement there in a way favorable to Washington and Seoul.

The December 1948 debate followed predictable lines. The socialist delegations made valiant efforts to obtain support for inviting delegates from the Democratic People's Republic of Korea (D.P.R.K.). This proposal was inevitably voted down. The socialist delegations went on to argue against accepting UNTCOK's endorsement of the May 1948 elections in the south and against the U.S. manipulation of the Commission's work. The socialist countries' case was based on a series of claims which certainly merited much more serious consideration than they were given, although it is also important to recognize the weakness in their case as it was usually presented.[46]

A key item in their argument was the whole social and political situation in the south, particularly as it affected the May election. Much of the socialist delegations' case was based on information derived from UNTCOK documents, and it is remarkable how this information was repeatedly brushed aside, without ever being directly refuted.[47]

The United States stood on its majority, ignoring the mass of specific criticism contained in the UNTCOK documents and the further evidence brought forward by the Soviet, Ukrainian and other socialist delegates (who also made available communications from the D.P.R.K. government in P'yŏngyang). The Indian delegate, too, although noticeably modifying the position taken earlier by the Indian chairman of UNTCOK, K.P.S. Menon, stressed that the government emerging from the May election in the south could not be considered a "national" one (as the November 14, 1947 General Assembly Resolution had stipulated): both because the UN had not verified an election in the north, and because of the massive absence of the anti-Rhee parties in the south, along with the fact that the Rhee regime subsequently had made no attempt at rapprochement or reconciliation.[48]

The U.S. delegation, headed by John Foster Dulles, rammed through a resolution which declared:

> . . . that there has been established a lawful government (the Government of the Republic of Korea) having effective control and jurisdiction over that part of Korea where the Temporary Commission was able to observe and consult and in which the great majority of the people of all Korea reside; that this Government is based on elections which were a valid expression of the free will of the electorate of that part of Korea and which were observed by the Temporary Commission; and that this is the only such Government in Korea.[49]

The resolution went on to set up a new commission, the United Nations Commission on Korea (UNCOK), with the same membership as UNTCOK, minus Canada.[50]

It must be noted that the resolution did not endorse the Seoul regime that emerged from the May 10 elections as a *national* government. But hair-splitting on this issue is not particularly productive, since the resolution was specifically crafted in order to pass the General Assembly and yet enable Rhee to use it to support his claims [51] (as he had already successfully manipulated UNTCOK in Korea after the elections). In view, too, of the supine behavior of the majority of UN members, who willingly went along with the whole fraud, their refusal to recognize the Rhee regime as a national government is itself worth rather little. But the point does need stressing, since the resolution was subsequently used by the Seoul regime to bolster its claims to be a national government, and the United States has actively gone along with Seoul's distortion. Indeed, this was the U.S. intention in formulating the resolution. The UN, too, repeatedly failed to dissociate itself from the claims being made by the Rhee regime, thus allowing Rhee to exploit this acquiescence. The December 1948 resolution served as the basis on which the United States, with the active complicity of Lie, rounded up UN support for South Korea after June 25, 1950. Other allies went along; less than two years after the December 12, 1948 resolution, the British Government was claiming that the resolution "recommended the recognition of the (Southern) Republic of Korea by members of the United Nations." [52] This is at least an exaggeration.

4. THE 1950–53 WAR

UNCOK, like UNTCOK, was a tiny group, lacking the skills and assets, as well as the political will, to accomplish any task except to provide cover, through its presence, for the consolidation of the Rhee regime. Its work in Korea is of minimal interest prior to the outbreak of the full-scale war in June 1950. However, it should be noted en passant that UNCOK specifically rejected any responsibility for endorsing (or not endorsing) the key events during this period, such as the partial withdrawal of U.S. troops [53] and the May 1950 elections in the south.[54] Yet, although powerless and ill-informed, it continued to transmit to UN headquarters reports which could be used by the United States to organize support for South Korea. This is hardly surprising in view of the fact that its predecessor had falsified its own reports in order to assist the installation of this regime.

Considerable controversy still rages over the immediate origins of the Korean War of 1950–53. The discussion here is limited to specific aspects of the question in which the UN was closely involved or where its actions are of particular relevance.

First, there was the failure to report the political dangers caused by the behavior of the Seoul regime. Whether or not the Rhee regime was in a position to initiate a war, it is indisputable that it repeatedly proclaimed that it would resort to force; moreover, its repressive internal policies were an outrage to Korean feelings north and south of the parallel. UNCOK chose not only to dismiss the likelihood of Rhee's invading the north, but consistently to downplay criticism of Seoul, and it ignored or obfuscated the wider political effects which Rhee's activities could reasonably be expected to produce.[55] In other words, the UN's Commission in Korea did not prepare the UN adequately for the virtually inevitable results of the UN intervention in Korea.

Secondly, there is the question of UNCOK's reportage on the events of June 25 and the immediately preceding period. Lie, MacArthur, and others frequently claimed that UNCOK was in a position to provide a reliable assessment of the military posture of the South Korean army at the time of the outbreak of the war. The main source for this claim was an UNCOK Field Observers' Report on their tour of the parallel between June 9 and June 23. Several points need to be stressed about this affair.

The observers' "team" in fact consisted of only two people—both Australian officers. Second, although it was subsequently claimed by MacArthur and others that the "team" toured the 38th parallel for two solid weeks,[56] scrutiny of the record shows that the two Australians were at or near the parallel for a maximum of nine, not fourteen days.[57] The assessment of troop dispositions (section 8) is utterly vague, and it is impossible to avoid the conclusion that these two men, depending anyway on South Korean officials for their information, were not in a position to assess accurately the real disposition of either South Korean or North Korean troops. In particular, it must be noted that on the crucial question of whether or not the South Korean army was disposed in depth, the Field Observers' Report is directly and fundamentally contradicted by MacArthur's subsequent testimony at 1951 Senate Hearings.[58] Although the report, which was extremely brief, was (allegedly) completed on June 24—i.e., before the outbreak of the full-scale war—it was not made available in full to UNCOK until June 26, after the Security Council had already condemned the D.P.R.K., and it did not reach the UN Secretariat until June 29. No convincing explanation for these delays has ever been forthcoming.

This ties up intimately with the third aspect: how the UN headquarters got its information and made its decisions about the start of the war and its own involvement in it. Lie records in his memoirs that he got his first information about the outbreak of fighting through the U.S. Assistant Secretary of State John D. Hickerson.[59] Lie's executive assistant, Andrew Cordier (an American), cabled UNCOK, which had not found it necessary to comment on the incident, for a report. During the rest of the night (June 24–25 in New York), Lie had at least four calls from U.S. Ambassador Ernest A. Gross, with whom he discussed procedures.

Quite apart from Lie's own political proclivities, it is of some importance that the U.S. government, with a virtual stranglehold on communications in this crucial initial stage, went to the trouble to edit the relatively cautious information which came from their Seoul ambassador, John Muccio.[60] Lie initiated action at UN headquarters on the basis of this information, transmitted and edited by U.S. officials. UNCOK, in Korea, did not send any information until after it had been specifically requested to do so by Cordier. The first cable from UNCOK gave no firsthand information about the origins of the fighting. And the first reports from the Commission's field observers about events on that day (June 25) did not come in until about 5 P.M. local time. Given UNCOK's political record and composition, it is quite striking that (a) its first message to headquarters on June 25 simply recorded Seoul's claim about being attacked by North Korea (although the Commission does go on implicitly to accept the South Korean version of events); and (b) for its rebuttal of the claim by P'yŏngyang radio that the south had attacked the north, the Commission in its report simply relied on the unchecked affirmation of Rhee, his foreign minister, and Muccio. If the Commission had other sources of information, it is hard to believe that they would not have been cited in preference to the unilateral and untrustworthy ones quoted.

In his memoirs, Lie records that he decided to act after receiving the first cable from UNCOK. But the record shows that Lie, in close alliance with the United States, decided to act upon receiving the American reports, transmitted through exclusively American channels. Technically the June 25 meeting of the Security Council was called at the request of the United States, but Lie's memoirs indicate that it was a coordinated operation between himself and the U.S. government. Lie, moreover, was closely surrounded by U.S. officials, and the June 25 proposals were drafted by Lie working together with Cordier and General Counsel to the UN Abraham H. Feller, both Americans. Lie arranged for the president of the Council to allow him to speak first so that he (Lie) could present his loaded report. Lie also worked on swinging the vote: "I believe I may say without risking any offence that my views probably influenced the Indian delegation, as well as the delegate of Egypt, Mahmoud Fawzi Bey, to vote in favor of the resolution." [61] Lie also pressured the vacillating delegate from his own country, Norway.

The June 25 Security Council meeting is of little interest. The United States presented its doctored version of the original Muccio report, falsely stating that it was giving the UN Muccio's relatively cautious message.[62] The U.S. juggernaut, aided by the Indian president of the Council, B.N. Rau (who seems to have been swung from a quasi-neutral position by the partial evidence presented),[63] then ensured the exclusion of any representative of the D.P.R.K., while allowing a Seoul envoy to appear. In light of the UN's consistent refusal in the past to hear delegates from the D.P.R.K., this decision is not very surprising, but here, where there were two utterly conflicting versions of the origin of a civil war, the exclusion of the D.P.R.K. from a hearing was a particularly grave act. Within the imperialist camp, only the U.K. delegate urged caution, stressing the limited evidence produced by UNCOK and calling for "as full a statement of the facts as we can [obtain] at the earliest possible moment." [64] In other words, he recognized that the information made available was not adequate. A principled motion put forward by Yugoslavia to hear representatives of both sides and adopt a neutral attitude until reliable information could be obtained was obliterated by the imperialist majority (6–1–3). The Soviet Union was absent, maintaining a boycott over the continued presence of the Kuomintang.

While the inadequate behavior of UNCOK in Korea must be noted, it is just as important to stress the lamentable and supine surrender of the majority of Security Council members. The surrender was particularly abject on two linked points: hearing both sides of the argument in the UN and investigating the D.P.R.K. side of the case in Korea. UNCOK's second cable (UN Doc. S/1503) suggested that the Security Council should ask both sides to agree on a neutral mediator. The Security Council brushed this suggestion aside. The Council, too, failed to investigate, or even try to investigate, the D.P.R.K. claim that

South Korea had started the war by launching an attack on Haeju on the morning of June 25. Admittedly, UNCOK reported the D.P.R.K. claim and dismissed it in a way that made it easy for the United States to write it off—even though the capture of Haeju by R.O.K. forces was confirmed by the ranking U.S. military officials in Korea.[65]

From here on, the UN followed a consistent policy of supporting the United States, not bothering even to go through many of the formalities usually associated with belligerence or even international diplomatic practice. Truman ordered American forces into action *before* the Security Council adopted its June 27, 1950 resolution (which called on member states to furnish assistance to South Korea). But this, wrote Lie, "did not anticipate its [the Security Council's] resolution of June 27 so much as it seemed to do, for diplomatic consultations before the issuance of the order had made it clear that there were seven votes . . . in the Council for authorizing armed assistance to the Republic of Korea." [66] In other words, Lie did not care if the United States waited for the UN authorization, since Washington knew what was going to happen anyway, and Lie agreed with the certain outcome.

On July 7 the Security Council passed a resolution setting up a "Unified Command" to direct military operations in Korea. Under this, the UN abdicated all responsibility and power to the United States, which was allowed to organize its own imperialist coalition under the UN flag, without being obliged even to inform the UN of what it was doing. General MacArthur was put in charge of this Unified Command.[67] In view of Washington's already troubled relationship with MacArthur over the bombing of North Korea and MacArthur's refusal to await Truman's orders before acting, it was highly irresponsible of the U.S. government to get the UN to give MacArthur this blank check. At the same time, it was craven of Britain and France, which proposed the Unified Command, to go along with such an outrageous maneuver, which they rapidly came to regret. Lie did his bit by appointing as his personal representative to the Unified Command (as well as to UNCOK and the South Korean government) one Colonel Alfred G. Katzin of South Africa, a former intelligence officer.[68] Having ensured that liaison would

e handled by a man with impeccable far-right credentials,
rther arranged a reorganization of the UN bureaucracy
imize the chances of UN interference in the Unified Com-
.[69]

From here on operations in Korea were out of the control of
the UN. UNCOK had neither the equipment nor the authority
to be of any effect. As is well known, the Korean People's Army
(KPA) liberated all of South Korea, except for a small area
around Pusan in the southeast, within a matter of weeks. On
September 15, 1950 the Inch'ŏn landing opened the way to the
fall of Seoul, which was captured by U.S. forces by the end of
the month, while the KPA was swiftly thrown back towards the
38th parallel. The main questions facing the UN by this time
were whether to invade the north and, if so, what *political* form
this invasion should take.

Since the UN had already signed away responsibility for what
might occur in the field, it is of slight value to rehash the argument about whether MacArthur technically jumped the gun in
moving across the parallel. There is anyway little evidence that
the UN as an organization was against this. Lie's personal representative, Katzin, had already filed a report on August 29 which
argued vigorously against stopping at the parallel. "This [would]
constitute a continuing military threat not only to our own
United Nations forces, but to South Korean freedom." [70] On
September 30 Lie and his advisors prepared a paper on "Suggested Terms of Settlement of the Korean Question." This called
for North Korea's surrender *via* a ceasefire, to be followed by
UN control of the D.P.R.K., and a UN-supervised election. U.S.
amendments to this draft led to the October 7, 1950 UN General
Assembly resolution, which endorsed the U.S. plan to destroy the
D.P.R.K.[71] The resolution also set up a new commission, the
United Nations Commission for the Unification and Rehabilitation of Korea (UNCURK), to replace UNCOK. UNCURK was
specifically entrusted (clause 2a, ii) with representing the UN
in the destruction of the D.P.R.K. Since UNCURK (although
its membership partly overlapped with that of UNCOK) could
not immediately go to work on the spot in Korea, an Interim
Committee was set up to act pending the arrival of UNCURK;
this Interim Committee assumed responsibility for North Korea.

MacArthur later defined his mission as "to clear out all North Korea, to unify it [presumably Korea] and to liberalize it." [72] Rhee pushed hard at once for an election to be held in North Korea alone. The Interim Committee adopted a fairly cautious statement on October 12, 1950 about interfering in the north. The key issue here was the use of South Korean officials in the occupied areas of the north. Rhee naturally wanted to expand his administration to the maximum possible extent. The Unified Command (i.e., MacArthur) complained to the Interim Committee that all the local North Korean officials had fled, and that therefore South Koreans were badly needed.[73] Rhee chimed in with a bitter complaint about the Committee's October 12 statement. The Interim Committee backtracked and on November 6 endorsed the already implemented use of South Korean officials, guards and police north of the 38th parallel. These Rhee officials at once initiated a vicious counterrevolution in the north, involving innumerable executions and other crimes against the local inhabitants.

Fortunately, the U.S.-UN occupation of the north was fairly brief. UNCURK did not reach Korea until November 26, well after the Chinese People's Volunteers had entered the war. UNCURK went along with the use of Rhee officials in the north and other measures, such as the use of South Korean currency in the D.P.R.K. But it could do nothing to assist Rhee in his plan to seize the north through another rigged election. UNCURK did, however, state that: "From its discussions with United Nations military authorities who were in North Korea, and from its own discussions with refugees from there, the Commission believes that, in fact, opinion in the north generally favoured joining the Republic of Korea [South Korea]." [74] This statement testifies both to UNCURK's appalling and wilful ignorance of the facts, as well as to its real, if necessarily limited, assistance to Syngman Rhee's policies.

The only other aspect of UNCURK'S activities which merits mention here is its whitewashing of Rhee's extermination of political opponents. The section on this in the first UNCURK report is actually entitled "Assistance to the Government of the Republic of Korea in questions connected with the administration of justice." [75] In this section UNCURK provides some information on two episodes of mass executions of civilians, at Hongjai-ri and Kuhchang (UNCURK spellings). The Commission was unable to do a complete whitewash of the Kuhchang massacre, but again it failed to emphasize to UN members the nature of the regime which they had voted to support, or to indicate that this treatment of political opponents was systematic and repeated. A qualitatively similar position was adopted by UNCURK over the May–June 1952 political crisis, where UNCURK reported that "the Constitution of the Republic of Korea has been violated in important respects," [76] but absolved Rhee (without adequate evidence) of part of the responsibility for some of the events.

The United Nations as such, including UNCURK, was largely irrelevant to the actual conduct of the war, including such important issues as the controversy over the dismissal of MacArthur. MacArthur himself put it bluntly in the Senate Hearings: "My connection with the United Nations was largely nominal. . . . The entire control of my command and everything I did came from our own Chiefs of Staff and my channel of communication was defined as the Army Chief of Staff. . . . I had no direct connection with the United Nations whatsoever." [77] Later in the hearings General J. Lawton Collins, army Chief of Staff, summed up the general position: on the one hand, the United States could do anything it wanted, without reference to the UN; on the other hand, something like a blockade of China or hot pursuit into Chinese air space necessitated consultations with America's allies. Collins noted, correctly, that this consultation was needed only with allies, not with the UN.[78] Hot pursuit seems in fact to have been the only policy advocated by the United States which was vetoed by its allies.

What is important as regards the UN, however, is the overall cover it gave to the entire Korean operation, an operation which was distinguished by massive destruction, incredible brutality, and the violation by the UN side of virtually every norm of warfare, including both the Geneva Convention and the criteria for war crimes which the United States had helped to establish at Nuremberg.[79]

The UN also allowed itself to be manipulated by the United States on a wider range of issues connected with the Far East, in particular the China question, which was skilfully entangled with the Korean war. The UN finally corrected its error on China in 1971. It is high time that it corrected its string of errors over Korea, ranging from the original assistance to U.S. plans in 1947, through the rigged 1948 election, to the condemnation of the People's Republic of China as an "aggressor" during the Korean war. South Korea, one of the most ferocious dictatorships on earth, was the United Nations' first creation, and it would be aberrant to imagine that the UN's actions over Korea had no influence on the UN itself. Moreover, while it was the unfortunate people of Korea who suffered most from the UN's servile behavior, the UN's actions also helped to mold a corpus of attitudes in the Far East and throughout the world. UNCURK was disbanded in 1973, but the UN continues to provide the cover for the presence of foreign troops in Korea against the wishes of the Korean people. Its record of intervention, ignorance, and deception hardly justifies its claim to be protecting the rights of a people who have only asked it to leave.

Notes

1. William Porter, Testimony, *United States Security Agreements and Commitments Abroad, Republic of Korea*, Hearings Before the Subcommittee on U.S. Security Agreements and Commitments Abroad of the Committee on Foreign Relations, U.S. Senate, Ninety-first Congress, Second Session, 1970, pp. 1579–82.
2. There is not space to argue this at length here. It emerges clearly from the well-documented liberal study of Dae-Sook Suh, *The Korean Communist Movement 1918–1948* (Princeton, Princeton University Press, 1967); it also emerges strongly from testimony by the U.S. Commander in Korea, General John R. Hodge, to the UN Temporary Commission in 1948, *First Part of the Report of the United Nations Temporary Commission on Korea* (hereafter cited as *UNTCOK Report*, First Part), Vol. 3, Annex 9, especially pp. 34, 134–42, in United Nations, General Assembly, Official Records (hereafter cited as *GAOR*), 3rd Session, Supplement No. 9 (A/575, Add. 2). See also Joyce and Gabriel Kolko, *The Limits of Power: The World and United States Foreign Policy, 1945–1954*

(New York, Harper and Row, 1972), pp. 278–89. The Kolkos' book gives an excellent survey of the Korean situation.

3. In 1948 General Hodge told the UN that Communist activity "has steadily diminished since the time we came in and found the communists actually ruling and controlling South Korea" (*UNTCOK Report,* First Part, Vol. 3, Annex 9, p. 34).

4. *Department of State Bulletin,* U.S. Department of State (Washington D.C.), December 30, 1945, p. 1030. Britain and China (Kuomintang) were also present at Moscow, and the Agreement stipulated that they were to be "consulted" on several matters, but this is irrelevant. The word used to translate "trusteeship" into Korean was the same word used for the Japanese "protectorate." It would seem that no firm agreement was reached at Moscow about the trusteeship. U.S. Secretary of State Byrnes said in a radio broadcast on December 30, 1945 that "the joint Soviet-American Commission, working with the Korean provisional democratic government, may find it possible to dispense with a trusteeship" (*Department of State Bulletin,* December 30, 1945, p. 1036).

5. These negotiations were carried on at several levels: the Joint Commission; direct talks between the Soviet and American commanders-in-chief in Korea; between the Soviet foreign minister and the U.S. secretary of state (or their deputies).

6. Soviet delegate Gromyko to the First Committee, United Nations, *GAOR,* 2nd Session, 87th Meeting (October 28, 1947), pp. 250–51.

7. The emergence of UNTCOK is documented fairly fully, from a pro-U.S. point of view, by Leland M. Goodrich, *Korea: A Study of U.S. Policy in the United Nations* (New York, Council on Foreign Relations, 1956), pp. 31–41; and, in more detail, by Leon Gordenker, *The United Nations and the Peaceful Unification of Korea: The Politics of Field Operations, 1947–1950* (The Hague, Martinus Nijhoff, 1959), pp. 13–21. That the United States move was designed to intrude UNTCOK in between the UN and the Korean people is clear from the language of the original U.S. resolution (A/C.1/229). As the socialist delegates pointed out, on the not dissimilar Palestine question, the UN had heard the direct representatives of the Palestinian people; the United States move to prevent Koreans being heard was therefore—apart from anything else —a move to alter UN policy.

8. The head of the Ukrainian delegation was Dmitri Manuilsky, formerly a leading figure in the Communist International and one of the most able foreign policy experts in the U.S.S.R. Manuilsky's speeches at the UN were consistently the best-researched, most mili-

tant and most inspiring; they still make much the best reading in the records.

9. Trygve Lie, *In the Cause of Peace: Seven Years with the United Nations* (New York, Macmillan Co., 1954), p. 325. Schmidt was soon to play a crucial role in suborning UNTCOK to the U.S. position after the Interim Committee ruling that the Commission should go ahead and "observe" in the south alone. Gordenker notes that the Secretariat's activities "became striking enough so that Mr. Schmidt's role . . . was called into question" (*Peaceful Unification of Korea*, p. 79). Schmidt reneged on a promise to the Canadian delegate George Patterson; Gordenker cautiously calls this only "pressure." "Rigging" or "sabotage" would fit equally well. Lie's role is detailed below. On the grounds that Lie originally favored restoring China's seat to the People's Republic, some on the Left have recently praised Lie as a friend of peace; this seems to me incorrect. See *Korea Focus* (New York), Vol. 1, No. 1 (Fall 1971), p. 17.

10. United Nations, Secretary-General, "Organization and Procedure of United Nations Commissions," Memo No. 8, *Memo on the United Nations Temporary Commission on Korea* (hereafter cited as Secretary-General, *Memo on UNTCOK*), pp. 13, 14. It is, of course, quite possible that Lie did not actually write this document, but it was put out under his official title. Lie tends to dismiss the seriousness of the U.S. Army Military Government in Korea opening mail, but once this kind of thing happens, particularly early on, the damage is done. Word gets around and insecurity is established.

11. This is not a minor point; for the crucial role of interpreters, see Kolko and Kolko, *The Limits of Power*, p. 283.

12. UNTCOK initially set up three subcommittees: Sub-Committee One (Canada, France, Syria, and later China) to consider means of ensuring a free atmosphere for an election; Sub-Committee Two (Australia, China, France, the Philippines, and later El Salvador) to examine communications and secure statements from Korean "personalities"; and Sub-Committee Three (Canada, France, the Philippines, Syria; later El Salvador replaced France, and China was added) to consider electoral laws and regulations. After the referral to the Interim Committee of the General Assembly in February 1948, a four-nation *ad hoc* committee of UNTCOK recommended that the three subcommittees be eliminated; they were replaced by a Main Committee on March 29, 1948 (see Gordenker, *Peaceful Unification of Korea*, pp. 36–37 for details).

13. *UNTCOK Report*, First Part, Vol. 3, Annex 9, p. 7. These "elections" were held in October 1946 for a provisional legislature

in Seoul. Half the ninety members were appointed by the USAMGIK. The other forty-five were "elected" on the basis of the Japanese franchise laws, so that only landlords, taxpayers, and village headmen could vote. In many places the election was held before it was even announced. For a detailed indictment of the real conditions under which this "election" was held, see Mark Gayn, *Japan Diary* (New York, William Sloane Associates, 1948), especially p. 426. No reading of official documents can substitute for the devastating detail provided by Gayn.

14. *UNTCOK Report,* First Part, Vol. 3, Annex 9, p. 6.

15. Gayn, *Japan Diary,* pp. 351–437, *passim.*

16. *UNTCOK Report,* First Part, Vol. 3, Annex 9, p. 36.

17. Quoted by J. and G. Kolko, *The Limits of Power,* pp. 295–96.

18. This emerges both from the actual testimony reproduced (mostly verbatim) in *UNTCOK Report,* First Part, Vol. 3, Annex 9, and from UNTCOK's own conclusions in *UNTCOK Report,* First Part, Vol. 2, Annex 6, *GAOR,* 3rd Session, Supplement No. 9 (A/575 Add. 1), pp. 64–66.

19. Goodrich, *Korea,* p. 44.

20. *UNTCOK Report,* First Part, Vol. 2, Annex 6, pp. 64–66.

21. Canadian delegate Patterson, chairman of Sub-Committee One, *UNTCOK Report,* First Part, Vol. 3, Annex 9, p. 7.

22. Secretary-General, *Memo on UNTCOK,* p. 17.

23. See, for example, the evasions by General William F. Dean and General Hodge, *UNTCOK Report,* First Part, Vol. 3, Annex 9, pp. 18, 37; Secretary-General, *Memo on UNTCOK,* p. 19.

24. On this, see *UNTCOK Report,* First Part, Vol. 3, Annex 9, pp. 13, 23–33. On the continued use of former Japanese police, see Gayn, *Japan Diary,* pp. 352, 423–24.

25. *UNTCOK Report,* First Part, Vol. 1, pp. 25–30.

26. Goodrich, *Korea,* p. 49.

27. See *UNTCOK Report,* First Part, Vol. 1, pp. 28–30; Goodrich, *Korea,* pp. 50–52.

28. Quoted by Goodrich, *Korea,* p. 50.

29. Gordenker, *Peaceful Unification of Korea,* pp. 83–84; the resolution is UN Document A/AC.19/Sr. 22, March 12, 1948.

30. *UNTCOK Report,* First Part, Vol. 1, p. 28; Gordenker, *Peaceful Unification of Korea,* pp. 76–85 for details.

31. Secretary-General, *Memo on UNTCOK,* p. 17.

32. There were 7,837,504 registered eligible voters; there is no sure figure for the total population of south Korea at this time, but estimates generally put it at about 20 to 21 million. See also speech by Ukrainian delegate Vadim P. Kovalenko to the First Committee of the General Assembly, *GAOR*, 3rd Session, Part I, First Committee, p. 982. See also note 41.

33. A detailed comparison was given by Weckerling to UNTCOK, *UNTCOK Report*, First Part, Vol. 3, Annex 9, p. 6; Weckerling's objective seems to have been to impress the Commission with its own feeble resources and thus persuade them to rely more heavily on the USAMGIK. "The limited staff of the Commission makes any discussion of ratio as a factor in determining the real situation patently absurd" (George McCune, *Korea Today* [London, Allen & Unwin, 1950], p. 229).

34. Secretary-General, *Memo on UNTCOK*, p. 17; for the Commission's own details of its observation, see *UNTCOK Report*, First Part, Vol. 3, Annex 9.

35. Secretary-General, *Memo on UNTCOK*, p. 21.

36. *Ibid.*, p. 22.

37. *Ibid.*, pp. 22–23.

38. *Ibid.*, p. 13. All this squares oddly with the later account given by Lie in his memoirs: "The Commission [UNTCOK], through extensive field investigation, ascertained that the atmosphere in South Korea was free enough for a free election, and then proceeded to supervise carefully the registration of voters, the campaigning, the voting, and the counting of ballots" (Lie, *In the Cause*, p. 326).

39. *UNTCOK Report*, Second Part, Vol. 1, p. 3.

40. *GAOR*, 3rd Session, Part I, First Committee, p. 1011.

41. Of course, the total population includes many under voting age, which has to be taken into account. The highest possible computation is that by the U.S. State Department: ". . . almost 80 percent of the eligible voters registered, and . . . an estimated 92.5 percent of these cast their ballots" (*Korea, 1945 to 1948*, U.S. Department of State [Washington, D.C., 1948], p. 15). The actual reported figures were that 7,036,750 people voted out of 7,837,504 registered voters; this was equal to about 72 percent of the qualified voters (Goodrich, *Korea*, p. 59; Gordenker, *Peaceful Unification of Korea*, pp. 105–6). For the massive violence, fraud and intimidation connected with the election, see J. and G. Kolko, *The Limits of Power*, pp. 295–98. The *UNTCOK Report*, First Part, Vol. 3, Annex 12, records many instances (in the few polling booths visited) of police inside the polling booths, booths without curtains or screens, and officials standing by "to help illiterates." The *UNTCOK Report*, First Part, Vol. 2, Annex 7, p. 80, records the invalidation of some elections on Cheju-do; this seems to have been a maneuver by the regime to smother the widespread abstentions (more than 50 percent) in parts of the island, which was heavily left-wing; Cheju-do was one of the most active areas during the great revolutionary uprising that started in autumn 1948.

42. Gordenker, *Peaceful Unification of Korea,* pp. 114, 117–20. The Commission first tried to move to Tokyo, but MacArthur claimed to be unable to find accommodation. That the decision to leave Korea altogether at this critical juncture may have been deliberately arranged by the more pro-U.S. members of the Commission is suggested by the information given by Gordenker (p. 120), although he himself rather unconvincingly disclaims such an interpretation.

43. *UNTCOK Report,* Second Part, Vol. 1, pp. 2–3; compare the detailed account of the Commission's negligence in Gordenker, *Peaceful Unification of Korea,* pp. 108–42; Goodrich, *Korea,* pp. 60–63. In a classic case of elision, the June 26, 1950 *Report* by the UN Commission on Korea (UNCOK, UNTCOK's successor) refers to: "the Government of the Republic of Korea *established under the auspices of the United Nations Temporary Commission on Korea . . .*" (emphasis added).

44. Gordenker, *Peaceful Unification of Korea,* pp. 121–34.

45. *Ibid.,* p. 140.

46. The socialist case was built on a combination of UNTCOK material and information largely supplied by the D.P.R.K. A reading of the UN debates demonstrates beyond the shadow of a doubt that the U.S. majority simply was not interested in facts or evidence. The socialist delegates presented an excellent case on the following points: (1) UNTCOK did not know what was going on in Korea; a reading of its evidence alone would not allow the interpretation the U.S. majority was attempting to impose; (2) the political situation in the south was one of complete turmoil, and the Rhee regime did not represent the Korean people; (3) a real majority did exist throughout Korea against splitting the country and for the immediate withdrawal of all foreign troops. This majority was most decisively demonstrated by the April 1948 P'yŏngyang conference attended by political leaders from both south and north Korea (the conference also called for the withdrawal of UNTCOK). The socialist presentation of the case for recognition of the D.P.R.K. was less convincing and, on the whole, less well argued.

47. It is noticeable that in the actual General Assembly debate the United States and its allies hardly bothered to make their case. Interestingly, the chief French delegate to UNTCOK, Jean-Louis Paul-

Boncour, had earlier urged that the records of the UNTCOK observation groups allegedly observing the elections not be sent to UN Headquarters, for fear that they would be useful to the socialist countries (Gordenker, *Peaceful Unification of Korea*, pp. 96–97).

48. *GAOR*, 3rd Session, Part I, First Committee, p. 973.

49. General Assembly Resolution 195, December 12, 1948.

50. Canada had been an unreliable appointee to UNTCOK. It had opposed the United States during the period of the Commission's hesitation before the southern election. Canada took a particularly independent line in the Interim Committee debate. The history of American purges of waverers would be worth writing. Later on Syria, which had been by far the most objective member of UNTCOK, was purged from UNCOK and replaced by Turkey, a solid U.S. liege (the Turkish delegate was made permanent chairman of UNCOK). Lie, already surrounded by U.S. aides, carried out a parallel purge within the UN Secretariat and reorganized bureaucratic channels so as to bypass anyone not thoroughly in favor of U.S. policy. See Lie, *In the Cause*, p. 343.

51. This is the opinion of Goodrich, *Korea*, p. 68, and other qualified observers.

52. *Summary of Events relating to Korea 1950* (London, H.M.S.O., 1950), Parliamentary Papers, Cmd. 8078, p. 7.

53. United Nations, General Assembly, *Annual Report of the Secretary-General on the Work of the Organization, 1 July 1948–30 June 1949, GAOR*, 4th Session, Supplement No. 1 (A/930), p. 20. The extent to which the withdrawal was only partial is emphasized by an official U.S. Army historian, Robert K. Sawyer, *Military Advisors in Korea: KMAG in Peace and War* (Washington, D.C., U.S. Department of the Army, Office of the Chief of Military History, 1962), p. 42.

54. *GAOR*, 5th Session, Supplement No. 16 (A/1350), *Report of the United Nations Commission on Korea, Covering the Period from 15 December 1949 to 4 September 1950* (hereafter cited as *UNCOK Report, 1950*), pp. 23–25.

55. *UNCOK Report, 1950*, pp. 15–16.

56. *Action in Korea Under Unified Command*, U.S. Department of State, First Report to the Security Council by the United States Government (Washington, D.C., July 25, 1950), p. 1.

57. *UNCOK Report, 1950*, Annex 4.

58. *Military Situation in the Far East*, Hearings before the Joint Senate Committee on Armed Services and on Foreign Relations,

U.S. Senate, Eighty-second Congress, First Session, 1951 (hereafter cited as *MacArthur Hearings*), p. 231.
59. Lie, *In the Cause*, pp. 327–28.
60. I. F. Stone, *Hidden History of the Korean War* (New York and London, Monthly Review Press, 2d. edition, 1969), pp. 46–47 for details.
61. Lie, *In the Cause*, p. 329.
62. As well as not forwarding the full report from Muccio (less than two hundred words long), the U.S. government had already prepared a draft resolution for the UN before the war even started; see Stone, *Hidden History*, pp. 53–56.
63. Excellent information on India's role is in Ross N. Berkes and Mohinder S. Bedi, *The Diplomacy of India* (Stanford, Stanford University Press; London, Oxford University Press, 1958), pp. 84–85, 93–97, 105–39; Shiv Dayal, *India's Role in the Korean Question* (Delhi, S. Chand & Co., 1959); and especially Karunakar Gupta, "How did the Korean War Begin?" *China Quarterly*, No. 52 (October–December 1972), pp. 699–716.
64. UN Security Council, *Official Records*, 5th Year, 473rd Meeting, June 25, 1950.
65. Much the best analysis of the Haeju episode is that by Gupta, "How Did the Korean War Begin?" On June 25–26 both the R.O.K. and ranking U.S. officials, including the head of KMAG, claimed that the South Koreans had captured Haeju, the seventh largest city in the D.P.R.K., just across the frontier. Haeju was an important road and rail junction. These R.O.K.-U.S. claims were confirmed by the D.P.R.K., and the incident was the immediate cause adduced by the D.P.R.K. for its counter attack. Subsequently the official histories of the war of both South Korea and the United States gave different versions. The South Korean history states that the claim that Haeju was taken was a false one. The U.S. history simply ignores the whole episode. In the absence of convincing evidence to the contrary, and given the political climate, Gupta's case must be treated with respect. In any case, neither UNCOK nor the UN ever produced satisfactory evidence to prove their case.
66. Lie, *In the Cause*, p. 332.
67. Stone, *Hidden History*, chap. 12, especially pp. 77–81, is excellent on the Unified Command. Much information is also available in the *MacArthur Hearings*. The U.S.-led coalition was a veritable gang of reactionaries and lackeys, including the United Kingdom, France, South Africa, and the United States' new counterrevolutionary protégés from Greece and Turkey.

68. Lie, *In the Cause*, p. 334; Gordenker, *Peaceful Unification of Korea*, pp. 47–48, records that Katzin had ready access to both MacArthur and Rhee and quickly ensured the further downgrading of UNCOK: Katzin, along with the newly arrived special political counselor, Constantin Stavropoulos (Greece), was "heavily" involved in heading off UNCOK criticism of Lie's negligence over Korea in July 1950. See Gordenker, p. 224.

69. Lie, *In the Cause*, pp. 337, 343.

70. Quoted by Lie, *In the Cause*, pp. 343–44. Katzin's rabid anticommunism oozes from the text; at one point he refers to "the practice of their own side [North Korea] in liquidating their troops who fail to meet their objectives."

71. On October 12, 1950 an Interim Committee resolution "authorized" the Unified Command and the United Nations Commission for the Unification and Rehabilitation of Korea (UNCURK) to interfere in the north. The utilization of the earlier resolutions is remarkable:

> Recalling that the Government of the Republic of Korea has been recognized by the United Nations as a lawful government having effective control over that part of Korea where the United Nations Temporary Commission on Korea was able to observe and consult and that there is consequently no government that is recognized by the United Nations as having legal and effective control over other parts of Korea . . . (United Nations, *GAOR*, 6th Session, Supplement No. 12 [A/1881], *Report of the United Nations Commission for the Unification and Rehabilitation of Korea* [hereafter cited as *UNCURK Report, 1951*], p. 13).

On the decision to invade the north and the election issue, see Stone, *Hidden History*, chaps. 16 and 17.

72. *MacArthur Hearings*, p. 19.

73. General J. Lawton Collins gave the Senate a fairly good idea of what really happened. The ban on using R.O.K. officials in North Korea applied only to Rhee, not to the UN. But even this was purely nominal. "Well, my understanding is that he [Rhee] could use South Korean officials but not as such. In other words, use them as civilians" (*MacArthur Hearings*, p. 1328). See also *Further Summary of Events relating to Korea, October 1950 to May 1951*, (London, H.M.S.O.) Parliamentary Papers, Cmd. 8366, pp. 7–8.

74. *UNCURK Report, 1951*, p. 16.

75. *UNCURK Report, 1951,* pp. 20–25.

76. United Nations, *GAOR,* 1952, 7th Session, Supplement No. 14 (A/2187), *Report of the United Nations Commission for the Unification and Rehabilitation of Korea,* p. 16.

77. *MacArthur Hearings,* p. 10.

78. *Ibid.,* pp. 1257–59.

79. For the degree of destruction, involving the deaths of probably some 4 million people (out of a total of about 30 million), see Stone, *Hidden History,* pp. 312–13. See also the testimony of Maj. Gen. Emmett O'Donnell, Jr., *MacArthur Hearings,* pp. 3063, 3075. MacArthur himself stated:

> The war in Korea has already almost destroyed that nation. . . . I have never seen such devastation. I have seen, I guess, as much blood and disaster as any living man, and it just curdled my stomach, the last time I was there. After I looked at that wreckage and those thousands of women and children and everything, I vomited. . . . (*MacArthur Hearings,* p. 82).

For the disdain for the Geneva Convention, see the frank statement by the former chief U.S. negotiator at Panmunjom, Admiral C. Turner Joy, in his *How Communists Negotiate* (New York, Macmillan Co., 1955), pp. 150–51; and also Walter G. Hermes, *Truce Tent and Fighting Front* (Washington, D.C., U.S. Department of the Army, Office of the Chief of Military History, 1966), p. 262: "The ICRC [Red Cross] . . . protested vigorously against the tactics of the United Nations Command. Violence, withholding food and water . . . and the use of force on hospital patients were heavily scored. . . ." (This referred to "clean-up activities" in camps at Pusan and Koje-do.) For war crimes, see Kolko and Kolko, *The Limits of Power,* p. 681 (U.S. bombing of five major dams in May 1953 in an effort to destroy the agricultural irrigation system).

The Korean Civil War
Robert R. Simmons

The Korean people will not abandon the struggle and
will reserve for itself the right to continue by any
maneuvers at its disposal the struggle . . . for the final
unification of the country by its own forces into a unified democratic state.
    Pak Hŏn-yŏng, P'yŏngyang, October 17, 1949.[1]

Even though some of our friends across the sea tell us
that we must not cherish thoughts of attacking the
foreign puppet who stifles the liberties of our people in
the north . . . we shall respond to the cries of our
brothers in distress.
    Syngman Rhee, Seoul, March 1, 1950.[2]

American government officials and, subsequently, scholars, have
described the 1950 Korean crisis as a battle in the Cold War.
President Truman, for example, wrote of his first reaction to the
fighting: "Communism was acting in Korea just as Hitler, Mus-
solini, and the Japanese had acted ten, fifteen, and twenty years
earlier. I felt certain that if South Korea were allowed to fall
Communist leaders would be emboldened to override nations
closer to our own shores." [3] The predominant view of the origin
of the war is that the Soviet Union completely controlled the
June 25 North Korean invasion. The war was a "Soviet war
plan" [4] that Stalin "planned, prepared and initiated." [5] Most
observers of this period have regarded the North Korean regime
as a mere satellite of the Soviet Union, and Kim Il Sung as an
instrument of the Russians. Stalin, so this version runs, pulled
the trigger that started the war. Such a metaphor, of course, ne-
glects the gun itself: the government in P'yŏngyang. Most cur-

143

rent writings on the origin of the Korean War continue to reflect this basic belief.[6]

Because the source of the war has been placed in Moscow, research on its Korean paternity has been largely neglected.[7] This article deals with factors present on the peninsula which had a fundamental bearing upon the initiation of the war. Focusing on the Democratic People's Republic of Korea (D.P.R.K.), it concludes that the P'yŏngyang government was neither a passive gun for an itchy Soviet trigger finger nor a monolithic political system totally subservient to Moscow that lacked its own dynamics. The conflict was not pure unprovoked aggression and it was not a complete surprise to Washington and Seoul. It was the Korean civil war.[8]

1. POLITICS IN THE DEMOCRATIC PEOPLE'S REPUBLIC OF KOREA, 1945–50

Five political clusters competed for power in post-World War II north Korea. First there were the Soviet-Koreans, Koreans who were born or resided in the Soviet Union before 1945. A leader of this group was Hŏ Ka-i, a graduate of Moscow University and a former secretary of the Tashkent Republic. Secondly, there was the Yenan faction led by Mu Chŏng and Kim Tu-bong, who had fought alongside of the Chinese People's Liberation Army (PLA). A third group vying for power was not physically located in north Korea. Pak Hŏn-yŏng, a respected communist revolutionary, led the Domestic faction, whose members had remained in Korea during the Japanese colonial period. Pak's group reestablished the Korean Communist party in Seoul on September 12, 1945. The fourth group were non-communist "nationalists" under Cho Man-sik.

The last group was the Kapsan faction, former guerrilla fighters against the Japanese led by the moderately well-known nationalist hero, Kim Il Sung.[9] Did the Russians have a design for Kim Il Sung? Was he a willing agent for Soviet machinations? Contrary to the oft-repeated assumption that Kim was a mere puppet, and analogous to the American experience with Syngman Rhee in south Korea, the Russians apparently entered north

Korea with no operational plan beyond establishing a friendly regime. Kim seems to have been chosen for largely negative reasons: most other potential communist leaders had been ruled out by the Russians, while at the same time they considered Kim a credible nationalist who would be malleably pro-Russian.[10] Kim Il Sung, however, owed sole allegiance to neither China nor Russia, a consideration which was undoubtedly appealing to Korean nationalists. He had served with Chinese Communist forces and with the Soviet Union's,[11] while his loyalty was to his comrades of the Kapsan faction.

The Kapsan and Yenan factions merged on August 28, 1946 with the formation of the North Korean Workers' party. The party chairmanship went not to Kim Il Sung but to Kim Tu-bong, leader of the Yenan group. Kim Il Sung's supporters had tried to elect him chairman, but the Soviet advisor present recessed the meeting. After a short break, Kim Il Sung personally nominated Kim Tu-bong; Kim Il Sung settled for first vice-chairman.[12]

During the turbulent period after liberation, most of the Domestic faction's leadership had stayed in Seoul, the traditional national capital. Pak Hŏn-yŏng committed a tactical error in hoping that he would be able to work with the American occupation authorities. His insistence upon remaining in the south siphoned off the energies of the most sizable and popular communist group on the peninsula. Meanwhile, the maneuvering for actual power within the communist movement took place in the north. The lesser-known communists of the Kapsan, Yenan, and Soviet factions rose to prominent positions in the north without a direct challenge from the Domestic faction.[13]

A witness to these events has described why the Soviet Union decided, in the end, to support Kim Il Sung's Kapsan faction:

> When the Domestic, Yenan and Soviet factions were running about in confusion in the political world of P'yongyang, the Kapsan faction, dispersed to local districts, was doing its utmost to establish its regional organizations. . . . There was no evidence that from the outset the Soviet occupation authorities had entrusted Kim Il-sung with the power to control North Korea. Even if the Soviet side had such an intention, it was not an absolute one. . . . It was, therefore, after the lower or-

ganizations were completed that the Soviet Union decided to entrust Kim Il-sung and his faction with the reins of government, or it may be said that such a decision was accelerated by the completion of the above organizations. . . . Many people ascribe the fame of Kim Il-sung to the Soviet decision. It may be one of the reasons, but the major reason was the Kapsan faction's completion of its lower organizations at this early stage.[14]

The resulting P'yŏngyang government, with Russian support, was a coalition of the Kapsan and Soviet factions, with Kim Il Sung in control.

The Democratic People's Republic of Korea was established on September 9, 1948, with Kim Il Sung as premier. Shortly thereafter, the southern regime of Syngman Rhee carried out a fierce purge of the South Korean Communist party. Many party leaders, foremost among them Pak Hŏn-yŏng, fled to the north. The North and South Korean Communist parties merged into the Korean Workers' party (KWP) on June 24, 1949. Kim Il Sung retained his leadership position, while Pak Hŏn-yŏng received lesser posts; according to one observer, the merger "appeared more like an incorporation of the Workers' Party of the South into the Workers' Party of the North than a unification of the two." [15]

Pak Hŏn-yŏng, however, still enjoyed widespread support among the newly unified KWP. Undoubtedly his arrival in the north spurred irredentist feeling toward the territory now controlled by Seoul. As both a symbol of the repression in the south and as a respected spokesman voicing the view that the Republic of Korea (R.O.K.) could be easily overthrown, Pak's presence probably encouraged military action against the south.

In mid-1949 Pak helped to organize the United Democratic Fatherland Front (UDFF), which carried out guerrilla activities in the south.[16] Concurrently, he was also the supervisor of the Kangdong Political Institute, which trained guerrillas sent to the south. From these two positions he monitored and encouraged revolutionary activities there.[17] His influence in the north, therefore, largely depended on the success of the anti-Syngman Rhee movement in the south.

Pak Hŏn-yŏng was also the vice-chairman of the KWP, a

vice-premier of the D.P.R.K., and foreign minister. Both the D.P.R.K.'s ambassador to Peking, Yi Chu-yŏn, and the ambassador to Moscow, Chu Nyŏng-ha, were members of Pak's Domestic faction.[18] Through them, Pak was informed about official policy in those countries and, perhaps, was able to communicate with China and the U.S.S.R. without Kim Il Sung's knowledge. Thus, although Pak Hŏn-yŏng occupied positions in the D.P.R.K. below Kim Il Sung, his very important posts and connections ensured his continued prestige and potential as a rival to Premier Kim.

In July 1949 the UDFF called for nationwide elections for September 15, 1949, but this demand was simply dropped on that date, probably due to the south's largely successful policy against the UDFF's guerrillas.[19] The UDFF failure was presumably a setback for Pak within the factional maze of P'yŏngyang. On June 7, 1950 the UDFF abruptly issued a new appeal for reunification combined with a proposal to hold nationwide elections between August 5 and 8. A national conference would be held in either Haeju or Kaesŏng from June 15 to 17 to discuss the mechanics of carrying out the election. The all-Korean legislature resulting from these elections would then meet in Seoul on August 15, the fifth anniversary of liberation from Japanese rule.[20] This plan was issued by the UDFF, rather than the D.P.R.K. Government, perhaps indicating that it was directed by Pak Hŏn-yŏng.

Russian awareness of the importance of the August 15 date is suggested by an *Izvestia* article of June 10, 1950 that declared: "On the fifth anniversary of the liberation of Korea, the people of South and North Korea can and should mark this day by celebrating it in the folds of one united democratic state." [21]

On June 19, 1950 the proposals calling for reunification and an all-Korean election suddenly shifted from the UDFF; they now originated from the Supreme People's Assembly of the D.P.R.K. Why was this campaign shifted from UDFF sponsorship? A reasonable explanation appears to be that Kim Il Sung acted to prevent Pak Hŏn-yŏng from receiving credit for Korean unification. Kim Il Sung's credentials of legitimacy rested upon his nationalist claims. When he returned to Korea in 1945, for example, Kim's first public speeches were not about communism, but rather about the aspiration common to all Koreans: the re-unification of an independent Korea. In 1950 this young (thirty-eight years old) leader, in a nation where age is correlated with respect and wisdom, needed to present himself as the leader of Korean nationalism and unification, particularly with regard to Pak Hŏn-yŏng, who had an impressive nationalist record and was the prime exponent of early reunification.

The hypothesis that Kim might have planned to use the invasion to undermine Pak's position in the south (which, despite Rhee's merciless hunt, remained Pak's natural power base) is supported by Kim's pre-June 25 actions toward the weakened southern wing of the KWP. A few weeks before the invasion, Kim sent Kapsan faction personnel south to take control of the remaining KWP apparatus. Aware that Pak's residual strength could coalesce with elements in the north if Pak emerged from the civil war as a nationalist hero, Kim moved into active control of the southern KWP.[22]

Pak Hŏn-yŏng was in a pivotal position to influence the strategic judgment to initiate hostilities by virtue of his near-monopoly on information from the south. It was through Pak that information on conditions in the south, including favorable dates for an invasion and the likelihood of success for such an attack, was funneled to the KWP. That Pak utilized his position to press for an early invasion date is indicated by the charges publicly brought against him *on the day after* the signing of the 1953 armistice. Item No. five of the incident stated: "In the June 25 war, he indulged in circulating a false report that in South Korea the South Korean Labor Party had an underground organization of 500,000 members, who were ready to take action in concert with the North."[23] North Korean agents who went south, it was charged, returned with reports that these 500,000 were eager for the war to start: "This was a major reason why the Kapsan faction decided to attack South Korea."[24]

Kim Il Sung and Pak Hŏn-yŏng (as well as Syngman Rhee) shared a moral imperative to unify the nation. Moreover, they both held a pragmatic desire to provide for the security and development of the north, as well as a common concern for the fate of the anti-Syngman Rhee forces in the south. Beyond these common beliefs, however, it appears likely that some of the tactics of the civil war, particularly the early *timing* of it, were dictated in part by the Kim-Pak rivalry.

2. SOUTH KOREA APPARENTLY PREPARES
TO MARCH NORTH

Koreans were divided by the 38th parallel but united in their desire for an early national reunification. The south was as determined to unify Korea as the north. Syngman Rhee consolidated his control of the south as a prelude to an apparent intention to invade the north. Consolidation brought increasingly autocratic rule. The judiciary, for example, was an "instrument of executive predominance, not the defender of rights or instrument of balance of forces, [and] forthwith became even more active than under colonial rule." [25] Between September 4, 1948 and April 30, 1949 over 80,710 people were arrested in the south. During this same period, more than one-third of the officers of the R.O.K. Army were discharged. By October, 1949, seven percent of the R.O.K. National Assembly had been jailed by Syngman Rhee's police.[26]

While the south's political situation became more harshly dictatorial, the economic condition and morale of the population worsened. Sporadic popular revolts developed which were brutally dealt with by Seoul. Conditions in the south seemed to augur a northern success. In the spring of 1950 the Seoul black market listed the wŏn at 4,200 to one U.S. dollar; the official rate was 600 wŏn.[27] In June 1950 the price of rice in the south had jumped 30 percent in one month.[28] The May 30 elections for the National Assembly resulted in a massive display of discontent with the Rhee regime; out of 210 seats, only 47 were now held by government supporters. It was this combination of anti-Syngman Rhee factors (added to the ardor for reunification) that led one responsible observer of North Korea's invasion to declare that it was a "*coup de grace* against a nation of people weakened by internal subversion, economic distress and political instability." [29] In short, the weakness and unpopularity of the Seoul regime probably reinforced Pak Hŏn-yŏng's hopes of an early and easy victory.

The south, meanwhile, was preparing for war. At the end of October 1949 the South Korean defense minister was quoted as saying: "If we had our own way we would, I'm sure, have started up already. But we had to wait until they [Americans] are ready. They keep telling us, 'no, no, no, wait. You are not ready.' " [30] William Sebald, a State Department representative in Japan, wrote of Rhee's belligerency: "It was feared that, properly armed for offense, Rhee promptly would punch northward across the 38th parallel." [31] This concern is frequently mentioned in military narratives of the war. The official history of the American Military Advisor Group in Korea (KMAG), however, presents a different view of why heavy tanks and more powerful artillery were not supplied to Seoul. Rather than solely an apprehension about Rhee's northern intentions, "it is much more likely that terrain factors and dollar limitations were actually responsible for the United States' failure to supply this type of equipment." [32]

Washington was not parsimonious in its support for the R.O.K. The Rhee regime received $495.7 million in military and economic aid between the end of World War II and the beginning of the Korean War; $53.7 million in economic assistance, the rest military aid.[33] The U.S. Army, moreover, maintained a 482-man permanent military assistance mission in South Korea.

Under the guidance of this military mission, Rhee was in 1949–50 rapidly expanding his armed forces. At the end of 1948 the South Korean army consisted of 60,000 men; when the war began it had grown to approximately 100,000.[34] American advisors were attached to thirteen military training schools. The R.O.K. Air Force also began to increase. The American mission's semi-annual report of December 31, 1949 requested forty F-51 fighter aircraft, ten T-6 trainers, two C-47 cargo planes, and $225,000 for supporting equipment.[35] It is, of course, true that the R.O.K. Air Force was not yet on a par with that of the D.P.R.K. when the war began. However, it appears that, given not too much more time, it would have reached parity. For example, during the first months of 1950 the air force grew from a few hundred men to 1,865 officers and recruits.[36] Seoul, during this same period, reportedly sought to acquire a ninety-nine plane air force.[37]

In April 1950 the R.O.K. decided to create twenty-one combat police battalions of 1,200 men each. The U.S. Congress had already voted a grant of $10,970,000 in additional aid for Seoul on March 15, 1950. Consequently, although by June 25 neither the R.O.K. Air Force nor the police battalions were totally operational, it seemed only a matter of time. After the war began, U.S. Army Brig. Gen. William L. Roberts, former head of the American advisory mission in Korea, was quoted as saying: "The only real flaw in K.M.A.G.'s plan in preparing [the South Korean Army] was that time ran out." [38] P'yŏngyang, listening to Seoul's provocative rhetoric and observing the R.O.K.'s increasing military capabilities, must have been concerned about Syngman Rhee's martial plans.

3. PRELUDE TO JUNE 25

In addition to Pak Hŏn-yŏng's advocacy of an early invasion, the perceived threat of a South Korean attack undoubtedly was the major factor in Kim Il Sung's decision to strike south. Well after the conflict had begun, on October 10, 1950, Kim came close to admitting that the north had initiated the civil war, albeit in response to tensions created by South Korea:

Having received reliable information early in May 1950 that preparations were under way for the northern invasion, the government of the Democratic People's Republic of Korea was able to take measures at the proper time to repel it. *At last,* toward the end of June, the Syngman Rhee armed forces invaded areas north of the 38th parallel. Not only did the people's armed forces repel the invasion, but they also dealt annihilating blows to the Syngman Rhee armed forces, with the support of the partisans and all the Korean people (emphasis added).[39]

There were constant and sizable armed clashes and border incursions between the north and south for over a year before the final crisis. A U.S. State Department official in April 1950 stated that: "The boundary at the 38th parallel . . . is a real front line. There is constant fighting. . . . There are very real battles, involving perhaps one or two thousand men." [40] Koreans were accustomed to the fighting and the possibility of war; each side believed that an early reunification was worth a war.

While the Seoul regime enjoyed little popular support, it had announced its intention to invade the north and appeared to be preparing to do so. It may be that the imminent arrival of additional U.S. arms and the progressive strengthening of the South Korean military prompted P'yŏngyang to advance its own invasion timetable in a pre-emptive strike. (There may have been a South Korean border incursion on June 25, as claimed by P'yŏngyang, but this would have been only a symbolic coincidence connoting the threat facing the north.) [41]

There are several indications that the decision to attack the south was made rather suddenly by a small core of the D.P.R.K. leadership. As Sectretary of State Dean Acheson later noted, "the Communists had far from exhausted the potentialities for obtaining their objective through guerrilla and psychological warfare, political pressure and intimidation." [42] A U.S. Army intelligence team that studied captured North Korean government documents found:

> Top secret work plans of the Standing Committee of the Labor Party headquarters dated January–June 1950 make absolutely no reference to the forthcoming invasion, although covering in some detail all other aspects of government policy. Second, a number of fairly highly placed North Korean officers that were interviewed, including the Chiefs of Staffs of two divisions, stated that they had only the barest presentiment of the coming of hostilities, and that they were given no concrete indication of their onset until approximately one week before the invasion took place. [43]

A further suggestion that the decision was a late choice comes from the fact that the Korean People's Army (KPA) had not been mobilized prior to June 25. General MacArthur's Tokyo headquarters reported that P'yŏngyang's army had only six full divisions mobilized on June 25, although "the North Korean war plans called for thirteen to fifteen." [44] The north actually invaded the south with a smaller (although better trained and equipped) force than Seoul commanded. The R.O.K. had a 95,000-man army and a paramilitary national police force of

48,000. P'yŏngyang had a 103,800-man army and 18,600 police.[45] The subsequent rapid North Korean victory was caused not by the size of its invading force, but rather a combination of superior firepower (tanks, artillery, and planes), surprise, higher morale, and the support of a significant part of South Korea's population.[46]

The KPA had been until the end of 1949, to quote an official U.S. Army history of the war, a "defensive-type army." [47] It was only when it seemed that South Korea was preparing a northern march in the spring of 1950, that P'yŏngyang began receiving offensive military supplies from the Soviet Union. But these arms were still in the "pipeline" in June; it was not until late July that the North Korean army received the necessary arms for a maximum-strength attack upon the south.[48]

4. WAS WASHINGTON DISMAYED?

The generally accepted interpretation of the U.S. reaction to the Korean civil war has been that Washington's leaders were surprised, dismayed, and unprepared. However, the record unambiguously demonstrates that Washington saw the war as the serendipitous instrument needed to resolve the vexing problem of how to implement the vigorous international military posture that had already been decided upon at the highest levels of the American government. A brief summary may help to place Washington's perspective in context. "Containment" had become the accepted doctrine shortly after the end of World War II; the problem, however, was to convince a weary public and a tax-conscious Congress of the necessity for Cold War expenditures.

The Truman administration soon found that such legislation would pass only if it were attached to a crisis. The pattern was set with the Truman Doctrine in the spring of 1947. The British withdrawal from Turkey and Greece was painted as a sudden catastrophe, although Washington actually knew of the British plan six months in advance. President Truman then went before the Congress and said: "At the present moment in world history nearly every nation must choose between alternate ways of life. The choice is often not a free one. . . . I believe that we must assist free peoples to work out their own destinies in their own way." [49]

Shortly before, President Truman and Under-Secretary of State Dean Acheson had met with key congressional leaders privately. The Republicans, who had intended to cut taxes by 20 percent, were not particularly receptive to an open-ended foreign aid program to help "nearly every nation"—until Acheson launched into the argument that the United States was not facing an isolated situation in Greece and Turkey but rather an implacable foe intent upon controlling all of Europe and, eventually, the United States itself. The congressmen then became amenable. As Senator Vandenburg explained, the administration had "scared hell out of the American people." [50]

The pattern was repeated. The celebrated 1947 Marshall Plan budget languished in committee. The president first asked for $17 billion and then lowered his request to $6.8 billion. In February 1948 the Communists consolidated their power in Czechoslovakia. On March 16 U.S. Army intelligence told the administration, in a grim tone, that war was not probable within the following sixty days. [51] Against this background, the Marshall Plan was finally funded with $4 billion, a comfortable election year compromise between concern over taxes and communism. (President Truman proposed his Point Four Program in January 1950; it was not acted upon until the summer of 1950.) On July 23, 1949 the president sent Congress a Mutual Defense Assistance Bill for $1.5 billion in military aid for Europe. It stayed in committee until after the president announced, on September 22, 1949, that the Russians had exploded an atomic bomb; then the bill raced through Congress.

It was in such an atmosphere of insecurity that President Truman authorized a crash program to develop the hydrogen bomb and instructed the secretaries of defense and state to undertake a re-examination of American objectives and priorities. The resulting short policy paper is known as NSC–68 (memorandum number 68 of the National Security Council). NSC–68 is still a classified document, but we have several credible summaries of its contents. [52] In general, its formulators accepted the premise that the confrontation between the two nuclear powers could only intensify. They believed that the Soviet nuclear arsenal would equal that of the United States within four years. During this same period, and of much more dangerous significance, the Russian conventional military capacity would continue to outstrip that of the United States. To cope with this forbidding future, the memorandum outlined four possible courses of action: (1) continue the low-scale defense budget, yet also continue to attempt to defend worldwide free-nation security; (2) continue the low-scale budget at the cost of forfeiting its commitments and withdrawing into a "fortress America"; (3) attempt to redress the trend toward an unfavorable balance of power by a "preventive strike"; (4) ". . . strike out on a bold and massive program of rebuilding the West's defensive potential to surpass that of the Soviet world, and of meeting each fresh challenge promptly and unequivocally." [53]

This last option was the one strongly preferred. In fact, given the main assumptions behind NSC–68, it was inevitable that the president's advisors would choose American rearmament:

> It must be assumed that these concepts and objectives of American life will come under increasing attack. If they are to be protected, the nation must be determined, at whatever cost or sacrifice, to preserve at home and abroad those conditions of life in which these objectives can survive and prosper. We must seek to do this by peaceful means and with the cooperation of like-minded peoples. But if peaceful means fail we must be willing and ready to fight.[54]

NSC–68 put a price tag on this program: a spectacular increase in the defense budget from $13.5 billion to $50 billion.[55] Thus, by the late spring of 1950 the top levels of the American government were emotionally and strategically committed to a dramatically increased defense posture. The question was how? Secretary of State Acheson later indicated how the "how" was achieved:

> The purpose of NSC–68 was to so bludgeon the mass mind of "top government" that not only could the President make a decision but the decision would be carried out. Even so, it is doubtful whether anything like what happened in the next few years could have been done had not the Russians been stupid enough to have instigated the attack against South Korea and opened the "hate America" campaign.[56]

After the war, the chairman of the committee that drafted NSC–68 explained that:

> The dilemma involved in choosing between an unbalanced budget, higher taxes, and more stringent economic controls on the one hand, and a more adequate military posture on the other was not *resolved* at the policy decision level until some three months prior to the outbreak of the North Korean aggression. Those decisions were *translated into specific action* only after the aggression into South Korea had given concrete and bloody confirmation to the *conclusions already introduced by analysis* (emphasis added).[57]

In June 1950, as before, it took a crisis to tap fully the financial and psychological resources already allocated on the drawing boards. Undoubtedly, the Truman administration sincerely believed in a Russian military threat and that in Korea it was witnessing only one more example of the compulsive, monolithic, and expansive nature of communism. (Washington consistently thought of nationalist movements in Asia only in terms of [evil] communism; e.g., China, Vietnam, and Korea.) Beyond those beliefs, moreover, it should be remembered that the administration was politically vulnerable about the recent "fall of China" and the charge that it was "weak on communism." These accusations meant that the Korean civil war offered the administration, at the start of a congressional election campaign, a chance to demonstrate its anti-communist zeal (in effect, to become its own Monday morning quarterback).

While much is made of the idea that the United States entered the war under the aegis of the United Nations, it would appear that this was not a necessity. Secretary of State Acheson, for instance, was later asked what the United States would have done if it had failed to receive the support of the UN in its military intervention. Acheson quickly responded: "We'd have gone in unilaterally. . . . We'd have gone in alone." [58]

Therefore, if the hypothesis that the decision to resist communist expansion by conventional means was taken before June 1950 is accurate, President Truman's judgment to enter the war has a significance different from that generally attributed to it. Rather than a decision of *strategic* proportions—should the

United States engage in a limited war with communist troops?—
the decision was *tactical*—did this particular crisis warrant, in
terms of expected costs and benefits, the use of American forces?
In short, the Korean War fit a pattern already developed by
Washington: the necessity of a Cold War crisis to pass large-
scale Cold War appropriation bills, in this case the spectacular
increase in the defense budget from $13.5 billion to $50 billion.
While *no* claim is being made here that the war was provoked by
the United States, it should be noted that Washington seized
upon it as an opportunity to carry out previously laid plans.

5. WAS MOSCOW SURPRISED BY
THE JUNE 25 INVASION?

It would have made more sense, at least from a Russian perspective, for the invasion to have begun in August while the
Soviet Union was chairman of the Security Council; Moscow
would have had additional leverage to utilize that forum in North
Korea's behalf. No pro-U.S. resolutions were passed by the
Security Council during the month of August. The hypothesis
that P'yŏngyang initiated the war without informing Moscow
might be challenged by the assertion that the Russian advisors
attached to the KPA before June 25 would have prevented an
"unauthorized" attack. However, there were very few Russian
advisors present who could have either counseled against or
forestalled an independent Korean decision. In 1948 there were
150 Russian advisors with each North Korean division (approximately one per company); in 1949 this number was reduced
to twenty per division. In the spring of 1950 there were only
between three and eight per division.[59] An alleged Russian de-
fector, who served in the D.P.R.K. shortly before June 25, stated
that the entire U.S.S.R. military advisory group at that time
totalled less than forty.[60] In short, the popular picture of Soviet
advisors carefully directing a North Korean invasion at every
level does not square with reality.

The domestic Russian response to the war also indicates that
it came as a surprise. Moscow issued no public announcements,
not even *pro forma* declarations in support of its ally, for thirty-

six hours. Moreover, the first full official statement of Russian attitudes was not released until July 4.[61] There were no mass meetings in support of the D.P.R.K. until July 3, although the Soviet Union was in the midst of a major "world peace campaign" that would have lent itself ideally to such demonstrations. In sum, the Soviet Union's public reaction—acutely atypical of its usual behavior during international crises—may well have been testimony to its surprise at the *timing* (although not the initiation) of the war.

The Russian reaction also helps to resolve one further problem: why did P'yŏngyang insist on claiming that it was invaded by South Korea on June 25 and that the North Korean attack was only a response? There is no persuasive evidence that a prior R.O.K. attack occurred, and the D.P.R.K.'s allegation has served only to cost it support in the West. The reason for P'yŏngyang's assertion may lie in Korean-Russian plans before June 25. If the Soviet Union anticipated an invasion date in early August, when its representative would be chairman of the Security Council, it is probable that Moscow would have urged P'yŏngyang to use a "legalistic" justification. If the north's invasion was, in fact, a pre-emptive strike, continued D.P.R.K. insistence on the rationalization is more understandable. North Korean consideration of Stalin's likely response to the war argued for a legalistic defense; Stalin favored such justifications in his own foreign policy.

Although the source lacks complete credibility, Nikita Khrushchev's alleged remark about the war's beginnings is a fair summation: "I must stress that the war wasn't Stalin's idea, but Kim Il-sung's. Kim was the initiator." [62]

The 1967 Middle East war provides a loose analogy, suggestive of some of the factors probably operating in June 1950: Israel, outnumbered and facing an implacable foe intent upon aggression with the support of a Great Power; Israel, possessing a superior military machine and fearful of an invasion; Israel, striking first but claiming that it was really the Arabs who had done so.

Were there factions within the Israeli leadership that argued about the best time to strike? Would an analysis of these debates aid our understanding of why and when the war began? Did

Israel not inform Washington beforehand about the date of the pre-emptive strike? Did it stick to its "victim of aggression" story in order, in part, to maintain the legal fiction which it knew Washington sought? Because the answers to each of these questions is "yes," it appears that many of the facets of the Korean civil war have not been unknown in the recent political-military records of the West.

Is the question of the timing of the war a matter of counting angels on the head of a pin? Not if one is interested in an analysis which goes beyond seeing the war as a mere tactic of monolithic communism. It also underlines the fact that the D.P.R.K. perceived that the south was preparing to march north; the war was a civil one with its roots in Korean nationalism. Moreover, the premise of independent Korean action goes a long way to explain the lack of substantial Russian aid during the war and later D.P.R.K. moves toward greater national autonomy.

6. THE D.P.R.K. AND ITS ALLIES, 1950

North Korean references to its two neighbors at the beginning of the war were vague; Kim Il Sung's major radio address of July 8, for example, made no mention of either the Soviet Union or China. On the other hand, both Peking and Moscow radios, broadcasting in Korean to Korea, clearly stated their desire to remain uninvolved in the war; each spoke only of their "moral" support of the D.P.R.K. Shortly after the war began, it became apparent that the American intervention had destroyed P'yŏngyang's expectation of an early victory. A general mobilization order was finally issued on July 1. On July 16 Premier Kim declared: "Had not the American imperialists intervened in our internal affairs and begun armed invasion, our country would have been unified and the war terminated." [63]

On August 15, 1950—Liberation Day—each of the three allies marked the day in a common ceremony in P'yŏngyang which clearly indicated its degree of commitment. The North Koreans spoke of an all-out fight for total victory. Russian ambassador Shtykov mentioned only the "technical assistance" which had "played an important role in strengthening the defen-

sive power of the Democratic People's Republic of Korea." [64]
The Chinese representative did not speak. A Chinese reporter
wrote:

> The stage was decorated with two large portraits of Kim Il-
> sung and Stalin, for it was on this day that the mighty Soviet
> Army ended the predatory rule of the Japanese imperialists.
> The ambassador of the Soviet Union and the People's Democ-
> racies brought warm words of their people's support for
> Korea's struggle for liberation. [65]

The writer stressed Russian accountability by almost completely
omitting any mention of China.

China and the Soviet Union shared one desire about the war
in its early stages: neither wanted to commit troops on the
peninsula. China's prime interests were in liberating Taiwan and
proceeding with her economic reconstruction after the civil war.
Consequently, the first official Chinese diplomatic mission did
not arrive in P'yŏngyang until July 10, 1950. The Chinese ambassador arrived in North Korea a month later. A further reason
for China's disinclination to come to P'yŏngyang's aid was that
its traditional influence, dating back a millennium, had been dis-
placed by that of the Soviet Union.

This fact had been signalled by the Soviet Union at the end
of World War II. In September 1945 Mu Chŏng, a leader of the
Yenan faction, attempted to enter North Korea through the
Manchurian city of Sinŭiju with an army of 2,500 men. They
were halted and disarmed at the border by Russian troops. Mu
Chŏng was told that he could not bring his armed forces into
North Korea, but that as a compromise his arms would be returned if he would take his army back into Manchuria and continue fighting with the Chinese PLA. [66] Because Mu Chŏng was
so closely connected with the Chinese Communists, the message
appeared to be unmistakable: North Korea was to be under
Russian influence. China therefore must have assumed that the
Soviet Union would defend the D.P.R.K. if necessary.

The Soviet Union, in a curious mirror image of American
protestations that the war was either a feint or a probe of Moscow's aggressive intentions, was mainly concerned with defending Europe. The U.S.S.R. was fearful that commiting Russian
troops to Korea would provoke a war with the United States. [67]

It is interesting to speculate upon what might have happened if only the South Korean army had crossed into North Korea in early October 1950. It was then a stronger force than the KPA, and probably would have been able to reach the Yalu by itself.[68] This still would have left a restive population in its rear, and the South Korean occupation probably would have prompted further years of civil war. However, the Chinese People's Volunteers (CPVs) probably would not have entered the war. As it turned out, of course, the use of American armed forces in North Korea ensured a reaction by China, which feared that the United States was pursuing the same predatory design toward China that Japan had a few years before.[69]

The decision which propelled China into the war was taken about October 9, 1950. The day before, two American fighter planes had strafed a Soviet airdrome sixty miles north of the D.P.R.K.-Soviet border.[70] Regardless of the cause of this armed incursion into Soviet territory, whether it was design or accident, it could only have served to solidify in the cautious mind of Stalin the firm resolve not to risk war with the United States. Additional irritating incidents by the United States only confirmed this resolve.[71]

Consequently, by the second week in October the Russians had decided to stay aloof from the war, while Peking observed the menacing sight of American troops racing toward the Chinese border. At this point the Chinese became the key members of the communist triangle. On October 9 the KWP daily organ, *Nodong sinmun*, published an article commemorating the first anniversary of Korean-Chinese diplomatic relations (three days late), after what must have been an "agonizing reappraisal" by the D.P.R.K. leadership about which of its neighbors it was to rely upon. Now, *for the first time*, the Korean media used the unequivocal term "aid" in reference to China; previously only the term "support" had appeared in P'yŏngyang's statements about China.[72] On October 11, *for the first time*, Pyŏngyang Radio expressed its thanks to China without coupling it with gratitude to the Soviet Union.

On October 12 Moscow Radio broadcast to Korea, in Korean, a message that indicated that Russian troops would not (although Chinese troops might) become involved in the war: "The

Americans will be ousted from Korea without fail in the same way as . . . they were kicked out of China." Shortly after this the Soviet Union pulled most of its men and equipment out of the war. Hanson Baldwin, in a dispatch to the *New York Times* of October 22, 1950, reported:

> There are increasing evidences that the Russians have cut their losses in Korea and are moving out altogether. The flow of traffic down the east coast highway from Vladivostok apparently has been halted altogether and the Russian advisors and technicians apparently have fled over the border after attempts to destroy or conceal the supplies and material they could not evacuate.[73]

With the Soviet Union abnegating any interest in defending her sphere of influence and with American forces rapidly approaching her borders, China reluctantly decided to intervene. The first announcement of the CPVs fighting in Korea, made over the North Korean Radio in Sinŭiju, reflected the D.P.R.K.'s appreciation of China's cautious entrance:

> Participating in operations along with the People's Armed Forces, under the unified command of the general headquarters of the People's Armed Forces, were volunteer units formed by the Chinese people who want to defend their homes and their fatherland, oppose the American aggressors, and support the struggle of the Korean people.[74]

Several interesting conclusions suggest themselves. First, the mention of the "Chinese people." A sophisticated distinction, it begs the question: why didn't similar "Russian people" volunteer? Secondly, the emphasis on the overall Korean control of the CPVs implies that the reality, especially taking into account the decimated nature of the KPA, was the reverse. Thirdly, the listed order of priorities of the CPVs underlined the fact that P'yŏngyang had no illusions about China's entry into the war: it was not primarily to preserve the D.P.R.K., but rather in reaction to a perceived threat to its own national security.

7. EMERGENCE OF STRAINS

P'yŏngyang was apparently worried that neither ally would come to her aid after the Inch'ŏn defeat and the subsequent swift U.S./UN drive north. This fear was indicated by the D.P.R.K.'s internal propaganda of late September and early October 1950. The three themes which this propaganda stressed implied that North Korea would have to fight alone: (1) the U.S.S.R. and China had offered military assistance, but Kim Il Sung had rejected the offer; (2) the conflict was a civil war; (3) Japanese troops were fighting with the UN forces. P'yŏngyang told its people that they must fight on without external help in order to prevent a third world war.[75] With the defeat of the D.P.R.K.'s army, China's military help, for whatever reason, was therefore very welcome.

On the other hand, the quantity and, more importantly, the *quality,* of the arms that the Soviet Union supplied to the D.P.R.K., and the CPVs during the war caused tensions. Much of the heavier Soviet military materiel, such as the 152 mm M1943 howitzer, the 152 mm 1937 gun-howitzer, the Joseph Stalin series of heavy tanks, and very heavy artillery, were not turned over to the communist forces during most of the war. The KPA's heaviest field artillery was the 122mm M1931/37 corps gun, and its largest mortar was the 120 mm M1938. North Korea's best tank was the World War II T-34/85. The bulk of the materiel came from Soviet surplus stocks and was obsolescent. Interestingly, production was recent (1948–50), but the models were outmoded; i.e., the stock often showed a recent year of manufacture, but the quality was of a decade-old weapon in terms of firepower.

Therefore, the weapons that the Soviet Union supplied to its allies during the war were inferior and vulnerable to American technology. For example, the North Korean and CPV tanks were no match for American anti-armor weapons; Soviet heavy tanks, which might have withstood U.S. firepower, were not used. The best Russian anti-tank weapons, e.g., 85 mm and the 100 mm M1944, were not used in Korea. The same held true of the Russian anti-aircraft artillery, which was not an equal match for the evasion capability of the American planes.[76] The D.P.R.K. realized early on that it was defending itself with inadequate Russian weapons. On North Korean Army Day, February 4, 1951, for example, P'yŏngyang Radio broadcast a speech by a "high ranking officer," Chon I-hwan: "Owing to Soviet assistance during the past five years, we learned how to drive tanks and how to fly airplanes. But for this assistance we could not have achieved our victories." Conspicuous by its absence was any "appreciation" for either Soviet troops or arms during the conflict. Russian troops who served as advisors or support forces later in the war for Soviet installations were reportedly unwelcome among both CPV and North Korean units.[77]

By September 1951 the United Nations estimated that Soviet forces in Korea consisted of: three anti-aircraft artillery divisions of 6,000 men; one 1,500-man security regiment; 2,000 military advisors; 2,000 engineers; 1,500 counterespionage guards; 1,000 signal and radar technicians; 400 civilian advisors; 5,000 air and ground troops; and 500 hospital and medical personnel.[78] This sizable number of Russians gave rise to widespread rumors in mid-1951 that the Soviet Union would enter the war about June 1952.[79] However, these were actually only token contributions, and P'yŏngyang's dismay at Russian aloofness toward the war increased as the battlefield stalemate continued.

Consequently, the D.P.R.K. was in the strained position of depending upon Chinese troops, whose main interest was not in pursuing Korean reunification, while being forced to defend its fatherland with inferior Russian arms. In this situation of inadequate Russian support, the D.P.R.K.'s gratitude toward China understandably became all the more pronounced as time went on.

China came to the aid of the D.P.R.K. at great cost to herself. She had been involved in civil wars since at least the beginning of the twentieth century, and the new regime in Peking in 1950 was eager to turn to the task of economic reconstruction and national unification. Involvement in a new war shattered the Chinese government's hopes for a period of domestic progress. The economic strain of maintaining a large army in Korea constituted a formidable difficulty. The money spent on the war not only caused a diversion from internal needs and priorities, but moreover was *borrowed* from the Soviet Union at interest! It has been estimated that China borrowed at least $2 billion from Moscow to finance her participation in the war.[80]

The war involved other costs for China. Taiwan's liberation was denied. Similarly, China's entry into the United Nations continued to be blocked because of her actions in Korea. Moreover, China's dependence upon the Soviet Union grew during the war. Finally, the CPVs suffered 900,000 casualties in the Korean civil war; it was a high price to pay for the defense of a neighbor that was now within the Soviet sphere of influence.[81]

The CPVs who entered P'yŏngyang in the fall of 1950 did not receive an enthusiastic welcome. To overcome this, they came supplied with receipts to pay for food and lodging. The receipts read: "Issued by the Supporters Society for Chinese Volunteers in Korea." The amount of the receipt was deducted from the next food levy imposed by the D.P.R.K. authorities.[82] From this point on, the CPVs worked fairly harmoniously with the North Koreans—allowing for the inevitable strains which accompany a wartime alliance. One example was reported in early 1952 when the CPVs refused to return Korean recruits to the North Korean army. Apparently the Chinese were dissatisfied with Korean combat efficiency and had been recruiting Koreans directly into the CPVs, using Korean-speaking interpreters.[83] Such tensions between China and the D.P.R.K., however, were not the norm.

Technically, control of the North Korean and CPV forces was concentrated in a joint command headed by Kim Il Sung and staffed by both North Korean and CPV officers. Actually, operations were controlled directly, particularly in the last two years of the war, by the CPV headquarters in Mukden.[84] Most significant, however, although it was these two armies which fought together to defend Korea, it was the Soviet Union that maintained ultimate direction of the war. For example, P'yŏngyang was apparently caught by surprise when Jacob Malik made his speech at the United Nations on June 23, 1951, calling for negotiations to end the war, not having been informed in advance of the Russian proposal.[85]

On September 7, 1951 at the Chinese border city of Antung, Chang Tsung-sun, a deputy commander of the CPVs, and the D.P.R.K. Minister of National Defense Ch'oe Yong-gŏn, reportedly met with General Malenchikoff, chief of the Soviet military advisory group in Korea, and demanded that the Russians rush fresh supplies to Korea and that the Soviet navy be used to counter the U.S. Navy.[86] These demands were largely turned aside by the Russians.

8. SOUTH AND NORTH KOREAN HAWKS

In early June 1953, as the armistice negotiations finally approached a successful conclusion, the R.O.K. threatened unilaterally to release prisoners of war held in camps guarded by South Koreans. Indeed, the actual release of these prisoners on June 18 did *not* come as a surprise. Rhee had been threatening such a step for several months. Reporters on the scene commented on the likelihood of such an event:

> A release was imminent and had been clear for some time. Several newspaper reports had even been published that South Korean guards at the camps were encouraging prisoners to break out of the stockades. Yet despite this advance information and despite the fact that there were sufficient American troops available for guard duty, in reserve areas of Korea and Japan, there had been only a token change in the procedure for handling prisoners in the camps.[87]

The same reporter wrote the following day that "officers in Tokyo had been warned such a measure might be taken by the Government of the Republic of Korea. However, the p.o.w. command was assured by higher headquarters that Dr. Rhee was 'bluffing.' "[88] The D.P.R.K. consequently had ample reason to suspect American connivance in Rhee's provocative action. In 1951 this might well have been cause for the communist side to break off the negotiations. But in their eagerness for an armistice in the summer of 1953, even though the released prisoners of war were never returned to their camps, Peking and Moscow reacted prudently.

P'yŏngyang, however, sensitive to the possibility of future

South Korean aggression, was furious at Rhee's precipitous move. On June 27, for example, P'yŏngyang Radio declared: "All provocative acts and all illegal actions by the traitor Syngman Rhee are scheduled with the connivance and guidance of his master, which is admitted by the world." Meanwhile, both Moscow and Peking Radios were blaming Rhee, not Washington. On July 9 P'yŏngyang Radio, in a sudden and dramatic softening of its position toward American responsibility, stated that it was indeed Rhee who was the culprit and that the continued American bombing of North Korea had become "an *unintentional* inspiration for Syngman Rhee" (emphasis added).[89]

The reason for this conciliatory expression became evident on the night of July 13–14, when the CPVs attacked and nearly destroyed the elite South Korean Capitol Division, while largely avoiding contact with nearby American forces, in this last major offensive of the war. The New China News Agency on July 20, 1953 described this attack as a lesson to "the Syngman Rhee puppet army which had been obstructing the Korean Armistice and provoking the People's Forces." China apparently had offered North Korea assurances that she would guarantee P'yŏngyang's interests; the attack upon the Capitol Division was meant as a demonstration of this intention.[90] Interestingly, in mirror image fashion, the United States offered the same guarantee to South Korea. Implicit, however, in these two foreign states' granting defensive assurances was the condition that they would not again support the nationalism of Koreans who still wanted an early reunification.

There were hawks on both sides of the 38th parallel who wished to continue the war. In the north, although the existing evidence is skimpy, it appears that Pak Hŏn-yŏng argued for a continuation of the war. At the Fifth Plenum of the KWP in December 1952, Premier Kim, without mentioning Pak, blamed a "certain individual" for disrupting the unity of the party. On August 7, 1953 P'yŏngyang Radio announced that Pak and his followers of the Domestic faction had been arrested on the charge of trying to overthrow the government of Kim Il Sung. Pak was accused of planning a coup d'état and being determined "to fight to the death rather than accept the armistice." [91] Pak, understandably, might well have wanted to continue the war to achieve victory in the south, his earlier power base.

The war ended as it had begun: its tactics linked in part to factional infighting with neither the north nor the south satisfied with the artificial division of one nation into two states.

9. UNLEARNED LESSONS

To a jaded North American public, to whom fragmentation bombs and televised napalm attacks have been everyday sights, the parallels between the Korean civil war and the Indochinese war(s) are numerous. In both cases the United States backed corrupt and unpopular governments, preferring to believe that "international order" was more important than the legitimate nationalism of the peoples involved.

The reader is urged to consult Washington's official histories of the Korean civil war which, in bureaucratic and stark description, detail the fruitless attempt to cut off enemy supplies—all the while, of course, inevitably striking at civilian targets as well. The air force generals apparently had not learned a lesson from their attempt to interdict enemy supplies in Korea. One official narrative, for example, after detailing the massive destruction of rails, roads, bridges, and cities through bombing, concludes that "despite the air force's efforts, the Communists were able to stockpile supplies to sustain themselves from thirty to forty-five days in the forward areas." [92] The devastation was awesome. By the end of September 1950, for example, the U.S. Air Force had dropped 97,000 tons of bombs and 7.8 million gallons of napalm.[93]

The results of the bombings, both south and north, rivaled Dante's *Inferno*. P'yŏngyang's population was 400,000 when the war started, 80,000 when the war ended. Only two public buildings in the capital remained intact by 1953.[94] An American source states that the North Korean population in 1949 was 9,622,000; by 1953 it had declined to 8,491,000.[95]

Another tactic familiar to the Indochina generation is the American bombing of North Korean dikes. This fact was buried within a twelve-paragraph daily communiqué about U.S. air action on May 15, 1953: "F-84s also struck an earthen dam at Tokchon, 10 miles north of Sukchon, with unobserved results." [96] The official military history of the war has a dryly interesting description of what happened:

> About twenty miles north of P'yongyang lay the big Toksan irrigation dam with a 3 square-mile lake behind it. Air Force planners had long realized that destruction of irrigation dams would have a serious effect upon the rice crop of North Korea, but humanitarian considerations had argued against the bombing of such targets. As the war progressed, however, more and more of the rice crop found its way into military and international barter channels and this knowledge overcame the objections against destroying the dams.[97]

After detailing the military tactics used, the history continues: "Floodwaters poured forth and left a trail of havoc. . . . Buildings, crops, and irrigation canals were all swept away in the devastating torrent."

The air force, "elated by the success of the Toksan mission," struck against other dikes. However, "the Communists had learned their lesson by this time and efforts in June to repeat the earlier success at Toksan found the enemy quickly draining the reservoirs under attack. The water was lost, but flood damage was averted." [98] A widely read history of the war regretfully notes that "the fifteen remaining irrigation dams could have been destroyed in as many days. Much too late, the USAF had at last found a possibly decisive target system." [99]

10. CONCLUSIONS

U.S. intervention in the Korean civil war had disastrous consequences for both America and the Korean peninsula. A swift and relatively bloodless Korean reunification was converted into a carnage. The United States suffered 142,091 casualties, including 33,629 killed. An even greater horror was inflicted by American technology upon Korea, both north and south.

The D.P.R.K.'s military casualties have been estimated at 500,000, with 1,000,000 civilians missing.[100] The R.O.K.'s situation, after being "defended" for more than three years, was similar. Their military casualty list officially reads 300,000, with 1,000,000 dead civilians. At the end of the war, 2,500,000 refugees roamed the south, and another 5,000,000 people were living on some form of relief.[101] It may be assumed that the bulk of North Korea's population was living at a subsistence level in 1953. Incredibly, the peninsula's total population in 1950 was only 30,000,000. In short, proportional to population, the 1950–53 war was perhaps one of the most destructive conflicts in history.

From an American perspective, non-intervention would have brought welcome consequences. First, the Chinese civil war would have ended with the liberation of Taiwan. And then, in all probability, Washington and Peking would have reached a working relationship, in contrast to China's forced alliance with the Soviet Union. Secondly, without the continuing identification of nationalism and communism that America's entrance into the Korean civil war reinforced, it is possible that the Indochina adventure might have been forestalled (given NSC–68, however, this is less likely).

The crisp certainties traditionally written about the origins of the Korean civil war are often fabulous fiction. And the intriguing factor in studying this event is the realization that many of the facts necessary for a complete understanding of the war are still classified. For example, while it seems clear that Washington did *not* "stage" the war, General Douglas MacArthur's role in its beginnings is more problematical. What were his relations with Syngman Rhee? Was MacArthur preparing to support a southern invasion of the north with American arms? Was he encouraging Seoul's hopes for a war of reunification? If so, were P'yŏngyang's fears of an early southern aggression justified? The answers to these pivotal questions must await publication of the complete record of South Korea's relationship with General MacArthur's Tokyo command.

Unquestionably, however, the origins of the war were rooted in the domestic politics of both halves of the peninsula. Both P'yŏngyang and Seoul sought the support of their patrons in pursuit of reunification. Each regime, further, utilized the irredentist issue to solidify its own power. In the south, the Syngman Rhee government, faced with large-scale dissatisfaction,

tried to rally public approval by promises to "march north."
That these pledges were not sufficient to counter anti-Rhee sentiment was demonstrated by the population's reaction to the
northern invasion in the summer of 1950:

> The invaders' Russian tanks could easily have been stopped in
> the hills by a resolute defense. . . . Communist doctrine had
> little appeal to a population familiar with the grim reports of
> Northern refugees. But millions of South Koreans welcomed
> the prospect of unification, even on Communist terms. They
> had suffered police brutality, intellectual repression and politi-
> cal purge. Few felt much incentive to fight for profiteers or
> to die for Syngman Rhee. Only 10 per cent of the Seoul pop-
> ulation abandoned the city; many troops deserted, and a num-
> ber of public figures, including Kimm Kiu Sic, joined the
> North.[102]

In the north, the *immediate* causes of the war were the perception of an early South Korean attack, combined with the rivalry
between Kim Il Sung and Pak Hŏn-yŏng. These two factors out-
weighed the twin probabilities that the Seoul government in the
summer of 1950 seemed about to fall of its own unpopularity
and that Stalin's cautious foreign policy would not have welcomed a June invasion date. The political price that Koreans
have paid for the American intervention has been autocracy
throughout the peninsula based upon the mutual fears of the
two governments. The human cost was much more drastic. In
the first three months of the war the entire peninsula was largely
devastated. General Emmet (Rosie) O'Donnell, head of the
Bomber Command in the Far East, put it succinctly: "I would
say that the entire, almost the entire Korean peninsula, is just
a terrible mess. Everything is destroyed. There is nothing standing worthy of the name. . . . Just before the Chinese came in we
were grounded. There were no more targets in Korea." [103]

Considering the next civil war in which the United States was
to intervene, Indochina, perhaps the most unsettling legacy of
the Korean War for North Americans is that many of the shib-
boleths about the conflict are still accepted, while often its lessons have been only partially learned.

Notes

1. *New York Times,* October 18, 1949.
2. *Ibid.,* March 2, 1950.
3. Harry S. Truman, *Years of Trial and Hope, 1946–1952* (New York, Doubleday and Co., 1956), p. 333.
4. David Rees, *Korea: The Limited War* (Baltimore, Penguin Books, 1964), p. 19.
5. David Dallin, *Soviet Foreign Policy After Stalin* (Philadelphia, J. B. Lippincott Co., 1961), p. 60.
6. An early, but neglected article which argues that the war was seeded in Korea itself is "North Korea Jumps the Gun," by Wilbur W. Hitchcock, in *Current History,* March 1951, pp. 136–44. A highly valuable recent work which presents a great variety of data on the complexities of the 1945–50 North Korean political system is *Communism in Korea,* by Robert A. Scalapino and Chong-sik Lee (Berkeley and Los Angeles: University of California Press, 1972), especially pp. 382–462.
7. There is a small but growing literature which is now dealing critically with the origins of the war. A work which summarizes much of this thinking is *The Limits of Power: the World and United States Foreign Policy, 1945–1954,* by Joyce and Gabriel Kolko (New York, Harper and Row, 1972), especially chapter 10. See also this writer's *The Strained Alliance: Peking, P'yongyang, Moscow and the Korean Civil War* (New York, The Free Press, 1974).
8. Only one popular history of the war has used this phrase and by putting it in quotation marks made it obvious that it was satirizing the idea: Carl Berger, *The Korea Knot* (Philadelphia, University of Pennsylvania Press, 1964). Chapter 7 is entitled "The March to 'Civil' War."
9. This would seem to be a reasonable middle ground between the absolute vilification of Kim by the South Korean government and the total adulation by the P'yŏngyang media. For a relatively balanced account, see Dae-Sook Suh, *The Korean Communist Movement, 1918–1948* (Princeton, Princeton University Press, 1967), pp. 300–29.
10. "There are grounds for doubting that the Soviet Forces entered Korea with a premeditated plan; it is more likely that the Soviet command possessed no more detailed instruction than to establish

a 'friendly regime' in Korea" (Chong-sik Lee, "Kim Il-sung of North Korea," *Asian Survey,* June 1967, p. 378).

11. Kim Ch'ang-sun, *Fifteen Year History of North Korea,* Joint Publications Research Service (Washington, D.C., 1965), p. 84.

12. *Ibid.,* pp. 99–104.

13. Suh, *Korean Communist Movement,* p. 301.

14. The Neighboring Countries Research Institute, "The North Korean Labor Party's Internal Factions," *Jiyū,* Tokyo, May 1967, translated by U.S. Embassy, Tokyo, in *The Selected Summaries of Japanese Magazines* (June 26–July 3, 1967), p. 4.

15. Dae-Sook Suh, "North Korea: Emergence of an Elite Group," in Richard F. Starr, ed., *Aspects of Modern Communism* (Columbia, University of South Carolina Press, 1968), p. 326.

16. See Pak Hŏn-yŏng, "Heroic Struggle of the People of South Korea for the Unity and Independence of the Country," in the weekly *For a Lasting Peace, for a People's Democracy* (Bucharest, March 24, 1950), pp. 4–6.

17. Roy U. T. Kim, "The Sino-Soviet Dispute and North Korea," Ph.D. dissertation, University of Pennsylvania, 1967, p. 71.

18. Suh, "North Korea," p. 328.

19. For the D.P.R.K.'s election proposal, see *History of the Just Fatherland War of the Korean People* (P'yŏngyang, Foreign Languages Publishing House, 1961), p. 24. For a reference to rebellions and guerrilla activities in the south, see Robert K. Sawyer, *Military Advisors in Korea: KMAG in Peace and War* (Washington, D.C., U.S. Department of the Army, Office of the Chief of Military History, 1962), pp. 73ff.

20. *History of the Just,* p. 30.

21. *New York Times,* June 28, 1950.

22. Writer's interview with Mr. Kim Nam-shik, Seoul, R.O.K., January 20, 1971. Mr. Kim was a former high-ranking cadre of the (South) Korean Worker's Party.

23. "The North Korean Labor Party's Internal Factions," p. 10. Although these charges must be treated with caution, the supporting evidence indicates that Pak was painting an optimistic picture of the KWP's condition in the south before the war.

24. *Ibid.,* p. 11.

25. Gregory Henderson, *Korea, the Politics of the Vortex* (Cambridge, Mass., Harvard University Press, 1968), p. 163.

26. *Ibid.,* p. 166.

27. *New York Times,* March 30, 1950.

28. *Ibid.,* June 29, 1950.

29. Hanson Baldwin, *New York Times,* June 27, 1950.

30. *New York Herald Tribune,* November 1, 1949.

31. William Sebald, *With MacArthur in Japan* (New York, W. W. Norton and Co., 1965), pp. 180–81.

32. Sawyer, *KMAG,* pp. 100–101.

33. U.S. Congress, Senate, Senator Millard Tydings, *Congressional Record,* Eighty-first Congress, Second Session, August 16, 1950, p. 12589.

34. Sawyer, *KMAG,* p. 98.

35. *Ibid.,* pp. 94–95.

36. *Ibid.,* p. 92.

37. Kolko and Kolko, *The Limits of Power,* p. 573: ". . . Rhee's energetic search for arms—especially for a 99-plane air force—must have caused anxiety in P'yongyang."

38. Sawyer, *KMAG,* p. 90.

39. P'yŏngyang Radio, October 10, 1950.

40. Philip Jessup in *Department of State Bulletin,* U.S. Department of State (Washington, D.C.), April 24, 1950, p. 627.

41. A quite unconvincing argument has recently been repeated that South Korea attacked the North Korean border city of Haeju on June 25, and that that action called forth a northern strike. Karunakar Gupta, "How Did the Korean War Begin?" *China Quarterly,* October–December 1972, pp. 699–716. This highly imaginative, but unpersuasive article was refuted by Chong-sik Lee, W. E. Skillend, and myself (followed with a rejoinder by Mr. Gupta) in *China Quarterly,* April–June 1973, pp. 354–68.

42. *Military Situation in the Far East,* Hearings before the Committee on Armed Services and the Committee on Foreign Relations, U.S. Senate, Eighty-second Congress, First Session, 1951, pp. 990–91.

43. *North Korea: A Case Study in the Techniques of Takeover,* U.S. Department of State (Washington, D.C., 1961), p. 114.

44. *New York Times,* July 31, 1950.

45. Sawyer, *KMAG,* pp. 105–06.

46. Kolko and Kolko, *The Limits of Power,* p. 578. After citing each of these factors, the Kolkos conclude that Kim Il Sung only meant to capture Seoul and then "open negotiations with the new Assembly on favorable terms."

47. Roy E. Appleman, *South to the Naktong, North to the Yalu,* U.S. Government Printing Office (Washington, D.C., 1960), p. 10.

48. For example, "Russian equipment is, of course, being used by the North Koreans, but there is probably more Japanese than Russian equipment in use, and the aggressors are also using some U.S. equipment" (*New York Times,* June 28, 1950).

49. *New York Times,* March 13, 1947. See also Richard M. Freeland, *The Truman Doctrine and the Origins of McCarthyism* (New York, Alfred A. Knopf, 1972).
50. Quoted in Walter LaFeber, *America, Russia, and the Cold War, 1945–1966* (New York, John Wiley & Sons, 1967), p. 45.
51. *Ibid.,* p. 64.
52. Paul Y. Hammond, "NSC–68: Prologue to Rearmament," in Warner R. Schilling, Paul Y. Hammond, and Glenn H. Snyder, eds., *Strategy, Politics and Defense Budgets* (New York, Columbia University Press, 1962); and Cabell Phillips, *The Truman Presidency* (New York, Macmillan Co., 1966).
53. Hammond, "NSC–68," p. 307.
54. *Ibid.,* p. 306.
55. Dean Acheson, *Present at the Creation* (New York, W. W. Norton and Co., 1969), p. 377.
56. Dean Acheson, *The Struggle for a Free Europe* (New York, W. W. Norton and Co., 1971), p. 106. Before June 25, 1950 the Bureau of the Budget was talking seriously of a budget ceiling below $10 billion for defense for fiscal year 1952. Hammond, "NSC–68," p. 331.
57. Paul H. Nitze, "The United States in the Face of the Communist Challenge," in C. Grove Haines, ed., *The Threat of Soviet Imperialism* (Baltimore, Johns Hopkins University Press, 1954), p. 374.
58. Robert A. Arthur, "Harry Truman Chuckles Dryly," *Esquire Magazine,* September 1971, p. 257.
59. *North Korea: A Case Study,* p. 114.
60. Lieutenant-Colonel Kyril Kalinov, "How Russia Built the North Korean People's Army," *Reporter Magazine,* September 26, 1950, pp. 4–8.
61. Adam Ulam, *Expansion and Coexistence: The History of Soviet Foreign Policy, 1917–1967* (New York, Frederick A. Praeger, 1968), p. 523.
62. Strobe Talbott, tr. and ed., *Krushchev Remembers* (Boston, Little Brown, 1970), p. 368. Either because of Khrushchev's faulty memory or because some of the book was fabricated, part of this section is probably in error. For example, it claims that Stalin withdrew all Russian advisors before the war began. Of course, on the other hand, there were not many advisors left in Korea by that time

and it is possible that Stalin's order had not been completely carried out by June 25.

63. P'yŏngyang Radio, July 16, 1950.
64. *Ibid.,* August 16, 1950.
65. Jack Chen, "People's War in Korea," *People's China,* Peking, September 16, 1950, p. 14.
66. *History of the North Korean Army,* Headquarters, U.S. Far East Command, Military Intelligence Section (n.p., July 1952), p. 6.
67. Adam Ulam, *Expansion and Coexistence,* p. 525: "One thing remains clear, and that is the extreme reluctance of the Soviets to become involved militarily in any phase of the Korean conflict."
68. Robert Leckie, *Conflict, the History of the Korean War, 1950–1953* (New York, G. P. Putnam's Sons, 1962), p. 146: "Only thirty per cent of the North Korean soldiers who had crossed the thirty-eighth Parallel on June 25 remained in action by September 15."
69. Edward Friedman, "Dealing with an Irrational Power," in Edward Friedman and Mark Seldon, eds., *America's Asia: Dissenting Essays on Asian-American Relations* (New York, Pantheon Books, 1971).
70. See the *New York Times,* October 9–11, 1950. The United States at first denied the incident, but two weeks later it apologized and offered to pay compensation.
71. For example, "Far East Air Force planes 'bombed' eighteen principal North Korean cities with copies of General MacArthur's demand for surrender. . . . Planes equipped with loud speakers and recordings of these declarations *soon will begin to fly over the Soviet Union*" (*New York Times,* October 7, 1950) (emphasis added). On October 12, "The biggest Allied fleet ever assembled off the Korean coast since the start of the war . . . blasted and burned a 105 mile stretch of the North Korean coast *just south of the Soviet border*" (*South China Morning Post,* Hong Kong, October 14, 1950) (emphasis added).
72. See editor's note in the *Foreign Broadcast Information Service Daily Reports,* Washington, D.C., October 10, 1950, p. PPP 29.
73. *New York Times,* October 22, 1950.
74. Sinŭiju Radio, November 4, 1950.
75. *United Nations and United States Far East Command Intelligence Summary,* Tokyo, December 21, 1950.
76. *United States Eighth Army Monograph,* untitled (n.p., January 18, 1952).
77. Pawel Monat, "Russians in Korea: The Hidden Bosses," *Life,*

June 27, 1960, pp. 76–102. Monat served with the Polish Embassy in P'yŏngyang after the beginning of the war.

78. *United States Army G–2 memorandum,* untitled (n.p., December 17, 1951). An American P.O.W. wrote that "We walked by big ack-ack batteries manned by Russians" on the outskirts of the border city of Sinŭiju on the Manchurian frontier (Morris R. Wills, *Turncoat* [New York, Prentice-Hall, 1966], p. 46).

79. *United Nations and United States Far East Command Intelligence Summary,* October 7, 1951.

80. Allen S. Whiting, " 'Contradictions' in the Moscow-Peking Axis," *Journal of Politics,* February 1958, p. 130.

81. Rees, *Korea,* p. 461.

82. *United Nations and United States Far East Command Intelligence Summary,* December 21, 1950.

83. *Ibid.,* March 14, 1952.

84. Walter G. Hermes, *Truce Tent and Fighting Front* (Washington, D.C., U.S. Department of the Army, Office of the Chief of Military History, 1966), p. 76.

85. *United Nations and United States Far East Command Intelligence Summary,* December 7, 1951.

86. *Ibid.,* September 28, 1951.

87. Robert Alden, *New York Times,* June 19, 1953.

88. *Ibid.,* June 20, 1953.

89. P'yŏngyang Radio, July 9, 1953.

90. General Mark Clark later wrote: "There is not the slightest doubt that one of the principal reasons—if not the one reason—for the Communist offensive was to give the ROK's a 'bloody nose,' to show them and the world that 'puk chin'—go North—was easier said than done" (Mark Clark, "The Truth About Korea," *Colliers,* March 5, 1954, p. 48).

91. Kim Sam-gyu, *Konnichi no Chōsen* [Korea today] (Tokyo, 1956), pp. 91–103. See also Koon Woo Nam, "The Purge of the Southern Communist in North Korea: A Retrospective View," *Asian Forum,* January 1973, pp. 43–54, esp. p. 50.

92. Hermes, *Truce Tent,* p. 400.

93. Cited in Kolko and Kolko, *The Limits of Power,* p. 615.

94. Wilfred Burchett, *Again Korea* (New York, International Publishers Co., 1968), p. 65.

95. American University, *Area Handbook for North Korea* (Washington, D.C., U.S. Government Printing Office, 1969), p. 63.

96. *New York Times,* May 15, 1953.

97. Hermes, *Truce Tent,* p. 461.

98. *Ibid.*
99. Rees, *Korea,* p. 382.
100. *Ibid.,* p. 461.
101. Kolko and Kolko, *The Limits of Power,* p. 615.
102. Alfred Crofts, "Our Falling Ramparts—the Case of Korea," *Nation,* June 25, 1960; cited in David Horowitz, *From Yalta to Vietnam* (Baltimore, Penguin Books, 1967), p. 121.
103. *Military Situation in the Far East,* p. 3075.

Regional Integration: Japan and South Korea in America's Asian Policy

Herbert P. Bix

1. INTRODUCTION

Ever since the late 1940s U.S. Asian policy has sought to use the southern half of the Korean peninsula and Japan to create a configuration of military and economic power that would enable the United States to contain the might of both China and the Soviet Union, while simultaneously ensuring its own hegemony over Pacific Asia. This basic strategy, which may be termed regional integration, has turned on making industrialized Japan dependent on the United States and economically backward South Korea dependent, ultimately, on Japan. Its psychological roots lay in a traditional, shared Japanese-American ruling class attitude of contempt for the Koreans and the other formerly colonized peoples of Asia. If Theodore Roosevelt exemplified such an outlook early in this century, John Foster Dulles was its exemplar by the middle of the century. Dulles, newly appointed Republican advisor to the secretary of state, wrote in his first memorandum on Japan, dated June 6, 1950, and summarized by Frederick Dunn, that ". . . it might be possible to capitalize on the Japanese feeling of racial and social superiority to the Chinese, Koreans and Russians, and to convince them that as part of the free world they would be in equal fellowship with a group which is superior to the members of the Communist world." [1]

Historically, the geographical closeness of Japan and Korea invited American policy makers to view them in tandem. As early as October 1871, for example, the United States attempted to use Japan as a tool to break Korea's self-imposed seclusion. [2] In 1882, when the United States finally signed an unequal trade

179

treaty with Korea, ". . . it followed from the fact that Japanese warships had forced the Koreans to submit to commercial agreements." [3] But the postwar pattern of America's effort to subordinate South Korea to its interests in Japan finds its direct historical precedents in the period after East Asia had been divided into spheres of Great Power influence. Theodore Roosevelt was the first president to see the utility of encouraging an expansive Japan to move onto the continent and away from America's forward military outposts in the Pacific—Hawaii and the Philippines. The secret Taft-Katsura Agreement of July 29, 1905 represented a grant of prior American approval for Japan's establishment of a protectorate over Korea. At the Versailles Peace Conference in 1919, members of President Woodrow Wilson's brain trust drew up a position paper which outlined how the United States should permit Japan to retain Korea and move deeper into Manchuria, away from America's sphere of interest in Pacific Asia.[4] The American effort to throw South Korea to Japan, which developed gradually in the two decades after 1945, represents essentially a return to a characteristic feature of early twentieth-century balance of power politics in East Asia. But the enormous human difficulty and the ultimate tragedy involved in the realization of that effort cannot be fully understood unless the Japanese colonial legacy in Korea is remembered.

Korea's reduction to protectorate status in 1905 immediately brought a national resistance movement that forced the Japanese to conduct a colonial pacification campaign, similar to the one the Americans were then bringing to a close in the Philippines. By 1910, the year Japan formally annexed Korea to its empire, the official casualty count was 17,779 Koreans killed and 3,706 wounded.[5] Less than a decade later, in March 1919, a new phase of Korean national resistance began, triggered by Japan's brutal suppression of the spontaneous protest demonstrations against its colonial rule. After crushing the 1919 independence movement, Japan made greater efforts to nurture various collaborationist strata within Korean society; but the Korean nationalist movement continued to grow—underground within Korea and as an armed diaspora in Siberia, Manchuria and China proper. It triumphed, ultimately, of course, with Japan's defeat in August 1945.

Out of their experience of great cruelty at the hands of the Japanese and their Korean collaborators, and from their gruelling resistance struggles to regain their lost independence, the Korean people built up a legacy of bitter anti-Japanese hatred which affected their relations with democratic Japan in the postwar period. With the Japanese, however, feelings of innate racial superiority, born of the previous forty years of exploitative rule over Korea, also lingered on, fueling attitudes of discrimination and unconcern. Thus, conservative leaders in Japan allowed their country to be used as a U.S. base against North Korea, while the desire of many Japanese business leaders and bureaucrats to re-establish economic domination over at least the southern portion of Korea bears unmistakable similarities to past relationships.

The following study of Japan and South Korea in America's Asian empire traces the evolution of the regional integration strategy from its weak beginnings in the late 1940s to a situation where it now seems that a partially independent Japan may be beginning to break out of the framework of integration and subordination to U.S. aims.

2. PLANTING THE ROOTS OF DICTATORSHIP

The history of how two separate states were formed in the divided Korean peninsula between 1945 and 1948 need not be repeated in detail here. Suffice it to say that the birth of the Syngman Rhee presidential dictatorship depended on the same forms of U.S. support later so well documented in the case of southern Vietnam. Under the U.S. Army Military Government in Korea (USAMGIK) the Koreans experienced famine, high unemployment and constant political terror from Rhee's thugs and American MPs. In order to create a client government, the USAMGIK passed ordinances restricting the political liberties of all but pro-American, right-wing Koreans and filled the jails with Rhee's opponents.[6] At the same time that it waged internal warfare against the Korean population, Washington began to turn the south into an advanced base for the containment of the Soviet Union. Operation "Bamboo," launched by the USAMGIK in January 1946, was a program to build the nucleus of a south Korean army from elements of right-wing vigilante groups and private landlord armies.[7] It would "contain" the indigenous population while military base construction, first announced by the Pentagon as early as June 1946, would help "contain" the Soviet Union.

In 1947, following the announcement by the U.S. government in March that it planned to intervene directly in civil wars throughout the world (the Truman Doctrine), U.S. military policy in south Korea began to change. In July Truman sent Lt. Gen. Albert Wedemeyer to East Asia to investigate the Chinese and Korean situations. In the section of his Korean report dealing with the strategic importance of the U.S. zone, Wedemeyer stressed that ideally the United States should "ensure the permanent military neutralization of Korea." However, as long as Soviet troops remained in the north, the United States "must maintain troops in South Korea or admit before the world an 'ideological retreat.' The military standing of the United States would decline accordingly; not only throughout the Far East, but throughout the world." Despite his cataclysmic perspective, Wedemeyer believed that the U.S. occupation garrison in Korea was a liability since it could not be defended in the event of a major Asian war. Seeking to *rationalize* the U.S. position in Korea from the perspective of an all-out war strategy, he recommended that American forces be withdrawn "concurrently with Soviet occupation forces" and that the United States continue with what he termed its policy of "Koreanization"—a policy which actually began in the fall of 1946. By no means did Wedemeyer's recommendations, which were accepted by Truman, signal an American intention to abandon south Korea.[8] They do indicate, however, that U.S. policy toward Korea had entered a period of redefinition during which there would be considerable uncertainty in Washington concerning south Korea's military importance in the event of nuclear war against the Soviet Union.

3. PREPARING JAPAN
FOR COUNTERREVOLUTION

At this point it is necessary to place Korea in the context of overall U.S. Asian policy. The disintegration of the Rhee regime during 1948–50 coincided with Chiang Kai-shek's ejection from the mainland. The Chinese People's Liberation Army (PLA) began its counterattack against larger, U.S.-armed and financed Kuomintang (KMT) armies in the fall of 1947; by October 1949 most of the mainland had been liberated and the Chinese People's Republic established. Viewed in the United States as a defeat for American policy—elements of two U.S. marine divisions had been intervening in the Chinese civil war since early October 1945, and the United States had given the KMT massive amounts of aid—the "fall" of China provoked powerful demands for a more "positive" foreign policy in Asia which no U.S. government could ignore.

Rhee's imminent collapse also coincided with stepped-up U.S. efforts to secure Indochina for French colonialism. The counterpart of the puppet Rhee regime in South Korea was the Bao Dai regime in the newly created state of Vietnam. This artificial entity—a *joint* contrivance of the United States and France to stem the revolutionary tide in Indochina—came into existence with the signing of an agreement between Emperor Bao Dai and the French on March 8, 1949 and was officially recognized by the United States and Britain on February 7, 1950. Its creation simultaneously escalated the French-Indochina war, which had been under way since December 1946, and inaugurated open U.S. participation in the war. There followed the Truman regime's publication of France's request for military assistance against the Democratic Republic of Vietnam led by Ho Chi Minh and the Vietnamese National Front (Lien Viet) on February 27, the arrival of the first U.S. warships in Saigon harbor on March 16, and, on March 19, the first demonstrations in Saigon against U.S. interference in the war. On May 25, exactly one month before President Truman internationalized the Korean Civil War, the U.S. Congress appropriated $30 million for the French war machine in Indochina. In short, the United

States helped move the first Indochina war into a more intensive stage of conflict even before it intervened massively in the Korean civil war; thereafter U.S. policy toward Korea and Indochina developed interdependently, with Washington paying for French (and other) mercenaries in Vietnam and employing its own American conscripts plus Koreans and an assorted "UN contingent" in Korea.

If the Korean problem is to be seen in an Asian and global context, however, one must focus not on Indochina, but rather on Japan. In the period before June 1950, Japan holds the key to understanding the origins of the Korean War.

Although Japan had figured as the critical linchpin in the entire U.S. strategic position in Asia from 1949, top American policy planners, both civilian and military, did not achieve a consensus on the importance of South Korea for Japan's defense until after the Korean War began. Before that time, American leaders were divided over South Korea's defensibility and assigned it a relatively low strategic priority, as seen in the Wedemeyer report and the American troop withdrawal of 1949. Yet this did not mean that the United States was ever willing to abandon South Korea politically, or that U.S. Asian policy during 1949 and early 1950 went on the defensive, or that when border warfare escalated along the 38th parallel the United States was unprepared to meet it with force. Secretary of State Dean Acheson's famous National Press Club speech of January 12, 1950, for example, was actually aimed at informing both Moscow and Peking that Washington intended to retain an indefinite military presence in Japan regardless of what peace settlement might be worked out. Though his domestic critics were attracted to that portion of Acheson's speech which defined the U.S. "defensive perimeter" in the Pacific in such a way as to exclude both Taiwan and South Korea, those to whom Acheson directed the speech regarded it differently. As John Gittings recently argued:

> What impressed Peking in its published analyses was not what was excluded from the "defensive perimeter" but the far greater expanse of territories which it did include. "It is clear," stated an editorial in *People's Daily* on 1 February 1950, "that the American imperialists have assigned a major and perma-

nent position to Japan in their defensive perimeter" and that the US intended to annex the Ryukyus. . . . On Korea itself, a Washington-watcher in Moscow or Peking would not have concluded so readily as his domestic critics that Acheson had washed his hands of the southern half of the peninsula. Acheson distinguished between American responsibilities in the northern part of the Pacific area, including Korea as well as Japan, and the southern part (Indo-China and South-east Asia) where "the direct responsibility lies with the people concerned." Korea belonged to the upper half of the league table, together with Japan although "in a lesser degree" than the latter. The exclusion of Korea from the "defensive perimeter" . . . stemmed from an essentially military definition of those interests. . . . It was not a political definition of those interests.[9]

While U.S. policy regarding the precise place of Korea in its overall Asian policy was, at this time, obviously ambivalent, the thrust of U.S. policy in Japan, especially after the middle of 1948, had a logic of its own. That is to say, Japan's transformation into a base for waging counterrevolution—the chief development in occupation policy in the year and a half preceding June 1950—carried its own momentum and might have eventually led the United States to reincorporate South Korea into its military defense perimeter even if the Korean War had not occurred when it did to illustrate the essential inconsistencies in Acheson's "defensive perimeter" speech. Many aspects of U.S.-Japan relations seem to bear out this interpretation and the evolution of Japan-R.O.K. relations after the Korean War certainly lends substance to it.

In November 1948,[10] three months after the creation of the R.O.K., the final decision was made to deal with occupied Japan as a potential military ally and member-in-good-standing of the U.S. empire rather than as a defeated enemy. Actually, however, this "reverse course" in U.S.-Japan policy had been under way almost since the inception of the Occupation. One of the first Asian peoples to feel its effects were the Koreans. For the Supreme Commander, Allied Powers (SCAP)—General Douglas MacArthur's headquarters in Tokyo—the Korean problem had two aspects: one was the question of the Koreans in Japan —approximately 2.4 million Koreans at the time of the surrender, of whom one million had been forced to emigrate after 1939 by Japanese colonial authorities; the other was that of steering Japan toward severing all remaining ties with the Russian zone of Korea. For three months after Japan's surrender, Koreans who could obtain sea passage returned to their homeland without any restrictions on the amounts of currency and valuables they could take with them. Wishing to end this unregulated movement, SCAP ruled in November 1945 that Koreans in Japan would henceforth be given free transportation back to Korea but permitted to take only 1,000 yen (equivalent to twenty packs of cigarettes), plus their personal effects. All of their other possessions, gained through hard labor at low wages in mines and factories, had to be left behind. This official repatriation program ended on December 31, 1946. By then the Korean community in Japan numbered from 600,000 to 700,-000, and was once again acquiring notoriety. The official repatriation program proceeded in the midst of an anti-Korean hysteria, paralleling the U.S. attack on radical elements in occupied south Korea. In a campaign that was actively abetted by SCAP, the Koreans became objects of attack from the American-censored Japanese press, the Diet and various branches of the Japanese bureaucracy. By the summer of 1946 they were being blamed for Japan's black market and an increase in crime, accused of being carriers of cholera, of paying no taxes, of "being brave today after having cowered in fright during the war," etc.[11] Koreans who chose to remain in Japan thereafter were on the defensive, objects in effect of dual occupation decrees.

On August 4, 1946 SCAP issued a memorandum for Japanese authorities entitled "On matters concerning the definition of allied nation, neutral nation, enemy nation, special position nation and nation of unsettled status." Korea was defined as a "special position nation." [12] By their unwillingness to recognize the Koreans as a liberated people, as reflected in this definition, and by their numerous open admissions of preference for Japanese over Koreans, Americans were contributing to the recrudescence of anti-Korean prejudice. On October 13, 1948, one month after the state of North Korea came into existence, SCAP ordered the Tokyo police agency not to let the North Korean flag or posters depicting it be displayed at any time within the territory of Japan.[13] This again called forth an enthusiastic response from the Japanese government. It proceeded to close privately operated Korean schools in Japan, oppress those Koreans who were pro-North Korea and push an assimilationist policy toward the small pro-Rhee minority in Japan.

While this reverse course in the treatment of Koreans in Japan was unfolding, a series of American missions and reports, beginning with the Clifford Strike report of March 1948, made it clear by 1948 that no reparations would be given to the victims of Japanese aggression in Asia. In 1948, with political tension escalating rapidly in South Korea and all-out civil war in China, General MacArthur finally ordered all interim reparations removals of Japanese industrial equipment stopped and the whole issue tabled until after the conclusion of a peace treaty. Thus U.S. Asian strategy, which made Japan first a "keystone," then a "workshop," and ultimately, after the Korean War, envisioned making it an "arsenal" for all of anti-communist Asia, implied Japan's restoration to a prewar position of superiority over its Asian neighbors. In particular, it ruled out the possibility of restoring Japanese-Korean relations on a basis of equality. These implications were clearly illustrated in the subsequent transformation of the meaning of Japanese war reparations from something negative—compensation for damage and injury suffered by Japan's neighbors and a reminder of Japan's past aggression—into a constituent element of its future economic reconstruction and even a cold war weapon.[14] The "reverse course" and especially the reparations issue reinforced Rhee's hatred of postwar Japan, a hatred derived partly from political expediency and partly from his long experience as an exiled nationalist. Hoping to restart economic relations with the Japanese on a cooperative basis, Rhee visited Tokyo as MacArthur's guest for the first time in October 1948 and again in February 1950. Each time he found the Japanese uninterested and the prospects of ever obtaining reparations bleak.[15]

In fact, Japan eventually settled the Korean reparations issue on its own terms, an outcome implicit in Washington's Japan policy by 1948 and, indeed, from the time it decided to reconstruct Japan within the conservative framework of its prewar

ruling class minus the military elite. Once Washington had reinterpreted the meaning of reparations to serve Japan's and its
own interests, once it had begun to capitalize on Japanese feelings of racial and social superiority toward Asian neighbors,
conservative Japanese governments were free to act. After Syngman Rhee passed from the scene, South Korea quickly shifted
its position from demanding "claims" to begging for "aid." The
Japanese first arrogantly rebutted R.O.K. property claims, aris-
ing from the Japanese plundering of the peninsula, with counter-
claims of their own. Later, they forced the R.O.K. to abandon
its concept of "property and claims rights" in favor of a fictitious
notion of "economic cooperation." With the signing of the Kim
Chong-p'il-Ohira Masayoshi "claims" memorandum on November 12, 1962, the R.O.K. acknowledged the impossibility of resisting its consolidation within the Japanese sphere of the U.S.
empire.

The "reverse course" policy distorted later Japanese-Korean
relations as well as Japan's own political development; the general crisis in U.S. Asian policy, in turn, determined the "reverse
course." During 1949 and the first half of 1950 the United
States accelerated its political, diplomatic and military preparations in Japan for launching counterrevolution in Asia, with
Korea as a primary target. These preparations began with General MacArthur's New Year's warning to the Japanese people
that their anti-war constitution did not preclude the right of self-
defense.[16] Three days later, on January 4, 1949, SCAP permitted the R.O.K. to establish a mission in Tokyo. This special
arm of the Rhee regime was charged with the task of winning
supporters among the 600,000-strong Korean community in
Japan.[17]

The combat effectiveness of MacArthur's Far East command
depended on the Eighth Army, whose main combat units were
all undermanned and assigned to occupation duties. In April
1949 MacArthur ordered the Eighth Army combat units—the
First Cavalry Division in central Honshu, the Seventh Infantry
Division in northern Honshu and Hokkaido, the Twenty-fourth
Infantry Division in Kyushu, the Twenty-fifth Infantry Division
in south-central Honshu and the Ninth Antiaircraft Artillery
Group in Okinawa—to divest themselves of all civil administra-

tive duties in order to concentrate solely on military training.[18] With an actual strength of 45,561 and a combat strength of 26,494 as of June 1950, the Eighth Army sought partially to offset its manpower deficiencies by employing over 150,000 Japanese personnel "in roles normally performed by service troops." [19] MacArthur's April policy directive was followed by a new training program announced on June 10. The Eighth Army's combat divisions, together with the Far East air forces and naval forces, were ordered to turn themselves into an integrated naval, air, and ground fighting team as quickly as possible. On August 8, 1949 SCAP acquired an area in the vicinity of Mount Fuji "which would accommodate limited division exercises over very rugged terrain." [20]

While the Far East command proceeded with its training preparations, on September 8 the Japanese government, on SCAP's orders, dissolved the leading Korean organizations in Japan—the Korean Democratic Youth Alliance and the League of Korean Residents—confiscated their property, and expelled their officials. In Washington the months between June and November 1949 witnessed an acceleration of preparations for a peace treaty with Japan that excluded the Soviet Union and was predicated on an anti-communist security principle.

In late October 1949 the United States commenced construction of expanded air base facilities on Okinawa with the $58 million that had been appropriated for that purpose by Congress in July. This strengthening of Okinawa was integrally related to the failure of American policy in China—that is to say, Chiang Kai-shek's retreat to Taiwan and the start of preparations for an invasion of that strategically situated island by the PLA. Viewed from General MacArthur's headquarters in Tokyo, the growing danger to Taiwan may have raised the prospect that nearby Okinawa would eventually be completely outflanked.[21] This meant that American air power based on Okinawa would be unable to guarantee Japan's defense. A perceived danger to Japan's Okinawan flank, in turn, may have led MacArthur to reassess the importance of South Korea.

Less speculative were the consequences of base construction on Okinawa and the improvement of existing air fields in Japan. These eliminated the "need to construct bomber fields in the

Far East" when the Korean War broke out. According to an official naval historian, "The capacity of Air Force bases in Japan and Okinawa exceeded the forces available, and shortly after the commencement of hostilities two B-29 bombardment groups were flown out from the United States to make up, with the 19th Group already there, the Bomber Command of the Far East Air Forces." [22] But already by June 1950 MacArthur had at his command "the largest aggregation of USAF units outside the continental limits of the United States." [23]

Throughout 1949 and the first half of 1950 the Far East command continued to implement a program informally known as Operation Roll-Up. Designed to equip the Eighth Army's infantry divisions with reclaimed equipment from World War II stockpiles scattered throughout the Pacific, the project involved transporting vehicles, weapons, ammunition and other types of supplies to Japan for repair and storage. Much of the repair work was done in specially designated Japanese factories under the supervision of a small American staff. In 1949 alone 200,-000 measurement tons of ordnance supplies were moved to Japan from Okinawa.[24]

While the Eighth Army stockpiled military equipment in Japan, America's leading oil monopolies were also busy establishing financial control over the Japanese oil industry. Between February and October 1949 agreements were concluded between the following Japanese and American oil companies: [25]

	Date	Estimated Percentage of Stock Acquisition
Toa Nenryo—Standard Vacuum Oil (a subsidiary of Standard Oil of New Jersey)	Feb. 11	55
Nihon Sekiyu ⎱ —Caltex Kōa Sekiyu ⎰	March 25; July 13	50
Mitsubishi Sekiyu—Tide Water Associated	March 31	50
Showa Sekiyu—Shell	June 20	–
Maruzen Sekiyu—Union Oil	Oct. 21	–

In this same period Japan's leading aluminum producers, Nihon Keiken Zoku and Toyo Aluminum, came under the financial control of Canada Aluminum, while Westinghouse Electric, together with International Standard Electric, reestablished prewar investment ties with Mitsubishi Electric and Japan Electric.[26] Completion of the framework for this subordination of Japanese capital was pre-eminently the work of Detroit banker Joseph Dodge, MacArthur's newly appointed economic advisor. In March 1949 Dodge translated the Occupation's "reverse course" economic policy into an austerity budget which the Japanese Diet then passed without revision on April 16. Its long-range aims were to foster reconcentration in Japanese industry, to assure economic ties with the United States and to achieve, eventually, limited remilitarization. To guide Japan along this path, Dodge introduced (April 1, 1949) the lever of the U.S. counterpart fund "special account," [27] which SCAP and Washington later used, after the Korean War began, to channel Japanese tax money into direct and indirect Japanese military production. (Fifteen years later, beginning in 1965, Japan would use this same technique against South Korea, creating a "counterpart yen fund" and a "claims fund special account" with which to guide Seoul's economic development along lines which served Japan's interests.)

Having created an economic-financial framework for Japan's long-term subordination to the U.S.-dominated capitalist bloc, SCAP thus began to revive Japan's industrial war potential, at the same time that America's leading defense contractors moved to bring key sectors of Japanese industry under their direct control. From Japan's long-term viewpoint this was perhaps the most significant development of 1949–early 1950. Initially SCAP had stopped reparations confiscations when only 30 percent of designated confiscations had been carried out. Of the untouched plant, 72 percent was directly related to the manufacture of armaments. At first only a few of the smaller arms manufacturers returned to the repair and production of conventional armaments and equipment for U.S. forces in Japan. But by January 1951, six months after the start of the Korean War, as much as 80 to 90 percent of Japan's intact war-related productive capacity may have been directly engaged in the manufacture or repair of weapons and Japan was started toward an embryonic military-industrial complex.[28]

During the first half of 1950 the counterrevolutionary momentum in U.S. Asian policy accelerated, stimulated by the Republican party assault on Truman's methods of implementing containment, the so-called "fall" of China, and the Soviet breaking of the U.S. nuclear monopoly. It appears that the United States by its actions in Japan (and in support of the French in Indochina, Chiang Kai-shek on Taiwan, and the former collaborationist elite in the Philippines) was emboldening Syngman Rhee to escalate his war provocations against North Korea and convincing the D.P.R.K. of the utter futility of pursuing national unification by peaceful means.[29]

The year 1950 began with the signing of the U.S.-R.O.K. Military Assistance Agreement (January 26), a two-day conference between Syngman Rhee and MacArthur (February 16–18) and visits to U.S. military installations in South Korea and Japan by America's top military leaders—Chairman of the Joint Chiefs of Staff Omar Bradley, Chief of Naval Operations Forrest Sherman, Army Chief of Staff Lawton Collins and Air Force chief Hoyt Vandenberg. When the military chiefs toured the Yokosuka naval base, on February 2, Rear Adm. Benton W. Decker, the base commander, told them of Yokosuka's critical importance as the only U.S. naval base west of Hawaii capable of repairing warships of any size during wartime and of its indispensability as a logistics support base for the army and air force. Decker reportedly requested at least $6 million for construction to bring the base up to its full potential and a guarantee of its indefinite use by the navy even after the ending of the occupation.[30]

MacArthur's anguish over the Truman regime's "weak" China policy, the near civil war situation in Korea, and his fear that the fall of Taiwan would outflank Okinawa and thus undermine the defense of Japan may explain his return to direct involvement in Japanese politics around this time and his efforts to make Japan a politically secure base for military operations *anywhere* on the periphery of China. Developments in Occupation policy certainly support such a view. In February 1950, for example, SCAP ordered a step-up in the anti-communist witch hunts in the Japanese labor movement and school system. In March, after conferring with Syngman Rhee and Prime Minister Yoshida, SCAP broached plans for forcing all Koreans living in Japan to return to Rhee's police state. In April John Foster Dulles, the man who "had played the leading American role in the creation of South Korea" in the UN,[31] was appointed chief Republican advisor to the secretary of state in charge of formulating Far Eastern policy. His appointment, as Jon Halliday has argued, was designed "to insure a radical shift of policy." [32] Dulles would end forever the uncertainty surrounding South Korea's importance for America's Asian strategy.

In the two months preceding the outbreak of the Korean War some of the most striking developments in Occupation policy were connected with the "red purge." MacArthur hinted that the Japan Communist party (JCP) was an illegal organization (May 3); he imposed an emergency martial law decree banning all public meetings and demonstrations in Tokyo (June 1–7); finally he purged the twenty-four-member central committee of the JCP and seventeen members of the editorial staff of its organ *Akahata* (June 6 and 7). The JCP had been a vigorous opponent of granting naval and air base rights to U.S. forces. In the wake of these actions over 12,000 union workers and government officials were fired from their jobs for political reasons. On June 16 Maj. Gen. Charles Willoughby temporarily banned all public meetings and demonstrations throughout Japan. Nine days later, on June 25, the Korean War broke out.[33]

But by this time Japan had been shifted by the "reverse course" into a position where the United States could safely use it as a "workshop" and base for waging counterrevolution. The Japanese and Korean Left were being suppressed or neutralized, plans were under way for a postwar Japanese military establishment, and Tokyo was being turned into an outpost for anticommunist delegations from all over Asia. The U.S. military— though unprepared for June 25 psychologically and in terms of manpower—was training and stockpiling to meet a future escalation of civil conflict in South Korea (or the fall of Taiwan) with military force.

4. JAPAN IN THE KOREAN WAR

The outbreak of the Korean War was the culmination of five years of a U.S. policy of violently repressing the national trend of Korean politics. It was a civil war which the United States, for its own foreign and domestic political reasons, immediately internationalized. Japan, which was being transformed into a supply depot for war long before June 25, was drawn into it as the main, direct base of operations for U.S. forces. Right at the start of the conflict MacArthur permitted Japan's embryonic army, the Police Reserve, to aid U.S. forces logistically in the war zone. While retired Japanese admirals and generals served in SCAP's Tokyo headquarters as "consultants," lesser ranking Japanese military experts served in Korea with the Eighth Army.* Robert Murphy, first U.S. ambassador to postwar Japan, claimed in his memoirs:

> The Japanese with amazing speed did transform their islands into one huge supply depot, without which the Korean War could not have been fought. . . . Japanese shipping and railway experts worked in Korea with their own well-trained crews under American and United Nations commands. This was top secret but the Allied Forces would have had difficulty remaining in Korea without the assistance from thousands of Japanese specialists who were familiar with that country.[34]

Like the origins and nature of the war itself, Japan's participation was kept secret in the United States and most Western

---

* On October 2, 1950 Japan's embryonic navy, the Maritime Safety Agency, also surreptitiously entered the war in a direct combat role. For the next two and a half months forty-six Japanese minesweepers, one large "guinea pig" vessel used for activating pressure mines, and twelve hundred former imperial naval personnel engaged in overseas combat in support of U.S. naval units at the Korean ports of Wonsan, Kunsan, Inch'ŏn, and Chinampo. (James E. Auer, *The Postwar Rearmament of Japanese Maritime Forces, 1945–71* [New York, Praeger Publishers, 1973], p. 66. Auer also notes [p. 66] that "Japanese forces swept 327 kilometers of channels and anchorages extending 607 square miles. Two ships were sunk, one exploding after activating a mine off Wonsan, another grounding off Kunsan. One Japanese sailor was killed and eight were injured in the sinkings.")

countries. Yet on July 1, 1950, just a few days after the United States intervened militarily, the secretary-general of the Yoshida cabinet, Okazaki Katsuo, announced cryptically at a press conference that "since the dispatch of U.S. troops is a United Nations police action, it is natural for some groups [*ichibu no hito*] to engage in hostile acts or other activities in compliance with Occupation orders." Formal cabinet approval to cooperate with the United States in Korea followed on July 4.[35] The enormous importance of Japan's subsequent contribution is stated in an army-commissioned study:

> The depots and other facilities for backing up supply activities in Korea were located [in Japan]. The essential rebuilding program depended on Japanese industrial facilities and labor —resources which also provided vital services in the transportation and handling of supplies and the movement, housing, and hospitalization of troops. . . . All forces in Korea depended mostly on World War II trucks during most of the conflict—and most of those came from rebuild and overhaul operations in Japan. . . . *without the use of Japanese workers, an additional 200,000 to 260,000 service troops would have been required* (emphasis added).[36]

In addition to supplying technical assistants and "engineering" troops in Korea, as well as being a logistics support base,[37] Japan was the major training area for U.S. forces bound for Korea; it was also the training area for R.O.K. soldiers.[38]

Japan's proximity to the war zone but safety from attack enabled American pilots to lead a "normal" home life: flying out in the morning to bomb Korean civilians and returning in the evening in time for "happy hour" cocktails at their officers' clubs in Japan. Moreover, by its utilization as a rest and recreation area for U.S.-UN combat forces, Japan prostituted itself to the task of counterrevolution in the most literal way possible. From the Miura peninsula to Yamigahama, from Hakone to Hakodate, wherever there were U.S. military bases, there were clusters of bars, cabarets, hotels, whore houses—honky-tonk ratholes teeming with the flotsam and jetsam of Japanese society. Yokosuka, headquarters of the U.S. Seventh Fleet, had approximately five thousand prostitutes and fifteen hundred whore houses in 1952, and nearby Sarushima (Monkey Island) was one of Asia's largest gambling sites, an early prototype of Seoul's notorious Walker Hill. So great was the symbiosis between the U.S. military and the Japanese power brokers of this former imperial naval base that in 1952 the city's Chamber of Commerce and Industry even thought it appropriate to establish a "Yokosuka Song Promotion Society" in order to create and popularize a "suggestive" Yokosuka song that "could be sung by both American soldiers and Japanese, adults and children." [39] "Yokosuka, Japan," the lyrics began, "a wonderful town,[40]

> Beer *beree naisu* and girls all around.
> Up on the hill where the "cherries" bloom
> I'm gonna make us a home sweet home.
>   Baby, what you do to me!
>
> A long time ago this town was full of fight,
> But now we've pretty rainbows to light up the night,
> Classy taxicabs to go scooting all about,
> And kisses in the rain when the moon comes out.
>   Baby, what you do to me!
>
> Up on the mountain I look down at the sea—
> Ships going, ships coming, and one ship of love for me.
> Rocking gently on the waves, rocking to and fro,
> Oh I want to get on board, to get on board and go!
>   Baby, what you do to me!

American planes, taking off from Japanese airfields, dropped napalm in Korea manufactured under license by Nissan Motors and Ishi Tekka Company; American artillery fired Japanese-made shells in prodigious quantities, while for nearly three years Seventh Fleet ships, operating out of Japanese ports, bombarded Korea's coast line. The Japanese people and their industry and merchant marine were mobilized to assist America's war effort. At the highest policy-making level the Korean War provided the first great opportunity for reviving Japanese monopoly capitalism and militarism. With the internationalization of the fighting, large-scale U.S. "special procurements" superseded GARIOA (Government Aid and Relief in Occupied Areas) and EROA (Economic Rehabilitiation of Occupied Areas) as the main forms of U.S. aid to Japan. "Special procurements" orders placed just with Japan's former zaibatsu industries averaged over

$746 million annually and accounted for nearly two-thirds of Japan's total exports between 1951 and 1953.[41] Total "special procurements" contract awards during the five years from the outbreak of the Korean War to June 1955 came to $1,619 million by unofficial count, and $1,723 million by official Bank of Japan statistics.[42]

U.S. "special procurement orders" were soon transformed from purchases of a temporary and emergency nature into semipermanent profits for Japanese business. Originally this term meant Pentagon orders to Japanese industry for war materials for U.S. forces in Japan and Korea and for Korean wartime relief. But by 1952–53 "special procurements" had expanded to include orders for the maintenance of U.S. forces in Japan, Okinawan base construction and relief, economic and military assistance to U.S. allies under the Mutual Security Agency program (in the form of "machinery for military base use," machinery and tools, steel materials, chemical fertilizer and textiles) and, lastly, Korean reconstruction. Included in the latter were sandbags, barbed wire, fuel tanks, incendiary bombs, steel materials, railway ties, freight cars, trucks, coal, chemical fertilizer, medicines and wool blankets. Most important of all, a new type of "special procurement order," called "educational orders," was added from about 1953. These chiefly concerned finished weapons (ammunition, small arms, machine guns and trench mortars) and were one of the concrete ways in which the United States spurred Japan's illegal rearmament and eventually locked Japanese industry into the role of arsenal for anti-communist Asia.[43] Thus not only had Japan secretly committed itself to supporting the division of the Korean peninsula by the end of the war; it had also embarked on indirectly furnishing guns and ammunition to the R.O.K. under the "special procurements" formula. Even in the postwar period, despite the objections of Syngman Rhee, Japan became the essential source of supply for South Korean reconstruction.

The Korean War marked a military and diplomatic turning point in Japan's relations with Korea and China, the two countries that had fought Japanese imperialism longest and hardest. During and immediately after the war, the United States systematized its anti-China containment policy centering on military-economic ties with Japan. On September 8, 1951 at the San Francisco Opera House, the same building where the UN Charter was signed, Washington and Tokyo signed a peace treaty and military alliance which simultaneously incorporated Japan into the U.S. imperial bloc and designated North Korea and China major "hypothetical" enemies, while maintaining a U.S. military presence in "free" Japan. On that day Prime Minister Yoshida Shigeru, in an exchange of notes with Secretary of State Dean Acheson, formally acknowledged Japan's involvement in the defense of South Korea. "In the Acheson-Yoshida notes . . . the Japanese Government agreed that the American bases in Japan would continue to support operations in Korea . . . for as long as there were American bases in Japan and a United Nations Command in Korea." [44] With the signing of the revised U.S.-Japan Treaty of Mutual Cooperation and Security in June 1960, these notes were also renewed as the Kishi Nobusuke-Christian Herter notes. Basically they signified that the Japanese government considered North Korea as a legitimate, direct object of attack from Japanese territory. They also symbolized the resurrection of a stripped-down version of Japan's traditional military policy toward Korea. With half the peninsula considered to be in "enemy" (i.e., independent Korean) hands, the Yoshida government and every Japanese government since has chosen to regard the Korean demilitarized zone as Japan's forward defense line and the existence of a separate South Korean state as essential to its own defense.

Thus the Korean War defined "Japan's"—that is to say, the Japanese government's—relationship with the Korean people. To South Korea, Japan became a military backstop, providing bases for the U.S.-R.O.K. military alliance, a staging area, a rest and recreation area, a logistics base extraordinaire—the silent but profitable partner, in short, of the United States in counter-revolution. To North Korea, Japan became the base for thousands of hostile military actions by U.S. intelligence-gathering ships and planes, of which the *Pueblo* (January 1968) and the EC–121 (April 1969) incidents would eventually become the most publicized. Japan has also been a hostile state in its own right, denying diplomatic recognition to the D.P.R.K. down to the present, even after recognition of China. Economically too, the Korean War rekindled an indirect Japanese business interest in Korea: first in "special procurement orders," then in "rehabilitation," and eventually, by the early 1960s, in a direct, old-fashioned desire to secure control of the Korean maket for the products of Japanese industry. By the 1970s Japanese economic expansion into South Korea would give birth to an autonomous dimension of activity beyond U.S. control.

To be sure, that outcome was implicit in the very concept of a regional military and economic integration of the basic U.S.-Japan dependency relationship, which was, ultimately, the most enduring legacy of the Korean War. But though Washington could immediately utilize both Tokyo and Seoul to project its military power outward towards the Chinese mainland (read "containment") and into Southeast Asia, it could realize the economic integration of the region only provisionally and in stages—that is, by gradually accumulating the material, political and ideological conditions for its realization. One obstacle here was Syngman Rhee. Though Washington could force Japan and South Korea to begin preliminary negotiations leading to eventual normalization of diplomatic relations as early as October 20, 1951—one month after the signing of the San Francisco treaties and in the midst of the Korean War—it could not prevent Rhee from aborting them by imposing a maritime defense line seventy-five miles out at sea around South Korea's coast from which Japanese fishing vessels were prohibited. Though Washington could see that only a unified U.S.-Japan-R.O.K. military alliance held the key to an all-Asian anti-communist military alliance, it could not make Rhee understand that fact and forswear anti-Japanism. Why? Because Rhee, who had long ago turned his back on the wishes and needs of the Korean people, needed national enemies to disprove his despotism. The "Communists," of course, because the system built to root them out conveniently served to ensure his dictatorship. But the Japanese even more, because an anti-Japanese posture was his one and only point of contact with the consciousness of the Korean people. It alone could procure some small measure of popular support.

The other obstacle to regional integration lay in Japan itself. Economically, Japan's industrial structure in the early 1950s was just not ready for concentration on overseas economic expansion. Militarily, article nine of its anti-war constitution stipulated that "land, sea and air forces, as well as other war potential, will never be maintained. The right of belligerency of the state will not be recognized." Reinforcing article nine throughout the occupation period was a Ministry of Education policy of inculcating a negative evaluation of war in Japanese youth. After the October 1953 Ikeda-Robertson talks, in which the U.S. and Japanese governments reached an understanding on the need to foster a greater defense consciousness in the Japanese people, this official policy underwent an about-face in order to meet the long-term military and ideological requirements of the United States-Japan military alliance; but the Japanese people would not permit formal constitutional revision.[45] This ruled out rapid remilitarization and made reliance on other regional armies an absolute necessity for the United States. Regional integration in the period ahead would have to take the form of a division of labor.

5. DIVISION OF LABOR I:
SOUTH KOREA IN THE U.S. EMPIRE

The Korean War ended with the Korean people ravaged and more divided than ever: the foreign-imposed barrier of the 38th parallel transformed into a demilitarized zone; their great dream of national unification temporarily set back by the enormous destruction wrought by the United States in the name of the UN. For the North Koreans, who suffered the greater proportion of deaths and destruction, the signing of the armistice agreement on July 27, 1953 meant the start of "socialist reconstruction" and rapid, independent economic development; for the South Koreans, whose land was also a ruined battlefield, it meant something entirely different: a billion dollars in U.S. "aid," to buy off Syngman Rhee, and a new U.S. effort to stabilize the south as a permanent anti-communist buffer state with a new role to play within America's Asian empire.

That role emerged from the various successes and failures experienced by the United States during the Korean War: Mac-

Arthur's failure to destroy the socialist regime in North Korea (September–November 1950), necessitating a reformulation of U.S. war aims (late 1950–early 1951); the partial achievement of reduced U.S. objectives; the lack of French success in Indochina, which was consistently viewed by American leaders as an extension of the Korean conflict; and the indisputable American success in consolidating the counterrevolution in South Korea by rearing a vast control structure of the R.O.K. army, paramilitary groups, and police forces under firm U.S.-Rhee control. In other words, after the Korean front had been stabilized around the 38th parallel and peace negotiations begun, the United States continued to fight a stalemated war in Korea for two years in order to realize specific objectives both within Korea and outside it. Internally, it Koreanized the fighting and reinforced the partition of August 1945. Externally, the United States was less successful. Prolonging the war and the misery of the Korean people created conditions within which an advantageous peace treaty for Japan was secured and the rearmament of both Japan and West Germany begun. But prolonging the war did not "deflate" China's political and military prestige throughout the Third World, a major U.S. war aim; nor could the U.S. military effort in Korea buy enough time to stave off a setback for imperialism in Indochina, another U.S. war aim.[46] It is in connection with these two failures, one ideological, the other military, that the initial rationale behind the U.S. plans for post-armistice Korea must be seen.

Although Washington continued after 1953 to use South Korea as a critical anti-communist buffer state for the protection of Japan, as early as 1952 U.S. leaders saw a potential role for the R.O.K. in another area. By then the Truman regime had succeeded in Koreanizing much of the ground fighting, and America was fighting two proxy wars: one in Indochina, the other in Korea. Thus when candidate Eisenhower charged, in the closing weeks of the 1952 presidential campaign, that there was "no sense in the United Nations, with America bearing the brunt of the thing, being constantly compelled to man [the] front lines. . . . If there must be a war, let it be Asians against Asians, with our support on the side of freedom," [47] Truman could answer, a few weeks later, "The United States is now support-

ublic of Korea military forces totaling approximately
men. Our training schools are turning out 14,000 South
oldiers a month. There are 50 per cent more South Ko-
ops in the battle lines today than there are Ameri-
cans." [48] The new potential value of South Korea, in short, lay in
its U.S.-trained army, the fourth largest in the world and the
largest native army in the U.S. "coalition." Touted by Pentagon
officials as the best "comparable return moneywise for the equivalent amount of money," [49] the R.O.K. Army had become by
1953 the primary model for the U.S. military assistance program
in Indochina [50] and its expansion, revitalization and support the
primary object of all U.S. policies in South Korea.

Thus while Japan became the object of massive U.S. investments in productive industries in the five years following the
armistice, South Korea became the object of a massive "defense
support program." [51] And while the United States concentrated
on building up Japan as the military arsenal of non-communist
Asia, an economic counterweight to China and a future military
ally, it conceived its Korean defense support programs much
more narrowly: to serve the interests of the dollar, to solidify
an imperial frontier by sustaining the military containment of
China, which had begun with the Korean War, and to have an
Asian army in waiting if it was needed in Southeast Asia.

Three main periods stand out in the history of U.S.-R.O.K.
relations after 1953. They are 1953 to about 1958: the period
of the R.O.K. military build-up; 1958 to 1960: the period of the
transition in U.S. global military strategy or of Syngman Rhee's
last days; 1961 to the present: the period of Park Chung Hee's
military dictatorship or the attainment of full mercenary status.

In the first period, from July 27, 1953, the signing of the
Korean Armistice Agreement to June 21, 1957, the day the
United States formally abrogated the arms limitation provisions
of that agreement, South Korea's development was shaped by an
American commitment to raise its combat strength to twenty
divisions—an amount which completely ignored Seoul's ability
ever to sustain such a force on its own.[52] Eisenhower and Dulles
may have considered this decision both in terms of securing
Rhee's approval for the armistice and inhibiting a major re-
deployment of Chinese forces from North Korea toward Indo-

china after the ending of Korean hostilities. Whatever the reason, North Korean sources, which I have not been able to confirm, charge that it was followed by a second decision to expand further the size of the R.O.K. military, which was made in the wake of the French defeat at Dien Bien Phu (May 7, 1954). In late July 1954, the same week that the Geneva Accords on Indochina were signed, Rhee arrived in Washington seeking additional aid. Protracted talks between R.O.K. and U.S. officials followed during which the South Koreans agreed, among other things, to purchase aid materials from their former enemy, Japan, and to retain their armed forces under American operational control. In return, the United States is alleged to have agreed to pay for a 320,000-man increase in the overall size of the R.O.K. military. These decisions were officially confirmed on November 17, 1954 in the form of an "Agreed Minute Between the United States and the Republic of Korea." In the unpublished "Appendix B" of the minute, the United States reportedly agreed to raise the R.O.K. armed forces to a total strength of 720,000. This included a 661,000-man army, a 16,000-man navy, 27,000 marines and a 16,000-man air force.[53] The published portions of the November 17 minute referred to a U.S. "intention and policy to . . . support a strengthened Republic of Korea military establishment as outlined in Appendix B, including the development of a reserve system. . . ." [54]

Whatever the size of the increase in R.O.K. combat strength after the armistice, the R.O.K. Army had grown so large as to force the United States to increase its control over it, if only to prevent Rhee from eventually using his forces to renew hostilities against North Korea. Thus two U.S. divisions (about sixty thousand men) and an American Military Advisory Group continued to advise, train and otherwise control the R.O.K. military. More importantly, control was achieved by keeping a tight rein on the amount of gasoline and ammunition supplied to South Korea. With U.S. "advisors" spread through every level of the R.O.K. military structure, determining everything from oil and ammunition levels to the annual size of the military budget, and each U.S. service branch in direct daily liaison with its R.O.K. counterpart, Americans directly shaped the ideology, training methods and organizational structures of the R.O.K. military.

ing embarked on a policy of furthering the full-scale
zation of South Korean society, the United States could
ignore the economic and legal contradictions that such a
policy entailed. Without an economic "defense support program"
through which to channel massive amounts of U.S. assistance,
the U.S.-R.O.K. military control structure would be unviable.
Without scuttling the key political-military provisions of the
armistice agreement, it would be difficult to turn South Korea
into a permanent anti-communist military base and achieve its
regional integration with Japan.[55] Yet industries constructed
primarily to meet the needs of America's Korean policy could
hardly be expected to contribute to the sustained, balanced development of the R.O.K. economy. Likewise, an arms build-up
in violation of the armistice would not only threaten North
Korea's very survival and leave the entire peninsula in a permanent state of crisis; it would also eventually undermine Rhee's
civilian dictatorship. All these contradictions became acute in the
second period of U.S.-Korean relations which began on June
21, 1957, when the United States formally abrogated sub-paragraph 13d, article two of the armistice agreement, and ended
with Rhee's overthrow on April 25, 1960. Sub-paragraph 13d
prohibited the further build-up of war materials by both sides
and directed inspection teams of a Neutral Nations Supervisory
Commission to supervise the military status quo at five ports of
entry in both North and South Korea.[56] Directly after abrogating
13d the United States brought its latest model jet fighters and
atomic weapons into South Korea, just as it had done in Taiwan
after the May 7, 1957 agreement with the KMT for the placing
of Matador tactical missiles.[57] By early 1958 the United States
had "Honest John" missiles, atomic artillery and a "Pentomic
Division" in South Korea and had acquired additional leases for
the construction of Nike missile bases on Okinawa. While China
was withdrawing its last "volunteers" from North Korea (completed in October 1958), a new stage of U.S. involvement in
R.O.K. internal affairs was about to begin.

On July 1, 1957 the Pentagon abolished its Far East Army
headquarters in Tokyo and moved its UN command headquarters from Tokyo to Seoul, where it continued to double as the
U.S. Eighth Army command. Simultaneously, the Defense De-

partment established a new Pacific command in Hawaii. Paralleling these Pentagon organizational changes, Washington pressed Japan to speed up its preparations for assuming a more active role in South Korea and Southeast Asia. Between 1956 and 1957 the U.S. military garrison in Japan was reduced from 117,000 to 77,000 in the first of several large-scale personnel reductions.[58] On June 14, 1957 the Kishi Nobusuke regime, which had come into office four months before, announced the start of Japan's first long-range Defense Build-Up Plan, programmed at 457.2 billion yen and supplemented by U.S. Military Security Assistance aid to the amount of 134.2 billion yen.[59]

Behind the renewal of the arms race in the Korean peninsula, the turning of South Korea and Taiwan into bases for waging atomic warfare and the start of Japan's first long-range military build-up lay the Soviet Union's success in launching the world's first unmanned satellite and its ICBM tests, which deprived the U.S. mainland of its vaunted nuclear sanctuary status. In the late 1950s the two largest imperialist powers entered a period of nuclear stalemate, their nuclear strategies showing the first signs of convergence. The psychological and strategic underside of this trend was the tendency for the United States to step up its counterrevolutionary activities in the smaller nations of the Third World, particularly in Southeast Asia. In short, changes in the nuclear balance of terror between the two "super powers" had ushered in an era of nuclear stalemate and thus diminished the *nuclear strategic significance* of America's perimeter bases ringing the Soviet Union and China, but not their *conventional military significance*. The new era of the 1960s would be one of preparing for "limited war," a fact reflected symbolically in 1957 with the publication of Henry Kissinger's book on the theory of limited war [60] and concretely in 1959 with the start of joint tactical exercises (involving the use of nuclear weapons) between U.S. Pacific forces and the client military establishments in Japan, South Korea, Taiwan, and South Vietnam.[61] Instead of leading to any abandonment of perimeter bases, nuclear stalemate led the United States to upgrade the value of its forward bases and client armies in South Korea, Japan, and South Vietnam. Overseas bases were now wanted primarily for control of the empire, while having client armies and client states to protect had become an end in itself.

The fact that Washington's balance of payments problem became chronic from 1958 onward was an important incentive behind its desire to subordinate South Korea to Japan. Equally important was Japan's desire for overseas economic expansion. In April 1959 the United States opened formal talks with the Kishi regime for revision of the 1951 U.S.-Japan Mutual Security Treaty. With Kishi actively cooperating in laying the foundations for a trans-Pacific military-industrial complex, and U.S. "non-grant" military assistance to Japan on the rise,[62] particularly after 1959, Washington anticipated a new era of increased Japanese military and economic participation in propping up South Korea—if only Rhee could be removed.

On March 15, 1960, in the twelfth year of his misrule, Rhee staged another fraudulent election, which touched off a series of demonstrations. On April 26, Rhee's bronze statue was toppled from its pedestal in Pagoda Park while he, in the presence of Ambassador McConaughy and U.S. Gen. Carter B. Magruder, the "UN" military commander, announced his decision to resign.[63]

Rhee's removal ushered in a brief interregnum of relative freedom in South Korean life during which many Koreans began to sense that the root cause of their misery was the domination of their country by America. A many-sided struggle against the status quo crystallized during April–May 1961 around the long-tabooed themes of peaceful national unification and anti-Americanism. The coup d'état of May 16 marks the beginning of the third period of America's Korean policy and can be called the period of R.O.K. performance. With the establishment of Park Chung Hee's military dictatorship, ruling class power was concentrated in the hands of a usurpatory segment of the military, the most Americanized institution in South Korean society, which was headed now by Park, formerly Lieutenant Okamoto Minoru of the Imperial Japanese Army.

Initially, Park had two tasks to perform for his new commander in chief, President Kennedy. First, to make the R.O.K. *politically* safe again so that R.O.K. armed forces could continue to serve U.S. interests, thereby realizing their own raison d'être.

Success came easily. Park replaced Rhee's ad hoc system of thought controls with an all-pervasive, thoroughly rationalized one, reaching down to every level of social organization. He began his reign with a ban on all political activities until the junta which he headed could complete its own political apparatus, a new "Anti-Communist Law" and, in June 1961, a new Central Intelligence Agency (R.O.K. CIA) with reported ties to its U.S. prototype. By the early 1970s the R.O.K. CIA, under Park's loyal assistant, Lee Hu-rak, controlled the nation's press, weekly magazines, radio, television, popular records, public billboards and even advertisements in local theaters and tea houses. Under U.S. tutelage, South Korea had become a nearly absolute "totalitarian" dictatorship.

Park's second task was to stabilize South Korea *economically*. He achieved this by: (1) dispatching R.O.K. troops and civilian workers to fight for the United States in Vietnam, thereby earning, among other things, "special procurements" and various "remittances"; (2) inducing large amounts of foreign loan capital; (3) exporting South Korean coal miners and nurses to West Germany; and (4) normalizing diplomatic relations with Japan, thereby securing Japanese "economic cooperation" as a constituent element of R.O.K. economic planning.

A new phenomenon in the typology of nation states would make its appearance on the world stage during the late 1960s: Venalia, or the mercenary state. But the conditions for its emergence were all in place by 1965. After fourteen years of pressuring Japan and South Korea to resolve their differences, the United States—in a final application of muscle necessitated by its deteriorating position in South Vietnam—had effectively fused the 1960 U.S.-Japan Mutual Security Treaty with the October 1953 U.S.-R.O.K. military alliance, thus laying the legal foundations for shifting the burden of empire in Northeast Asia to Japan. His flanks protected by the R.O.K.-Japan normalization treaty, Park tied South Korea's fate to the "limited war" in Southeast Asia and, simultaneously, opened it wide to domination by U.S. and Japanese capital. The U.S.-Japan dependency relationships, axis of America's Asian strategy since the late 1940s, could be regionalized thereafter in the most concrete way. It could be used to foster a hierarchic pattern of

integrated military-economic relations between the two industrially advanced partners, who were cooperating in counterrevolution, and industrially backward, relatively impoverished South
Korea, whose armed forces served the common interests of both
in Vietnam. In this pattern, which was conceived in the late
1940s but emerged clearly only after 1965, the South Korean
people were on the bottom, their interests constantly sacrificed
to American-Japanese objectives; the Japanese, while remaining
in a definite dependency relationship vis-à-vis the United States,
played the role of "junior partners," able to act autonomously in
their economic relations with the R.O.K. and gradually relieving
the United States of its military "burdens" there as well.

But to understand the content of the regional integration that
is being fostered today in Northeast Asia, it is necessary to turn
to the Japanese dimension.

6. DIVISION OF LABOR II:
JAPAN'S POLICIES TOWARD SOUTH KOREA

Japan's objectives in South Korea after 1953 were diplomatic,
military and economic.

1. The major thrust of Japanese diplomacy throughout the
early 1950s was toward joining the international organizations
of the U.S. bloc; normalizing relations with the former subject
peoples of Asia, particularly the Koreans, was a low priority
item. The World Bank, then shifting its attention from repressing communism in Western Europe to preserving as much of the
Third World as possible for the system of private capitalism,
accorded Japan formal membership in August 1952.[64] COCOM
(the Coordinating Committee), an organization of the major
trading nations, established under U.S. leadership in 1950 to
wage economic warfare against Communist bloc countries,
made Japan a member in September 1952. Membership in
COCOM's China Committee (CHINCOM) came that same
month, though Japan had been forced to subscribe to an em-
bargo on trade with Communist China ever since the start of the
Korean War. Full-scale compliance with the CHINCOM em-
bargo on trade with China was, reportedly, enforced after April

18, 1952 (the day Japan regained its formal independenc
means of the secret "Takeuchi-Linden Agreement." [65] The
eral Agreement on Tariffs and Trade (GATT) reluc
granted Japan associate membership status in October 195
"full membership," though under restricted conditions, in September 1955. Finally, in 1956, Japan became a member of the United Nations, the most nearly universal of the organizations created by the United States to manage the post-World War II world in its own interests. Thus, in terms of achieving its major objective—reintegration in the imperialist world system—Japanese diplomacy was both successful and rapid.

Against this record of rapid successes in inter-imperialist diplomatic relations stands Tokyo's record of vacillation and slowness in normalizing relations with the Koreans. The basic Japanese policy toward divided Korea has always been one of favoring the south and discriminating against the north. But for a long time the Japanese government was content simply with the de jure recognition which it had granted the R.O.K. by signing the San Francisco peace treaty and subscribing to the December 12, 1948 UN General Assembly resolution on R.O.K. independence. In 1956, after becoming a UN member, the Japanese government began to uphold the UN resolutions on Korea which legitimized continued U.S. occupation of the south and violated the UN's own charter principles of national self-determination and non-interference in the domestic affairs of other countries. Almost a decade later, on June 22, 1965, the government of Sato Eisaku signed the basic treaty normalizing diplomatic relations with the R.O.K. Immediately thereafter, commencing with the 1966 UN General Assembly, the Sato government became a joint sponsor, along with the United States, of the annual Korean resolutions. [66] Meanwhile, in the ten-year interval between joining the UN and becoming an annual sponsor of pro-R.O.K. resolutions on the Korean question, Japan's military and economic interests in South Korea gradually deepened.

Militarily, as noted earlier, Japan continued to give logistics support to U.S. forces in South Korea long after the signing of the Korean Armistice Agreement. However, beginning in 1960, with the renewal of the U.S.-Japan military alliance, Japan's involvement in the U.S.-R.O.K. defense set-up gradually deepened. One way to understand the new trend is to contrast the military function of the original San Francisco treaties with that of the revised Mutual Security Treaty of 1960.

The 1951 peace treaty with Japan gave the United States a legal foundation for continued military rule over Okinawa (article three) and allowed it to proceed with the forcible expropriation of Okinawan land for military use. At that time B-29s were taking off regularly from Okinawa's Kadena air base to bomb targets in the Korean peninsula. The U.S. pre-condition for the peace treaty was the first security treaty; it granted U.S.-UN forces in Japan and Korea unlimited use of Japanese military bases and helped rationalize the system for channeling Japanese resources into the Korean War. Continued U.S. military aid, integrally linked to the treaty in the form of direct aid grants and "educational orders," helped modernize Japanese industry and fostered the development of the Self Defense Forces. By 1958 Japan had advanced economically, militarily, and politically to the point where it required a more formally equitable relationship with the United States. The Mutual Security Treaty and accompanying Kishi-Herter notes of January 19, 1960 reflected these facts as well as the awareness of ruling circles in both countries of the need to assuage a Japanese public opinion increasingly divided over the treaty renewal. The new security treaty, consequently, deleted the more objectional features of the first, shifted the burden of suppressing domestic disturbances to the Self Defense Forces, and stipulated that henceforth "major changes in the deployment into Japan of US armed forces, major changes in their equipment, and the use of [Japanese] facilities and areas . . . as bases for military combat operations to be undertaken from Japan . . . shall be the subjects of prior consultations with the Government of Japan." [67]

However, the treaty's real significance did not lie in such equalizing features, which were contrived, in any case, solely to assuage Japanese public opinion, but in its underlying premise, designed to support American policy aims under the new conditions of the 1960s. Whereas before the United States assumed complete responsibility for Japan's "defense," henceforth, as stipulated innocuously in article three, Japan itself assumed that responsibility. The 1960 treaty appeased the Japanese government's desire for a larger measure of military power and the American desire for a joint strategic system in which Japan's Self Defense Forces would, at long last, act as a dependent, subordinate unit within the newly reorganized Pacific command structure. Such a strengthened security system was needed, according to article five, in order "to meet the common danger" of "an armed attack against either Party in the territories under the administration of Japan," though, of course, there was no military threat to Japan then, just as there is none today. But as the Kennedy regime began to expand its air base and missile facilities on Okinawa, the key island base situated in the center of America's Asian military coalition—approximately 800 miles from Tokyo, 750 from Seoul, 725 from Manila, 310 from Taipei and 1,300 from Saigon—and as it began to implement the policy of "special war" in South Vietnam, the real meaning of the revised treaty became clear. Just as the original one had been a device to ensure continued Japanese support for the Korean War, so the revised treaty was a device for ensuring Japan's official support in the waging of war against the peoples of Indochina.

During the late 1950s a U.S. Military Assistance Advisory Group, established in March 1954 at Self Defense Forces headquarters at Ichigaya, Tokyo, had helped concretize the U.S.-Japan military alliance. The revised treaty now supplemented it with a U.S.-Japan Consultative Committee on Security, whose function it was to provide an exchange of intelligence at a higher level and to foster joint analysis of the military situation in East Asia.[68] It was in this committee that Washington renewed its pressure on Japan to begin coordinating defense planning with South Korea. On February 1, 1963, at the urging of the Pentagon, the Defense Agency began its first full-scale study of Japan's military role if a revolt within the South Korean army, such as brought Park to power, escalated into a renewed Korean war. Given the code name Three Arrows Study (*Mitsuya kenkyŭ*) and designated top secret, it was brought to light by a Socialist memeber of the Diet in 1965, revealing for the first time the interlock between the Self Defense Forces, the revised security treaty, and the Korean situation. It also showed that neither the Pentagon nor the Defense Agency had complete confidence in the R.O.K. military.[69]

The Three Arrows Study provides a convenient benchmark for gauging Japan's growing military-operational responsibilities for the defense of South Korea. In late June 1963, when the study was completed, Tokyo assumed that in the event of renewed Korean hostilities, the role of the Self Defense Forces would be supplementary in nature, limited, at most, to joint or combined operations with U.S. forces; today it anticipates playing the main role. In 1964 U.S. pressure on both Seoul and Tokyo increased in proportion to the worsening U.S. position in South Vietnam. Three Arrows was thus followed by the Japan-South Korea normalization treaty of 1965, which, though it contained no military provisions, was viewed by top policy planners in both Washington and Seoul as laying the foundation for further Japanese-R.O.K. military collaboration. It is not without interest to note that prior to the conclusion of that treaty, the Cabinet Investigation Office (the Japanese equivalent of the U.S. CIA) expressed this view of South Korea in the September 1964 issue of *Research Report,* a government publication.

> Japan is an indispensable base for the defense of South Korea. Conversely, South Korea controls the entrance to the Japan Sea and is extremely important for the security of Japan. Viewed historically, not allowing South Korea to fall to hostile forces had become the number one goal of Japanese foreign policy. Since Meiji two [legitimate] wars were fought—the Sino-Japanese and the Russo-Japanese Wars—in order to prevent South Korea from falling under the control of hostile forces.[70]

A short time later, as the Japan-R.O.K. talks entered their final stage, Assistant Secretary of State William P. Bundy stated in a press interview in Seoul on October 3, 1964 that "in the event the R.O.K. is attacked by the communist side, both the American and Korean governments, of course, and Japan too, within the limits permitted by its constitution, will assist South Korea to repel the communist armies." [71] On March 28, 1965, five months before Park forced ratification of the normalization treaty through South Korea's National Assembly, the R.O.K.

defense minister, Kim Sŏng-ŭn, while enroute to Saigon, stated to newsmen at Tokyo's Haneda airport that "if agreement is reached in the Japan-Korea talks, it will naturally give rise to cooperative relations between the R.O.K. military and Japan's Self Defense Force." [72] Four years later, on November 21, 1969, came the Nixon-Sato Joint Communiqué which stipulated that the defense of South Korea was "essential" to Japan's own security. Thereafter it remained for Washington to implement the actual transference of the main military supervisory duties for South Korea from the Pentagon to the Defense Agency.

During 1970 the Pentagon announced plans to reduce the U.S. garrison in South Korea from 64,000 to 50,000 and to give the Park dictatorship approximately $1.5 billion in military aid from 1971 to 1975. [73] In April 1968 President Park Chung Hee had established a 2.3 million-man "Homeland Reserve Force." On July 5, 1968 he inaugurated his first "Three Year Plan for Completion of War Preparations" and "First Defense Industry Consolidation Plan," while accelerating the training of his essentially mercenary forces. [74] Between January 1967 and December 1969 a total of 107 joint and combined training exercises were conducted between U.S. and R.O.K. forces, [75] with peripheral Self Defense Force participation. In the spring of 1971 the United States, Japan and the R.O.K. conducted "Operation Freedom Vault," a nine-day-long combined war exercise involving U.S.-R.O.K. airborne units and utilizing Okinawa and Japanese homeland bases.

The R.O.K. moved for the first time toward self-sufficiency in the production and repair of conventional weapons—tanks, military vehicles, and ammunition. It acquired up-to-date weapons from America's Vietnam arsenals and readied itself to independently aid other anti-communist regimes in Asia. The Japanese Defense Agency increased its preparations for assuming the main military role in *supporting* South Korea and also U.S. troops and bases on Okinawa after reversion to Japan. In 1971, the year the Defense Agency hired three hundred "civilian" ferry boats for exercises designed to transport tanks and troops to South Korea and dispatched a large military mission to Seoul, these preparations were just getting under way. But by the end of the decade, when Japan will be nearing completion of its fifth

Defense Build-Up program, the Self Defense Forces will have been transformed from a *dependent* unit within the American alliance system into an *independent* one, able to assume primary responsibility for backing up South Korea and defending U.S. bases on Okinawa.[76] The dictatorship in Seoul will have advanced its military preparations to where it can conduct limited military interventions of its own in so-called post-Vietnam Asia: either in support of U.S.-Japanese monopoly capital, as it has been set up to do, or even to protect Japan's economic interests against America's, as U.S.-Japanese economic competition may someday give it the encouragement to do.

The very existence of such options suggests at once the inherent instability and contradictions of regional integration. Japanese big business, beginning in the late 1960s, advanced rapidly into Southeast Asia (Thailand, Indonesia and the Philippines) and East Asia (Taiwan and South Korea). In Korea the purpose was to secure the demilitarized zone as Japan's front line of defense. It also was anxious to realize high profits from exploiting Korea's cheap wage labor—the same reason that prompted Yankee merchants to step up their capital investments throughout Pacific Asia at the same time. For Japan the turning point was, of course, the 1965 treaty and claims settlement. Before that time the United States alone had been responsible for thwarting balanced industrialization in South Korea by policies which were extremely effective: in nurturing the premature development of monopolies in the R.O.K. export sector, widening the market for U.S. surplus manufactures and relieving America's subsidized farmers of their surplus agricultural products—by making Korean peasants subsidize them. Now Japan entered the act.

The 1965 treaty settled the long-outstanding reparations issue between the two countries. Japan agreed to give Seoul $200 million in public loans, $300 million in free grants and at least $300 million in commercial credits over a ten-year period beginning in 1966.[77] Though the reparations were called "economic cooperation" or the "congratulatory fund for independence" by the Japanese negotiators and "reparations" by the Koreans, it was a good deal for both sides. For Japan the $300 million in grants included trading debts that Seoul had accumulated since 1948; the funds were put into a special account that could be utilized only with prior Japanese government approval. Japanese goods and services destined for Korea under the terms of the agreements had to be carried by Japanese ships and insured by Japanese firms.[78] For the monopolists of the Korean Businessmen's Association, who had been lobbying for a Japan treaty since 1961, the economic opening to Japan was a godsend, while for the Park regime it may have seemed a step toward a future political alliance as well as a necessary defensive measure in case its participation in the Indochina war led to renewed hostilities with North Korea.[79]

After 1965 the Japanese government established a committee system to coordinate state political interests and private economic interests in dealing with Seoul. It consisted, initially, of an annual Japan-R.O.K. Ministerial Conference and the Japan-R.O.K. Economic Committee; later, beginning in January 1969, a Japan-R.O.K. Cooperative Committee under the chairmanship of former prime minister Kishi Nobusuke was added. Naturally, Japanese capitalists regarded this three-tiered structure as a guarantee by *their* political representatives of their future "private" investments in South Korea. At the first Ministerial Conference (August 1967), the Sato government agreed to furnish Seoul with $200 million in private loans; at the second Ministerial Conference (August 1968), it agreed to supply $90 million in private loans; at the third Ministerial Conference (August 1969) it agreed to cooperate in building the P'ohang integrated steel works and to furnish a $5 million private loan; at the fourth Ministerial Conference (July 1970) Tokyo agreed to provide loans totaling $160 million to help finance the construction of four heavy industry plants and the development of small industries, agriculture, and export industries.[80]

Direct Japanese investment in South Korea increased from only $1.2 million in 1965 to $27.1 million in 1969, while South Korea's trade gap with Japan during the same period climbed from 3.8:1 to 6.7:1.[81] By March 1970 Japanese companies had acquired control of about 90 percent of South Korea's fertilizer industry, 64 percent of its chemical fiber industry, 62 percent of foodstuffs, 48 percent of glassmaking and cement and 43.5 percent of its chemical industry. In the field of joint ventures with

South Korean companies, Japanese capital controlled less than half the stock in 19 percent, half the stock in 33 percent, over half but less than 100 percent of the stock in 22 percent, and 100 percent of the stock in 26 percent.[82] While tied to the United States militarily and still dominated by American capital, South Korea had also clearly reentered the Japanese economic sphere.

Behind the enormous influx of Japanese direct investments in South Korea lay the attraction of cheap Korean wage labor made available to foreign investors under ideal conditions of exploitation. In 1970, for example, the average monthly wage of Korean workers in manufacturing was only 13,950 yen or *one-sixth* the 86,540 yen monthly wage of Japanese manufacturing workers.[83] The Park regime denied Korean workers employed in foreign-owned enterprises the right to strike and was creating "free export zones" in the interior and along the coast (i.e. inland and coastal "treaty ports") where 100 percent foreign-owned factories, employing strikeless Korean labor, could export their products free of tax.

Against this background, and after five years of open dealing with a dictatorship anxious to facilitate the influx of foreign capital, a leading Japanese capitalist made one of the most significant disclosures of the thinking of the Japanese business world on the future of R.O.K.-Japan economic relations. In April 1970 Yatsugi Kazuo, longtime friend of dictators Park Chung Hee and Chiang Kai-shek and a member of Japan's "Korea lobby," prepared a report for the second general meeting of the Japan-R.O.K. Cooperative Committee. The Yatsugi Report or the "Draft Plan for Japan-Korea Long-Term Economic Cooperation" called, in effect, for a concentration of effort in two key areas.[84] In one area South Korea was urged to expand its "export free zones" and "bonded land areas" and "take more efficient charge of processing Japanese manufactured goods" in middle and small industries. Eventually, as Japan-R.O.K. economic cooperation progressed, a "model case of an Asian EEC" would come into being. The first step would involve linking South Korea's Namhae coastal industrial region south of P'o-hang, where Japanese firms are constructing a Korean steel industry, with Japan's Chugoku industrial region: specifically,

Tottori and Yamaguchi prefectures in southern Honshu and a portion of Oita and Fukuoka prefectures in eastern and northern Kyushu respectively. A striking feature of this plan for an East Asian EEC is the dominating role implicitly envisioned for Japanese industrial groups who have their headquarters in Osaka and Nagoya. Historically, ex-samurai businessmen and politicians from southwestern Japan took the lead in advancing Japan's interests in Korea. The same is true today: the original "Korea lobby" which formed during the period of the Kishi regime centered on conservative politicians in alliance with Kansai capitalists; in 1970 Kansai industrial groups again took the initiative in trying to rationalize the economic gains Japan had made in Korea since 1965.[85]

The other area where the Yatsugi Report sought R.O.K. cooperation was in developing so-called "specialization and cooperative industry" (*bungyō to kyōgyō*). This involved transferring to the R.O.K.'s new "treaty ports" the labor-intensive and processing sectors of such main Japanese industries as steel, aluminum, oil and zinc refining, chemicals, plastics, electronics and even shipbuilding. In other words, if South Korea "cooperated" in solving the contradictions of Japan's economic development by furnishing greater amounts of land and cheap labor (for Japanese industries which were finding it difficult to expand within Japan from the viewpoint of land utilization and environmental pollution), then R.O.K. industry would receive, in return, the benefits of Japanese capital and advanced technology. With Japan supplying the imported parts, raw materials, capital and technology and South Korea the labor and territorial space for processing it all for re-export, a "vertical international division of labor" would be realized and the Japan-R.O.K. trade imbalance rectified, eventually.

And so to the South Korean question: how does a basically rural, underdeveloped country which is functioning in the international arena as a mercenary state, but is committed to the goal of a high GNP, relate to its economically advanced neighbor? The Yatsugi Report and, by extension, the Japanese business world, replied: by again becoming its economic colony and its source of proletarian wage labor.

7. CONCLUSION: RECENT DEVELOPMENTS

Diplomatic events of the past few years have tended to under-line the historical rather than the structural nature of the U.S.-Japan-South Korea alignment. Can the ending of overt American aggression in Vietnam, the return of R.O.K. mercenaries to South Korea, and new diplomatic configurations in Asia dissolve overnight an interconnected military-economic-political formation that has been twenty years in the making? The evidence presented here certainly does not support a positive answer to that question, yet it would be foolish to ignore the new dimension that has been added to Japan-R.O.K. regional integration by the current restructuring of international relations in East Asia.

That restructuring began in 1971 and was revealed to the world during the U.S. election year 1972 when Nixon made two precedent-shattering trips to Peking and Moscow in connection with his plans for extricating the United States from direct involvement in the Vietnam war. Russia and China began tacitly to cooperate with the United States in dampening down revolutionary movements in Southeast Asia and exploring possible areas of future cooperation with the United States. In so doing they raised the specter of a united front of giant continental powers seeking to govern the world jointly in their own interests while still maintaining a certain level of confrontation and competition, if only to satisfy their respective domestic needs. It was in this context that Japan's newly installed prime minister, Tanaka Kakuei, responding to Peking's initiative, quickly normalized diplomatic relations with China, Japan's geographically natural trading partner, and dumped Taiwan, its erstwhile ally ever since the Korean War.

The change in Sino-American relations from confrontation to rapprochement, the normalization of Sino-Japanese diplomatic relations and the Japanese withdrawal of formal diplomatic recognition from Taiwan represented one side of the restructuring process. The other was the apparent easing of tension in South Korea's diplomatic relations with various communist countries and, most importantly, the start of talks with North

Korea on the problems of north-south reunification. It is difficult to believe that a regime which is committed, of necessity,
to reliance on U.S. and Japanese military and economic assistance and takes anti-communism as its only raison d'être can
strive seriously for national unification—the basic goal of every
nationalism. Yet it may well be that the current talks between
Seoul and P'yŏngyang are genuine and will lead, eventually, to
procedures and a timetable for national reunification. Or it may
be that P'yŏngyang intends at this stage to use the unification
issue to speed the departure of the U.S.-UN presence in South
Korea, weaken the loathsome Park dictatorship, and lighten the
oppression of Koreans in the south. There is also the possibility
that the ongoing conversations between Seoul and P'yŏngyang,
together with the recent signs of a quasi-rapprochement between
Japan and North Korea,[86] will serve merely to stabilize rather
than undermine regional integration.

One can, of course, never predict the future but this much
is certain: the United States shows no signs of reassessing its
role in Korea, though American policies since 1945 are more
responsible for creating and perpetuating the Korean tragedy
than any other single factor. Moreover, the start of north-south
talks has coincided with more repression in the south: imposition of martial law, outlawing of all opposition parties, dissolution of the National Assembly, rewriting of Park's own constitution in such a way as to strip the people of their few
remaining civil liberties while granting him permanent dictatorial powers, and even the harassment, intimidation, and in certain cases, kidnapping of Korean dissidents living abroad. The
Park regime, fearful of a violent upheaval which may yet overthrow it, has tightened its military and CIA control over every
aspect of life and thought in the south [87]—to the point where
it is now as isolated politically at home as it once was abroad.
Unification of the Korean people will surely be achieved someday, but probably not before this client regime goes the way of
its predecessor.

Notes

1. Frederick S. Dunn, *Peace-Making and the Settlement with Japan* (Princeton, Princeton University Press, 1963), p. 100.

2. Kim Hŭi-il, *Amerika teikokushugi no Chōsen shinryaku shi* [The history of American imperialism's aggression in Korea] (Tokyo, Seinen Shinsho 7, 1964), pp. 12–13.

3. William Pomeroy, *American Neo-Colonialism: Its Emergence in the Philippines and Asia* (New York, International Publishers Co., 1970), p. 14.

4. I am indebted to Frank Baldwin for this information from his Columbia University Ph.D. thesis.

5. C. I. Eugene Kim and Han-Kyo Kim, *Korea and the Politics of Imperialism, 1876–1910* (Berkeley and Los Angeles, University of California Press, 1967), pp. 137, 205.

6. See Joyce and Gabriel Kolko, *The Limits of Power: The World and United States Foreign Policy, 1945–1954* (New York, Harper and Row, 1972), pp. 277–99; and "Our Record in Korea—In the Light of the Increasing Hostility of the Korean People to our Military Government," *Amerasia*, No. 5 (November 1946).

7. Robert K. Sawyer, *Military Advisors in Korea: KMAG in Peace and War*, ed., Walter G. Hermes (Washington, D.C., U.S. Department of the Army, Office of the Chief of Military History, 1962), pp. 11, 13–14.

8. *Report to the President Submitted by Lieutenant-General Albert C. Wedemeyer, September 1947—Korea*, U.S. Government Printing Office (Washington, D.C., 1951), pp. 24–27.

9. John Gittings, "Touching the Tiger's Buttocks—Western Scholarship and the Cold War in Asia," in Roger Morgan, ed., *The Study of International Affairs* (London, Oxford University Press for Royal Institute of International Affairs, 1972), pp. 231–32.

10. Dunn, *Peace-Making and the Settlement with Japan*, p. 77.

11. Richard H. Mitchell, *The Korean Minority in Japan* (Berkeley and Los Angeles, University of California Press, 1967), pp. 102–3; David Conde, "The Korean Minority in Japan," *Far Eastern Survey*, February 26, 1947, pp. 41–45.

12. Rimu Bon, "Sengo Nitchō kankei shi I" [The history of postwar Japanese-Korean relations], in *Chōsen kenkyū* [Korean studies], No.

117 (August 1972), pp. 22–23: Rimu Bon may be the pseudonym of a Japanese scholar.

13. Rimu Bon, "Sengo Nitchō kankei shi II" [The history of postwar Japanese-Korean Relations II], *Chōsen kenyū,* No. 118 (September 1972), p. 26.

14. Noguchi Yūichirō, "Nikkan keizai 'kyōryoku' no kyokō" [The fiction of Japan-R.O.K. economic "cooperation"], pp. 138–41, in Saitō Takashi and Fujishima Udai, eds., *Nikkan mondai o kangaeru* [Considerations of Japan-Korea problems] (Tokyo, Taihei Shuppansha, 1965).

15. Kwan Bong Kim, *The Korea-Japan Treaty Crisis and the Instability of the Korean Political System* (New York, Praeger Publishers, 1971), p. 44.

16. Suzuki Masashi, *Sengo Nihon no shiteki bunseki* [Historical analysis of postwar Japan] (Tokyo, Aoki Shoten, 1969), pp. 116–17.

17. Rimu Bon, "Sengo Nitchō kankei shi I," p. 26.

18. James F. Schnabel, *United States Army in the Korean War—Policy and Direction: The First Year* (Washington, D.C., U.S. Department of the Army, Office of the Chief of Military History, 1972), p. 55.

19. *Ibid.,* p. 54.

20. *Ibid.,* p. 55.

21. See Russell Brines, "US Bases in Japan," *Nippon Times,* January 18, 1950, p. 1.

22. James A. Field, Jr., *History of United States Naval Operations: Korea* (Washington, D.C., U.S. Department of the Navy, 1962), p. 88.

23. *Ibid.,* p. 55.

24. Schnabel, *U.S. Army in the Korean War,* p. 59.

25. "Gendai Nihon sangyō hattatsu shi kenkyūkai," *Gendai Nihon sangyō hattatsu shi* [History of modern Japan's industrial development] Vol. II: Inoguchi Tosuke, ed., *Seikiyu* [Oil] (Tokyo, 1963), pp. 384–85.

26. *Nihon shihonshugi kōza—sengo Nihon no seiji to keizai* [Study series on Japanese capitalism—the politics and economy of postwar Japan], Vol. II, *Kōwa kara MSA e* [From Peace to MSA] (Tokyo, Iwanami Shoten, 1953), pp. 152–53, 229.

27. The key provisions of the SCAP memorandum to the Japanese government establishing the counterpart fund (SCAPIN 1988 of 1 April 1949) read as follows:

1. The Japanese Government will establish as of 1 April 1949 a special account in the Bank of Japan in the name of the

Japanese Government to be designated the U.S. Aid Counterpart Fund for Japanese Stabilization (hereinafter called the Fund) and will make deposits in Japanese Yen in this account in amounts commensurate with the dollar cost to the Government of the United States of American Aid (including any cost of processing, storing, transporting or other services incident thereto) furnished Japan by the United States.
2. The Supreme Commander for the Allied Powers will from time to time notify the Japanese Government of the dollar cost of the United States Aid and the Japanese Government will thereupon deposit in the Fund a commensurate amount of yen computed at a rate of exchange which will be indicated to the Japanese Government by the Supreme Commander.
3. The Japanese Government will be permitted to draw from the Fund only such amounts and only for such purposes as may be approved by the Supreme Commander.
4. The Japanese Government will be required to submit to the Supreme Commander separate and specific proposals for any desired use of the Fund.

In preparing these proposals the Japanese Government will take into account the imperative need for promoting and maintaining internal monetary and financial stability, for stimulating exports and for carrying out the other objectives set forth in the letter of 19 December 1948 from the Supreme Commander to the Prime Minister. . . .
5. . . . . proposals by the Japanese Government to advance Counterpart Funds for private and public investment programs will be considered in the light of achievement by the proposed recipients of specific programs of rationalization and economic stabilization.

SCAPIN 1988 is printed in Takaishi Suekichi, *Oboegaki shūsen zaisei shimatsu* [Notes on financial circumstances at the termination of the war], Vol. XII, *Beikoku no tai-Nishi enjo to mikaeri shikin* [U.S. assistance to Japan and the counterpart fund] (Tokyo: Okura Zaimu Kyōkai, 1971), pp. 584–85.

28. Takahashi Ryozo, "Bōei seisan keikaku no zenbō" [The entire picture of the Defense Production Plan] in *Chūō kōron* [Central review], April 1953, pp. 77–78.
29. On this point see Yamada Hiroshi, "Chōsen sensō zenshi o meguru jakkan no shomondai—toku ni Amerika no Ajia seisaku to

no kanren ni oite" [Some problems in the pre-history of the Korean War, particularly in connection with America's Asian policy] in *Rekishigaku kenkyū*, No. 338 (July 1968), pp. 21–31.

30. Kanzaki Kiyoshi, "Kichi shūhen—Yokosuka ni kansuru danpenteki nōto" [Base outskirts—fragmentary notes on Yokosuka], in *Shisō* [Thought], No. 348 (June 1953), pp. 135–36. A special edition on "The Occupation and Japan."

31. I. F. Stone, *The Hidden History of the Korean War* (New York, Monthly Review Press, 1970 paper edition), p. 16.

32. See Jon Halliday, *Three Articles on the Korean Revolution 1945–1953*, p. 17. Stimulating essays calling for a rethinking of the meaning of the Korean War, brought together in a single pamphlet by The Association for Radical East Asian Studies, 6 Endsleigh Street, 3rd Floor, London W.C. 1, United Kingdom.

33. Suzuki, *Sengo Nihon*, p. 119; for a convenient chronology of events in Japan at this time see Toyama Shigeki, ed., *Shiryō sengo nijū nen shi* [Historical materials on twenty years of postwar history], *Nempyō* (Chronology), Vol. 6 (Tokyo: Nihon Hyōronsha, 1967), pp 226–27.

34. Robert Murphy, *Diplomat Among Warriors* (New York, Doubleday and Company, 1964), pp. 347–48.

35. Rimu Bon, "Sengo Nitchō kankei shi II," pp. 32–33.

36. James A. Huston, "Korea and Logistics," *Military Review*, February 1957, pp. 19, 25.

37. In 1952 at the height of the Korean War, the United States had unrestricted use of 1,212 "military installations" in Japan proper. These consisted of 579 military barracks, 54 housing complexes, 69 air bases, 37 port facilities, 83 practice ranges, 42 factories, 140 warehouses, 26 medical facilities, 129 communications facilities and 53 "other facilities." In addition, the U.S. military command barred Japanese fishermen from hundreds of miles of specially designated naval and air force gunnery target ranges in the rich fishing waters surrounding Japan (*Kōwa kara MSA e*, p. 157). A more up-to-date American study, however, mentions a figure of 2,500 U.S. "military installations" in Japan in 1952 (*Global Defense—U.S. Military Commitments Abroad*, A Publication of Congressional Quarterly Service, September 1969, p. 34).

The whole question of US bases and troops in Japan during the Korean War deserves an independent study.

38. Asahi jānaru, ed., *Showa shi no shunkan* [Moments of Showa history] (Tokyo, Asahi Shimbunsha, 1966), Vol. 2, p. 273.

39. Quoted in Takamure Itsue, *Josei no rekishi II* [The history of

224   HERBERT P. BIX

women II], in *Takamure Itsue zenshū* [The collected works of Takamure Itsue] (Tokyo, Rironsha, 1966), Vol. 5, pp. 978–79.
40. Protests by Yokosuka housewives soon stopped the Chamber
of Commerce from disseminating the song.
   I am indebted to Professor Edward Cranston of Harvard University for this translation.

Tamaran Bushi

1. Jyapan, Yokosuka *wandafuru*
   Biya mo garu mo *berinaisu*
   Cheri saiteru ano oka ni
   Suito homu o tsukuritai
   Tamaran tamaran

2. Mukasha don to utsu iki no machi
   Ima jya nana iro niji no machi
   Iki na *haiya* no yukikaeri
   Tsuki no deru yo ni *kisu* no ame
   Tamaran tamaran

3. Yama no ue kara umi mireba
   Defune irefune koi no fune
   Nami ni yurarete yurayura to
   Washi mo noritaya ano fune ni
   Tamaran tamaran

41. Enatsu Michiho, *Kokusai shihonsen to Nihon* [The warfare of
international capital and Japan] (Tokyo, Iwanami Shinsho, No. 731,
1971), p. 150.
42. Arisawa Hiromi and Inaba Shūzō, ed., *Shiryō sengo nijū nen
shi* [Historical materials on twenty years of postwar history], Vol. 2,
Keizai [Economy] (Tokyo, Nihon Hyōronsha, 1966), p. 160.
43. Nakahara Tone, "Tokuju no sannenkan—tsunagareru Nihon
keizai" [Three years of special procurements and their connection
with Japan's economy], in *Sekai* [World] No. 90 (June 1953), pp.
141–43; Yamada Hiroshi, *Sengo Amerika no sekai seisaku to Nihon*
[Postwar American world policy and Japan] (Kyoto, Hōritsu Bun-
kasha, 1967), p. 140.
44. Martin E. Weinstein, *Japan's Postwar Defense Policy, 1947–
1968* (New York and London, Columbia University Press, 1971),
p. 52.
45. Ōe Shinobu, *Nihon gendai shi ni okeru kyōkasho saiban* [The
textbook trial in contemporary Japanese history] (Tokyo, Aoki Shoten, 1971), p. 11.

46. Truman to MacArthur, January 13, 1951, quoted in Robert Leckie, *Conflict, the History of the Korean War 1950–1953* (New York, G. P. Putnam's Sons, 1962), p. 251; also see Jon Halliday's comments on U.S. war aims, *Three Articles on the Korean Revolution*, pp. 58, (v), n. 59.

47. *New York Times,* October 3, 1952, p. 16.

48. *New York Times,* October 19, 1952, p. 12.

49. Although the cheapness of the R.O.K. soldier is a constant Pentagon theme from at least 1953 onward, the quoted words are those of General Lemnitzer, chairman of the Joint Chiefs of Staff, in an exchange with Senator J. William Fulbright during the March 23, 1960 Senate Foreign Relations Committee hearings on the U.S. defense program in South Korea.

THE CHAIRMAN [Fulbright] I am informed that we supply about 110 per cent of the total defense costs of Korea. In other words, we supply more than the Korean Government does.

GENERAL LEMNITZER Well in the case of Korea . . . you have a special situation of a suspended war. The security of the Republic of Korea is being provided primarily by a rather large number of [R.O.K.] divisions, 18 to be exact. . . . I believe that the record will show beyond any doubt that we do get more soldiers along the Demilitarized Zone in Korea per dollar than we are able to get in any other way. . . . we get more return per dollar in defense of Korea and also in the defense of the United States in that part of the world than we do probably in other areas where greater emphasis is being placed on more modern and more expensive types of weapons and equipment.

THE CHAIRMAN You think that in spite of the fact that in Europe they themselves pay 92 per cent of the cost and we only pay 8 per cent, whereas in Korea we pay 110 per cent; is that right?

GENERAL LEMNITZER In Korea we have . . . 18 divisions— 18 full-strength divisions—along that 155 mile front, and I don't know of any area where we get a comparable return militarywise for the equivalent amount of money (*S. 3058* [The Military Security Act of 1960], Hearings Before the Committee on Foreign Relations, U.S. Senate, Eighty-sixth Congress, Second Session, 1960, pp. 125–26).

50. See General O'Daniel's "Report of U.S. Joint Military Mission to Indochina," July 14, 1953, in *U.S. Vietnam Relations 1945–67,* U.S. Department of Defense (Washington, D.C., 1971), Book 9 of 12, pp. 69–106.

51. See Major General Marquat's testimony on the Mutual Security Act of 1954 in *Hearings Before the Committee of Foreign Affairs,* U.S. House of Representatives, Eighty-third Congress, Second Session, April 5–June 8, 1954, pp. 453–55. In explaining the purposes of the postwar U.S. aid program for South Korea, Marquat stressed that its intent was to

> . . . strengthen the [R.O.K.] economy to permit it to assume a greater portion of the load of maintaining both its military and economic requirements. The new program is not just to prevent disease and unrest, I repeat, but an economic buildup which will enable them to develop gross national product. . . . The second thing it does . . . is to check inflation. Now . . . as our input of funds into the support of the defense of Korea increases, we will ultimately have to pay for the maintenance of our forces that are there . . . and we will also have annual costs of maintaining our troops in the Korean economy.
>
> So, as the inflation is checked, the value of our dollar increases and we get more for our dollar . . . it is difficult to separate the economic and the military because the whole thing is really a defense-support program plus, of course, what we do recognize as a growing inflation which must be met in the interests of our dollar.

52. In his memoirs, General Maxwell D. Taylor, the Eighth Army commander from January 1953 to mid-1954, gave the general terms of the deal whereby the United States secured Rhee's support for the armistice:

> In the end Rhee compromised, and on July 12 he gave [Walter S.] Robertson written assurance that he would not obstruct the implementation of the terms of the armistice. . . . In exchange, he received a number of important concessions from us: the promise of a bilateral security pact, of long-term economic aid, and of continued support for the twenty division program; also, an understanding that the United States and South Korea would withdraw from the postarmistice political conference after ninety days if no substantial progress

had been made by that time (Maxwell D. Taylor, *Swords and Plowshares* [New York, W. W. Norton and Co., 1972], p. 147). Fifteen pages earlier, however, Taylor stated that the R.O.K. army had reached twenty divisions by 1953.

53. Kim Hŭi-il, *Amerika Chōsen shinryaku shi* [History of America's aggresion against Korea] (Tokyo, Yūzanka Shuppan Kabushiki Kaisha, 1972), p. 356. Tranlated from Korean by the Translation Group, Historical Division of the Korean Scientists Association in Japan; also see Kim Byong-sik, *Gendai teikokushugi to Minami Chōsen* [Contemporary imperialism and South Korea] (Tokyo, Miraisha, 1972), pp. 343–45.

The military build-up in South Korea immediately following the Korean armistice should be considered in the context of the Eisenhower regime's Indochina policy at the time of the Geneva Conference which ended the French (U.S.-supported) Indochina War. What strikes one immediately, of course, is the coincidence between the expansion of the R.O.K. military in violation of the Korean Armistice Agreement, and the start of direct U.S. military intervention in Indochina, in violation of the Geneva Accords. Just as the Korean Armistice Agreement—a fragile document signed only by the military representatives of the Chinese and "UN" sides, with Rhee refusing to participate—was nevertheless a "legal" obstacle to U.S. plans for perpetuating Korea's partition and turning the south into a permanent anti-communist buffer state, so also the election and military demarcation provisions of the Geneva Accords were "legal" obstacles to U.S. plans for reproducing a Korea-type partition in Vietnam. Yet in both cases America's leaders regarded their own foreign policy objectives as higher than any international agreements and quickly resorted to tactics of sabotage and reinterpretation to nullify both.

54. *American Foreign Policy 1950–1955: Basic Documents,* Vol. 2, Publication 6446, General Foreign Policy Series 117, U.S. Department of State (Washington, D.C., 1957), pp. 2734–36.

55. These were articles four and two (sub-paragraph 13d). The former called for "the convening of a political conference of a higher level of both sides . . . to settle through negotiation the question of the withdrawal of all foreign forces from Korea [and] the peaceful settlement of the Korean question, etc." It was the first item of the armistice agreement that U.S. policy demanded be reinterpreted. When the Geneva Conference convened on April 26, 1954, ostensibly for the purpose of discussing Korea, the United

States quickly demonstrated its disinterest in seeing genuine peace return to either Korea or Indochina. It refused permission for neutral nations to participate in the Korean talks as voting members; it insisted, contrary to fact, that the Soviet Union had been a belligerent and hence could not participate as a neutral; and it rejected the principle that all political conference decisions required mutual agreement by both sides to the armistice. In this way, by insisting that individual countries that disagreed with conference decisions need not be bound by them, Eisenhower and Dulles sought to give Syngman Rhee a veto over any Korean political conference. Lastly, the United States stubbornly insisted that Korean unification could occur only through peninsula-wide elections supervised by the UN— the same organization that legitimized the fraudulent elections of May 1948, that branded North Korea an aggressor without a hearing, that covered the U.S. war of aggression with its own mantle of internationalism and had even attempted to destroy the north.

Interesting material on the political conference can be found in Wilfred G. Burchett, *Again Korea* (New York, International Publishers Co., 1968), p. 137; *Hearings Before a Subcommittee of the U.S. Senate*, Eighty-fifth Congress, First Session, *Committee on Foreign Relations, Part II*, January 9–10, 1957, p. 989; Kim, *Amerika teikokushugi no Chōsen shinryaku shi*, pp. 179–80, 184–85.

56. On the U.S.-R.O.K. side the first step in formally abrogating 13d came as early as December 25, 1954, when the United States curtailed operations of the Neutral Nations Inspection Teams at Seoul airport, Kunsan and Kangnung. The illegal R.O.K. military build-up was by then under way and the United States had begun to improve its airbase facilities at Masan, Taegu, Kimp'o, P'yŏngt'aek and Kunsan, and its naval facilities at Chinhae, Pusan and P'ohang. Construction of the giant U.S. air base on Cheju island, known today as the second Okinawa, began in 1955. And in May–June 1956 the U.S. command stopped the operations of the Inspection Teams entirely throughout South Korea (*Nippon Times*, December 26, 1954, 1; Kim Hŭi-il, *Amerika Chōsen shinryaku shi*, pp. 357–58). Violations of the armistice agreement on the North Korean side during the same period, according to American officials, took the form of bringing in new model armaments and jet fighters. See *U.S. News and World Report*, July 5, 1957.

57. The agreement with Taiwan is mentioned in G. King and C. MacDougall, "Asia and the Far East," in G. Barraclough, ed. *Survey of International Affairs 1956–1958* (London, Oxford University Press, 1962), p. 339.

The placing of atomic weapons in South Korea was long hinted at by Dulles and finally conceded in Congressional testimony on February 3, 1958, by Nathan F. Twining, chairman of the Joint Chiefs of Staff:

SENATOR WILEY What is the situation in Korea?
GENERAL TWINING About status quo. It is pretty quiet over there. We still have our same forces. We are, you know, putting atomic weapons in Korea ("Review of Foreign Policy 1958," in *Foreign Policy,* Hearings Before the Committee on Foreign Relations, U.S. Senate, Eighty-fifth Congress, Second Session. *Part I,* February 3, 1958, p. 15.

58. Following the conclusion of the Korean War, U.S. troop strength in Japan decreased as follows:

Year	Total	Army	Navy (including Marines)	Air Force
1953	250,000			
1954	210,000			
1955	150,000			
1956	117,000			
1957	77,000	17,000	20,000	40,000
1958	65,000	10,000	18,000	37,000
1959	58,000	6,000	17,000	35,000
1960	46,000	5,000	14,000	27,000
1961 (Aug.)	45,000	6,000	14,000	25,000
1969 (Feb.)	40,700	9,400	12,000	19,300

Source: Fujii Haruo, *Jieitai—kono senryoku* [The Self Defense Forces—this fighting power] (Tokyo, San Ichi Shobō, 1970), p. 132.

59. *Ibid.,* p. 130. The yen-dollar exchange rate at the time was 360:1.
60. In *Nuclear Weapons and Foreign Policy,* first published in June 1957, Kissinger argued against a cost-conscious approach to "national security policies"—in other words, the "New Look"—and for development of tactical forces for waging limited war. In 1958 his book received the Woodrow Wilson Award from the American Political Science Association.
Another early advocate of "limited war" was Townsend Hoopes.

In a 1958 *Foreign Affairs* article Hoopes argued that overseas bases were needed in order to support the "fire brigades" that would soon be formed to wage "limited war" far from America's shores. In his view, the two essential requirements were:

> . . . our possession of highly mobile, stringently practiced "fire brigades" capable of effective limited action with appropriate weapons, and . . . the will to defend our interests and those of our friends through the application of military force for rational and restricted purposes. . . . The situations most likely to confront us on the boundaries of Eurasia will call for modern ground forces supported by tactical air and naval forces and employing primarily what are called "conventional" weapons. . . .
>
> Only if we face up squarely to the problem of limited war, show a willingness to enter upon "joint" military planning with our non-European allies and declare ourselves ready to commit appropriate forces to local and limited defense actions are we likely to hold together our alliances in Asia and the Middle East. Conversely, only if we retain forward positions of advantage overseas will we be able to maintain a valid capability for military action on the boundaries of Eurasia and thus to hold a favorable local power balance in selected areas ("Overseas Bases in American Strategy," *Foreign Affairs,* Vol. 37, No. 1 [October 1958], pp. 78, 82).

61. Hayashi Katsuya, "Nikkan jōyaku no gunjiteki kikensei" [The military dangers of the Japan-Korea treaty] in Saitō and Fujishima, *Nikkan mondai o kangaeru,* p. 175.

62. "Non-grant" assistance consisted of two types: one involving the purchase of a finished weapon at a fixed price, as in the case of the Sidewinder missile for the F-104J, the other type an arrangement whereby the United States would furnish Japan parts of a complex weapons system and then sell Japan the technical licensing rights to "home-produce" the remainder of the system. Total "non-grant" military assistance contracts jumped from 2.5 billion yen in 1958 to over 7 billion in 1959 (Shishido Fumitake, "Nihon no kokubō ryoku—sono senryoku to keizaiteki haikei" [Japan's national defense power—its fighting power and economic background], a special research report in *Chūō kōron,* July 1960, p. 243).

63. Matsumoto Hirokazu, *Gekidō suru Kankoku* [Agitated South Korea] (Tokyo, Iwanami Shinsho, 1963), p. 69.

64. For an interesting study of the World Bank, see *World Bank Report,* distributed by the International Information Centre, Grønnegade 37, DK-1107, Copenhagen K, Denmark.

65. Yamada, *Sengo Amerika,* p. 138.

66. Fujishima Udai, "Namboku Chōsen tōitsu to gaibu seiryoku" [North-South Korean unification and outside forces], in *Ajia* [Asia], October 1972, p. 53.

67. George R. Packard III, *Protest in Tokyo: The Security Treaty Crisis of 1960* (Princeton, Princeton University Press, 1966), Appendix D, p. 369. This academic study avoids throwing any light whatsoever on the political aspects of the security treaty itself. The appendixes, however, are useful.

68. Yamada, *Sengo Amerika,* p. 359.

69. Fujii, *Jieitai,* pp. 83–84. For the text of the Three Arrows Study and other important secret documents relating to the Self Defense Forces, also seen by the same author, *Nihon no kokka kimitsu* [Japan's state secrets] (Tokyo, Gendai Hyōronsha, 1972).

70. Quoted in Fujii, *Jieitai,* p. 73.

71. Quoted in Fujiwara Akira, "Ni-Kan-Bei no gunji taisei to Nikkan jōyaku" [The Japan-South Korea-U.S. military system and the Japan-South Korea treaty], in Saitō and Fujishima, *Nikkan mondai o kangaeru,* p. 157.

72. *Ibid.,* p. 157.

73. *Washington Post,* July 1, 1971; Morton Abramowitz, "Moving the Glacier: The Two Koreas and the Powers," *Adelphi Papers,* No. 80 (London International Institute for Strategic Studies, 1971), p. 4.

74. Sasaki Ryūji, "Ajia ni okeru shinshokuminshugi no aratana kyokumen ni tsuite—Betonamu e no tairyō hahei igo no Minami Chōsen shihai taisei no henka o chūshin ni" [On the new phase of neocolonialism in Asia—centering on the changes in South Korea's control structure after its large-scale troop dispatch to Vietnam] in *Rekishigaku kenkyū,* No. 363 (August 1970), pp. 9–10.

75. *United States Security Agreements and Commitments Abroad,* Hearings Before the Committee on U.S. Security Agreements and Commitments Abroad of the Committee on Foreign Relations, U.S. Senate, Ninety-first Congress, Second Session, *Part 6* (February 24–26, 1970), p. 1750.

76. For a discussion of the meaning of Japan's fourth Defense Build-Up program, see the author's essay, "Japan: The Roots of Militarism," in Mark Selden, ed., *Remaking Asia: Essays on the American Uses of Power* (New York: Pantheon Books, 1974).

77. *New York Times,* October 3, 1971, p. 8.
78. Mura Tsuneo, *Kankoku gunsei no keifu—Ri Shō-ban kara Boku Sei-ke e* [The genealogy of the R.O.K. Military Government —from Syngman Rhee to Park Chung Hee] (Tokyo, Miraisha, 1966), p. 235.
79. Kim, *The Korea-Japan Treaty Crisis,* p. 87.
80. On Japan's economic expansion in South Korea after 1965, see the chapter by Sakurai Hiroshi in Satō Katsumi, Kajimura Hideki, and Sakurai Hiroshi, *Chōsen tōitsu e no taidō* [The quickening of Korean unification] (Tokyo, Sanseidō, 1971).
81. Kino Junzō, "Japan-Korea Economic Cooperation—The Actual Condition of Neo-Colonialism," in *Chūgoku kenkyū geppō* [China Research Report], August 1970, p. 7.
82. *Chūō Nippo* [Central daily news], April 9, 1970.
83. *International Labour Organization—Yearbook of Labour Statistics 1970* (ILO Office, Geneva, 1970), p. 563.

However, according to a household budget survey conducted by the government statistics bureau, the average monthly salary of Japanese wage earners in manufacturing in fiscal 1970 was 93,498 yen (*The Oriental Economist,* January 1971, p. 13).
84. Kino, "Japan-Korea Economic Cooperation," pp. 3–6. The author quotes extensively from the Yatsugi report.
85. Kim, *The Korean-Japan Treaty Crisis,* p. 88.
86. One of the more significant may have been the establishment in Tokyo on November 16, 1972 of a "League of Elected Officials to Promote Friendship Between Japan and North Korea." Among its members are Liberal Democratic party dietmen and the governor of Tokyo, Minobe Ryōkichi.
87. Although North Korea reportedly reduced its defense spending for 1972 by almost half, from 30 to 17 per cent, South Korean defense spending remained unchanged: in the 1973 R.O.K. budget defense expenditures will account for 28 percent of the total (Kiyoshi Takase, "Shakaishugi Chōsen keizai no ronri to genjitsu" [The theory and reality of the socialist economy of the Democratic People's Republic of Korea], in *Ajia keizai* [Asian economy], Vol. 13, No. 8, August 1972), p. 18; *Ashai shimbun,* December 3, 1972, p. 2.

Capitalism in South Korea

Gerhard Breidenstein

1. INTRODUCTION

This article attempts an overall interpretation of the economic, social, and political situation of the Republic of Korea (R.O.K.). I have tried to establish a comprehensive analytic framework for other more detailed and specialized studies of South Korean society. The broad scope of this essay does not permit detailed examination of all aspects of South Korea. Other essays in this collection will provide the historical background for this two-dimensional photograph and throw some light on the question of *why* capitalism became the dominant system in the R.O.K.

The term capitalism is used for this interpretation. Not all aspects of South Korean society can be related to capitalism; there are still elements of a preindustrial culture. But it is the intention of this essay to show that South Korea can be understood properly only as a capitalistic country.

A definition of the term capitalism as used in this article is not provided at the outset. An understanding should emerge from the article itself and will be clarified in the concluding section. For some readers the use of this term might appear too apologetic. But one should keep in mind that capitalism was, for too long a time by too many (liberals), identified with "free world goals" and its value taken for granted. Except for Marxist literature, capitalism was hardly more than a slogan; serious efforts are necessary to reestablish its analytic and critical implications.

This is particularly true for the literature on the so-called underdeveloped or developing countries. The unwary reader easily gets the impression that "the development" of Third

World nations is a universal process where the food, population, education, industrialization, and urbanization problems that have to be solved are more or less the same everywhere and their solution is basically a question of investment strategies, "social change," and "modernization."

However, there are at least three major groups of countries which follow very different, in fact opposing, strategies of development. There are communist-led developing countries, such as the People's Republic of China, the Democratic People's Republic of Korea (D.P.R.K.), the Democratic Republic of Vietnam, and Cuba, for whom building socialism is the only humane way of development. There are a variety of non-communist developing countries that also chose socialism as their basic program but built it with different political methods. Some examples are Sri Lanka, Burma, Tanzania, most of the Arab nations, Chile, and Peru. Finally, there are developing countries with a clearly capitalist pattern, such as Taiwan, the Philippines, Brazil and most Latin American nations, Kenya, the Ivory Coast, Turkey or Greece. These three main types of developing countries, to say nothing of the many intermediate or mixed types (such as India), suggest that the term developing country must be modified by its *type,* that is, communist-socialist, socialist, or capitalist.

The following analysis of "developing" South Korea is intended as a case study of capitalist development. Therefore, general and theoretical comments are interspersed with the data on South Korea. By this blend, which reflects the reality of R.O.K. "development," we may reach a deeper understanding of both South Korea and capitalism.

2. GNP GROWTH AND SECTORAL DEVELOPMENT

The most frequently mentioned economic data on the Republic of Korea are the impressive, almost unbelievable, growth rates of the Gross National Product (GNP) over the last decade and particularly the last five years: 1966: 13.4 percent; 1967: 8.9 percent; 1968: 13.3 percent; 1969: 15.9 percent; 1970: 9.7 percent; 1971: 10.2 percent. The 1962–71 average was 10 percent.[1] Per capita income also increased remarkably: 1966: $131; 1971: $253. These figures have probably been exaggerated to support the South Korean success story, "The Miracle of the River Han"; the official inflation rates considered in these growth data are certainly too low.

But the statistics are not pure fantasy. International creditors watch the R.O.K. economy carefully and could not be deceived completely. There can be no doubt that the economy did expand rapidly, making South Korea one of the most successful developing countries—as long as high GNP growth is taken as a criterion for development success. This usually unquestioned presupposition needs serious scrutiny, as does the human price paid for this growth and the social consequences resulting from it. Such questions will be raised in this article. We begin by examining the nature of this remarkable economic growth.

The growth rates by industrial sectors show an unbalanced development. The average GNP growth rate for 1962–69 was 9.9 percent. During this period agriculture and fishery grew by an annual average of 4.3 percent, mining and manufacturing by 17.9 percent, and social overhead and services by 11.4 percent. Thus the industrial structure changed drastically from 1962 to 1969: the agricultural sector's share of GNP declined from 39.7 percent to 28.4 percent, while the manufacturing industries' share rose from 15.0 percent to 24.6 percent.[2] Of course, this shift from agricultural to manufacturing production is a necessary step in the process of modernization. The creation of new and basic industries, such as fertilizer plants, oil refineries, cement factories and power plants, which were successfully established in South Korea during the First Five-Year Plan (FFYP) (1962–66) and the Second Five-Year Plan (SFYP) (1967–71), and the infrastructure investments in roads, railways, water and electricity supply, communication, etc., are inevitable features of development in any economic system.

However, the speed and the mode of this change in the industrial structure of countries varies enormously, as do the social implications. In South Korea, as in many other developing countries, the neglect of agriculture has led to rural poverty, mass migration to the cities, and the growth of urban slums. We will discuss below whether these are typical phenomena of a capitalist development pattern.

Another significant phenomenon of South Korea's economic development is the rapid expansion of consumption and service industries, such as textile and clothing, electronics, automobiles, pharmaceuticals, plastic utensils, banking, insurance, and tourism. Such industries may not have top priority in development theory, but for private investors they are decidedly more attractive than investment in agriculture, education, or health care.

Finally, there is a striking imbalance in the geographical distribution of economic development. In 1969, 80 percent of all new firms were established in Seoul. Besides the Seoul-Inch'ŏn-Suwŏn area, there is only one other region of major industrial investment: the cities of Masan, Pusan, and Ulsan on the southeast coast. These port cities are the closest to Japan. Furthermore, they are in President Park's home area and favored in economic development in return for strong electoral support.

The economic reason for the high concentration of investment in two urban-industrial areas is obvious. Private investment in rural areas is not profitable, in spite of tax favors promised by the government for such investments. The infrastructure outside the big cities is not sufficiently developed, and the supply of cheap labor in rural areas is not as concentrated and exploitable as in the urban slums.

3. INVESTMENTS AND THEIR SOURCES

If then private capital prefers investment in manufacturing and service industries and in the existing industrial centers, could not the government balance this out through its public investments? The government in a capitalist system does not have much investment funds to allocate. Only one-fourth of South Korea's annual total investments are public investments, while three-quarters stem from private sources.[3] This proportion of public and private in South Korea's capital formation reflects partly the nature and influence of foreign capital coming into South Korea. This "foreign saving" accounts for at least half of South Korea's gross domestic investments (see note 10). By the end of 1970, 29 percent of the foreign capital was public loans,[4] while the remaining 71 percent consisted of mainly commercial loans and some direct private investment (7 percent).[5]

Commercial foreign loans as well as private investments, both national and foreign, go where "the business is": into the manufacturing industries, particularly the labor-intensive ones where the investor can profit most from low wages and obtain a return on his investment within a relatively short period.[6] The R.O.K. used part of its investment funds plus foreign capital to establish urgently needed key industries (fertilizer, oil, petro-chemicals, iron and steel). Some government investment went into social overhead (education, health, housing). However, most of the public investments, as well as the majority of the public foreign loans, were used for infrastructure. Since private investors do not care about infrastructure but expect it to be provided as a precondition for their investments, public savings have to be used mainly in this sector.[7]

In summary, most of the available capital was invested by private, profit-oriented investors. This predominance of private national and foreign investment (70–80 percent of total investments) has led to a one-sided expansion of the profitable secondary industries. On the other hand, investments with no profit—infrastructure—or low profit—agriculture—or high capital requirements—basic industries—necessarily have been neglected in South Korea.

Thus in the cities of South Korea one can buy almost anything a consumer dreams of (or advertisements make him dream of). Urban middle-class people spend their money on clothes, shoes, handbags, neckties, electrical appliances, fancy food, and beer. At the same time, there are not enough schools, hospitals, public transportation, roads, drinking water, and electricity. This is particularly so in the rural areas where half of the population still lives. This is certainly not rational development! We notice a basic contradiction between the necessities of development and the internal dynamics of capitalism.

Consumption expenditures in South Korea, both private and public, are very high.[8] Accordingly, the national saving rate is very low; it averaged 11.3 percent of GNP in the years 1964–69.[9] Therefore, foreign capital had to be induced to finance those investments necessary for desired growth. As mentioned above, one-half of the annual total investment, according to official figures, is being paid with foreign capital.[10] In reality, certainly more than half of South Korea's investments are foreign financed, openly or hidden, directly or indirectly. By the end of 1970 more than $3 billion had been introduced into the R.O.K. (since 1959 and excluding grant-type aid), of which $2.5 billion stood as foreign debts.[11] Since most of this foreign capital had come as short-term, high-interest commercial loans,[12] debt servicing has become an ever increasing burden for the R.O.K.[13] Also, this heavy inflow of foreign capital (as far as it increases the money-supply) is one of the causes of South Korea's permanent high inflation which, according to conservative government figures, runs at more than 10 percent annually.

Direct foreign investment has been surprisingly low; only $225 million by the end of 1970.[14] In spite of attractive tax exemptions [15] and other financial favors granted by the government, an extremely low wage level,[16] and special "protection" of companies with foreign capital against labor disputes (see note 81), the investment climate was not considered attractive. Excessive bureaucratic red tape and the military tensions on the peninsula deterred foreign investors. The situation, however, is changing. A desire to attract more foreign investors was certainly one of the motives behind South Korea's surprising response in July 1972 to North Korea's longstanding offers of détente.

In 1971, 58 percent of all foreign investment was American and 31 percent was Japanese. But this pattern, too, is changing and Japanese capital soon will take the lead.[17] In February 1970 a ban on 100 percent Japanese equity ownership was lifted. In the same year a Free Trade Zone was opened in the port city of Masan that proved particularly attractive to Japanese investors. Furthermore, investment projects which meet public resistance in Japan because of their pollution effects are welcome in the R.O.K.[18] Some big Japanese concerns turned away from investment plans in South Korea following Chou Enlai's declaration of Four Principles on Trade, one of which discriminates against firms investing in South Korea. But there are many other ways to gain influence and control: investment through Korean residents in Japan, "Korean" companies actually owned by Japanese, license and supply contracts, and open and hidden loans.[19] The Japanese grip on the South Korean economy is strong and more pervasive than it appears.

Foreign capital poses a perhaps mortal contradiction for the R.O.K. government. Many foreign investors will not put money into South Korea unless they are allowed to produce not only for export but also for the domestic market. If the government permits entry into the local economy, Korean firms will almost certainly be destroyed by their stronger foreign competitors. Can the South Korean regime afford to lose the support of frustrated Korean capitalists? Or should we rather ask: how long will it take until Japanese, American, European, and multinational corporations have swallowed up Korean capital and made South Korea their market and the R.O.K. government their instrument?

Because South Korea's industrialization is in an early stage, it is quite easy, capital provided, to control the market of a certain product and dictate profitable prices. The markets for many important products are monopolized by one, two, or a handful of manufacturers, quite a few of them foreign.[20] There is no military industry yet, but it is a potential area for foreign expansion and control. In 1971 construction of an M-16 automatic rifle plant was begun with U.S. assistance. It is obvious that for military supplies, as well as for most other markets, there are many favorable opportunities for expanded American and Japanese investment.

A crucial investment resource for South Korea has been the grant-type economic aid which South Korea has always received. Under various programs, such as the United Nations Korean Reconstruction Agency (UNKRA), U.S. Public Law 480, and the Agency for International Development (AID), South Korea has received approximately $4.5 billion in grant aid from the United States since 1945.[21] Some of this aid was in the form of agricultural products and other commodities, but much was given as Supporting or Stabilization Assistance (SA), that is, as a direct financial contribution to the South Korean budget. In some years (1953, 1956–58) half of the government's revenues, in other years a third or more, were pumped in from the United States.[22] Since 1966 this grant aid support has been gradually phased out and replaced by loan aid. Except for smaller amounts earmarked for technical assistance, grant-type aid ended in 1970.

There is probably no way of determining how much of this money and commodity values was actually used for development investments. In any case, these funds meant tremendous additional resources for the R.O.K. government and the South Korean economy. The same is true for the $3 billion military assistance given to South Korea.[23] Though spent in military consumption and to a great degree for purchases in the United States, this money freed R.O.K. resources. Finally, the South Korean economy received an estimated $2 billion from the "UN" Forces in Korea (to 1970) including some of the receipts the R.O.K. got for her troops in Vietnam.[24]

In summary, $3 billion in loans and investments, $4.5 billion as grant aid, $3 billion in military assistance, and $2 billion from U.S. troops in Korea; altogether $12.5 billion had been poured into South Korea by 1970. Considering the fact that in 1969 gross investment in South Korea was about $2 billion [25] one can realize the tremendous size of this external support. Or to put it more bluntly: these figures give some idea of how much the Republic of Korea is a product of U.S. "investment" since 1945, with increasing Japanese help since 1965. It should be noted that most of this "aid" was given under the condition that it be used for purchases in the United States or Japan respectively. One wonders who was aided in the end.

4. FOREIGN TRADE

South Korea, unlike most other less-developed countries, is poor in raw materials. The R.O.K. must import some of the basic raw materials for industrialization, such as iron and steel, good coal, and petroleum. Approximately 12 percent of all imports in 1969 were such raw materials. Like most other developing countries, South Korea has a tremendous need to import capital goods—that is, machines, transport equipment, instruments (1969: approximately 36 percent of imports). Finally, South Korea has a great and increasing need to import foodstuffs, mainly wheat and rice (1969: approximately 17 percent of imports). The remaining 35 percent were imports of other raw materials and manufactured goods less necessary for industrialization.[26]

To pay for these imports South Korea had to develop her originally very weak exports. This was achieved with striking quantitative success: in 1960 exports totaled only $33 million; in 1968 they rose to $455 million; in 1969 to $622 million; and in 1970 to $835 million.[27] Exports expanded by about 40 percent annually. However, this success was mainly achieved with manufactured goods that required imported raw materials.

For example, plywood, the most important single export item (1969: 13 percent of all exports) is made entirely from imported lumber. Textiles, clothes, shoes, and wigs (47.5 percent of 1969 exports) are almost completely made from imported wool, cotton, and synthetic materials. Furthermore, to produce export quality products, advanced machinery had to be imported. Thus, Korea's exports are highly import-inducing [28] and have a very low and decreasing foreign exchange earning rate, 51.5 percent in 1970.[29] (An export worth $100 results, because of previous expenses for imports, in net foreign exchange earnings of $51.) No wonder that with rising exports, imports grew also: 1968: $1.468 billion; 1969: $1.823 billion; 1970: $1.984 billion. The gap between imports and exports was closing very slowly; in 1970 imports were still more than double exports. The balance of payments deficit was covered with loans and a diminishing surplus in invisible trade from goods and services supplied to U.S. troops in South Korea and R.O.K. troops in Vietnam. South Korea's manufactured exports—about 80 percent of all commodity exports—face strong competition. This is particularly true in their main market, the United States, which has imposed special import restrictions since 1971. This raises serious doubts about the R.O.K. export policy. Finally, it must be noted that South Korea's manufactured goods are competitive only as long as her workers' wages remain extremely low.

An alternative strategy would be to emphasize import substitution (for food, machinery, semi-processed material) and the export of raw and processed agricultural and fishery products, such as fish, oysters, seaweed, tobacco, ginseng, raw silk, mushrooms, and fruits. These have been relatively successful export items without government support. Agricultural and fishery exports have a very high foreign exchange earning rate (100 percent and 88 percent respectively),[30] so that with only one-half of the manufactured goods' export volume they would net the same amount of foreign currency.[31]

Since such exports could directly benefit South Korean farmers and fishermen and would stimulate decentralized small and medium-sized processing industries, one wonders why the R.O.K. government does not resolutely promote these exports rather than those of manufactured goods which increase imports in a vicious circle. One answer is that farmers and fishermen do not have political power in Seoul. Another answer is that most South Korean export producers—and many are driven into export production because import permits and foreign loans are tied to export achievements—can no longer survive without the government's overseas trade promotion and domestic subsidies in the form of tax and customs favors, preferential tariffs, and loans. In 1968 these subsidies amounted to fifty-one wǒn or eighteen cents per dollar exported and covered an average loss of 16 percent of the export prices.[32] Difficulties have increased since. But these exporters, including foreign investors, do have power in Seoul.

South Korea's trade partners are the United States, which in 1970 absorbed 47 percent of South Korea's exports and supplied 29 percent of her imports, and Japan, with a 28 percent share of R.O.K. exports and 41 percent of her imports. The trade deficit with the United States was not high, but Japan scored a 10:3 advantage, some improvement at least after years of a 6:1 imbalance.[33] Three-quarters of the R.O.K.'s exports go to these two countries; South Korea is obviously dependent on the two giants, economically and politically.[34] Thus the South Korean government, in its desperate search for new trade partners, decided in 1971 to start trade with "non-hostile communist" countries. The 1972 move toward coexistence with North Korea may have been motivated by trade interests, too; South Korea could sell its surplus consumer goods to the north and buy machinery, raw materials, and even grains from the D.P.R.K.

5. AGRICULTURE

Before the division of the Korean peninsula the south used to be the rice supplier for the whole country. Under Japanese colonial rule great amounts of rice were shipped to Japan by extortion from Korean farmers whose own rice consumption shrank by one-half.[35] Today the R.O.K. has to import large quantities of rice, wheat, barley, and sugar.[36] Self-sufficiency in food was one of the main targets of the SFYP, but the Third Five-Year Plan (TFYP) (1972–76) no longer envisages full self-supply in grains. In fact, South Korea's grain self-supply rate dropped from 97 percent in 1965 to 81 percent in 1970.[37] According to 1972 forecasts, the rate was to be 75 percent.[38]

Another symptom of South Korea's weak agricultural policy is the widening gap between rural and urban income. In 1965 the farmers' average income equaled that of urban wage earners, but it dropped to 60 percent in 1967 and reached only 65 percent in 1969, although wage earners are certainly the lowest income group in the cities.[39] This is a direct consequence of the low purchasing prices of grains, which are set and influenced by the government and which do not even meet production costs.[40] Inadequate agricultural production and low productivity stem mainly from structural reasons: (1) farmland units are too small—the average holding is 2.25 acres (0.9 hectare) per farm household, but one third of all farmers own less than 1.25 acres; (2) fields are too small and irregular to utilize farm machinery; (3) one-fourth of the nation's rice paddies (1969) were not insured against drought; and (4) South Korea's farm economy is not sufficiently diversified. To expand profitable cash crop farming (vegetables, fruits, mushrooms, mulberry trees for sericulture, etc.), farmers need capital, technical aid, and marketing assistance. The same is true for livestock breeding and dairy farming. However, loans available for the agriculture and fishery sector, though increasing in absolute terms, sharply decreased from 40 percent of all loans in 1963 to 14 percent in 1969.[41]

The government has made some efforts to develop agriculture. Seven modern fertilizer plants have been established since 1960 which fully meet domestic needs. Most pesticides and insecticides are now available on the domestic market. Land rearrangement, land reclamation, and irrigation programs have been accomplished. Since 1970 large-scale river development projects have been started with the help of international loans. Yet the hundreds of thousands of farmers who desert their land only to find themselves living in urban slums indicate that these efforts have been far from satisfactory. When the government announced the Third Five-Year Plan, it claimed that special emphasis would be given to the agriculture-fisheries sector. The plan figures for the annual growth of the primary sector, 4.5 percent, and the share of total investments allocated to this sector, 11.8 percent, are higher than the performance figures of the SFYP, 3 percent and 9.7 percent respectively.[42] However, they are even lower than the original SFYP figures of 5 percent and 16.3 percent, which were not met.[43] The UN's Food and Agriculture Organization stated that the planned growth rate of 4.5 percent for South Korea's primary sector is much too low for satisfactory development.[44]

The main obstacle to an increase in agricultural productivity seems to be the small size of the farm units. A plan has been prepared to remove the land ownership ceiling of 7.5 acres (3 hectares), which was established in the 1949 land reform.[45] This would allow some bigger farmers and urban businessmen to accumulate land and invest in profitable sectors of agriculture. But it certainly would ruin the vast majority of poor farmers. Twenty percent of South Korea's farm land is already under short-time tenant farming, although tenancy is banned by law.[46] The only alternative to this capitalist approach would be to encourage and support a genuine movement to form production cooperatives.[47] The merger of small fields, the joint use of equipment and facilities, collective work which allows for specialization, and the use of available capital for concentrated investment are all advantages of production cooperatives that would raise productivity even without extra capital input.

The same is true for the urgently needed modernization of the nation's fishery industry. A few big deep-sea fishing companies have received government support since tuna proved to be a successful export item. The rest of South Korea's fishermen can hardly make a living.[48]

6. URBAN LIFE

The cities of South Korea are exploding with people and problems. Seoul, with an annual growth rate of 8 percent (2 percent natural increase, 6 percent immigration), is among the fastest growing cities in the world. The population doubled within ten years from 2.5 million people in 1960 to 5 million in 1970. It surpassed 6 million in 1972. A thousand newcomers stream into the overcrowded city every day. Even the most effective city administration could not provide housing, employment, transportation, schools, water, electricity, and garbage collection for such numbers.

Most obvious in daily life is the transportation problem. In spite of great efforts to widen roads and build elevated highways, the streets are jammed with taxis, private cars, and buses, the only means of mass transportation. (A subway is now under construction with Japanese assistance.) Here we note a typical capitalistic feature of life in South Korea. While the nation's total number of cars increased from 50,000 in 1966 to 109,000 in 1969, the number of Seoul's cars rose from 20,000 to 50,000. During the same three years the number of private cars tripled from 8,000 to 24,000.[49] In 1971 private cars for the privileged were 60 percent of all the cars in Seoul. Why was this permitted when more than 80 percent of the people must travel on buses packed like chicken coops? [50] There is only one convincing answer: three foreign car producers (Toyota, Ford and Fiat) are competing to sell locally assembled passenger cars in the South Korean market, and the Seoul city administration would not jeopardize the auto makers' profits by refusing licenses for private cars.[51] That would have been a reasonable policy considering that two cars with a few passengers take as much space as a bus which serves dozens. Another irrational but very capitalistic phenomenon is that about two hundred small bus companies compete for passengers in the downtown area of Seoul, while the outskirts are neglected. These private owners profit when buses are overcrowded and poorly maintained.

A similar basic conflict between the interest of the people and those of private entrepreneurs exists in the staggering problems of air and water pollution. Paradoxically, they are worse in this underdeveloped country than in the highly industrialized nations.[52] A U.S. pollution expert called the Northern Han River, which serves as the main source of drinking water for Seoul, worse than New York's sewage.[53] Seoul and other cities do not have human waste treatment facilities or sewage systems, and the unchecked disposal of untreated industrial waste exacerbates the problem. Seoul's air pollution is partly caused by industrial smoke and the widespread use of briquettes for heating, but the main sources are automobile exhaust due to the traffic density, the use of poor quality gasoline and diesel oil, and old and poorly maintained engines. This pollution is not a matter of technical know-how or being a poor or a rich country, but of whether the government is willing to force car owners and companies to use anti-pollution devices. Of course, anti-pollution costs would reduce profits.

Housing is another tremendous problem for South Korea's cities because of rural-urban migration. In 1970 there were only 600,000 houses for the one million households in Seoul, and 180,000 of them were illegal. The city administration estimated that in the slum areas an average of three households, comprising twelve to fifteen people, occupied each little house. According to this estimate, 2.5 million people, half of Seoul's population at the time, were living as squatters. Some of these illegal houses are well constructed and have been inhabited for ten or twenty years, but most are merely wooden shacks or even tents.[54] Slum houses have no water supply, no sewage disposal, often no electricity, and no garbage collection. Their inhabitants depend on a few public toilets. Experts say that other Asian slums are much worse than South Korea's. But it must be remembered that Korean winters are extremely cold, with temperatures often dropping to zero Fahrenheit.

Seoul's city administration made two attempts to clear away slums. In 1968–69, four hundred apartment buildings with sixteen thousand housing units were built on city-owned steep hillsides formerly covered with slums. Although the buildings were cheaply built, prospective residents had to pay more than $1,000 per apartment unit. Therefore, many sold their eligibility right; others moved in, improved the apartments, and then sold them.

By 1971 less than 60 percent of the occupants were former slum dwellers. The city had to stop the program in 1970 after one apartment building collapsed, killing thirty-three people. Most of the other four hundred buildings were found to need repair and reinforcement. Some even had to be demolished because of slipshod construction, a consequence of large-scale embezzlement of funds.

The city administration also attempted another policy. Beginning in 1969 tens of thousands of slum dwellers were removed to Kwangju, a new town two hours by bus from Seoul. Those who had owned their own shacks in Seoul were given a small piece of land and a tent for four families. But many families in the slums were renting their huts.[55] Such people were not entitled to new land and had nowhere to go. There were no jobs for the people moved to Kwangju and no transportation to Seoul either. In August 1971 the situation in this new slum city got so bad that the residents rioted. A thousand riot policemen were needed to crush the demonstrations. Land speculation, another capitalistic feature fully operating in South Korea, also hampered this "solution." An estimated 60 percent of the people removed to Kwangju sold their pieces of land and moved back to Seoul—into another slum.

To build enough apartments is apparently beyond the city's financial power. To remove slums from the inner city to other places is certainly not a solution either. There is no solution to slums once they exist. One must seek the causes: where do the slum dwellers come from and why?

Reliable, comprehensive data are not yet available, but some surveys (see note 54) suggest that, aside from some small groups of war refugees, most squatters come from rural areas, either directly to Seoul or via provincial cities. Their motivations are diverse; "pushing" and "pulling" factors are present. It appears that urban immigrants are basically of two types: (1) young people who have no jobs or prospects in their rural areas, and (2) whole families with insufficient land to sustain themselves. Both are attracted by a rather vague but glamorous image of the city (created by government propaganda) where there are "opportunities for everybody." Thus urban problems are closely interrelated with rural problems.

We return to our earlier criticism that the South Korean government has failed to develop agriculture. To our previous explanation that this failure is because investment policy neglected agriculture, we now add the strong suspicion that the unchecked rural-urban migration is in fact not unwelcomed by the government, since it provides unlimited reserves of people willing to work for any wage (32 percent of the household heads in Seoul's slums are unemployed or without regular jobs).[56] The government's "export first" policy and its attempt to attract foreign investors depend on a continued low wage level. It is logical, then, not to do much to prevent poor farmers from coming to the cities.[57]

How do these hopeful migrants make a living in the city? A few typical examples will illustrate what life is like at the bottom of the capitalistic society in South Korea.

If the father of a family is strong enough, he will borrow an A-frame (a wooden holder for carrying loads on the back) and try to get occasional work as a porter. If he is lucky enough to find work, he will make twenty-five cents an hour for brutal physical labor. His wife works at home cracking nuts while caring for a young child. She works twelve hours to make fifty cents. The oldest son gets a bundle of neckties from a dealer and tries to sell them on the street. He has to pay 5 percent daily interest on the goods he borrows for his little "shop," so that his net income may be less than a dollar per day. The daughter of the family is lucky to have a "permanent" job in a small garment work shop. She works twelve to fifteen hours every day and receives ten dollars a month. This family has a daily income of about two dollars.[58] This is just enough to buy simple food and pay the rent to the "landlord" of their one-room "apartment" in a shack dwelling.

Another example is a single girl from the countryside who came to Seoul. She found work as a housemaid, first in a middle-class family, later in a small inn. In neither place did she receive cash wages; her salary was free room and board for a fifteen-hour workday. She finally could not stand it any more and ran away. After days of hunger, she found a private "employment center" which promised her a good job in a beer hall. After a few days of work, she was forced to serve as a prostitute. Because of her debts to the "employment center" she could not leave. A policeman to whom she tried to tell her story was paid off by the brothel owner.

This is exploitation at the grass roots level. These examples show the dehumanizing effect of the profit principle, which according to development theories stimulates people for economic activities, but which in reality drives people, even on the lowest levels, to squeeze those who are one step lower. These examples represent the plight of several million in the R.O.K.'s large cities. They do not starve on the streets, but, living in the most primitive conditions, they struggle hard from day to day to match their uncertain income with the soaring prices of the most basic necessities of life.[59]

Poverty does not stir people who know of no other life. But poverty is agony and frustration when others nearby live lavishly. Such is the situation in South Korea's cities. There is a relatively broad urban middle class who earn enough money to be able to waste it on fashionable clothes—imitating the *dernier cri* of the West—in costly restaurants and expensive beer halls. Above this middle is a small upper class of politicians, senior bureaucrats, business tycoons, and military leaders, who lead a provocatively luxurious life in ostentatious villas equipped with elevators, swimming pools, imported private cars, and a host of servants. This elite meets on the golf courses and at the horse races; they frequently travel abroad. Thus we note a gap not only between rural and urban living, but also an even wider gap within urban society.

7. THE EDUCATIONAL SYSTEM

Education in South Korea is theoretically free (and compulsory) for the first six years. In reality, there are school support fees and additional expenses that quite a few families cannot pay, resulting in early dropouts. Moreover, from middle school through the university, education becomes more and more expensive.

In 1970 monthly expenses for a child in public middle or high school amounted to about twenty dollars; in a good private school, which a student has to attend if he wants to get into one of the good universities, expenses were approximately thirty dollars. Private tutoring for high school students to enable them to pass the difficult university entrance examinations—a ubiquitous practice—costs thirty to fifty dollars a month. Enrollment in one of the numerous private universities cost $200–300, and tuition was $500 per year. The student's monthly living costs were additional. Government schools are less expensive, but only Seoul National University, with the country's most difficult entrance examination, has genuine prestige. In 1969 the average monthly income for farm households was about seventy-five dollars and for urban wage earner households approximately ninety dollars, of which at least half had to be spent on food.[60] Higher education, then, is out of reach for the vast majority of South Korean children.

Higher education in South Korea must be bought from institutions which often make a good profit from the business. This "educational transaction" reinforces the separation of classes. While a child's education depends on his father's income, it is the child's education which in turn determines his future income and his children's education. Low-income people get little education and only low-paying jobs. Children from the middle and upper classes get more and better education, which "entitles" them to get well-paying and influential jobs. Only a few exceptionally intelligent children are able to break this cycle by getting one of the very rare scholarships. They do not invalidate the rule that in the R.O.K. higher education costs private money and therefore is inaccessible for whole classes of people. This is one of the negative social aspects of capitalism, a system which requires that each individual pay for what he wants—even when the desiderata are as basic as learning. It should be noted that a completely free education is not a luxury for rich countries, something South Korea could not afford; it is a matter of social values and political choice, as can be seen in socialist developing countries.

8. THE HEALTH CARE SYSTEM

We observe the same structural problem in the field of medical care. Like education, medical care in South Korea costs private money and one has to buy it from private doctors and hospitals. Doctors usually are financially successful from their health "business." Most Americans and South Koreans will find this "natural," but in fact this is another unnatural feature of a capitalist society. The consequences are threefold.

First, masses of people have inadequate or no medical care. In July 1970 almost half of South Korea's townships (*myŏn*) were without a qualified doctor, the same situation as four years earlier.[61] These areas are without doctors not because of a general lack of doctors in South Korea but because of a lack of purchasing power in the villages. Private doctors cannot make a living in a rural area since the farmers cannot afford to pay for their expensive services. The cities have an ample supply of doctors and hospitals.[62] Nevertheless, the urban poor see the fancy clinics and hospitals only from the outside. Fifty to sixty percent of the population, urban and rural, consult only a pharmacist or drugstore when they are sick.[63] There are not only doctorless rural areas but also doctorless classes within the cities.

The striking inequities in medical care are not due to an underdevelopment of the field of medicine in South Korea. The doctors are there and are well trained; in fact thousands have been allowed to emigrate.[64] Rather, it is again a consequence of the capitalist health care system. Doctors who invested much private money in long and overly specialized training go where the money is: to the urban middle and upper classes, or abroad. The system, not the individual physician, is at fault.

A second consequence of capitalist health care is that the product—health—is sold on the market. The doctor-patient relationship is marked by distrust. The patient is often afraid that the doctor is trying to sell him a treatment he does not really need, while the doctor, against his best intentions and professional ethics, is tempted to prescribe treatments which make his clinic more profitable. The same is true of the pharmacist, who is a businessman, not to mention the profit-minded pharmaceutical industry and its advertising efforts. (At least three major foreign pharmaceutical concerns—Pfizer, Hoechst, and Bayer—are flooding the unregulated Korean market with medicines produced in Korea.

The third deleterious result of a capitalist health care system is severe negligence of public health and preventive medicine. Hospitals, and young physicians choosing their fields of specialization, are not interested in these important branches of medicine. A hospital that is expected to recover at least its costs cannot afford a public health or preventive medicine program for which no one pays. Can one expect a young, able doctor to choose a career in a government health center at a salary of $130 a month when society allows his colleagues to earn several times more as private practitioners?

The government has established health centers, one in each *gun* or *gu* (administrative units below the province or city respectively). But in March 1971, of the 1,220 positions available for doctors, 370 were vacant. The sub-health centers—on paper there is one in each *myŏn*—are very short of medical personnel. There is supposed to be one tuberculosis, one family planning, and one mother-and-child-care worker in each *myŏn*. However, 90 percent of the staffs are hired on a temporary basis, are unqualified, or not doing medical work.[65] A survey revealed that very few people visit the health centers, despite their low fees, because of the bureaucratic procedures and rude treatment.[66] The latter reflects poor doctor and staff motivation and morale.

Finally, the capitalist ideology that everyone is responsible for himself is contrary to the idea that medical service should be available to all who need it. As long as health care is decided by one's private financial situation, medical attention, recovery from illness, and life span will be as unequally distributed as income. Only a national health care system where dues are paid according to financial ability, medical service is free, and doctors are employed by communities like teachers, is able to distribute health care equally to all classes and areas and meet the medical needs of the country. Other developing countries, poorer than South Korea but with different priorities, have adopted this socialist system in health care: Sri Lanka, Tanzania and Cuba to name but a few. North Korea has such a system, too.

9. THE WORKING CLASS

Housing problems, a lack of educational and health care opportunities, inadequate transportation, and pollution plague the low-income urban populace. But their life is really determined by their job situation. It is a characteristic of capitalist industrialization that it creates a new class: the industrial worker. Unlike the farmer or the craftsman, and more than the feudal farm worker, the industrial worker's total life situation in a capitalist society depends on having a job. Being unemployed in an urban slum exposes a man and his family to extreme physical and psychological hardships. In a capitalist industrializing country, sickness, disobedience to the employer, actively working for a labor union, or even getting older than forty may result in loss of job. Thus, belonging to the working class implies more than a low income; it means dependency on a place of work owned by a private owner. Likewise, belonging to the class of capitalists means more than having a relatively high or very high personal income; it implies power of disposal over jobs. The latter have personal, economic, and political power over the former—individually and as a class.

The employee in an office, a shop, a restaurant, or other service enterprise is basically in the same situation of dependency as the industrial worker. The fact that at least the male white-collar employee usually has a higher income, better working conditions, and more chances for promotion than a blue-collar worker might conceal but does not alter his situation. It makes white-collar employees, however, more easily co-opted and integrated into the system.

In quantitative terms the R.O.K. labor force of ten million can roughly be classified as follows: five million work in agriculture and the fishery industry (mainly as self-employed and family workers); one million in the mining and manufacturing industries (mainly as laborers); two million in tertiary industries; while almost two million are self-employed or family workers in the non-agricultural sectors. The official figure of five hundred thousand unemployed (5 percent) is certainly too low.[67] Though most of the "self-employed" farmers, fishers, small traders, and street vendors are in many ways as badly off as the industrial workers, or in even worse positions, I shall comment mainly on the roughly three million workers in the mining, manufacturing, and service industries.

Sixty percent work in small and medium-size firms that account for 98 percent of the total number of industrial establishments.[68] Big companies, particularly if they depend on skilled workers, tend to offer more or less regular working conditions. But in the thousands of middle-size and small factories, workshops, restaurants, and inns, work is inhuman. A workday of ten to twelve hours with one short rest break is the rule and up to eighteen hours is quite common.[69] One or two days off a month is standard; many workers get no holidays except national holidays. Daily wages of a dollar or less for skilled workers and fifty cents or less for unskilled workers and "apprentices" are the norm.[70] Extra pay for overtime or night work, though prescribed by law, is an exception. Many companies withhold wages and severance pay for several months.[71] Illumination, ventilation, heating, and noise-protection in most factories are so poor that the worker's health frequently suffers.[72] Industrial accidents, due to the absence of safety precautions and overwork of the laborers, are frequent and increasing annually;[73] compensation pay, if given, is nominal. Assault, mistreatment of young workers, and sexual exploitation of female workers are common.[74] Even child labor still occurs.[75]

These inhuman, exploitative working conditions were shockingly brought to the nation's consciousness on November 13, 1970. Chŏn T'ae-il, a twenty-three-year-old worker, burned himself to death in a desperate protest against sweatshop conditions in a huge garment center in the middle of Seoul. Two years earlier he had been fired from a textile shop for trying to organize a labor union. In October 1970 Chŏn had made public statistics showing that in the P'yŏnghwa garment district, a center of sewing and garment workshops, twenty-seven thousand workers, half of them below fifteen years old, were employed in nine hundred small garment shops. These young people worked thirteen to sixteen hours a day in overcrowded, poorly lit and unventilated rooms, many mere cubicles five feet high. A daily wage of thirty cents was their reward.[76] (A survey revealed that 90 percent of the youthful workers suffered from some kind of disease.) There was no reaction from the government's Office of Labor Affairs to Chŏn's revelations. On November 13 he and a small number of friends demonstrated in the market area demanding enforcement of the existing labor law. When police interfered, Chŏn poured kerosene over his body and set himself on fire.[77] His death stirred student demonstrations, a broad public debate, and lofty promises from the Office of Labor Affairs. Months later very little had changed. Chŏn T'ae-il was not an isolated case.[78]

The R.O.K. has very modern labor laws—on paper. The Labor Standard Law prescribes all the usual protections of advanced nations. The law does not apply to small shops, however, where the situation is the worst. But the government does very little to enforce this law. Sixty percent of the companies employing more than sixteen workers never received the required inspection. Of those checked, 98 percent were found to be violating the Labor Standard Law.[79] There were no reports of punishment of the violators. The inspectors, the authorities responsible for enforcing the law, and the government are in collusion with management.

Labor unions, whose rights are theoretically guaranteed by the Labor Union Law, are too weak to protect the workers. Large companies illegally prevent workers from organizing or set up company-sponsored unions. The salary of the union representative and his office are provided by the company, thus leaving little room for independent action. Many of the top union leaders are affiliated with the party in power and not a few have been corrupted enough to cooperate with the R.O.K. Central Intelligence Agency (R.O.K. CIA). Thus strikes are very uncommon.

The history of the existing labor organizations is not that of a genuine labor movement. From the time of the anti-Japanese struggle through the years of Syngman Rhee, the democratic government of 1960, and the military coup of 1961, unions were organized from the top down to serve as instruments of those in power. The U.S. Military Government outlawed communist unions in March 1947, a measure reinforced by all later regimes in South Korea; socialism, the natural ideology for a true labor movement, was a forbidden alternative.[80]

At present the unions are shop-oriented and solely concerned with wage questions. There are signs that a new orientation is growing among the leaders, a consciousness of a wider responsibility for social justice in South Korea. However, before the unions can become a powerful force in South Korea's sociopolitical system, they will have to double their membership. (At present the Federation of Korean Trade Unions has about five hundred thousand members in seventeen industrial unions. Fortunately, there is no competing labor organization in the R.O.K.) And they will have to strengthen the workers' class consciousness to establish the solidarity necessary for an effective labor movement.

Since skilled laborers are increasingly demanded by industries, there is theoretically a chance for unions to gain some power. On the other hand, the "army" of unemployed, unskilled or semi-skilled workers is so large and growing so fast, that it is very difficult to organize workers.

Foreign capital, which the government wants to attract for investment, enjoys special protection against labor disputes.[81] This protection was extended to all private capital in South Korea in December 1971, when President Park was given special emergency powers, including the right to freeze wages and interfere in labor disputes. As long as this "emergency" lasts, there is not much room for an independent free labor movement to develop.

10. THE POLITICAL SITUATION

The December 1971 incident shows how economic and political questions are interrelated. A free labor movement and other political activities had been suppressed before that date. Nevertheless, economic difficulties and social unrest increased during 1971. On December 6 Park Chung Hee declared a State of Emergency, giving as reasons an unspecified "threat from the North" and international developments, "including Red China's entrance into the UN." But the special bill that his ruling party "passed" in a secret, illegal session on December 27 clearly indicates the crisis was domestic. The president was granted the right to ban public assemblies and demonstrations (which were prohibited anyway), to control "irresponsible debates" in the mass media (which were censored anyway), to freeze wages, rents and prices, to interfere in labor disputes, and to mobilize any material or human resources for national purposes.[81a]

Not much democracy had existed before this declaration of dictatorship. The three secret services were omnipresent in labor organizations, political parties, universities, and newspaper offices threatening any opponent of the government with the loss of his job, brutal investigation, or arbitrary arrest. The Anti-Communism Law and the State Security Law were handy instruments against those who refused to be intimidated. Any criticism of the government could be declared "aiding the communists"; as "evidence" for alleged espionage activity, extorted "confessions" sufficed.

The government regularly issued stories of captured "armed agents" or infiltration groups from the north, with special frequency at election times. Many of these stories seemed fabricated to independent observers; others could have had a basis in South Korean attempts at resistance.[82] At times of extensive student demonstrations, "spy-rings" have been uncovered and hundreds of intellectuals arrested. They were later proved innocent of the fabricated charges.[83] The regime again and again encouraged the people to fear "the Red Devils." Brutal excesses by local, irregular communist forces during the Korean War provide an underlying factual basis for these fears. But they are mainly a product of systematic anti-communist education and propaganda at all levels of the school system, in news media, through posters, slogans in the streets, and indoctrination during military service.

The Korean War is treated in another essay of this book. The D.P.R.K.'s policy towards the south after 1953 and the R.O.K.'s policy towards the north merit additional research. But from observation of South Korea it is very obvious that "the threat from the North," if it ever existed, was used to establish and maintain anti-communism among people of the south. The identification of anti-communism with freedom and democracy, and these again with capitalism ("free enterprise"), helped to make any criticism of social and economic injustices "pro-communist, destructive and dangerous." Thus the ideology of anti-communism, under Syngman Rhee as well as under Park Chung Hee, functioned to support capitalist policy and to suppress any opposition to it. Not only was any communist or non-communist socialist alternative eliminated from political life in South Korea, but even criticism from within the system was severely hampered under the pretext of anti-communism. At the same time, fear of "the Communists" was repeatedly used to mobilize the masses behind a government which otherwise gave the people little reason for loyalty. Intensive anti-communism became an ideology to cover up the ruptures and tensions which inevitably occurred in capitalist development. It is an open question how long this will work.

11. SUMMARY AND CONCLUSION

Capitalism serves as the interpretive framework of this analysis. A summary of the major features noted above will clarify its meaning for South Korean development.

Among the aspects of the economic system we found most striking was the tremendous growth of South Korea's GNP. This growth was, however, achieved at the price of a neglect of agriculture, high inflation, and a very high inflow of foreign capital, mainly as loans. The expansion occurred predominantly in the secondary industries, more precisely in the consumption-oriented industries. Since the domestic market could not absorb their overproduction, the government vigorously encouraged and heavily subsidized exports of these commodities, although their production increased imports and foreign debts. The predominance of manufacturing industries in South Korea's economic development stems from the fact that the biggest share of all available capital, domestic and foreign, was at the disposal of private investors interested in the fastest maximum profit. Under such a system agriculture, infrastructure, and "investment in man" (health, education, culture) necessarily were neglected.

Therefore, we conclude that capitalism is not a suitable eco-

nomic system to develop a country in the broad sense of human development. It may be effective at creating rapid GNP growth rates, since the profit motive of private investors directs the investments where the fastest growth can be expected. But this produces a sectorally and regionally unbalanced economic development which creates tensions within the system and leads a temporary boom into a structural crisis, as has occurred in South Korea. Is it not true that maximum GNP growth is itself a capitalist goal? We must reject the assumption that development—humane development—can be measured in GNP growth or per capita income. The social aspects of South Korea's development warn us to be wary of meretricious "development" statistics.

We observed the problems of an uncontrolled urbanization: growing slums, air and water pollution, traffic congestion, a housing shortage exacerbated by unrestricted land speculation, and the widening gap between the wealthy and the destitute. This urban explosion is related to the neglect of agriculture. Both phenomena serve to guarantee the manufacturing industries, particularly the export industries, a large cheap labor force. In addition to income and wealth polarization (the accumulation of capital favors only a few), a new class of workers and employees has emerged which is extremely dependent upon employers. This dependency makes them easy prey for exploitation. Discrimination and inequalities in the education and health care systems were noted. Both areas are concerned with basic human needs that a purely capitalist society is unable to meet equitably. It creates and protects classes of privileged people.

The main elements of South Korea's political system, which were not dealt with in detail in this essay, complete the picture: the dictatorial concentration of power in the hands of the president, a well-organized government party, manipulated elections, a large military machine, efficient secret services, controlled mass media, elimination of student protest and the labor movement, and an omnipresent ideology of anti-communism for obvious domestic purposes.

This political system functions to maintain a social-economic structure full of inner tensions and contradictions. If a government boasts of economic successes which the vast majority can only observe but not enjoy, strict control of the inevitable social unrest will be needed. If a government creates a high rate of inflation but cannot allow wages to rise because otherwise export products would no longer be competitive and foreign capital no longer forthcoming, the control and corruption of labor unions is unavoidable. If a government pretends to be democratic but is bound to break the rules in order to stay in power, manipulation of elections, elimination of student protests, and suppression of public criticism is inevitable. In fact, an economic system which benefits the few and exploits the masses cannot afford to have free elections, a free press, and free mass movements. This is the basic contradiction between capitalism in the narrow sense of an economic system and parliamentary democracy as a political system. This contradiction occurs also in other capitalist developing countries such as Taiwan, Thailand, South Vietnam, the Philippines, most Latin American states, and the "white" African countries. We even rediscover it in the perhaps only superficially democratic societies of Western Europe and North America.

Whether capitalism is a term which can be universally applied to all non-socialist industrializing and highly industrialized societies without becoming a mere slogan is beyond the scope of this article. However, we have found the term germane to the South Korean case for several reasons.

First, it indicates that the core of this economic-political system is the fact that the wealth of a nation, although collectively created and accumulated, is gathered in the hands of a few, the private owners of productive capital. (This, and not just excessively hard working conditions, is the true meaning of exploitation.)

Secondly, the term capitalism means the private disposal of profits. Even if the owners of private capital, domestic or foreign, spend only a small portion of their wealth in consumption of luxurious goods or in capital transactions out of the country, and even if they reinvest most of their gains, still the private owners' profit-oriented investments are generally not in the people's long-range interest. This is true in a capitalist developing country like South Korea as well as in the waste-making "advanced" Western economies with their private material affluence but public poverty.

Thirdly, the term capitalism indicates a class structure in which workers and low-ranking employees are kept in a dependent and underprivileged position to facilitate their exploitation. The workers, poor farmers, small traders, and low-level officials stand on one side of the basic class conflict; the leading politicians, high-ranking bureaucrats, and domestic and foreign capitalists are on the other side. In between is the class of middle-level employees and officials, managers, technicians, scientists, and military leaders—the people who at present serve the small ruling class and obtain some of its privileges.

The term capitalism does not mean that capitalists, that is, the owners of productive capital, are directly running the country. The R.O.K. government has so many ways of granting or refusing privileges in taxation, loan distribution (control of foreign capital!), foreign trade licenses, public investment allocation, and price policy that the South Korean capitalists depend on the government rather than dominating it. The case is different with foreign capitalists who do not invest in the R.O.K. unless their basic conditions are fulfilled. At the same time, the ruling R.O.K. political-military elite also depends on the capitalists, both domestic and foreign, to finance its expensive structure of control, manipulation and suppression. Furthermore, any anti-capitalist policy would discourage domestic and foreign investment, thus depriving the government of its economic basis and international support.

Of course, South Korea's government is stronger than England's at the time of Manchester liberalism. Among other reasons this results from the different international situation. Industrialization in Europe and Japan occurred partly through the exploitation of colonies, and in America capital was first accumulated through expropriation of the Indians, extreme exploitation of black slaves, and later through exploitation of economic colonies. Contemporary industrializing countries, most of them having been exploited as colonies themselves, have no outside resources to exploit. They therefore depend on foreign capital for a faster accumulation than the exploitation of their own farmers and workers would allow. Only their governments can successfully solicit such international support. And while the early European capitalists had only each other as competitors when they began to develop world trade, capitalists of developing countries meet highly superior powers who already control world markets and sometimes their own domestic markets, too. For these and other reasons, capitalists in newly industrializing countries need and tolerate more governmental economic activity than their early European or North American predecessors did. One might call this a "government-directed capitalism." But is that much different from what we observe in the United States or Western Europe today, where Big Business needs and expects more and more economic interference by government in order to avoid severe crises?

There are differences between the capitalism Karl Marx analyzed and the kind we now see in developing countries like South Korea. But they do not seem to be very important or fundamental. The alliance of interests between those with political power and those with economic power to maintain their joint rule as a system of exploitation and suppression is best characterized by the term capitalism. It appears to be accurate and concise enough, in fact, indispensable to characterize a social, economic, and political system like South Korea's.

Notes

1. These and most following data are, unless otherwise indicated, derived from government statistics, mostly from the *Korea Statistical Yearbook 1970,* Economic Planning Board of the Republic of Korea (Seoul, 1970). Most 1970 data are from *Monthly Statistics of Korea,* No. 3, 1971, Economic Planning Board of the Republic of Korea. The growth rate for 1971 is from the *Korea Times,* December 25, 1971.
2. *Korea Statistical Yearbook 1970,* table 56.
3. This is an average share for the years 1967–71 as calculated from *Economic Statistics Yearbook 1972,* The Bank of Korea (Seoul, 1972), table 15.
4. From the governments of the United States and Japan and from international institutions such as the International Development Association (World Bank) or Asian Development Bank.

5. *Korea Times,* January 24, 1971. Grant aid foreign capital is not included here.

6. By June 1971, 51 foreign firms had invested $50 million in electronics and electrical equipment and $37 million in petroleum, while chemicals, fertilizers and textiles/garments had attracted $20 million each (*Far Eastern Economic Review [FEER]*, August 28, 1971, p. 71).

7. For the different use of the various investment resources, compare *Report of the United Nations Commission for the Unification and Rehabilitation of Korea,* General Assembly, Official Records, 26th Session, Supplement No. 27 (A/8427), United Nations (UN-CURK 1971 Report), p. 23. For the use of various types of foreign capital by industries, see table 15 in *Industry in Korea 1970,* The Korea Development Bank (Seoul, 1970), p. 18.

8. Military expenses, to mention one of the major public consumption items, amounted to 30 to 40 percent of government spending, according to published figures (*Korea Statistical Yearbook 1970,* table 53).

9. *Ibid.,* table 44. In recent years it was somewhat higher.

10. The foreign saving rate between 1964 and 1968 varied between 40 and 50 percent. Before 1964 it was much higher, as high as 83 percent in 1962. In 1969 and 1970 it dropped to 37 and 35 percent. But in 1971 it was again 44 percent. National saving is indicated for 1969 and 1970 as 57 and 59 percent respectively, leaving a high "statistical discrepancy" as in most other years (*Economic Statistics Yearbook 1972,* table 17).

11. *Korea Times,* January 24, 1971.

12. *Korea Times,* January 24, 1971. Commercial loans: 63.5 percent; public loans: 29 percent; direct investments: 7.5 percent.

13. Interest and principal to be repaid in 1971 amounted to $350 million (*Korea Times,* October 10, 1971). Experts predict that by 1976 foreign debts will account for 31 percent of GNP and debt servicing will use 17 percent of foreign exchange earnings, if exports develop as planned (*Korea Times,* January 24, 1970).

14. *Korea Times,* January 24, 1971. Foreign investment in Taiwan (1970) exceeded $500 million.

15. Foreign investment receives a five-year tax holiday from all taxes and three additional years at half the normal tax rates (*FEER,* August 28, 1971, p. 55).

16. Gavan McCormack and Jon Halliday, "The Tokyo-Taipei-Seoul Nexus," *Journal of Contemporary Asia,* Vol. 2, No. 1 (1972), pp. 36–55. On page 54, n. 56, the authors quote U.S. government data which shows a wage ratio for the average wage per hour of textile workers of 1:6 for Korea vis-à-vis Japan and of 1:24 for South Korea vis-à-vis the United States.

17. In 1971 approved Japanese investments were higher than those from the United States (*FEER,* August 28, 1971, p. 71).

18. Two examples are a huge oil refinery built exclusively to supply Japan and a zinc plant (*Korea Times,* June 1, 1971).

19. A case in point is the P'ohang integrated iron and steel mill. Plans for this first Korean steel plant were evaluated as unfeasible and unprofitable by the World Bank and a European consortium of firms. The Japanese, however, leaving profitability considerations aside, rushed to take over the project. It will allow them to control future Korean steel production and the resultant machine and military industry. On December 3, 1969 Japan and the R.O.K. signed a $124 million grant and loan agreement for the plant construction (*Korea Times,* December 4, 1969). The Nihon Steel Corporation later worked out a compromise with China which enabled it to continue "technical cooperation" with the project in spite of Chou's Four Principals (*Korea Times,* November 26, 1971).

20. In 1970 the production of explosives, soda ash, aluminum, rayon yarn, and three-wheeled trucks was completely monopolized by single firms. Two firms each shared the market of buses, trucks, sugar, glutamate, electric wires, plate glass, and beer. Five companies dominated 80 percent of the market for the following products: automobile lubricants, auto tire tubes, cement, transformers, antibiotics, multivitamin pills, television receivers, reinforced steel, plywood, and electric generators (*Korea Times,* April 3, 1971).

21. *Korea Times,* November 22, 1970. The exact figure given was $4.881 billion. Other R.O.K. government statistics for 1948 to 1969 amount to $4.037 billion. (*Korea Statistical Yearbook 1970,* table 228); see also note 23.

22. *Economic Statistics Yearbook 1969,* The Bank of Korea (Seoul, 1969), table 16.

23. *United States Security Agreements and Commitments Abroad,* Hearings before the Subcommittee on U.S. Security Agreements and Commitments Abroad of the Committee on Foreign Relations, U.S. Senate, Ninety-first Congress, Second Session, 1970, p. 1562. The exact figure given there is $2.9 billion and a total of $7.46 billion for all military and economic aid.

24. *Korea Statistical Yearbook 1970;* table 237 shows "Foreign Currency Receipts from U.N. Forces (includes receipts from Vietnam)" of $1.057 billion for the years 1960–69. It seems safe to assume that in the period from 1950 to 1960, when many more U.S. troops were in South Korea, receipts were at least the same amount. Also, one can be sure that the Vietnam "earnings" are not all included in this table. McCormack and Halliday, citing a 1971 U.S. House Hearing on Foreign Aid, give the figure of $8.6 billion for the maintenance of U.S. forces in Korea from 1954 to 1970. Probably most of this money did not go into the South Korean economy but stayed in the United States or was spent in Japan. The same is true for the $18 billion Korean War expenses. Thus the total of $34.7 billion cannot be called U.S. expenses *in* Korea, but rather U.S. expenses *for* Korea. There is no difference for the U.S. taxpayer, but there is a difference for the South Korean economy (McCormack and Halliday, "The Tokyo-Taipei-Seoul Nexus," p. 53, n. 52).

25. *Korea Statistical Yearbook 1970,* table 55.

26. The percentages are my own evaluation of *Korea Statistical Yearbook 1970,* table 224.

27. *Monthly Statistics,* March 1971, table 119.

28. In 1970 Korea imported $405 million worth of raw and semi-processed materials in order to export $835 million (*Korea Times,* March 27, 1971).

29. According to a Bank of Korea report, contradicting a higher government figure (*Korea Times,* March 27, 1971).

30. According to a survey of the 1968 exports (*Korea Times,* August 15, 1969).

31. There certainly is a foreign market for tobacco, silk, and refined and processed food products. Japan, because of her polluted coastal waters, is now forced to import marine products that she formerly exported.

32. *Korea Times,* August 15, 1969. Of course, this is related to the overvaluation of the Korean wŏn, which is maintained because imports are twice the cost of exports.

33. *Monthly Statistics,* March 1971, table 46.

34. After two and a half years of negotiations the R.O.K. had to give in to America's demand that textile exports to the United States be restricted. It was estimated that the quotas adopted would cut South Korean textile exports by almost $1 billion over five years (*FEER 1972 Yearbook,* p. 296).

35. McCormack and Halliday, "The Tokyo-Taipei-Seoul Nexus," table, p. 52.

36. In 1970, in spite of a bumper crop in 1969, one-fifth of the nation's rice demand had to be imported from the United States and Japan. The cost was $140 million, while total commodity exports that year earned $835 million. Total grain imports in 1971 (2.4 million tons) cost $282 million; in 1972 imports of 2.9 million tons, worth $258 million, were expected (*FEER 1972 Yearbook*, p. 296).

37. According to a Bank of Korea report from December 1970 (*Korea Times*, December 3, 1970).

38. *FEER 1972 Yearbook*, p. 296.

39. *Korea Times*, December 6, 1970.

40. This was shown for rice by a 1970 survey of the Korean Farm Culture Research Association. For barley and wheat, even government figures for production costs are considerably higher than the prices the farmers received (compare tables 112, 113, 114 with table 216 in *Korea Statistical Yearbook 1970*).

41. *Korea Times*, February 25, 1970.

42. Figures from *Korea Times*, January 1, 1972.

43. *The Second Five-Year Economic Development Plan 1967–1971*, Government of the Republic of Korea (Seoul, 1966), pp. 41, 44.

44. *Korea Times*, December 26, 1970.

45. *Korea Times*, November 30, 1971.

46. *Ibid.*

47. The present National Agricultural Cooperative Federation (2.2 million members) is a state-run and virtually compulsory organization for fertilizer distribution, government rice collection, and marketing of some farm products.

48. Of 223,000 households engaged in fishing, only 61,000 had enough income to meet expenses (*Korea Statistical Yearbook*, table 115). A 1970 census revealed that of the 149,000 fishing "enterprises," 6 percent owned motor-power boats, 13 percent had non-motorized ships, and the remaining 80 percent operated with set nets, worked fish farms or used no special equipment (*Korea Times*, June 26, 1971).

49. *Statistical Yearbook of Seoul 1970* (City Administration of Seoul, 1970).

50. Early in 1972 the Seoul government ordered that all seats be removed from public buses so they could carry more passengers!

51. In April 1971 the Transportation Ministry lifted the existing "restrictions" on private car license approvals (*Korea Times*, April 11, 1971).

52. Dust fallout in Seoul averages 38 tons per month per square kilometer; in downtown areas it is 67.7 tons. The safety level is 6.5

tons. Taegu averages 48 tons. In Japan's major cities it was 14 tons in 1965 (*Korea Times,* May 20, 1970).

53. *Washington Post,* December 18, 1970. The Han River around Seoul has a BOD of between eighteen and thirty-nine PPM. The international standard for safe water is four to five PPM (*Korea Times,* January 1, 1971).

54. *A Study in Urban Slum Population,* College of Medicine and School of Public Health, Seoul National University (Seoul, 1967), table I/68. More recent and more comprehensive data can be expected from *A Low Income Housing Area Survey* by the Institute for Urban Studies of Yonsei University, Seoul, which was making an evaluation in the fall of 1971.

55. In 1967 half of the slum families were renting (*Study in Urban Slum Population,* table I/67).

56. A tentative finding of the 1970 Yonsei survey mentioned in note 54.

57. The New Village Campaign of 1972 (*Saemaŭl undong*), essentially a beautification movement, apparently has not changed the flow.

58. In 1969 the average daily household income in slum areas was 300 wŏn (one dollar) (Yonsei survey).

59. The consumer price of rice, the staple food for Koreans, almost doubled from 1970 (6,000 wŏn per 80 kilograms) to the spring of 1972 (11,000 wŏn). For people who have to spend 70–80 percent of their income on food, the government's allegation that the wholesale price index rose by "only" 10 or 12 percent a year is derisible.

60. *Korea Statistical Yearbook 1970,* tables 109 and 201 (the wŏn dollar rate is 300:1).

61. According to a government survey (*Korea Times,* July 18, 1970).

62. According to information provided by the Ministry of Health and Social Affairs, there are twelve doctors for every ten thousand people in Seoul, while there are two to four physicians per ten thousand people in the rural provinces (including the provincial cities). The statistical doctor-patient ratio is 1:833 in Seoul and 1:5,000 in the provinces. About twenty-five hundred of South Korea's fifty-four hundred hospitals and clinics are located in Seoul and Pusan (*Korea Statistical Yearbook 1970,* table 401).

63. From a government survey (*Korea Times,* November 22, 1969).

64. *Health Manpower Study,* School of Public Health, Seoul National University (1970) (figures rounded off). There were 8,000 physicians registered in 1967 for a population of 30 million. About

2,000 were inactive or abroad; 1,250 were serving in the army (resulting in a doctor-patient ratio of 1:480 young healthy men!); and approximately 2,000 were practicing in Seoul. There were less than 3,000 for the rest of the country.

65. According to a report from the Ministry of Health (*Korea Times,* March 30, 1971).

66. Only 6.6 percent of rural people make use of health centers, according to a Health Ministry survey (*Korea Times,* November 22, 1969).

67. The exact figures for 1970 (derived from *Monthly Statistics,* March 1971, tables 3 and 6) are in millions: economically active population—10.020; "employed"—9.574; in agriculture, forestry, and fishery—4.834; in mining and manufacturing—1.369 (of which 0.393 were self-employed or family workers); in social overhead and other services—3.371 (of which 1.359 were self-employed or family workers), leaving 0.446 as officially "unemployed."

68. This refers to firms with assets of less than 200 million wŏn or $540,540 (*FEER 1972 Yearbook,* p. 297).

69. This statement is based on a number of newspaper reports, my own inquiries, and information from industrial social workers. A survey of mining and manufacturing enterprises by the R.O.K. Industrial Health Association shows: an eight-hour workday in 43 percent; up to twelve hours in 23 percent; and more than twelve hours in 33 percent.

70. This statement is based on a number of newspaper reports (e.g., *Korea Times,* January 14, 1971) as well as other reliable information. It is backed by government statistics which give as average gross (!) monthly earnings of regular employees in manufacturing industries 11,270 wŏn (1969). This is $1.25 per day (*Korea Statistical Yearbook 1970,* table 217).

71. The law prescribes severance pay of one month's salary per each year of employment. In December 1970 the government was compelled to give 350 million wŏn in emergency bank loans to 128 enterprises that had failed to pay wages to 24,600 employees (*Korea Times,* December 12, 1970). These figures do not include enterprises with less than sixteen employees and show only the tip of the iceberg.

72. A government survey of twelve thousand workers revealed that 31 percent had hearing difficulties and 37 percent had poor eyesight (*Korea Times,* December 30, 1969).

73. According to government statistics, in 1969 there were 34,000 accidents that resulted in the death of 454 workers and injuries to

33,800. This was an increase of 68 percent over 1968 (*Korea Times*, January 27, 1970). In 1970 accidents increased 30 percent over 1969 (*Korea Times*, August 26, 1970).

74. This information is based on reliable reports from industrial social workers. These problems, of course, were never really surveyed.

75. Though employers usually conceal their young employees' ages, a government survey of 5,000 firms with fifty or more employees discovered 1,430 cases of the hiring of minors (children under thirteen years of age) (*Korea Times*, November 30, 1969). In smaller establishments (particularly restaurants, inns, and small workshops) child labor is much more frequent.

76. *Korea Times*, October 8, 1970.

77. *Korea Times*, November 14, 15, 22, 1970.

78. In May 1971 a fifteen-year-old boy in Pusan killed himself after having been beaten and fired by the factory owner. He had asked for a raise in his $13 a month salary (*Korea Times*, May 16, 1971). In August 1971 a young worker in Anyang tried to kill himself in front of the factory's director. He and some colleagues had been discovered sleeping after having been working nineteen hours daily for twenty days with twenty-minute lunch breaks (unpublished report). It should be noted that suicide is not at all common in Korea; in fact, it is alien to the Korean culture. In May 1971 another young worker in Yŏngdŭngp'o was beaten to death by hooligans hired by the employer because of his labor union activities.

79. *Korea Times*, November 30, 1969, January 22, 1971, March 27, 1971.

80. For the history of Korean unionism, see Park Young-ki, "Unionism and Labor Legislation in Korea," *Korea Observer*, Vol. 1, No. 2 (1969), pp. 94–102.

81. If a company has more than $100,000 in foreign capital, all labor disputes are subject to immediate compulsory arbitration by the government (*Korea Times*, May 10, 1970). In the Free Trade Zone now under construction around the southern port city of Masan exclusively for foreign export producers, labor unions are completely banned.

81a. In the fall of 1972 President Park gave such "State of Emergency" permanence by issuing a new constitution which eliminated all formal rests of democracy and "legalized" his personal dictatorship. The "Revitalization Reforms" proclaimed at the same time proved to be another futile attempt to fool the people. Only a year later anti-government protest and social unrest rose again in spite of most severe repression.

82. For example, the repeated story that North Korean agents carried bottles of poison to put in public wells and kill hundreds of people is simply unbelievable since it is against any conceivable communist strategy. The R.O.K. allegation that North Korea ordered cholera germs in Japan and sent them to the south was later silently dropped. There have been numerous cases of "espionage boats" being sunk without a trace, that is, no evidence that they even existed. A mutiny of South Korean espionage agents at a secret training site on August 23, 1971, was reported to be an armed infiltration from the north.

83. In April 1971, ten days before the presidential elections, Korean students from Japan were arrested for alleged espionage activities. The leaders of anti-government student demonstrations were arrested at the same time but later released. In the subsequent trials only "confessions" were offered as evidence. Indications of torture were obvious. In October 1971, when students again demonstrated against the government, more than a thousand were arrested. Four student leaders were accused of having attempted to overthrow the government. Their trial had still not opened in the summer of 1972. The 1967 case of the so-called East Berlin–based spy-ring, which involved hundreds of arrests in western Europe and South Korea, also occurred at a time of student demonstrations against the rigged elections.

The Plight of the South Korean Peasant

Bernie Wideman

1. INTRODUCTION

South Korea is a beautiful country—short, jagged mountain ranges with narrow valleys where morning mists settle on thatch-roofed villages. The people are inherently a joyous people. Their faces are intent; their bodies are strong from an invigorating climate and hard work. They deserve a better life than the present political system offers them.

I have been served bowls of steaming rice by hospitable villagers who normally eat potatoes. They sell their rice for cash to send their children to distant cities for an education. I have also been to villages where no rice was grown because there was no road to send it to market. People sat and waited for the crops to grow while government-painted slogans against drinking and gambling faded on the decaying wall around the village meeting hall. I have seen fresh-faced country girls by the hundreds forced by the system to sell their bodies in the alleys around Seoul Station. I have seen young men from the countryside come to Seoul with hopes and a little money, only to lose both as they attempted to buy a job in the surplus-labor job market. I have seen young boys working long hours on dangerous machines in dimly lit machine shops, and young girls working for eleven hours a day at eight dollars a month in garment sweatshops. And I have seen these people, refugees from the countryside, living in their wood and tar paper shacks, without water or sanitation facilities, without room to be human beings.

I have also seen the wealthy, who eat so much that they are continually taking medicine for upset stomachs. I have seen them, termed by the popular Korean poet Kim Chi-ha "those who can shit giant turds," riding by in their chauffeur-driven Mercedes Benzes. I have seen them barricaded in their high-walled, barbed-wired, well-guarded houses. I have even seen President Park Chung Hee go by in his long Cadillac. The street was cleared of vehicles, and pedestrians were ordered by police to stop walking and face away from the street. President Park would notice only the policemen every ten yards, maybe not even them. His entourage sped by so rapidly, he probably could not pick out a single face. Nor was I able to distinguish his face behind the darkened glass.

But there is more to life than motorcades. President Park has launched the New Countryside Movement (*Saemaŭl undong*), which is going to provide a better life for the peasants, if the peasants do what the bureaucrats tell them to.[1] The president has also directed that urbanites help out by sweeping their streets and straightening up their morals, which are corrupting the peasants. He has also directed students to go to the country-side to teach modernization, and creative artists to celebrate the movement in picture and story. He himself has led the way by supposedly writing the New Countryside theme song.[2] However, it is interesting to note that he supplies his own table with milk from a foreign missionary farm.[3]

But my purpose is not to criticize President Park. He is prob-ably similar to most men, although a bit more ambitious. My purpose is to criticize a system that stifles people on the bottom because all the weight is on top. By focusing on the peasantry, I hope to show how they are being sacrificed for the benefit of the small number of the wealthy and powerful. I hope to demon-strate that they, like the workers, are being exploited by the Republic of Korea (R.O.K.) government to increase the regime's power and that though new programs with new names may be enacted, the regime's basic agricultural policy is anti-peasant and pro-industrialist.

2. THE CURRENT SCENE

General

The economic development of the R.O.K. has been lauded as a U.S. success story in Asia.[4] After a decade and a half (1948–

63) of pouring an average of over $200 million in aid a year into the country, the United States saw the economy stop sputtering and begin to show signs of life.[5] From the mid-1960s on, the economy has raced ahead with real Gross National Product (GNP) increases (that is, GNP adjusted for inflation but not for population growth) of over 10 percent yearly.[6] This has been due to luck, shrewd planning, and the rape of the peasantry.

The military coup led by Park Chung Hee and Kim Chong-p'il that toppled the Chang Myŏn government in 1961 unveiled its First Five-Year Plan (FFYP) (1962–1966) in 1962. Although modest in scope, the planners soon realized that the plan's goals would not be met, and the goals were therefore adjusted downward.[7] However, increasing U.S. involvement in Vietnam from 1964 brought windfall profits to South Korea. American use of South Korean mercenary troops and construction workers, as well as the purchase of commodities for the war, boosted R.O.K. foreign exchange earnings remarkably beginning in 1965. While the exact figures are closely guarded by Seoul and Washington, judging by the leaps in invisible trade receipts and receipts from UN (i.e., U.S.) forces, it seems that the war enriched Seoul by approximately $85 million in 1966, $210 million in 1967, $275 million in 1968, $335 million in 1969, and $300 million in 1970.[8] This is close to the total arrived at by the U.S. Senate.[9] This windfall, in addition to the $500 million from normalizing relations with Japan in 1965, started the process of capital accumulation and investment that has spurred the South Korean economy. It ensured that not only the goals of the trimmed-down FFYP were exceeded but, to the government's surprise, even the original FFYP was surpassed.[10]

There has also been shrewd planning. The 1961 military coup lacked legitimacy. It had overthrown a relatively democratic government in order to "protect the fatherland," but it was not fully accepted at home or abroad. The foreign opinion that counted was mainly that of the U.S. government. The change to civilian clothes for the 1963 election did not markedly increase its prestige. To gain legitimacy the Park regime touted itself as the government that would modernize South Korea. The basic measure of modernization used by the regime's policy planners was a high rate of GNP growth with visible effects in the capital city. To achieve this the Park regime has settled upon, since the revision of the FFYP in 1963, an "export-first" policy.

Since South Korea's most abundant natural resource is cheap and plentiful labor, the government has sought to utilize this resource to produce export goods to earn foreign exchange. The foreign exchange is used to purchase the raw materials needed for the export industries to process into manufactured goods. Moreover, the structure of the South Korean economy and the nature of the R.O.K. political system militate against rational saving and investment, most money being used for consumption or speculative investment, such as real estate.[11] Investment for economic growth, unless there was a social and political revolution first, had to be with foreign money.[12] This money has been sought through foreign loans and investments. To be able to appear a profitable area for foreign loans and investments, South Korea has had to normalize relations with Japan and maintain low wages, political stability, and high exports. Foreign loans and investment not only bring in needed funds in lieu of domestic savings, but also carry foreign political backing.[13]

South Korea has done well in terms of the Park regime's development goals and policies. Through 1971 the R.O.K. government has induced $3.734 billion in foreign loans and investment. Of this amount, 59.4 percent was commercial loans, 33.5 percent was public loans, and 7.1 percent was investment.[14] This foreign capital, plus the $1 billion windfall profit made on the Vietnam war, has been the financial underpinning for the new export industries, the skyscrapers, and the freeways.[15]

Rural areas

Yet the so-called modernization policies of the Park regime have not resulted in modernization—that is, improved food, clothing, shelter, education, and opportunity for the people. The booming GNP growth rate masks gross maldistribution of income and social benefits; the fancy industrial plants, skyscrapers, and freeways divert attention from the more than one million slum dwellers in Seoul who live two and three families per temporary shack.[16] But the absence of real modernization is felt nowhere more than in the rural areas.

South Korea is still a rural country even though industry provides slightly more to GNP than agriculture does. Half of the population live in South Korea's approximately thirty-three thousand villages. Of the remainder, 10 percent live in small towns, and 40 percent in cities of over 50,000. Of the total population of thirty-two million, approximately one-sixth live in Seoul. Yet the budget of Seoul city is approximately equal to the combined total of all other provincial and city budgets.[17] Seoul has half of the country's colleges and universities, approximately half of the nation's telephones, and approximately half of all motor-driven vehicles.[18] In the countryside, not only are there few vehicles but hardly any roads to drive on. In country areas away from cities, the proportion of paved roads to total length of roads is 0.5 percent.[19] One-third of the villages do not even have roads that can accommodate small trucks.[20]

In 1970, of the 33,000 villages, only 3,040 had telephones,[21] and only 1.2 percent had electricity in every house.[22] At present most rural people are forced to do without medical care: 80 percent of all doctors and 90 percent of all nurses are in urban areas.[23] Of these, over half of both categories are in Seoul.[24] More shameful, four thousand doctors and six thousand nurses (approximately half of the total nursing graduates) have been sent abroad in order to earn foreign exchange.[25]

Although there are grade schools within walking distance (walking distance can be up to two hours each way) for most village children, sending a child to middle or high school usually requires that the family be prepared to board the child in the local town or city.[26] Boarding, plus tuition and other costs, places a middle school education out of the reach of most village children. If a student shows academic promise and the family has money, he is usually sent to a high school in Seoul to prepare for college.[27]

The reason that all roads, no matter in what endeavor, lead to Seoul is that the capital is the source of all political and financial power. Two-thirds of the nation's banking deposits are in Seoul,[28] capital investment per employee is higher in Seoul,[29] and good white-collar jobs are either in Seoul or staffed by Seoul college graduates.[30] As is truly said, "Seoul is a republic in itself."[31]

The overconcentration of social benefits in urban areas, i.e., a half-dozen large cities, especially in Seoul, not only depresses the growth of the rural areas but actually forces them to subsidize the growth of the urban areas. This is so because rural families must pay for boarding their children in urban centers during their school years. They also must pay school expenses—PTA, books, donations to teachers, etc.—to the urban area. Finally, when a child or family migrates to an urban area (approximately three hundred thousand migrate from rural to urban areas yearly), the migrant either takes money with him or is supported by the rural family until he can find a job.[32] Moreover, since the manufactured goods that farmers need are produced by factories clustered in big cities rather than dispersed throughout the provinces, these funds also evaporate away from the rural areas.[33] The total transfer payment from the rural to the urban sector results in a subsidy to industry that the peasantry can ill afford to pay.

At the same time that the government concentrates its investments (and thus, social benefits) in the cities, its policies also have forced farmers to live at decreasing levels of income and nourishment relative to urban citizens. The average daily caloric intake of city dwellers is 2646, whereas peasants average 2511.[34] Although this does not indicate undernourishment for peasants, other studies show that the protein content is much higher in urban than in rural diets. In my own discussions with villagers, I have been told that they almost never have meat but do occasionally have fish.

The primary food in South Korea is rice. If one has the money, he expects and is expected to eat rice. Interestingly, although per capita rice consumption has been increasing in South Korea, among peasants it has been declining. In 1964, among the total population, per capita rice consumption was 135 kilograms [297 pounds]. By 1971 this had risen to 157 kilograms [345 pounds].[35] An average peasant family in 1964 consumed 1023 liters [29 bushels] of rice. By 1970, consumption had dropped to 820 liters [23.3 bushels]. In fact, peasant family consumption of all staples dropped from 1766 liters [50 bushels] to 1506 liters [43 bushels].[36] Farmers produced approximately the same amount of grain in 1970 as they did in 1964, yet they sold approximately 25 percent more of it, reducing their own consumption.[37] It has been necessary for farmers to market more of their grain each year because the cost of living is rising faster in the countryside than in the cities. For example, if we compare education costs and establish an index number of 100 for costs in 1965, by 1971 we find that a city family's cost index for education had risen to 224, while a farm family's index had risen to 260. For medical care, a city family's index stood at 192 in 1971; a farm family's index was 235. The overall cost-of-living index in 1971 stood at 205 for urban dwellers and 227 for farmers.[38] The higher cost of living in the rural areas is of course due to the government's concentration of social services and industries in the cities.

Peasant income has lagged far behind the income of urban citizens. In 1965 an average farm household's yearly income was $411, or 112,000 wŏn; an urban wage-earning household's income was $413, or 112,500 wŏn. (The 1965 exchange rate was 272 wŏn to one dollar.) By 1970 urban wage income was $782, or (in 1965 prices) 212,736 wŏn, but farm income was only $445, or 121,275 wŏn.[39] This does not mean that life for a worker in the city is good. Nor does it mean that the average farmer will be tempted to migrate. But many peasants, especially the one-third with holdings of less than one-half hectare (one hectare equals approximately two and a half acres), come very close to financial disaster each year. An educated guess would be that one-fifth of all peasant households had net losses in 1970.[40] These farmers would be tempted to migrate even though life in the city holds no great hope for the newly arrived migrant. At present the unemployment rate in the cities is 9.4 percent.[41] Among the newly migrated population, most reach the city without jobs and remain jobless for a number of months.[42] Still the poorer peasant has no choice but to migrate. As Bishop Ji Hak-sun describes it: "I see men who have failed in agriculture. . . . In the end, they could not help leaving their homes to migrate to the slums of large cities without security, without shelter, without hope for a better life in the future." [43]

As noted above, this migration takes capital away from the countryside and transfers it to the cities and takes even more precious labor away from farming. The unemployment rate in rural areas is estimated at only 2.7 percent.[44] This is somewhat misleading though, since at peak labor seasons (rice transplanting and harvesting) much work must be accomplished in a short period of time, and consequently there is always an acute shortage of labor.[45] Thus it is no surprise that wages for farm laborers have risen faster than for any other agricultural input.[46]

The cities

At a quick glance this situation—the rural sector being shorn of money and workers for the benefit of the urban sector, which already has a disproportionate share of both—seems to make no sense at all. One would think that the planners have made a miscalculation somewhere. But in fact this is just the situation that the planners hoped to foster. As noted at the outset, the Park regime has identified itself with rapid GNP growth. The easiest way to achieve this was to lure foreign loans and investments with cheap labor and to repay these debts with earnings from cheap exports. Although industrial labor productivity has increased yearly by 15.9 percent, labor has been able to obtain only 8.8 percent yearly wage increases.[47] The government is able to hold down wages by maintaining a large unemployed labor pool in the cities. This hinders workers' efforts to obtain wage increases and form labor unions. As the R.O.K. government boasts, "the wage scale in Korea is one of the lowest in Asia," and although "unions are recognized by law . . . unionization is not well developed in Korea because of a large reserve labor force." [48]

Grain price policies

The major government policy that ensures low incomes for farmers (and thus a steady migration) also provides cheap food for the urban workers. It is one thing to get cheap labor to the city; however, if the migrants cannot buy food on their low wages or on money rural relatives contribute, they will demand higher wages. The government makes sure that the workers can eat and work on their low salaries. The policy which accomplishes both these ends—urban migration and cheap food—is the grain price policy. The farmers' grain is purchased at below-market prices and sold, along with imported grains, in industrial cities at below-market prices.[49]

Most crops are marketed through private channels, and price is determined by supply and demand. The major exception is grains, especially rice and barley. Although grain is also marketed mainly through private dealers, the government announces its own purchase price at the time of harvest. Private dealers will normally offer the peasants a higher price, but not too much higher, because the government will later release the grain it has purchased (plus imported grain) if it feels that the selling price of private dealers is threatening the low-wage policy in industry. Thus dealers must be able to judge how much they can pay the peasant and still make a profit without prices rising to the point where the government releases grain and quashes prices. Most peasants do not sell to the government because of the low prices offered. However, the government is able to get the peasants' grain by forcing them to repay government loans in grain and using the official price as the rate of exchange between money and grain. The government also collects the peasants' land taxes in grain.[50] When these methods fail to garner enough grain, the authorities simply close the commercial channels, thus forcing the peasants to sell to the government.[51]

Some examples of what the peasant can expect after he harvests his grain (in constant 1965 prices): in 1965, a 100-liter bag of polished rice [about 2.8 bushels] brought the producer $11.80, or 3,210 wŏn; in 1971, a bag brought $12.10 or 3,306 wŏn. For polished barley, a 100-liter bag brought $7.80, or 2,133 wŏn in 1965 and only $7.70, or 2,112 wŏn in 1971.[52]

The above prices are for polished grains, and published government purchase prices are for unpolished or unhusked grains. The government estimates that polishing increases the value of a bag of rice by 72 percent and a bag of barley by 67 percent. Using these ratios, I have developed comparable government polished grain purchase prices.[53] Analyzing the grain purchase prices paid to farmers, we note that for most harvests between 1965 and 1971, farmers did not even obtain adequate cost-of-living increases for their grain. This was directly due to the low government purchase price. Dealers generally offered farmers 25 percent higher prices than the government. Even this figure masks the truth, however. The market figures published by the government are the *arithmetic* mean of the entire year's prices.[54] Most peasants have to sell their crops right after harvest in order to pay off debts. Prices, of course, are at their lowest right after harvest. The government also seems purposely to depress the price at harvest time by dumping stored grain on the market.[55] A pro-government newspaper observed:

> The gap of wealth between cities and countryside has been deepening, and poverty-stricken farmers have been deserting their farmland in increasing numbers. The price of farm products is being kept below production cost, making farming a losing business, and thus compelling farmers engaged in small-scale farming to leave their farmland.[56]

In response to such criticism, and in realization that migration to Seoul was proceeding more rapidly than necessary to hold down wages and in fact was leading to social unrest, the government announced in 1971 that it would purchase the 1972 early summer barley crop at higher prices. Since barley prices had been declining steadily, peasants had been steadily decreasing the area planted to barley, growing the crop mainly for their own consumption, and selling more of their rice crop to make up for the loss of income.[57] In response to the government's promise and with the help of excellent weather in the spring of 1972, peasants produced more barley than in 1971. However, the government's purchase price did not match its promise, seemingly because it did not have the funds to carry out the purchase.[58] Apparently responding to this double-dealing, peasants sold only a little more than half the barley that the government wanted.[59]

Government officials debated whether or not to set a higher rice purchase price in 1972. Those in favor of giving farmers an incentive to stay on their farms and produce more favored a price that would at least match the 18 percent rise in the cost of living from June 1971 to June 1972. Those who feared what higher grain prices would do to the wage demands of urban workers were opposed to a cost-of-living increase in the rice purchase price.[60] The final decision was forced by political events. After announcing a 5 percent price increase in September, the government suddenly changed this to a 13 percent increase just before the November 1972 referendum in which President Park needed a large voter turnout to confirm his seizure of greater power.[61] While 13 percent did not match the increase in the cost of living, it was higher than the peasants had expected and tended to ease resentment toward the government.

Price stabilization through the purchase and sale of government grain has a long history in East Asia, having been institutionalized by the Former Han Dynasty in China (206 B.C.–23 A.D.). Governments bought grain at above-market prices when prices were depressed at harvest time and released grain stocks at below-market prices when prices got too high due to hoarding or natural scarcity. The R.O.K. has corrupted this rational system by buying at low prices. This depresses the farmers' receipts for grain and also reduces the farmers' incentive to plant and produce more. The result is that South Korea has been forced to import more and more grain each year in order to check rising prices caused by scarcity. In 1954, after production had recovered from the Korean War, South Korea had to import 202,-000 metric tons of grain. By 1965 grain imports had inched up to 669,000 metric tons. But by 1970 they had zoomed to 2,115,-000 metric tons. This was approximately one-fifth of South Korea's grain consumption.[62] In 1971 and 1972 there were continued shortages, and grain imports finally jumped to 3,600,000 metric tons for 1972, or approximately one-fourth of consumption requirements.[63]

The R.O.K. would be unable to manage its program of grain price manipulation and foreign grain purchasing if it were not for the help of the U.S. government. The Agency for International Development (AID) PL 480 grain loans permit the R.O.K. to import U.S. grain on a long-term deferred payment basis. The sale of this imported deferred payment grain provides the R.O.K. government with the funds necessary to buy grain from South Korean peasants.[64] If it were not for AID largesse, the R.O.K. would have to think twice before spending its precious foreign exchange on foreign grain. It might also be forced to allow the peasants to sell their crops through normal commercial channels. In effect, AID allows the government to maintain its stranglehold on the country's grain supply.[65]

In fiscal year 1972 PL 480 grain loans to South Korea were

approximately $222 million. This amounted to $90 million for the import of 1.3 million tons of wheat, $13 million for 240,000 tons of corn, and $119 million for 800,000 tons of rice.[66] These loans are repayable with a down payment of 20 percent in wŏn and the remainder in dollars over a forty-year period (including ten years' grace) plus 3 percent interest.

Since these PL 480 loans help to hold down domestic grain prices, thus stifling the income potential of peasants and the wage demands of workers, they obviously are of no benefit to the South Korean people. The main beneficiary, aside from the R.O.K. government, is the U.S. farmer. The R.O.K. uses the PL 480 loans to import grain from commercial channels. U.S. agricultural circles are delighted that, thanks to PL 480 loans, South Korea is the fastest growing market for U.S. farm goods in the Far East.[67] Next in importance to PL 480 grants are rice credits from Japan. Since 1969, Japan has supplied the R.O.K. with 750,000 tons of rice on a deferred payment basis.[68]

The grain shortage resulting from the 1972 harvest is compounded by steeply rising world grain prices. Although government figures have not yet been released, it seems that South Korea will be short approximately 500,000 tons of rice, 2 million tons of wheat, 250,000 tons of barley, and 500,000 tons of corn. Although the shortages are not greatly different from the 1971 harvest shortfall, the increase in international prices will require South Korea to make purchases of about $410 million ($100 million more than the previous year) in order to meet her needs.[69] Since PL 480 loans are not expected to rise, the drain on South Korea's foreign exchange holdings will be considerable for the first time. This prospect angered Park Chung Hee to the extent that he criticized his agriculture minister for "a wrong method of policy implementation." [70] In reality, it is not the implementation that is wrong, but rather the policy itself. As long as the government tries to keep its grain prices below market prices in order to feed the urban proletariat, peasants will not increase production.

Farmers are responsive to changing prices and highly motivated by the chance to make a profit. We have seen this with the 1972 barley crop, and it was also true with the 1965 sweet potato crop. When the government promised to purchase sweet potatoes at a high price, peasants produced so many that the government had to renege on its promise due to a shortage of funds.[71] But certainly the money spent on grain imports could be more profitably spent in giving peasants decent prices. The major drawbacks are that the peasants would have added incentive to stay on their farms, stopping the flow of poor peasants to the factories, and the urban workers would demand higher wages to pay for the increased cost of living.

The Republic of Korea's closest neighbors, Japan and the Democratic Peoples' Republic of Korea (D.P.R.K.) have both become self-sufficient in rice, and the latter in all grains. Both were rice importers (whereas South Korea was a rice exporter) but induced their farmers to produce more by offering price supports.[72] To be sure, this was not the only policy used. Both countries have invested in mechanization, and in Japan demand for rice has slackened as diets have become more diversified. But the chief means for increasing production is to offer higher prices to the producers. To determine South Korean peasant attitudes toward profit, I asked (by means of a written questionnaire) a selected sample of peasants, varying from poor to rich, what influence higher grain prices would have on their planting patterns. With hardly an exception, they indicated that higher prices would lead them to plant more grain. A high grain price policy would also be good for industry since the rural sector would earn more money and be able to purchase more manufactured goods.

3. DESCRIPTION OF PRODUCTIVITY DEVELOPMENTS

In the above section I have tried to describe the lives of peasants and their urban counterparts to show the effects of a government policy designed to destroy citizens for the sake of inducing foreign capital and illusory GNP growth. I will now attempt to relate government policies more directly to production by examining the inputs to agriculture: land, labor, and capital.[73]

Land

Not only are land holdings naturally small (each consists of fragmented plots due to the inheritance and purchase pattern), but agricultural methods—intensive farming using oxen and human labor—are suitable only for small plots. Approximately one-third of all peasants have holdings below one-half hectare; another third have holdings between one-half and one hectare, while the other one-third have holdings above one hectare. According to the R.O.K. landholding law, land is supposed to belong to the tiller, and since in unmechanized, intensive agriculture a peasant household can cultivate only about one hectare, there is an upper limit of three hectares for any family.[74] Still there is a wide divergence between those who use the land and those who own it. At the lower end of the scale, 35.4 percent of the peasants use only 11.4 percent of the total land. At the upper end of the scale, 1.5 percent of the rural population owns at least 7.0 percent of all land.[75] Moreover, this figure of 7 percent is grossly inaccurate because rich landowners conceal their excess holdings by registering them under the names of relatives. Private surveys have shown that rich landowners acknowledge owning only the three-hectare limit, even though in some cases they actually own as much as fifteen hectares.[76] Therefore, we can probably double the government figure and assume that the wealthy 1.5 percent of the peasantry must own about 15 percent of the total farmland. This figure is supported by the fact that the total amount of land farmed by tenants is between 15 and 20 percent, and it is safe to assume that most of the rented land belongs to the richer peasants and absentee landlords.[77] Although most of those renting land to others are middle or rich peasants, at least 32 percent are absentee landlords.[78]

While tenancy does not seem to be a major problem in South Korean agriculture, the fact that the government accepts it (even though it is prohibited by law), and is presently abetting it by considering an increase in the upper limit on holdings from three to four hectares, indicates the government's general attitude toward the well-being of the peasant.[79] Tenancy in South Korea was supposedly ended by the land reform of 1950–53. This land reform was originally opposed by the Syngman Rhee government but was finally instituted because the peasants were organizing, expropriating lands, withholding rents, and killing landlords. In order to defuse a volatile situation while trying to fight a war, the government had no choice but to implement a land reform program. At the time the tenancy rate was about 50 percent, and rent was paid in kind, usually about half the crop.[80] Although the land reform ended tenancy, it gave such small amounts of land to the former tenants, while allowing rich peasants illegally to retain large holdings, that the basic structure of the countryside was not changed. Consequently, tenancy reappeared very quickly. By 1965, 7 percent of all peasants were landless tenants, and another 23.5 percent were renting some of the land they tilled. The percentages have been going up yearly.[81] The rent paid by tenants is still 30–50 percent of the crop and is still paid in kind.[82]

Although tenancy has not yet grown to be a major cause of social unrest in the countryside, the disproportionate size of holdings causes gross misallocations of labor and lower than optimal production, even given the present level of technology. For example, on a country-wide basis, of the 2.5 million peasant households, the poorer 600,000 households farm the same amount of land as the richer 40,000 households.[83] In terms of economic efficiency, too much labor is used on some land and too little on other land. On the low end of the scale, the productivity of labor could be raised by adding more land; on the upper end of the scale, the productivity of land could be raised by adding more labor. My questionnaire survey revealed that a family can farm approximately one hectare before it needs to borrow or hire other labor. Government figures show that small holders, even though they are farming poorer quality land (more upland and less paddy), use their land more intensively (especially through double-cropping) and get higher yields per acre by investing more capital and labor per land unit than do large holders. An extreme example is barley. Small holders produce five times as much barley per acre as large holders.[84] It is a case of work hard or starve on the small holdings.

If the government truly wanted to help the peasants and boost agricultural output at the same time, it would carry out a thoroughgoing land reform in which the 2.5 million peasant households would equally share the 2.1 million hectares of farmland. But the government is not interested in helping the peasantry or in increasing agricultural output if it detracts from the major goal of producing exports with cheap labor. Thus the government has a vested interest in continuously forcing poor peasants off the land so that the industrial labor pool stays filled. The government's recent decision to allow large holders to increase their holdings, at the expense of the small holders, must be seen in this light.

Labor

Land and labor is wasted through inefficient distribution among peasant households. Labor is also wasted through inefficient distribution between rural and urban areas. We have seen that the unemployment rate in the cities is three times higher than in the countryside; even this statistic is far from accurate for urban unemployment, or rather underemployment. As one walks the streets of Seoul, a striking feature is not only the vast number of men doing nothing, but especially the large number doing minute, uneconomic tasks. A count of the men who serve as A-frame carriers, those who stand on the streets selling lighter flints, combs, belts, shoe horns, pocket dictionaries, candy, maps, ball pens, etc. (all items purchasable in regular stores), those who shine shoes, dust taxis, sell ice water to thirsty passers-by, on and on ad infinitum, would produce a staggering total. These are people without capital, without real jobs, without hope. But since they spend their days struggling to earn a few pennies, they are not counted as unemployed.[85] Their productivity in the cities is almost zero. In the countryside they were productive, but land and price policies forced them to migrate.[86]

Since 1965, although the employable population has increased by one million, the number of peasant workers has actually declined by three hundred thousand.[87] The total population has increased from 29 million in 1965 to 32 million in 1970, but farm population in absolute terms has actually decreased. In relative terms, the decrease is very marked: from 55 percent to less than 50 percent. This is the most precipitous relative decrease in South Korea's recent history; [88] as a consequence, farming is done increasingly by women and older men.

To make up for the shortage of labor, women farm workers increased from 37.3 percent of total farm workers in 1963 to 43.1 percent in 1971.[89]

Urbanization is not necessarily undesirable, although urban sprawl and pollution, characteristic of South Korean cities, certainly are.[90] In a well-planned or well-regulated society the opposite is often the case. Urban industries produce manufactured goods for the rural area, thus increasing agricultural mechanization and freeing rural labor for use in urban industry. However, this is not the pattern of change in South Korea. Industries produce for export and foreign exchange. Farm labor is not replaced by machinery; rather, as labor leaves for the cities, farmland becomes fallow for lack of labor to cultivate it. Since 1966 the amount of land under cultivation has been steadily decreasing, from 2.3 million hectares in 1967 to 2.1 million hectares in 1970.[91]

Surveys show that the labor shortage is most acute in the poorest regions, that is, those regions with the highest tenancy rates. It is these regions, most notably Kangwŏn and North Ch'ungch'ŏng provinces, where land-poor peasants are forced to desert their villages.[92] Although these regions are among the poorest in the country, wages for rural labor are the highest due to labor scarcity.[93]

Capital

Government investment policies are another example of how the government is ruining the peasants and agricultural production. Given the nature of South Korea's household farming, the individual household has little ability to increase the capital stock of its operation. For instance, there is little that the individual household can do to raise the productivity of its land through building irrigation facilities, or to improve its seed stock through a seed development program, or to build a tractor, or to construct a road to transport crops to market. These are capital improvement projects that must be financed by a larger social-economic unit. In South Korea only the government has the power and resources. However, the government has directed investments toward manufacturing rather than agriculture. Manufacturing could be beneficial to the agricultural sector and to the country as a whole, but the investments have been in the processing industries that produce exports and bring in foreign exchange.[94] From 1964 to 1970 (in constant prices) investment in agriculture rose one and a half times, but investment in manufacturing quadrupled.[95] As noted earlier, investment in social overhead also overwhelmingly favors the industrial sector. Assuming similar capital-output ratios, it is not surprising that productivity per worker is more than twice as high in industry as in agriculture.[96]

Agriculture was relegated to surviving on manpower alone in the first two five-year plans.[97] The Third Five-Year Plan (TFYP) (1972–1976) has been designed to give "top priority" to the agricultural sector.[98] However, although agricultural investment has been boosted to a total of $1.2 billion (10 percent of total investment),[99] manufacturing investment is set at $3.1 billion (25 percent of total investment).[100] Also, it should be noted that the agricultural sector was supposed to be stressed in earlier plans as well.[101] By contrast, in North Korea agriculture receives 20 percent of total investment.[102]

In investment requirements the family farm is not very different from the industrial firm, except in scale. If the industrialist is going to produce a certain line of goods, he needs to obtain credit in order to purchase machinery and raw materials. Each spring the peasant has to borrow money to buy or rent an ox for plowing, to buy seeds, and to buy fertilizer. Since these are essential but costly inputs for both the peasant and the industrialist, the credit terms partly determine whether they make a profit. Government policies are nowhere more evident than in the fact that export industrialists obtain credit at 6 percent per annum, while the peasant pays 59 percent per annum.[103] The August 3 Decree (of 1972) was yet another shift of government resources away from agriculture and to the export industries. It authorized additional bank credit of 200 billion wŏn ($500 million) for industry and a meager 15 billion wŏn ($38 million) for agriculture.[104]

Quite clearly, President Park's concept of economic development is rapid GNP growth fueled by foreign capital and aided by the foreign political support behind that capital. This is not economic development. It is subterfuge to conceal the fact that the masses give their sweat and blood for the benefit of the elite. The R.O.K. will go to any length to bring in foreign capital, whether by exporting medical personnel who should be caring for Koreans, selling soldiers to die in Vietnam, or diverting AID money earmarked for public housing for the poor to build fancy apartments for foreigners.[105]

Production

Given the maldistribution of land, labor, and capital caused by government policies, it is no wonder that agricultural production has been disappointing. In the all-important rice harvests, production from 1961 to 1970 increased only 22 percent or 2.2 percent per year.[106] This is the same pace as the population growth rate.[107] Significantly, this increase was due to increased land cultivation until the late 1960s when, due to the effects of government policies, farmers began to take land out of cultivation. Therefore, a more important statistic is the yield per area. From 1961 to 1970 the per hectare yields increased by an annual rate of only 1.5 percent.[108] The government's goal of a 4 percent annual increase in grain production during the TYFP seems overly optimistic.[109] The 1972 rice harvest of 3.6 million tons, compared to 4 million tons in 1971, gives added cause for pessimism.[110]

If South Korean peasants have slacked off on grain production, they have seemingly worked overtime on the production of fruits, vegetables, and industrial crops. Significantly, these crops do not face the obstacle of government pricing. From 1961 to 1970 vegetable production increased by 132 percent, fruit production was up 185 percent, and silk cocoons increased by 333 percent.[111] To accomplish these feats peasants devoted more of their resources to the more profitable crops. Vegetable and fruit acreage increased significantly, while the acreage for industrial crops such as sesame and rape increased as much as tenfold during the decade.[112] The peasants are excellent profit maximizers and bypass government obstacles any way they can to maintain their livelihood.

Since peasants obviously do respond to profit incentives, there is very good reason to believe that grain production could be increased remarkably if the government would either set grain prices high enough for the peasants to make a profit, or simply refrain from tampering with grain prices and allow market demand to pull up prices to a realistic level. Of course, this is the minimum that government could do. Additional impediments such as landholding inequities, lack of credit, lack of social overhead, and lack of local control will also have to be removed. However, the government prefers to keep the peasants under economic pressure and provide cheap grain to city dwellers by foreign imports. Meanwhile the yearly importation of over $400 million worth of grain, amounting to over 3 million tons or about one-fourth of domestic consumption, is a terrible record for a country where almost half the population is engaged in food production.

4. DESCRIPTION OF INSTITUTIONAL DEVELOPMENTS

Governing

In South Korea money goes from the local level to the upper level, but political power goes the other direction. Local areas contribute their taxes to finance the central government; the central government returns a portion of these taxes to the local areas.[113] The peasant pays his taxes in grain through the local government to the central government at the rate of 6 percent of his crop yield.[114] The provincial government, which is responsible for the peasant's schools and roads, receives few of his taxes. Thus it is no wonder that the peasant receives few services from local government.

Democratic local governments were abolished by the Park regime.[115] Although Korea has historically been an autocracy, villages were largely self-governing (especially with the easing of status distinctions from the eighteenth century on), and townships had elected mayors and councils. In 1961 the election of mayors and councils was ended. Now the township mayor (*myŏn-jang*) is appointed by the county executive (*kun-su*), who is a central government appointee, as is his boss, the provincial governor (*tojisa*).[116] Villages used to select their own leaders, called village chiefs (*ri-jang*). While the selection process was not necessarily a democratic election, especially in villages where one or two strong clans predominated, it was at least local control, and the village chief represented the village to the government rather than vice versa. This is rapidly changing, and the government is choosing the village chiefs.[117] Consequently, the only officials whom peasants, or any other citizens, can vote for are the president and the members of the National Assembly.[118]

South Korean villages are beautiful examples of how people can organize themselves socially and economically for the common good. Villagers protect one another from social or economic embarrassment as best they can. While status distinctions, especially between age groups, are maintained, work and decision-making are collective endeavors, and autocracy is unacceptable.[119] Yet the government approaches the village as an autocrat. The three institutions that provide contact between the village and political-economic power are all controlled by the central government. These institutions are: the agricultural cooperatives, the Office of Rural Development (ORD), and the New Countryside Movement. While there are a host of other organizations in the villages, such as 4-H and women's groups, these exist in name only, having been set up by the government and then left to wither by the villagers, since they were not locally controlled and served no real needs.[120] Only the cooperatives, rural guidance, and New Countryside Movement still exist because of continuing government efforts to bring the villages and peasants under closer government control.

Cooperatives
Agricultural cooperatives in most countries are farmer-organized and farmer-controlled. Their purpose is to give farmers a stronger bargaining position than they would have as individuals vis-à-vis agriculture input suppliers and agricultural product buyers. Specifically, by buying seeds, fertilizer, and farm machinery in bulk, they realize savings unavailable to the individual farmer. By using cooperative grain storage facilities, the farmer does not have to sell his crops right after harvest when the price is lowest. R.O.K. cooperatives are not of this type at all.

In 1970 there were 5,859 cooperatives "serving" South Korean peasants. These are all branches of county cooperatives and are authorized by the National Agricultural Cooperative Federation (NACF), a government organization.[121] Almost all of South Korea's peasants maintain membership in these cooperatives even though they have no control of them. National, provincial, and county cooperative officials are all political appointees. Policies are directed from the top down.[122] The cooperatives actually serve the government by separating the farmer from his grain. We have already seen that the government gets some of the farmer's grain by collecting taxes in kind. The cooperatives get the remainder of the government's requirements by selling fertilizer for grain and through direct purchase. Since there is no other source of supply for fertilizer, because fertilizer production and sale is a government monopoly, the peasant is forced to buy from the cooperative. This is also the reason that farmers join the cooperatives in the first place—to guarantee the availability of fertilizer.[123] Also, since they have to repay grain at the (below-market price) grain/cash equivalency rates set by government, they lose additional grain.[124] The cooperatives purchase grain right after harvest at government prices and store the grain for the government. Most farmers prefer to sell their grain to private merchants. Their reasons are mainly higher prices, flexibility in selling time, and absence of red tape.[125]

The other major role that the cooperatives play in farmers' lives is as a supplier of credit. The government provides the cooperatives with money to lend. The interest rate to the peasant is nominally 15 percent a year, but bribery of officials is often necessary to get the loans. This is because the amount of credit in rural areas is extremely limited, the amount of cooperative credit is very small, and the NACF interest is relatively very low. Farmers are either forced to bribe the cooperative officials to obtain the cheaper loans or borrow from private sources at usurious rates. The scarcity of the cheaper credit is obvious from the fact that the average interest rate on *all* peasant loans is 59 percent per annum.[126] Much of the scarce cooperative credit is not even available to the farmers; in fact, almost two-thirds of all cooperative loans go to business and industry.[127]

Technical assistance

In addition to the agricultural cooperatives, the government also maintains an Office of Rural Development, whose purpose is to help the peasants with technical assistance as the cooperatives supposedly help the peasants with capital assistance. But the peasantry ranks low in receiving technical assistance too; the R.O.K. sends Korean agricultural technicians trained in the United States through AID programs to South Vietnam to gain foreign exchange.[128] Although every field guidance worker is responsible for nine to thirteen villages, only the most accessible villages receive the authorized weekly visit from their technical advisor.[129] Most villagers never see him except at election time. Half of ORD guidance funds are actually handouts to farmers to build up the image of a benevolent government, and these funds are conspicuous at election time.[130] Moreover, since ORD is a bureaucratic organization run from the top down for the benefit of government rather than peasants, the guidance workers are forced to spend their time pushing government-sponsored programs, such as 4-H, women's Home-life Improvement clubs, and *Saemaül,* rather than dispensing technical guidance.[131]

The South Korean peasant uses farming techniques that have been handed down from father to son. However, he is not bound by tradition to these techniques but rather by his own lack of organization and the absence of meaningful governmental assistance. For example, the farmer realizes that improved seeds are the quickest and easiest way to increase production,[132] but he has not the time, capital, or knowledge individually to undertake a seed improvement program. Although seed improvement is one of the major activities of ORD, the peasant does not benefit from ORD research because the improved seeds do not usually get to him.[133] When they do, as in the case of the new Miracle Rice, bureaucratic autocracy wrecks the expected results.[134]

The Miracle Rice, IR 667, called the *tongil* (unification) variety, was experimentally grown in 1971. Since the preliminary results were encouraging, the government ordered it planted on two hundred thousand hectares of paddy even though researchers, both Korean and foreign, advised that more experimental data were needed, and farmers were hesitant because of lack of knowledge of its characteristics. The harvest results were disastrous. Just how bad the damage was has not been announced by the government, but it is instructive to note that plans for expanding IR 667 cultivation from two hundred thousand hectares in 1972 to four hundred thousand hectares in 1973 have been scrapped, and the current plan is to resume experimental cultivation.[135] Meanwhile, the probable five hundred thousand peasant families who suffered due to this bureaucratic heavy-handedness are forced to survive as best they can.[136]

Saemaŭl undong

The zenith of bureaucratic meddling, mismanagement, and autocracy has been reached with the implementation of the New Countryside Movement. This movement is a last-ditch effort to use coerced labor power in place of government investment for the improvement of agricultural production. President Park has termed the NCM a "spiritual revolution"—that is, the government is not going to back it with capital investment.[137] In fact, however, some capital is being invested, notably concrete for construction projects. But the mainstays of the NCM are "self-reliance, self-help, and mutual cooperation." [138]

The NCM got underway in late 1971, and the first phase lasted through April 1972, the end of the farmers' slack season. The first phase was mostly beautification projects. They seem to have been intended to get the farmers used to working together on government-directed projects and to enable the government to show immediate results. Half the country's villages were involved. Although involvement in the NCM is supposedly voluntary (if a village wants to participate, the government will provide cement), there is actually strong coercion by all levels of the government on local officials and villages to force participation.[139] A National Assembly committee investigation found (before the October 1972 closure of the assembly) that "a large percentage of the local population [were forced to] bear a heavy portion of work" in the NCM.[140] The power of township and county officials over the lives of villagers is enormous because of their connection with the cooperatives which the peasant has to rely on for fertilizer and cheap loans; therefore, coercion is a simple matter. The lack of a real feeling of participation was voiced by a farmer in North Chŏlla province: "Why does there suddenly have to be a New Countryside Movement?" [141]

NCM projects are designed in the Ministry of Home Affairs; all officials, down to township mayors, are controlled ultimately by this ministry. The township mayor and his assistant are responsible for securing the services of the village chief, a village Movement Leader (*saemaŭl chidoja*), and a women's leader, and getting them to enlist the villagers in carrying out the designated projects. The Movement Leader holds meetings in the village to discuss the projects and get the villagers to vote for them, but it is clear from the fact that all villages do the same projects that the villagers do not actually select their own projects.[142]

I visited a model NCM village, one of the best in its province. The projects undertaken and completed were: clearing the village stream, placing white stones as road boundaries to the village road, building a concrete bridge over the stream, building three concrete washboards by the stream, and building a concrete bulletin board for government notices. In addition, a team of college students built a seesaw and two chinning bars in a play area. The projects, while decorative, made no changes in production or in village life. The projects for the second phase, to begin after the harvest season, were construction of a cow pasture on a hillside and development of compost piles. The latter was supposed to be done on a large scale, substituting compost for fertilizer. This apparently is in keeping with President Park's teachings that fertilizer is not the most suitable nourishment for crops. "The more it is used, the more it is needed." [143] And the less it is used, the less government has to divert industrial resources to the countryside and the more it can export. The drive to save government fertilizer is being pushed very forcefully with officials visiting all villages weekly to check on the progress of the compost piles.

In my formal survey of two villages, farmers were asked to indicate what improvements would make countryside life better. Out of eight choices, the three most numerous responses were: better roads, higher grain prices, and electricity. What the government thinks is good for the countryside and what the peasants want are very different. The government is demanding that peasants substitute labor for capital, while the peasants are asking for capital inputs to make their labor more productive. This contradiction was shown clearly in a recent "restricted" NACF report. Responding to a question about the reason for problems with NCM projects, 49 percent of the responding peasants blamed a lack of capital investment. Another 21 percent blamed a lack of materials and equipment.[144] Even the government party has admitted that the government's economic program is not giving financial support to the NCM.[145] What the peasants cannot do with their hands and backs will not get done, which is probably just as well, since they did not want the projects in the first place.

If the NCM was simply wasting coerced labor, it would not be more than an exercise in futility, but it is also causing financial hardship for the peasantry. In order to widen and beautify village roads, lands are confiscated without payment, sometimes forcibly. To improve the appearance of villages near major roads, to give a good impression to bureaucrats and foreigners, peasants are being forced to replace their thatched roofs with tile roofs. If they do not comply, their houses are torn down.[146] The "modernizing" of roofs has nothing to do with peasant well-being or production efficiency. It is a "hastily conceived" plan designed to compete with D.P.R.K. successes in modernizing the North Korean countryside.[147]

The bureaucratic autocracy that has marked the NCM has been criticized by newspapers and officials.[148] Even President Park took officials to task for being overbearing. But the system in South Korea fosters autocracy; there are no checks against it. A village cannot stand against a township mayor who has influence with the cooperative and controls the supply of fertilizer and credit. Likewise, a township mayor cannot stand against a county executive, and so on. Moreover, the government's view of the peasantry is of a tradition-bound, drinking, gambling, superstitious, and lazy people.[149] This view reinforces the autocratic institutions because the people on top do not believe that the peasants and other people on the bottom know what is in their own best interests.

5. THE FUTURE OF THE PEASANTRY

The South Korean peasant is being backed into a corner. He can endure his poverty or move to the city—and endure poverty there.

I discussed this dilemma with one young farmer. He was going to move to Seoul. I asked him why. His answer was, "So that I can eat rice." Since he lived in a rice-producing area, I asked him why he did not eat the rice his family grew. He said it had to be sold to earn money. I then asked him why money was so necessary to a farm family. He said they needed it to send the children to school.

I could have asked him why it was necessary to send the children to school, but he was a little embarrassed already, and besides, I knew the answer. Peasants want to educate their children so that they will not have to be farmers. So that they can move to a city and eat rice.

The following is an excellent critique of the problems plaguing the South Korean agricultural economy.

> Although an agricultural economy, Korea has had to import large quantities of food-grain annually. Corrupt and inefficient agricultural and forestry administration brought about impoverishment of the rural economy. . . . Farm prices were kept at levels considerably lower than those of other prices, with the result that farmers hardly managed to recover the actual costs of production, and, in the end, lost the will to produce. . . . The impoverishment of the rural economy reduced the purchasing power of the domestic market for products of small and medium-sized industries.

This statement castigating earlier agricultural policies was made in 1962 when the Park regime announced the First Five-Year Plan.[150] It went on to promise: "By developing agriculture, the largest segment of the Korean economy, self-sufficiency in food grain will be attained by the target year. This will free the country from the present dependence on imported food-grains, and at the same time enhance the welfare of farmers as well as improve the market for domestic products." [151] But this never happened.

The Second Five-Year Plan made the same promise: "Production of food grains has increased considerably since 1962, thus facilitating achievement of the target of self-sufficiency by 1971." [152] Even though the relative paucity of grain and the relative impoverishment of the countryside was more acute in 1971 than before, the Third Five-Year Plan amazingly proclaims: "We introduced long-term development planning for the first time in our history in 1962 and have successfully completed the first two five-year plans." It goes on to again promise that "the production of food grains will be increased and self-sufficiency will be achieved in the major food grains." [153]

There is no chance of this happening. The R.O.K. five-year plans are more sets of wishes than actual operational plans committing resource allocation to match hoped-for results.[154] A special team of agricultural economists from Michigan State University estimated in 1972 that the TFYP will still leave South Korea 20 percent short of its rice requirements by 1976.[155]

For peasants to produce more grain they must have the incentive of higher grain prices. These higher prices can come either through government subsidies or through curtailing imported grain and allowing urban demand to raise prices.[156] Neither of these policies is acceptable to the present regime. Both would make farm life liveable and thus reduce the flow of rural labor to the urban labor pool.[157] This would result in higher wage demands by urban workers, thus raising the cost of export goods.[158]

What would happen if export costs rose due to higher wages? First, exports and foreign exchange earnings would decrease. Foreign loans would slow down because South Korea would be unable to repay the foreign exchange. Foreign investment would decrease because the wage level would no longer be the second lowest in Asia. However, the economy would not collapse. Peasants and workers, with their higher incomes, would be able to purchase more manufactured goods so that export production could be shifted to domestic production. In addition, hundreds of millions of dollars of foreign exchange would be saved as peasants produced more grain, reducing grain imports. If capital were invested in rural social overhead, such as roads, schools, electrification, and hospitals, the cost of living for peasants would decline. Industries could also then locate in rural areas. If industry were diversified in this manner, the rural population could use its energies in industry during the slack season in agriculture. This is basically the development plan used by the D.P.R.K.

These are not secret formulas for success; the R.O.K. government knows all this.[159] But since it is not a government of the people or for the people, it cannot be expected to pursue policies beneficial to the people. Rather, it will continue to drain the people's energy and sell it for foreign exchange and foreign political backing.[160]

The South Korean people put up with these policies under protest. Nineteen seventy-one was noted for "the increase in violence and group protests as frustration mounted among people passed over by fruits of spectacular economic development." [161] Nineteen seventy-two produced the same, not only because of economic hardship, but also because of increasing governmental autocracy. In July five hundred fishermen in South Chŏlla province destroyed oyster beds planted by the government-run Agriculture and Fishery Development Corporation because the government had expropriated the fishermen's anchovy beds.[162] Peasants of a village on Cheju island protested the summary dismissal of their village chief by the provincial governor. The governor had ordered him fired after a young peasant of the village complained about the NCM's coerced labor policy.[163] Numerous villagers in South Ch'ungch'ŏng province failed to raise their flags on Memorial Day as required. One township mayor was fired and five others were reprimanded.[164] In North Chŏlla province farmers disobeyed government instructions to plant soybeans on the ridges of their rice field; three township officials were dismissed.[165] Sixty peasants from six villages in Kyŏnggi province staged a sit-in at the National Assembly to protest confiscation of their lands in the NCM. They were forcibly dispersed by the police.[166] These protests were all dared even under the government's 1971 State of Emergency. Since the 1972 October coup, protest has become more difficult, and protests are not allowed to be reported in the press.[167]

As the economy stagnates and the government sinks ever more investment into the overbuilt export industries, unemployment, new inflation, and reduced earnings for peasants are becoming menacing. The new measures embodied in the August 3 Decree are a contradictory blend, aimed at spurring industrial investment with newly printed money while at the same time holding prices and wages in check by government fiat. The axe will fall hardest on those least able to protect themselves—the peasants. Without organization, without elected officials, without economic power, the peasants are bound to suffer greater indignities than before in the current economic crisis.

As if to add insult to injury, the NCM has developed a scheme for setting up small workshops in the countryside. These workshops will provide profitable work for farmers in the slack season, but, more importantly, they will earn foreign exchange for the government. The workshops will not produce farm implements, but rather handicraft goods for export. By 1976, the government hopes to be earning $480 million from these exports.[168] This may be enough to pay for the grain the government will be importing by then as a consequence of its repressive agricultural policies.

POSTSCRIPT

South Korea's poet Kim Chi-ha writes of R.O.K. government ministers, "waddling from obesity," scrawling "INCREASED PRODUCTION, INCREASED EXPORT, and CONSTRUCTION" on the breasts of their mistresses. Three editors who published Kim's poem, "Five Bandits," in 1970 were found guilty of violating the Anti-Communist Law. Kim is still under indictment on the same charge. In his poem, "Groundless Rumors," (the March 1972 issue of *Sasanggye* [The realm of ideas] containing the poem was confiscated), Kim portrays the South Korean masses as trapped in a system run by rich men, swindlers, and bureaucrats. For the common man:

> nothing turned out, not even a love affair . . . not even earning meals. . . . Nothing turned out because of no backer; nothing turned out because of no school ties; nothing turned out because of no cash to buy a position; nothing turned out because of no money for bribes . . . nothing turned out because of so many rakeoffs into so many hands

When this common man realizes that it is the system and not just bad luck, he is immediately incarcerated, bound, gagged, and castrated. Yet having understood the system, he rolls (the only movement possible) with anger and rebelliousness against the walls of his cell "KLAANNG!", protesting till the end.

> And there were persons who had money and who could shit
> giant turds
> But who each time they heard that sound could not go to sleep
> for some unknown reason
> and who finally put out an order to execute this fellow at
> once . . . but still KLAANNG!
> It's strange
> For that KLAANNG! KLAANNG! which is driving some
> persons crazy never stops
> It's strange indeed
> Even now, day and night, it's heard.
> Some people say it's the work of a ghost,
> Others say that it's him that he didn't die but is still alive
> somewhere
> rolling his body against the wall.
> The people say this stealthily in low whispers with a
> strange fire in their eyes.

This essay was written with those good people in mind.

Notes

1. There are various translations for *Saemaŭl undong*. New Village Movement would be the most exact, but I prefer New Countryside Movement (NCM) because projects (such as provincial bridge construction) are being carried out in rural areas outside the boundaries of any particular village. The government uses the term New Community Movement, but aside from mobilizing a few city students to sweep their neighborhood streets, and aside from chastising the city people, the movement is, obviously, being carried out in the countryside. For example, President Park called "on the urban people to participate in the new community movement spontaneously," and to "at least not get in the way." Also, as the government newspaper commented, "In view of the fact that the cities spread the

tendency of decadence, such as waste, luxury, and lavishness, which are all anti-social practices, to the rural communities, it is high time for all the urban residents to ponder seriously what they have done for the rural communities" (*Seoul sinmun*, May 18, 1972). Throughout this essay, all references and quotations from South Korean vernacular daily newspapers are based on the daily *Press Translations* published by New Asia Press and its predecessor, North Asia Press, Seoul.

2. *Korea Times*, July 9, 1972.

3. *Korea Times*, July 16, 1972.

4. "USAID Report on Korea for Fiscal 1973," summarized in *Korea Times*, May 17, 1972.

5. Bank of Korea (BOK), *Economic Statistics Yearbook, 1971* (Seoul, 1971), p. 308. The U.S. ambassador to South Korea offered the figure of $5 billion as the total economic aid given, presumably from 1945 to 1972. U.S. Information Service (USIS), "Remarks by Ambassador Philip C. Habib" (Seoul, December 8, 1972).

6. Paul W. Kuznets, "The Korean Take-off," *Korea Journal*, January 1972, p. 16. First National City Bank (FNCB) Seoul, *Monthly Economic Letter*, June 1972, p. 2.

7. Paul W. Kuznets, "Korea's Five-Year Plans," in Irma Adelman, ed., *Practical Approaches to Development Planning: Korea's Second Five-Year Plan* (Baltimore, The Johns Hopkins Press, 1969).

8. BOK, *Yearbook*, pp. 270–71. I have taken the "Government Transaction" receipts and "Military Procurement" figures for 1964–65 as a baseline and calculated receipts above that baseline to be war profits.

9. *New York Times*, March 29, 1970, p. 1, and April 1, 1970, p. 1; *Korea Times*, September 13, 1970. Noted in Kuznets, "Take-off," n. 33.

10. "USAID Report on Korea for Fiscal 1973."

11. Lee Hyo-jae, "Life in Urban Korea," *Transactions of the Royal Asiatic Society, Korea Branch*, Vol. 46 (1971), p. 46.

12. Foreign capital as a percentage of gross investment increased from 33.2 percent in 1965 to 44 percent in 1971 (*Performance of the Korean Economy in 1971*, U.S. Embassy, Seoul [February 1972]; *Sanŏp kyŏngje sinmun*, January 20, 1973).

13. My view of the South Korean economy relies heavily on materials and analyses presented in the two Kuznets articles and in David C. Cole and Princeton N. Lyman, *Korean Development: The Interplay of Politics and Economics* (Cambridge, Mass., Harvard University Press, 1971). The latter tend to see development in terms of growth rates rather than social benefit distribution. Kuznets' "The

Korean Take-off" is the best single analysis of the South Korean economy, although Kuznets' approach to the problem is with a healthy cynicism (and sound economic theory) rather than with a political point of view. Also see my own analysis of economic changes in the more immediate period, "Lopsided Development," *Far Eastern Economic Review (FEER)*, February 26, 1973, pp. 39, 41.

14. FNCB Seoul, *Monthly Economic Letter*, April 1972, p. 3.

15. FNCB Seoul, *Monthly Economic Letter*, January 1972, p. 1; Kuznets, "Take-off," p. 17.

16. The number of shacks, according to the *Korea Times*, July 12, 1972, is 173,904. Since most hold more than one family (three to five persons), I have estimated the Seoul slum population at over one million. One of South Korea's Catholic bishops describes the situation as follows:

A small group of powerful men, who are unjust and corrupt, can accumulate unlimited wealth, enjoy a luxurious life and unrestrained freedom—better called license—while the majority of people suffer injustice, poverty and hunger. The so-called economic development is chiefly for persons backed by power. They arrogate to themselves special privileges in the name of economic growth, whose other face is recognized by most people as the accumulation of a vast foreign debt (Bishop Ji Hak-sun, "Demonstration for Social Justice," *Impact*, February 1972, p. 48).

17. Ministry of Home Affairs (MOHA), *Municipal Yearbook of Korea, 1971* (Seoul, 1971), p. 84.

18. *Ibid.*, pp. 462, 508, 524.

19. Park Jin-hwan, "The Growth of Taegu and Its Effects on Regional Agricultural Development," in Lee Man-gap and Herbert R. Barringer, eds., *A City in Transition—Urbanization in Taegu, Korea* (Seoul, Hollym Corporation, 1971), p. 146.

20. *Korean Agricultural Sector Analysis and Recommended Development Strategies, 1971–1985*, Korean Agricultural Sector Study Team, Michigan State University (East Lansing, 1972), p. 29.

21. Government of the Republic of Korea (R.O.K.G.), *The Third Five-Year Economic Development Plan, 1972–1976* (Seoul, 1971), p. 88. Villages with phones usually have only one, in the village chief's house.

22. *Sector Analysis*, p. 29.

23. *Korea Times*, May 21, 1972.

304   BERNIE WIDEMAN

24. MOHA, *Municipal Yearbook,* pp. 274–75.
25. *Korea Times,* May 21, 1972; *Sina ilbo,* January 1, 1972; *Sanŏp kyŏngje sinmun,* January 23, 1972; *Kyŏnghyang sinmun,* April 8, 1972.
26. Herbert R. Barringer, "Migration and Social Structure," in *A City in Transition,* p. 316.
27. Yu Si-joong, "Educational Institutions," in *A City in Transition,* p. 437.

Table 1

Rural Education in 1970

School	No. of children in age group	No. of students
Grade School	3,214,000	3,118,000
Middle School	1,280,000	452,000
High School	1,012,000	146,000

Source: *Sector Analysis,* p. 110.

28. MOHA, *Municipal Yearbook,* p. 342.
29. Kim Jae-jin, "Characteristics of Manufacturing Industries," in *A City in Transition,* p. 168.
30. Yu, "Educational Institutions," p. 448.
31. C. I. Eugene Kim, "Political Behavior of the Citizenry," in *A City in Transition,* p. 227. As a Seoul daily notes, "People move to Seoul to seek a means of livelihood in spite of the higher cost of living in Seoul than in other areas. They move to Seoul because administration, service and other systems of Korea are concentrated in this city" (*Chungang ilbo,* January 30, 1973).
32. Park, "Regional Agricultural Development," p. 126; *Sector Analysis,* p. 11.
33. Park, "Regional Agricultural Development," p. 152. *Sector Analysis,* p. 111.
34. Ministry of Health and Social Affairs survey, reported in *Korea Times,* July 4, 1972.
35. G. S. Tolley, "Research Needs for Korean Grain Price Policies," mimeographed (Seoul, USAID, 1971), p. 15.
36. Ministry of Agriculture and Forestry (MAF), *Report on the Results of Farm Household Economy Survey and Production Cost Survey of Agricultural Products, 1971* (Seoul, 1971), p. 90.
37. *Ibid.,* pp. 90–91.
38. National Agricultural Cooperative Federation (NACF), *Monthly Review,* April 1972, pp. 8–9, 14–15.

39. *Ibid.*, pp. 80–81, 82–83. I have deflated the 1970 figures to 1965 values with the "all item" indices on pp. 8–9 and pp. 14–15.
40. MAF, *Farm Household Economy Survey*, pp. 56–57, 64–65. The household sample for 1970 was 1180 households. Those with net losses totaled 249. However there is a bias in the sample, in that "under ½ hectare" peasants, who equal one-third of the peasantry, receive only one-quarter representation in the sample. Thus, my estimate that one-fifth suffered losses should be conservative.
41. *Korea Times*, July 28, 1972.
42. Barringer, "Migration," p. 305.
43. Bishop Ji, "Demonstration for Social Justice," p. 48. This forced migration is nowhere more movingly described than in the poem "The Road to Seoul" by Kim Chi-ha.

> I am going, don't cry,
>   I am going,
> Crossing the thirsty passes
>   that make even the sky tired,
> Along the wearisome road to Seoul,
> I am going to sell my body.

Rōnin, Vol. 1, No. 2 (March 1972) (in English).

44. *Korea Times*, July 28, 1972.
45. Park, "Regional Agricultural Development," pp. 134–35 discusses this point.
46. NACF, *Monthly Review*, p. 15.
47. According to an R.O.K. government report noted in *Korea Times*, July 28, 1972.
48. "Questions and Answers on Foreign Investment in Korea," *Korea Business*, August 1972, pp. 27–28. An average textile worker (the major export industry is textiles) earns just over $30 a month. However, unskilled textile workers (mostly young women) earn the equivalent of $7.50 to $15 a month. Wage information is according to BOK, *Yearbook*, p. 343, and conversations with Catholic priests and textile labor union leaders. Recently, workers at the Kumgang Slate Company in Suwŏn (near Seoul) attempted to form a union. The company retaliated by locking out all four hundred workers. The company also forced its workers to sign statements saying they would not seek compensation for injuries sustained on the job. See *Tonga ilbo*, June 14, 1972.
    Lest there be any doubt about the life of the migrant looking for a job in the city, the social explosion of August 1971 is instructive.

On August 10, thirty thousand slum dwellers who had been removed from their eyesore shanties in Seoul to a resettlement camp rioted. They demanded jobs and places to live. In the demonstration government buildings were destroyed and eighty-two policemen were injured. See *FEER 1972 Yearbook* (Hong Kong, 1972), p. 294.

49. A Michigan State University report states: "The program has been oriented toward maintaining reduced consumer prices as the marketing year progresses and not toward price support for farmers" (*The National Agricultural Cooperative Federation: An Appraisal*, Korean Agricultural Sector Study Team, Michigan State University [East Lansing, 1972] [hereafter cited as *NACF: An Appraisal*], p. 35).

50. *Ibid.*

51. *Tonga ilbo,* January 25, 1973.

52. NACF, *Monthly Review,* p. 24. Prices have been deflated using the "Index of Prices, Wages, and Charges Paid by Farmers," p. 14.

53.

Table 2

Rice Prices
(in wŏn)

1 Year	2 Gov't. Price (unhulled)	3 Gov't. Price (polished)	4 Private Dealer (current/constant)	5 Percentage Increase 4 over 3
1965	1533	2636	3210/3210	21%
1966	1608	2765	3386/2985	22%
1967	1746	3003	3730/2921	24%
1968	2043	3513	4390/2889	25%
1969	2505	4309	5435/3242	26%
1970	3405	5857	6000/3082	2%

Barley Prices
(in wŏn)

1	2	3	4	5
1965	1005	1678	2133/2133	33%
1966	1005	1678	2026/1792	20%
1967	1090	1820	2342/1898	28%
1968	1333	2226	2564/1728	10%
1969	1466	2448	2974/1834	21%
1970	1686	2816	3282/1792	16%

Sources: See note 52. NACF, *Agricultural Yearbook, 1971,* p. 74; MAF, *Yearbook of Agriculture and Forestry Statistics, 1971,* pp. 332–33; NACF, *Monthly Review,* pp. 12, 14, 24.

54. NACF, *Monthly Review,* p. 25, n. 1.

55. *Korea Times,* June 20, 1972.

56. *Kyŏnghyang sinmun,* June 21, 1972.

57. *Ibid.;* MAF, *Farm Household Economy Survey,* p. 90; MAF, *Yearbook of Agriculture and Forestry Statistics, 1971* (Seoul, 1971), p. 146. The area planted to barley decreased from a high of approximately 545,000 hectares in 1965 to approximately 425,000 in 1970.

58. *Kyŏnghyang sinmun,* July 22, 1972; *Korea Times,* June 21 and June 29, 1972; *Kukche sinbo,* July 26, 1972. Press reports stated that the government was paying 6357 wŏn for a 200-liter bag, rather than the 7130 wŏn President Park had promised. My own questioning of peasants revealed that they were receiving only 5900 wŏn per 200-liter bag.

59. *Seoul sinmun,* August 17, 1972.

60. *Sanŏp kyŏngje sinmun,* June 30, 1972; FNCB Seoul, *Monthly Economic Letter,* July 1972, p. 1.

61. *Han'guk ilbo,* September 13, 1972; *Korea Times,* November 10, 1972.

62. NACF, *Agricultural Yearbook,* pp. 37, 84–85.

63. *Foreign Agriculture,* U.S. Department of Agriculture, quoted in *Korea Times,* June 14, 1972 and February 9, 1973.

64. *Sanŏp kyŏngje sinmun,* November 18, 1972.

65. The first minister of agriculture under Park Chung Hee, in criticizing the grain policy of the former government, said: "It [the government] had not been willing . . . to take direct measures to support farm prices at higher levels. Instead the Government had followed an import policy which had had the effect of substantially weakening the competitive position of Korean grains in the domestic market." Foreword to Chung Nam-kyu and Oh Heung-keun, *An Introduction to Korean Agriculture* (Seoul, The American-Korean Foundation, 1962). This basic policy has remained unchanged, except that it has broadened in scope.

66. Conversations with U.S. Mission (Seoul) officials in January 1973.

67. *Foreign Agriculture,* quoted in *Korea Times,* June 14, 1972.

68. *Japan Times,* December 10, 1972, p. B6; *Korea Times,* February 9, 1973.

69. *Korea Times,* January 28, 1973.

70. *Korea Times,* January 17, 1973.

71. U.S. Operations Mission to Korea (USOM/K), *Rural Development Program Evaluation Report, Korea 1967* (Seoul, 1967), p.

125; Adlowe L. Larson and Helim H. Hulbert, *Study of Agricultural Cooperatives in Korea,* USOM/K (Seoul, 1966), p. 53.

72. The situation in North Korea is clearly presented in Harald Munthe-Kass, "Progress under Kim," *Far Eastern Economic Review,* July 1, 1972, p. 38. A somewhat more scholarly presentation (but with a hostile bias) is Joseph Chung, "Economic Development of North Korea, 1945–70," in Kim Se-jin and Cho Chang-hyun, eds., *Government and Politics of Korea* (Silver Spring, Maryland, The Research Institute on Korean Affairs, 1972), pp. 224–27. Chung believes that $12 million grain imports in 1967 indicate that the D.P.R.K. could not be self-sufficient now. South Korean agricultural economists often point to the Japanese government's subsidy policies as a model to follow. "Korea can become self-sufficient [in grain] . . . if Korean farmers have the same assurance of a protected market that the Japanese farmer has." See Chung and Oh, *An Introduction to Korean Agriculture,* pp. 160–63, especially p. 163. Conversely, as long as grain prices are forced down with cheaper imports, there will be no improvement.

73. This section has been previously published in part under the title "Political Economics of Factor Inputs in Korean Agriculture," *Korea Journal,* Vol. 13, No. 1 (January 1973), pp. 19–24.

74. Pak Ki-hyuk and others, *A Study of Land Tenure System in Korea* (Seoul, Korea Land Economics Research Center, 1966), p. 10.

75. NACF, *Agricultural Yearbook,* pp. 14–15.

76. Pak, *Land Tenure,* pp. 220–21.

77. *Ibid.,* p. 126; Koo Jae-suh, *A Study of the Regional Characteristics of Korean Agriculture* (Seoul, Korea University, 1967), pp. 379, 387, 435.

78. Pak, *Land Tenure,* p. 135. This statistic is for 1965, the most recent available. Informed Korean observers, however, note that absentee landlordism rose remarkably between 1969 and 1971.

79. *Korea Times,* June 28, 1972.

80. Robert B. Morrow and Kenneth H. Sherper, *Land Reform in South Korea,* USAID Country Papers (Washington, D.C., June 1970), pp. 5–6, 15, 19–22, 35.

81. Pak, *Land Tenure,* p. 131 and n. 4. In a small survey done in 1958, pure tenants were 9.8 percent and partial tenants were 13.4 percent of the sample (Lee Man-gap, "Politics in a Korean Village," mimeographed [Seoul, 1969?], p. 16).

82. Pak, *Land Tenure,* pp. 146–48.

83. MAF, *Yearbook,* pp. 46–47.

84. Pak, *Land Tenure*, p. 163; Yoo Chin-sok, *Report on Field Study in Employment and Income Pattern of Farm Household in Rural Community in Korea* (Seoul, Korean Social Science Research Institute, 1969), pp. 132–33; MAF, *Farm Household Economy Survey*, pp. 60, 63, 66, 70, 71, 74.

85. My own questioning in January 1973 of a South Korean Red Cross official in Majang-dong, one of Seoul's large slum areas, revealed the following statistics concerning the employment of the local population: employed in business establishments, 20 percent; self-employed (i.e., A-frame carriers, etc.), 50 percent; unemployed, 30 percent. If these percentages are applicable to Seoul's other slums, and I assume they are, they indicate that 70 percent of the males in the slum population of one million are unemployed or underemployed. Anyone who has dealt with R.O.K. government labor statistics realizes that they are simply fantasies. Since there is no unemployment compensation or other means of registering those unemployed, the R.O.K. government simply subtracts the number of people working (a figure arrived at by spot checks) from the number of people in the population assumed to be in the job market.

86. According to a 1968 survey, 62.2 percent of those migrating to Seoul came directly from the countryside. One scholar states categorically: "Industrial labor demand has not been the major factor pulling the rural population into the cities. . . . Most migrants coming into cities leave the village with no definite prospect of employment in the cities" (Lee Hyo-chai, *Industrialization and the Family in Korea* [Honolulu, Social Science Research Institute, University of Hawaii, 1971], pp. 6–7). For a different view, see Lee Man-gap, "Pushing or Pulling," *Report of the International Conference on Urban Problems and Regional Development* (Seoul, Yonsei University, 1970). But Professor Lee Man-gap's view that "pulling" is more of a factor than "pushing" is due mainly to semantic difficulties and his choice of a middle-class rather than a lower-class sample. See especially pp. 117–18.

87. NACF, *Monthly Review*, pp. 80–81.

88. BOK, *Yearbook*, p. 6.

89. *Korea Times*, February 4, 1973. In an article of uneven quality, Woo Ki-do has demonstrated that South Korea's economic growth has been due mainly to the influx of cheap labor into export industries. The author also shows that wages have been held at subsistence levels in manufacturing by building a pool of unemployed and underemployed persons in urban service industries, i.e., porters and the like, who are transferable to manufacturing. The main weakness of Woo's article is his assumption that the underemployed persons who migrated into the tertiary (service) sector had previously been underemployed in the primary (agricultural) sector. In fact, the author disproves his own assumption by noting that women have had to take the place of men in agriculture to make up for rural labor shortages. Since Woo's research also discloses that the monthly wage in agriculture is higher than in industry, his contention that labor has left the rural areas for better opportunities in industry seems unfounded. However, his conclusions regarding the need for a continued supply of cheap labor are very important. See Woo Ki-do, "Labor Force, Wage Level and Economic Growth in Korea," *Asian Economies,* September 1972, pp. 12–51.

90. Kim Sam-o, "Industrial Fallout—South Korea," *FEER,* January 22, 1972, p. 34.

91. NACF, *Agricultural Yearbook,* p. 14.

92. The percentage of persons in the economically active age group (i.e., over twenty) is 56.8 percent of the total population in Seoul, but only 46.8 percent of the population in Kangwŏn and North Ch'ungch'ŏng provinces (*Kangwŏn ilbo,* December 12, 1972).

93. See discussion of tenancy above; also, Yoo, *Report on Income Pattern,* p. 17.

94. Kim Seung-hee, "Economic Development of South Korea," in *Government and Politics of Korea,* pp. 157–61.

95. BOK, *Yearbook,* p. 29.

96. Kuznets, "Take-off," p. 10.

97. Kim, "Economic Development," p. 170.

98. R.O.K.G., *Third Five-Year Plan,* statement by President Park, n.p.

99. *Ibid.,* pp. 41, 181.

100. *Ibid.,* pp. 19, 187.

101. Han Nae-bok, "Third Five-Year Plan and Green Revolution," *Korea Journal,* March 1972, p. 4.

102. Munthe-Kass, "Progress under Kim," p. 38.

103. *Sector Analysis,* p. 28; *Daehan ilbo,* July 14, 1972; Pak, *Land Tenure,* p. 476.

104. *Korea Times,* August 3 and August 19, 1972. (In 1972 the exchange rate was W400-$1.) Most Asian policy makers in "free" Asia tend to favor industry at the expense of agriculture, but developmental economists point out that "the sensibility of such a policy is questionable." See Uma J. Lele, "Agricultural Development in Asia," *Economic Development and Cultural Change,* July 1972, pp. 754–55.

105. Concerning the AID fund diversion, see *Korea Times,* May 17, 1972. Possibly the height of venality was reached by the Kunsan city government (a major U.S. airbase is nearby), which forbade older women from engaging in prostitution for U.S. troops because they were lowering the attractiveness level of Korean prostitutes and thereby causing a loss of foreign exchange (*Chungang ilbo,* June 14, 1972).

106. NACF, *Agricultural Yearbook,* p. 34.

107. Although the R.O.K. Economic Planning Board calculated the population growth at only 1.9 percent, U.S. experts consider 2.2 percent to be closer to reality (*Kyŏnghyang sinmun,* January 19, 1973).

108. MAF, *Yearbook,* p. 128. In 1968 the per hectare rice yield was 4180 kilograms in Taiwan and 5720 kilograms in Japan. It was only 2790 kilograms in South Korea (*ibid.,* p. 489).

109. R.O.K.G., *Third Five-Year Plan,* p. 12. The government plans to have 7.8 million tons of rice and barley in 1976. South Korea produced 6.3 million tons in 1970. By way of contrast, the D.P.R.K. has set a grain target of between 7 and 7.5 million tons for 1976 (the end of its current six-year plan). In the mid-1960s, North Korea produced 5 million tons. It should be remembered that the north has only half the population of the south. See Munthe-Kass, "Progress under Kim," p. 38.

110. Harvest figures for 1972 have not been released at the time of writing. My information is from Western diplomats.

111. NACF, *Agricultural Yearbook,* p. 34.

112. MAF, *Yearbook,* pp. 216, 218, 223.

113. Edward R. Wright, Jr., "Perceptions of Community Power," in *A City in Transition.* For example, the city of Taegu in 1967 presented the central government with 4 *billion* wŏn of taxes. In return, the central government gave Taegu 8 *million* wŏn in transfer taxes and subsidies. See p. 244. Local taxes provide only 20 percent of provincial budgets; 70 percent is central government subsidy (*Rural Infrastructure,* Korean Agricultural Sector Study Team, Michigan State University [East Lansing, 1972], p. 34).

114. Pak, *Land Tenure,* pp. 358–59, 371–72.

115. Cho Chang-hyun, "Bureaucracy and Local Government in South Korea," in *Government and Politics of Korea,* p. 123.

116. *Ibid.,* pp. 106–12.

117. *Ibid.,* p. 113; Vincent S. R. Brandt, *A Korean Village Between Farm and Sea* (Cambridge, Mass., Harvard University Press, 1971), p. 164; Larson and Hulbert, *Study of Agricultural Coopera-*

tives, p. 2. In my conversations with village chiefs, they insisted that they were elected by the villagers. However, my survey was in a different region from Brandt's. Professor Lee Man-gap points out that selection procedures are still not firmly institutionalized (Lee, "Politics in a Korean Village," p. 20).

118. This was the situation when this essay was first written in the summer and early fall of 1972. The October 17, 1972 coup by Park Chung Hee wiped out these voting rights as well. The South Korean people, according to the new constitution forced on them in November 1972, can no longer select their own president. Instead, he is selected by a hand-picked group of delegates called the National Conference for Unification (NCU), the chairman of which is Park Chung Hee. Also according to the new constitution, the South Korean people can no longer truly elect the members of the National Assembly. One-third of the assemblymen are appointed by Park Chung Hee. The other two-thirds are "elected" by the people, but since only government-controlled campaigning is allowed, the chance for a true election is gone. Moreover, the new constitution and new National Assembly Law effectively disembowel the National Assembly.

119. Brandt, *A Korean Village,* pp. 70ff., 75, 91, 103–4.

120. USOM/K, *Rural Development Evaluation,* pp. 292–93.

121. NACF, *Agricultural Yearbook,* p. 145. That the cooperatives do not actually serve South Korean peasants is reflected in the fact that the majority of peasants have little confidence in them. See *NACF: An Appraisal,* pp. 46ff. The Korean language version of this report was labelled "restricted" by NACF and suppressed.

122. Larson and Hulbert, *Study of Agricultural Cooperatives,* pp. 5, 9, 79; USOM/K, *Rural Development Evaluation,* p. 242.

123. Larson and Hulbert, *Study of Agricultural Cooperatives,* p. 11.

124. For example, in 1969 and 1970 farmers lost 20 percent of the market price on each bag of rice paid to the cooperatives in exchange for fertilizer (*Sector Analysis,* p. 18, n. 3).

125. Information obtained from my own questionnaire. The questions were: "Do you prefer to market your grain through the cooperative or through private individuals? Why?"

126. *Sector Analysis,* p. 28. Answering questions on my written questionnaire, villagers who had cooperative loans indicated that they were paying between 18 and 23 percent per annum, but mostly 18 percent. The interest rate quoted by the government is 15 percent. See NACF, *Agricultural Yearbook,* p. 179. Significantly, those households in my sample receiving the cooperative loans were exactly the largest landholders in the village, mostly with holdings above the government-set three-hectare limit. In contrast to the NACF interest rate, borrowing from other farmers requires interest averaging 68.3 percent yearly, while borrowing from professional moneylenders carries interest charges averaging 121.7 percent yearly (*NACF: An Appraisal*, p. 16).

127. Of the total funds available to NACF for lending, only about 25 percent go to agriculture. The bulk of the funds, about 60 percent, go to non-agriculture loans. The result is that only one-third of all farmers seeking loans can get them from NACF. The remaining two-thirds must obtain them from private channels (*ibid.*, pp. 15, 21, 22). The NACF states that only 30 percent of its loans go to non-farm enterprises (NACF, *Agricultural Yearbook*, p. 177).

128. USOM/K, *Rural Development Evaluation*, p. 66.

129. *Ibid.*, p. 289, and conversations with a foreign advisor to the R.O.K. government's agricultural development program.

130. *Sector Analysis*, p. 27; USOM/K, *Rural Development Evaluation*, p. 285; Brandt, *A Korean Village*, pp. 193–94. According to a foreign advisor working with ORD, in the period just prior to the November 1972 constitutional referendum, all the district cadre were out in the villages going from house to house badgering the peasants to vote in favor of the new constitution.

131. *Sector Analysis*, pp. 27, 105; Yu Wan-jae, "Survey of the Administrative System of Rural Extension Works in Kangwŏn-do," mimeographed (Seoul, 1967?), pp. 11–12.

132. On my questionnaire, villagers were asked to indicate those farming improvements that would increase production. Of eight choices, the most frequent response was "seed improvement."

133. Yu, "Rural Extension Works," pp. 14–15.

134. *Ibid.*, pp. 13–14. For example, new seeds demand new and varied additions of fertilizers, but fertilizer production is controlled by government monopoly, and distribution by the NACF, neither of which the ORD researchers can influence.

135. Information is mainly from conversations with U.S. Mission officials and foreign technical advisors. Also see *Korea Times*, July 18, 1972, January 25, 1973.

136. The government announced that 3000 hectares of IR 667 planted by 15,000 families were a total loss. Assuming that half the total 200,000 hectares planted yielded poor harvests, and using the 5:1 proportion given by the government report of families per hectare, I have concluded that those suffering poor harvests would number around 500,000. Only the 15,000 families which suffered total loss will receive government compensation (*Korea Times*, November 18, 1972).

137. Quoted in *Sin tonga*, July 1972, p. 180. An official of the government-controlled Agriculture and Fishery Development Corporation notes that the New Countryside Movement is "an attempt to convert rural labor into capital in the form of improved roads, better housing, more sanitary environment, and other visible assets conducive to higher productivity and efficiency in agriculture" (Han Nae-bok, "New Community Movement," *Korea Journal*, July, 1972, p. 4).

138. *Seoul sinmun*, May 18, 1972; MOHA, *Saemaŭl undong* (Seoul, 1972), p. 6.

139. The governor of South Ch'ungch'ŏng province dismissed a county official for "slow progress" in the NCM (*Tonga ilbo*, July 7, 1972). The government of Cheju City replaced ninety-nine neighborhood chiefs (*pan–jang*) for failure "to push ahead" with the NCM (*Korea Times*, June 23, 1972). Nor are these isolated incidents; approximately 5 percent of all township mayors and deputy mayors were replaced.

140. *Korea Times*, October 15, 1972.

141. Quoted in *Sin tonga*, July 1972, p. 194.

142. The projects are listed in the Ministry of Home Affairs' brochure, *Saemaŭl undong*. I know of an incident where a precocious middle school student questioned her social studies teacher about this issue of free will. The social studies textbook states that NCM projects are decided upon by each village. The student told the teacher that she had heard that the government actually decided upon the projects and wondered what the situation actually was. The teacher got angry and told her not to question what was in the textbook.

143. *Korea Times*, June 21, 1972.

144. NACF, *Nongch'on kyŏnggi tonghyang chosa pogŏ, 72.2/4 punki, yowŏl* [Second quarter 1972 research report on agricultural conditions and trends—a summary] (Seoul, July 1972), p. 34.

145. *Korea Herald*, June 8, 1972. On the other hand, the government explanation for problems associated with the completion of NCM projects is that village leadership and participation are weak. See MOHA, *Saemaŭl undong*, p. 13.

146. The excesses of bureaucratic autocracy in the NCM are amusing, instructive, and tragic. In one province alone, 834 people sued for compensation for confiscated lands (confiscated by the military).

They were denied compensation by the court. See *Korea Times,* May 21, 1972. In another province, seventy-two hectares of ripening barley were destroyed by county officials for a landscaping project. See *Tonga ilbo,* June 3, 1972. In a separate incident in the same province, eleven thatch-roofed houses were torn down by the county government because high-ranking officials were scheduled to pass by a few days later to attend a Farmers' Day ceremony (the rural equivalent of Labor Day). See *Tonga ilbo,* June 3, 1972. A Western diplomat in Seoul related to me in the summer of 1972 how he was repeatedly asked, beseeched, and commanded during that spring to replace the thatched roof on his countryside house. He adamantly refused, and the local officials finally gave up. All his Korean neighbors had to change their roofs. The Ministry of Home Affairs has admitted that excesses in the NCM have included no compensation for property loss, inferior materials, forcible collection of money from villagers who refused to participate, discontent over forced labor practices, and forcing villagers into debt in order to carry out projects. See *Kukche sinbo,* April 18, 1972.

147. Conversation with an AID contract employee in Seoul. Another reason for the drive to change to tile roofs, according to a Seoul bank official, is that the firm making the most profit from roof tile sales is the Hyundai Group, a huge conglomerate whose owner is a close friend and backer of President Park.

148. For example, see the *Chosŏn ilbo,* May 15, 1972.

149. MOHA, "Saemaŭl undong iran?" [What is the New Countryside Movement?] Pamphlet No. 2 (Seoul, 1972), pp. 21–24; MOHA, *Saemaŭl undong,* p. 8. The government newspaper speaks of correcting "their chronic evil practices and traditions inherited from generation to generation" (*Seoul sinmun,* May 18, 1972).

150. R.O.K.G., *Summary of the First Five-Year Economic Plan, 1962–1966* (Seoul, 1962), pp. 9–11. The sad fact is that the record of agricultural growth was better before the FFYP. See Han, "The New Community Movement," p. 4.

151. R.O.K.G., *First Five-Year Plan,* p. 25.

152. R.O.K.G., *The Second Five-Year Economic Development Plan, 1967–1971* (Seoul, 1966), p. 20.

153. R.O.K.G., *Third Five-Year Plan,* Preface, p. 2.

154. George L. Mehren, "Preliminary Analysis of the Third Five-Year Plan for the Agricultural Sector, Republic of Korea," mimeographed (New York, 1969). This is a consultant's study undertaken for the R.O.K. government. See p. 19.

155. *Sector Analysis,* pp. 74–75. The TFYP is referred to as Alternate I.

156. Mehren, "Analysis of the Agricultural Sector," p. 38.

157. *Sector Analysis,* pp. 84, 92.

158. Mehren, "Analysis of the Agricultural Sector," p. 23.

159. *Ibid.,* pp. 38–39; Koo, *Regional Characteristics,* p. 713; Pak, *Land Tenure,* p. 468. Park Chung Hee's first minister of agriculture pointed out in 1962:

> In the process [of industrialization] . . . it appears that the economic well being of the farmers was more or less taken for granted, so that very little was done to correct the situation which resulted from falling prices and inadequate farm incomes. . . . The farmers' plight might be dismissed as a part of the cost of building up a new economy for Korea, if it were not for the fact that the same farmers comprise approximately 60 percent of Korea's potential market for industrial products. Consequently the farm depression had a repressive effect upon Korean industry.

These remarks have never been heeded by the Park regime, and in fact the "farmers' plight" *is* dismissed as a cost of aiding the industrialist. See "Foreword" to Chung and Oh, *An Introduction to Korean Agriculture.*

160. Foreign countries (such as the United States and Japan) with heavy loans and investments in South Korea are not in a position to normalize relations with the D.P.R.K. easily. More importantly, the United States and Japan would not look favorably on a revolution in South Korea that would repudiate the Park regime's policies and indebtedness. Many current U.S. policies directly and indirectly aid the Park regime's ability to control the people. The most important is the $1 billion donated to this regime for bolstering the U.S. position in Vietnam. Second is the $400 million annually in military and economic assistance. Third is the stationing of troops in South Korea and the $180 million spent on their upkeep. Fourth is the PL 480 grain, which makes it possible for the Park regime to fleece the peasants with relative impunity. Pertinent information can be found in USIS, "Remarks by Sen. Charles H. Percy," News Release (Seoul, December 2, 1972), p. 2.

161. *FEER 1972 Yearbook,* p. 292.

162. *Korea Times,* July 18, 1972.

163. *Tonga ilbo,* June 1, 1972.

164. *Tonga ilbo,* June 13, 1972.
165. *Tonga ilbo,* July 20, 1972.
166. *Chosŏn ilbo,* July 27, 1972.
167. Numerous people in the countryside, and in the cities as well, protested the government's autocracy in handling the constitutional referendum and the campaign prior to it. One villager near Namwŏn, North Chŏlla province, was arrested for complaining in the voting line. As the villagers have not seen him since, they assume he was killed while being beaten in the police office. People throughout the country complained to newspapers and ministers that their referendum ballots had been cast for them before they arrived at the polling places.
168. *Korea Times,* November 17, 1972.

"Democracy" in South Korea, 1948-72

James B. Palais

If there is one lesson to be learned from a study of Korean history, it is that the reality of Korean politics has always been masked and obscured by a facade of borrowed political institutions. In the dynastic period that lasted to 1910, Chinese institutions of a centralized despotic monarchy were taken over by a native Korean hereditary aristocracy. The result was the creation of a hybrid political form that attained an extraordinary degree of stability. In the twenty-five years since the establishment of the Republic of Korea (R.O.K.) in the southern part of the peninsula in 1948, political life has been structured almost totally through democratic institutions borrowed directly from the United States and the West. The Republic of Korea was born in 1948 with all the accouterments of a democratic republic. Its new constitution provided for a popularly elected legislature, a president elected indirectly by the legislature, universal suffrage and the secret ballot, an independent judiciary, local self-government, and guarantees of civil liberties including freedom of speech, press, and association.

Yet in the past twenty-five years South Korea has at no time really possessed democratic government, even though some of its borrowed democratic institutions appeared to be functioning reasonably well. Except for the brief hiatus of military rule from 1961 to 1963, elections for the presidency and National Assembly were held on time, political parties were organized, and the press seemed relatively outspoken. These developments, however, merely distorted the reality of Korean politics by directing the attention of outside observers to the superficialities rather than the substance of political power. Of what use are elections of legislators to a National Assembly if real power is vested in the executive, and the legislature performs merely a marginal function as a forum of debate for frustrated politicians? Of what use are presidential elections if they serve only to legitimize the power of a dictator who either manipulates the electoral process to guarantee victory or changes the constitution at will to prevent the possibility of defeat at the polls? Of what significance is an ostensibly independent judiciary if in fact it is subject to control and coercion from the state and used as a means of repression of the government's political enemies? Of what consequence are political parties if they are prevented from extending their organizational base among the people as a means of winning power in open competition with the political establishment? And of what value is a press whose freedom of expression is limited only to politically innocuous topics?

There are several conditions which are at least necessary, if not sufficient, for democratic government. If a constitution is used as the expression of the fundamental principles governing the organization of a democratic state, respect must be shown for its sanctity if it is to serve as a legitimizing force for the exercise of political power. The mass of the population must have the right to participate in government by running for office, organizing political parties, and selecting political leaders through the electoral process. There must be freedom to express one's views on public affairs so that the electorate at least has the opportunity for a rational choice of leaders and issues. The people, political actors, and the media must have freedom from oppression and intimidation by the state and the protection afforded to individual rights by due process of law. And the elected representatives of the people should be able to serve in a legislature that has the power to make laws. If too many of these necessary conditions are absent, there is little chance for the true functioning of democratic process. In the history of the Republic of Korea very few of them have, indeed, been present.

There is no single reason for the failure of democracy in South Korea in the last quarter century. In the past, one could have pointed to low levels of urbanization, industrialization, education, and a small middle class as causal factors. It is, however, no longer so clear to many students of developing nations that high percentages in these aspects of social mobilization are sufficient for democratic development. In South Korea's case, an urban population of about half the total population, high rates of literacy and education, and growth in per capita income have not been sufficient to overcome other obstacles to democratic politics.

The South Korean regimes have constantly been subjected to immense pressures and strong desires to achieve certain goals. The uninterrupted threat of war, invasion, and internal subversion has created intense anxiety over problems of security—a burden that Japan has not had to bear since the end of World War II in her search for stability and democracy. South Korea has also been engaged in a desperate struggle to escape poverty and create an industrialized and prosperous nation. Her people have always needed to overcome feelings of national inferiority and gain a sense of value in the eyes of the world, and they have ardently desired national reunification for their divided peninsula. South Korean political leaders have almost always stressed that national concerns and national goals have been too important to be obstructed by the legalistic niceties of democratic process. One suspects that the majority of the population has agreed.

More fundamental, possibly, than the overriding urgency of national goals as an explanation for the failure of democracy has been the absence of attitudes and values necessary for viable democratic government. Democracy requires a respect for political process that outweighs the desire for the achievement of specific goals. It requires a patience for the delay and inefficiency that are the usual concomitants of open debate and legislative procedure. Political leaders must be willing to play by the rules of the political game, to tolerate opposition, and to concede defeat in peaceful political competition. Political leaders must also recognize that competition is the essence of democratic politics; they must have confidence that the democratic process will transform apparent disharmony and disunity into cohesiveness and consensus rather than lead to disintegration and chaos. They must also be willing to accept restraints on the use of their power lest they establish precedents for authoritarian and undemocratic action. And they must have confidence in the validity of honest mass election politics; that is, they must be willing to abide by popular and majority decisions whether they believe the masses are the true possessors of political wisdom or not. Syngman Rhee, Park Chung Hee, lesser political leaders, and probably the vast majority of the Korean population have not shared these essential values.

To the contrary, the opposite situation is closer to the truth. In addition to the demand for rapid economic growth, national security, and reunification, political leaders have not been willing to play by the rules of the game. They have not tolerated opposition, they equate competition with disharmony and disunity, they are not willing to accept restraints on the use of power, and they have no confidence in the political wisdom of the masses. Although the political styles of Rhee and Park have been markedly different in many respects, both men shared similar attitudes toward politics. A fundamental transformation of values is therefore necessary if democracy is ever to succeed in any part of Korea, but at the present time the prognosis is not good.

1. THE RHEE REGIME, 1948–60 [1]

Syngman Rhee was the father of the Republic of Korea, but he was anything but the father of Korean democracy. He spent over thirty years in exile in the United States during Japanese colonial rule (1910–45) and took an advanced degree at Princeton under the tutelage of Woodrow Wilson, but his political behavior after his return to Korea in 1945 demonstrated that he had either failed to assimilate the lessons of American democratic politics or found them irrelevant to Korean circumstances. Rhee came to power in the three years of internecine political strife between Korea's liberation from Japanese rule in 1945 and the founding of the Republic of Korea in 1948, an act which helped to seal the political division of the Korean peninsula at the 38th parallel. During this period Rhee outmaneuvered, discredited, and repressed the socialists and communists with the aid of the police, right-wing youth groups and gangs, and the American military government. In a situation in which only disorganized conservatives remained as participants in politics, Rhee emerged as the single most powerful political leader.

No sooner did Rhee come to power as the first president of a nominally constitutional democratic republic than he set about forging the tools of autocratic power in almost total disregard for the constitution and democratic process. When constitutional limitations stood in his way, Rhee ignored them or amended the constitution at will. When the legislature proved recalcitrant, he arrested and jailed its members and unashamedly coerced it into the passage of legislation. Rhee regarded electoral politics as nothing more than a tool to be used to perpetuate his rule. At the outset he possessed a contemptuous disdain for political organization and viewed himself as a national leader who transcended the demeaning competition of political parties and factions. And he preferred to use agencies of coercion—the police and the army—to ensure his power rather than to try to persuade his political opponents.

By ruthlessness, force, and manipulation Rhee was able to stay in power for twelve years until overthrown by the student uprising of 1960. Yet for all his political skill, he possessed glaring weaknesses. Rhee failed to realize that subtle tactics were necessary for the manipulation of an ostensibly democratic system if it was to retain its value as a source of legitimacy. His violation of the electoral system was so flagrant that it provoked the 1960 mass uprising. His police were also heavy-handed in the use of violence against both political opponents and students. Rhee did little to check overt corruption in the civil and military bureaucracies, and he was almost totally concerned with political problems to the neglect of economic development and growth.

A significant clue to understanding the subsequent success of Park Chung Hee is that Park learned from Rhee's mistakes and thereby created a more impregnable base of political power. Where Rhee was clumsy in his manipulation of democratic institutions, Park was skillful and subtle. After 1963 Park developed a political party and used the bureaucratic structure to help win elections. He restrained his police from the more overt forms of violence. Park used better tactics in quelling and preventing student demonstrations. He appealed to his policies of economic development, utilized the fears of the people, appealed to their nationalist consciousness, and catered to their desires for unification not only to win elections but to guarantee popular support for his constitutional amendments and for his transformation of the political system itself. The two men thus represent two different stages in the evolution toward modern autocratic authority.

The first stimulus to Rhee's undermining of constitutional democracy came with the Yŏsu rebellion in October 1948. After the rebellion was put down, Rhee passed the infamous National Security Law in December. The security law became a model for future legislation of the same type by defining sedition and treason in such vague terms as to allow the government and the police the utmost license in the persecution of political enemies as well as communists and revolutionaries. The law was constitutional because of the phrase in the constitution that civil liberties would be subject to "the provision of law." Under the new security law, "disturbing the tranquility of the nation" was made a crime against the state, and on these grounds and others ninety thousand persons were arrested in the aftermath of the rebellions. School teachers were investigated, the army was purged, and some newspapers were closed and reporters arrested.

In 1949 the National Assembly began to assert its independence by passing resolutions calling for the withdrawal of foreign troops from Korea and the institution of local self-government, by voting no confidence in Rhee's cabinet, and by overriding his veto of land reform. Rhee responded by arresting and trying over a dozen legislators. By these means Rhee exhibited almost total disdain for the dignity of the elected legislature and helped to undermine the integrity of the courts by exerting improper pressure for the prosecution of the assemblymen. Rhee was determined to subjugate both the legislative and judicial branches of government to his will.

In the spring of 1949 Kim Koo, a leading right-wing politician, leader of the Korean Provisional Government in exile during the colonial period and a political opponent of Rhee, was assassinated under circumstances that suggest Rhee's complicity or approval. Shortly thereafter Rhee announced that the elections scheduled for May 1950 would be postponed, but under pressure from the United States he was forced to retract this order. By early 1950 opposition to Rhee in the National Assembly had gained momentum. The opposition bill for conversion of the presidential system to a cabinet responsible to the legislature was narrowly defeated, and in the May elections Rhee emerged with only a few legislators committed to his leadership. Despite Rhee's efforts it appeared that the structure of electoral politics was operating to topple him from power, but he was saved from political disaster by the outbreak of the Korean War.

When the North Koreans invaded the South on June 25, 1950, political issues were postponed as the Republic of Korea struggled for its very life. After the tide had turned and a degree of stability had been restored, Rhee turned his attention back to political matters. By the end of 1951 Rhee had organized the Liberal party to support him in the legislature, a mild concession to the realities of parliamentary government. Although the Liberal party had an extraparliamentary component, Rhee's main objective was to organize forces within the legislature to gain his political objectives.

Rhee's power and prestige were enhanced considerably by the war. He maintained his control over the police and the army, which by the end of the war had grown to about 700,000 men. Rhee was now the national leader in charge of the struggle against invasion and communism, and he used the opportunity to obliterate the Left by force. Many were killed in the routine violence of war. Thousands more were rounded up and rushed through trials, and five hundred were executed. Migration to the north of other leftists rid the regime of those it could not catch and incarcerate. The war thus provided an opportunity for the elimination of the left wing in politics and the creation of ideological conformity.

In 1952 Rhee resumed his attack on the National Assembly by pushing through, by methods that were tantamount to a political atrocity, constitutional amendments for the direct election of the president and the creation of a bicameral legislature. Both measures were designed to increase his power and weaken the legislature, the first by removing the legislature's power to elect the president and the second by dividing and expanding the assembly to make it easier to control. Rhee mobilized youth groups and gangs to organize "spontaneous" demonstrations on behalf of his measures. He then used the demonstrations to justify the imposition of martial law in Pusan, where the government was then located. When the assembly voted to lift martial law, military police surrounded the assembly building and arrested several dozen legislators. On July 3 the police rounded up legislators who were boycotting the assembly in protest, took them and previously arrested assemblymen to the assembly building, surrounded the meeting place with guards, and forced the legislature to approve Rhee's constitutional amendments. Under coercion the assembly also passed new election laws and scheduled a presidential election for August 5, allowing hardly any time for opposition campaigning. Not surprisingly, Rhee won the presidential election with 72 percent of the popular vote. Armed with control over the police and local administration, and supported by a politically unsophisticated populace threatened by the insecurity of war, Rhee could hardly lose. In the midst of a war being fought in the name of democracy, Rhee dealt a disabling blow to the democratic process and strengthened the foundations of authoritarian rule.

By this time Rhee had discovered the utility of the political party backed by the apparatus of the central government as the means of perpetuating his power in an electoral system, but despite his overwhelming advantage in electoral competition he watched with dismay as his popular support dwindled in subsequent elections. When it became obvious that party and election politics alone could not guarantee his power, he decided to ensure victory by increased repression and election rigging.

In the elections of May 1954 Rhee's Liberal party won over half the seats in the National Assembly and by the use of bribery and cajolery of independent legislators attempted to acquire the two-thirds majority necessary for constitutional amendments. When Rhee's proposal to abolish the two-term limitation on the presidency fell short of the necessary two-thirds approval by a mere one-third of a vote, he had the speaker declare that the fraction could be "rounded off" and the amendment passed. This marked the second time in two years that Rhee had subverted the legislature and the constitution in order to achieve his ends.

In 1956 Rhee suffered another setback when the opposition Democratic party candidate, Chang Myŏn, won the vice-presidential election. Most of Chang's support came from the urban population discontented by inflation, economic hardship, and bureaucratic corruption. Rhee responded to the new threat with repression. The first casualty of the new wave of reaction was Cho Pong-am, leader of the Progressive party, the only representative of the moderate Left on the national scene, and presidential candidate in 1952 and 1956. Cho had obtained an impressive two million votes in 1956, and his party had advocated a program of socialist democracy, a planned economy, and peaceful unification. By the summer of 1959, the Progressive party was broken up and Cho was executed on trumped-up charges of collusion with North Korean agents. There was obviously no room for democratic socialism under Rhee.

Cho's arrest in 1958 was only a prelude to the passage of a new National Security Law in December. Once again the dignity and sanctity of the legislature had to be violated to secure passage of the law. Outnumbered in the legislature, the opposition assemblymen resorted to a sit-down strike to block passage of the legislation. The government used police to clear the opposition from the hall. The Liberal party legislators then rammed through twenty-two bills, including the new National Security Law.

Under the terms of the new security law, the criminal libel law was extended to include derogatory statements or criticisms by the press of the president, speaker of the House of Representatives, or the chief justice of the Supreme Court. The law also allowed for extended detention of individuals suspected of crimes and for the arrest of civilians by agents of the armed forces intelligence agencies.

The Rhee regime now approached the 1960 presidential elections determined to win both the presidential and vice-presidential posts. Rhee was left unopposed on the ballot when, in a repetition of the events of 1956, his chief opponent died in an American hospital a month before the election. Had Rhee and his Liberal party been content with another victory for the presidency, they would undoubtedly have remained in power, but they chose to rig the elections to ensure the defeat of Vice-President Chang Myŏn. Police suppression of riots that followed announcement of the lopsided defeat of Chang kindled the flames of rebellion. Thousands of students took to the streets in protest, and when the police defending the presidential mansion fired into the crowd of students killing over a hundred of them, the death knell was also sounded on the Rhee regime.

Rhee declared martial law, but to no avail. Army troops refused to fire on the people in the streets and the commanders remained neutral. The Americans withheld ammunition from the martial law command and put pressure on Rhee to compromise. The newly elected Liberal party vice-president committed suicide with his family, and Rhee himself resigned and went into exile in Hawaii. The first Republic had come to an end.

The so-called April student revolution of 1960 marked the defeat of Rhee's autocracy, but it did not signify a victory for democracy. There were several sources of discontent in the late Rhee years: corruption and profiteering among government officials, economic distress, police brutality, profligate and ostentatious expenditure, and decadent morality in a *sauve qui peut* atmosphere produced by the continuing threat of renewed war. The election process itself had also become sufficiently legitimized in South Korean politics that a completely and openly fixed election was too much for many people to bear. The legitimation and institutionalization of electoral procedure must, however, be separated from the inculcation of democratic values and legitimation of the democratic process in the minds of the people. Many South Koreans demanded fair elections, but they were not that concerned about what happened between elections. The fact that the elected representatives of the people had been ignored, degraded, arrested, and jailed had stirred no one to violent opposition. The fact that the legislature had been completely dominated by the executive, that the judiciary was a helpless pawn in the hands of the administration, or that guarantees of freedom of speech, press, and association had been flouted had never stirred any mass demonstrations in defense of democracy.

The Korean people had been given little opportunity to develop respect for democracy or to develop strong institutions to support a democratic system. In addition to the subjugation of the courts and the legislature to the executive, local government remained under central control; political parties were weak and disorganized, and of little use in integrating urban and rural masses into political participation; and little leeway had been allowed for the healthy development of a free and responsible press.

2. THE SECOND REPUBLIC, APRIL 1960–MAY 1961 [2]

With Rhee removed from power, South Koreans seemed to have been provided with the best opportunity since 1945 for the establishment of a truly democratic order. The constitution was amended in June 1960 for the fourth time since 1948, but the amendments were now designed to remove restraints on civil liberties and make the executive and legislative branches of the government responsible .to the people. The new amendments made the president a figurehead and provided for a prime minister and cabinet responsible to the National Assembly. The emergency powers of the president and prime minister were weakened. A central election committee was established to ensure fair elections. A special constitutional court was established for judicial review, and legal restraints on civil rights were removed. Finally, in the National Assembly elections of July, the Democratic party won an overwhelming victory; the Liberal party had evaporated with the removal of Rhee.

But the experiment in democracy lasted only a year, brought to a sudden end by a military coup d'état in May 1961; and while there were undoubtedly many intellectuals who mourned democracy's passing, the coup was accepted with resignation by most of the populace, including the students. How did it happen that the obliteration of the whole apparatus of democratic government in one stroke elicited hardly a murmur when the rigging of a vice-presidential election under Rhee had led to a massive convulsion?

In the first place, many have explained that the student uprisings of 1960 did not represent a protest against the flouting of democratic principles and practices but a negative reaction to brutality, corruption, and vice.[3] Secondly, the new government of the Democratic party was unable to establish unity, eliminate corruption, solve the nation's economic problems, and establish a base of support among the people. Finally, the mass of the people had not become sufficiently politically socialized to regard democratic government and civil liberties as both legitimate and indispensable.

The weaknesses of Democratic party leadership were the most obvious of the three factors. The party had always been composed of a coterie of factions organized around prestigious individuals bound together by personal ties of loyalty. The Democratic party hardly differed from the Liberal party in its failure to form a solid organization with grass-roots support. It soon split into two major groups, one under President Yun Po-sŏn and the other under Prime Minister Chang Myŏn. Furthermore, the reemergence of a number of small left-wing parties under the new conditions of freedom may have confused and upset a populace unused to open competition. In fact, however, the political developments of this period may have been only an unavoidable first stage in any evolution toward stability under a system of open competitiveness, but competition and struggle were still not honored values in Korea. Harmony and order had always been the traditional goals of the Korean political community, and these seemed as far as ever from realization under the Second Republic.

The general mood of confusion and disruption was exacerbated by continuing student activity through November of 1960. Although the students were disorganized, they were highly motivated and filled with an important sense of mission. They demonstrated constantly to achieve their demands, which were directed to the accomplishment of specific objectives rather than the preservation of democratic process. They were strongly committed to the punishment of the "criminals" of the Rhee regime; in one famous incident, student mobs invaded the National Assembly in October and forced passage of laws for the retroactive punishment of members of the Rhee regime. Neither the students nor the party and government leadership were concerned about the violation of civil liberties that these laws represented or the fact that they were hardly different in kind from the national security legislation of the Rhee regime. While the students accomplished their objective in this instance, they made the government appear helpless and discredited the dignity of the legislature itself. Although student activity declined sharply after November 1960, the police had been weakened and demoralized, and it appeared that the government was unable to maintain law and order.

The press enjoyed greater freedom under the Second Republic than at any time before or since; and yet this, too, probably had negative effects on the morale of the populace. Some students of the period have noted that the press engaged in irresponsible journalism and blackmail, but further study may well reveal that this aspect of public expression has been exaggerated.[4] The irresponsibilty of 1960 was probably a necessary prelude to the development of a responsible press, and the suppression of the press after 1961 came as a result of the military government's policy of stifling criticism, a far more serious detriment to healthy democratic politics than irresponsible journalism. It is, nevertheless, still true that to political conservatives and the military the press may have appeared to be an unhealthy symptom of a disorganized and rootless society.

The new government was also unable to contain corruption and provide quick solutions to the economic problems bequeathed by the Rhee regime. To its credit, the Democratic regime introduced concepts of economic planning for the first time; Rhee had neglected long-range economic planning altogether. In economics as well as in other areas, had the new regime been given more time, it might have succeeded.

The new freedom also gave rise to spokesmen for national reunification and peaceful negotiation with the north, especially among student groups at Seoul National University. But many of the political and social elite, and the army in particular, were not ready in 1960 for an easing of tensions. The memories of the Korean War were still too vivid to be forgotten, and the anxiety and insecurity caused by the legacy of mutual hostility between north and south undoubtedly produced fear among a large segment of the population at the slightest mention of conciliation with the north. In 1972 the issue of reunification was a force that could bind the nation together behind a government-sponsored policy of compromise; but in 1960 a student-backed movement for reconciliation appeared threatening and subversive to the military and the right wing. Furthermore, the political confusion of the time undoubtedly inspired the fear that the country would be unable to resist an invasion from the north.

Dissatisfaction with the developments of 1960–61 was greatest among the middle ranks of the army's officer corps. During most of Rhee's regime the military had been corrupted and subordinated to Rhee's political control. By 1960 the military were ready to emerge as a political force in South Korea, but they had to postpone plans for a coup because of the student uprising in April. The military had not remained apolitical and quiet during the Rhee regime because they valued military noninterference in democratic politics, but because they were late in developing the political consciousness and the clandestine organization necessary for a lateral move into politics.

When the Chang Myŏn regime faltered in its first attempts to provide leadership and unity in conjunction with democratic politics, a small group of army officers sensed that the opportunity for a coup d'état had arrived. Their venture into politics involved three risks: that the downswing in public temperament since the heady days of the student uprising would reduce discontent with a military takeover, that the United States would not intervene directly in Korean affairs to preserve democratic institutions, and that the Chang government would not have the power or resolution to defend itself by a resort to force. The coup leaders were proved right on all three counts. When they took over control of the government, they justified their action on the grounds that their purpose was to save the nation from aimlessness, weakness, and inefficiency. No matter how noble the pretext for the coup, however, the fact remained that the military had become the strongest political force in South Korea and their seizure of power constituted another serious setback for the growth of democracy.

3. THE MILITARY REGIME, 1961–63 [5]

The military regime, which lasted for about two and one-half years, appears significant in retrospect for the following reasons. It brought the military into government and politics as administrators and members of political parties. It produced a new national leader, Park Chung Hee. It led to the introduction of state planning in the economy and the beginning of rapid industrialization. In politics, it marked a retreat to constitutional authoritarianism and a dominant-party system. Although the constitution was amended specifically to eliminate minor parties and produce a two-party system, it represented a desire by Park and a segment of the military to maintain power in a political system based on and legitimized by presidential and assembly elections. The Democratic Republican party (DRP) emerged as the main base of government power with a more complex organization than that of Rhee's Liberal party, but Park's commitment to party politics and party organization was a temporary phase in his political thinking, as was shown by events in 1972. Finally, the period of military rule witnessed the initial use of the national referendum, first to approve the constitutional amendments of December 1962, and secondly as a proposal (later retracted) to approve a continuation of military rule in the spring of 1963. Park sowed the seeds of a new pattern of politics that emerged full-blown only in 1972—strong-man rule with direct mass support untrammeled by intervening competitive political organizations.

The military regime represents the zenith of authoritarian government in the history of South Korea, in structure as well as content, and one suspects that Park Chung Hee in subsequent years nostalgically longed for a return to the security and political order of this period. The government was run by a committee of military officers on active duty, the Supreme Council for National Reconstruction (SCNR), and Park soon emerged as chairman. The president and constitution of the Second Republic were retained without change to lend the military regime an air of continuity and legitimacy, but the Law for Extraordinary Measures for National Reconstruction took precedence over any conflicting constitutional provisions.

The SCNR was superimposed over the regular administration and was divided into committees. All local administration was placed under direct central control. All political organizations were disbanded and political activity disallowed. The press was muzzled and subjected to strict censorship, the slightest violation of which was punished by arrest. A new anti-communist law, in the tradition of the older vaguely worded security and sedition laws, was promulgated, granting legal justification for the perse-

cution of leftists, intellectuals, and political opposition. A powerful new Republic of Korea Central Intelligence Agency (R.O.K.
CIA) was created to maintain surveillance over all elements in
society, and political crimes were handled by a special revolutionary tribunal. Under the military, in other words, order replaced confusion, control replaced competition, and coercion
replaced persuasion. The constitution was worth little more than
the paper it was printed on; law was utilized by the state for the
accomplishment of its objectives and afforded little protection
to the individual, and civil liberties were discarded altogether.

The abandonment of democracy was justified on several
grounds and by no means without sincerity of intent. The ideology of the military leaders was filled with appeals for moral
regeneration, nationalist unity, increased efficiency for economic
development, and political stability. In their view, individual
freedom, liberty, and democratic competition interfered with
these objectives, and the controlled and regimented state was the
best vehicle for the achievement of their goals.

The military sought to attain their goals by fiat. Sumptuary
regulations were passed outlawing ostentatious display and decadence. In the economic field orders were issued to lower interest
rates and increase private savings by converting demand deposits
in banks to long-term deposits. The bureaucracy and the army
were purged of "corrupt" and politically suspect individuals;
gangsters, leftists, and other recalcitrants were paraded before
the courts in an attempt to sweep society clean of its worst elements. The style of rule was more reflective of Yi Dynasty and
colonial authoritarianism than the democracy of the First Republic.

Nevertheless, stark military rule could not be sustained for
long. The high moral standards of the military leadership could
not be maintained, the economic measures created inflation and
stagnation in the economy, and political repression stimulated
resentment without creating widespread public support. Moreover, there was continuing and increasing pressure from the
United States for a return to civilian rule. Park and some other
military leaders realized from the outset that a return to civilian
politics or at least the "civilianization" of government would
have to be carried out at some time in the near future, and prep-

arations soon got under way for the transition. The military government prepared for this in three ways: by an attempt to purify politics by eliminating the older generation of politicians, by the revision of the constitution, and by the organization of the Democratic Republican party.

The Political Purification Law of 1961 banned several thousand persons from political activity, although many were subsequently released on petition. The law was justified on the grounds that the physical removal of the old politicians would eliminate the corruption, factionalism, and self-interest that characterized political behavior under the first and second republics. In many ways, the politics of the ensuing decade proved these to be vain hopes, although the fault was not exclusively that of the politicians. The idea that healthy democratic politics could be ensured by undemocratic means—even assuming that Park's ultimate objective was really the attainment of democracy—was fallacious to begin with. The resort to coercion and violence for the supposed achievement of democratic ends was as subversive to democracy as political misbehavior.

The same might also be said of the revision of the constitution in 1962. Respect for the constitution and law was certainly not enhanced by amendments imposed by fiat in contravention of the legal processes for amendment as provided by the constitution, no matter how well-intentioned the purpose. The amendments of 1962 were the fifth major revision of the constitution in a decade (1952, 1954, 1958, 1960, and 1962), and they contributed to the declining prestige of the constitution and its utility as a source of legitimacy.

The revised constitution was designed to increase the power of the president and the executive branch at the expense of the legislature. The principle of cabinet responsibility, a main feature of the 1960 revision, was abandoned. The president was now elected directly by the people, and he appointed cabinet ministers. He was granted the power to rule by decree whenever he saw fit to declare a national emergency. Both the legislature and the judiciary were weakened. The legislature lost its control over the prime minister, the cabinet, and the budget. The chief justice of the Supreme Court was appointed by the president for only a six-year term, but at least the Supreme Court retained the important functions of judicial review and the power of decision over the dissolution of political parties that failed to conform to law.

The guarantees for civil liberties were again so hamstrung by limitations and loopholes as to render them virtually meaningless. Censorship of the press was allowed for the preservation of public morality and ethics. The constitution also enabled the president to curtail liberties of speech, press, and association during periods of national emergency. Indeed, this provision for the declaration of national emergency at the whim of the president proved to be the most serious weakness of the revised constitution. Park used it with impunity at the mere suggestion of crisis, or even in anticipation of a crisis, in particular in 1971 and again in 1972, when the constitution was virtually suspended. The main purpose of the provision was obviously to enable the government to maintain or strengthen its power against domestic political challenges.

One of the most significant aspects of the revisions of 1962 was a new approach to political parties. The constitution allowed for the dissolution of parties by government request to the Supreme Court if their goals and activities were judged not to be in conformity with "the basic democratic order"—whatever that meant. The constitution also required that candidates for the presidency and the National Assembly had to be nominated by a party and that an assemblyman would lose his seat if he resigned from his party or if his party dissolved. A proportional representation system also awarded extra seats to parties based on the total national popular vote they received in district elections. These provisions were designed to eliminate small parties, prevent frequent changes of allegiance and factionalism, and introduce a measure of stability into party politics. In practice, they also tended to strengthen the centralized control of the major parties over their members but had little effect in reducing factionalism. The reform of the political party system also indicated that Park, as opposed to Rhee, had come to realize the necessity of political parties as a means for creating a stable political order.

The new attitude toward parties was reflected by the efforts of the military regime to begin the organization of a strong party to provide the basis for the continuation of the military's policies and power in a civilian regime. Kim Chong-p'il, the founder of the R.O.K. CIA, began organizing the Democratic Republican party in 1962, long before the regime announced its willingness to return to civilian rule.

Between February 18 and April 19, 1963 there was some confusion about Park's plans, as he vacillated over the decision to revert to civil rule. No doubt Park's hesitancy only reflected the struggle that was taking place within the military; some were in favor of continuing military rule and others preferred that the military stay out of politics altogether after a return to civilian rule. At first Park promised not to participate in politics after reversion to civil rule if all politicians promised to take no retributive action against members of the military regime, approve the constitutional amendments, and follow the major policies of the SCNR. On February 27 Park and the ex-politicians even took an oath to support the conditions of this agreement. In March, however, it appears that the government instigated a phony crisis (an alleged assassination plot) and rigged demonstrations for the continuation of military rule; on March 16 Park announced that military rule would be extended for four more years. Nevertheless, public denunciations, demonstrations, and pressure from the United States forced him to honor the original agreement. On April 19 he announced that elections for the presidency and the National Assembly would be held at the end of the year. Later, however, Park reneged on part of his pledge and ran as the presidential candidate of the Democratic Republican party.

In the October 15 presidential elections, Park defeated his opponent, Yun Po-sŏn, with only 46.6 percent of the popular vote. The fact that the combined popular vote of the opposition presidential candidates was greater than the vote for Park indicates that if the opposition had ceased its factional squabbling and united against Park, they would have turned him out of office. Park won handily in the rural areas, but Yun had a large edge in the cities. Despite the setback for the opposition, the vote suggested that rapid industrialization and urbanization might turn the tide in favor of the opposition in the near future.

In the National Assembly elections of November 1963, the

Democratic Republican party was victorious and won a majority of seats in the legislature; but there was a tremendous discrepancy between the elected representatives and the popular vote. The DRP, aided by the at-large proportional representation seats it received, obtained a total of 110 out of 175 seats in the assembly, seven seats short of a two-thirds majority. The Democratic Republican party had thus won almost two-thirds of the assembly seats while receiving only one-third of the popular vote.

The main reason for the discrepancy between the popular vote and the results of the assembly election was that opposition parties each ran candidates in many districts. In the absence of a run-off system, votes for the minor parties were thus wasted. The failure of the opposition to unite against the Democratic Republican party was thus the major cause for the unrepresentative nature of the assembly election.

Park received about 13 percent more votes in the presidential election than the combined total of the votes for members of his party in the assembly elections. This phenomenon reflected the relative weakness of the government party. Park was the dog that wagged the tail of the party rather than the other way around. He appealed to many voters because he appeared as a national leader who transcended party politics even though he was associated with the DRP. This situation probably also reflected Park's feeling of independence from his own party and his growing view of himself as an indispensable national leader. As the events of the ensuing decade show, these trends were intensified: the Democratic Republican party was ultimately not able to build up its strength, and Park became less rather than more dependent on his own party. By late 1972 Park decided to revise the constitutional structure to increase his autocratic powers as the transcendent leader and to decrease the role of all parties in the political process. In retrospect it is easy to see the origin of this development in the transition to civilian rule in 1963.[6]

4. THE THIRD REPUBLIC, 1963–72 [7]

Three important trends in the political history of South Korea
are evident in the decade of the third republic. Park began the
skillful utilization of national goals and policy, such as normalization of relations with Japan, industrial development, national
defense, and reunification, in order to build up his political
power. He abandoned his initial commitment to two-party politics in favor of plebiscitary dictatorship backed by a strong executive and the military. And he waged a continuous campaign
against freedom of speech and political action, students and
intellectuals, and suspected subversives.

The first example of Park's utilization of national issues of
foreign policy, economics, and defense in order to secure his
political power came during his campaign in 1964–65 to achieve
the normalization of relations with Japan. To accomplish this
objective, Park had to ignore the political opposition, manipulate
the National Assembly, suppress student dissent, and stifle newspaper criticism. At the time it appeared that these measures were
taken exclusively to accomplish the specific objective of achieving ratification of the treaty with Japan. From the standpoint of
political development, however, it would appear that the events
surrounding the normalization of relations with Japan also illustrate a recurrent phenomenon in the politics of the third republic—the justification of the repression of the political opposition and the curtailment of civil liberties for the achievement
of higher national goals.

In August 1965 the Democratic Republican party majority
voted the R.O.K.-Japan normalization treaty out of committee
in the National Assembly while physically barring the opposition
from the rostrum. The DRP then approved the treaty when
opposition members were absent from the assembly.[8] While this
action was technically legal, since the DRP possessed a majority
of seats in the legislature, it reflected Park's disdain for political
opposition and compromise.

The crisis over normalization also marked the beginning of
the suppression of students and the press. Park developed new
techniques for breaking up student demonstrations and confined

the student-police confrontations to the campuses themselves rather than the downtown areas of the capital. Park censored the press during martial law, but he retreated from passage of a law to perpetuate overt censorship. Nevertheless, the press emerged from the events of 1965 under a form of self-censorship that was most effective in stifling dissent.

After the normalization crisis was settled, Park turned his full attention to economic development. Economic planning began with the military regime, but it did not produce visible results until 1965–66, when a spectacular rise in the percentage annual increase in the Gross National Product (GNP) made economic development a useful political tool.[9]

Park displayed the utmost skill in the use of economic development for political purposes. Throughout the decade he emphasized the importance of industrialization and exports. This policy stimulated rapid urbanization, the growth of a wealthy upper class of industrial and commercial entrepreneurs, and an increasing gap in the distribution of wealth between city and countryside. Although the peasantry escaped from starvation during this period, it did not advance much higher than poverty or subsistence levels of existence. Despite differential growth and discrimination against the rural sector for the benefit of industry and the cities, however, Park retained the political support of the rural classes in elections and national referenda through the end of the third republic.

This political phenomenon was partially due to the effects of land reform carried out in the early 1950s. Tenancy was reduced significantly, and a new class of petty landowners was created in the countryside. The ownership of small plots of land kept the rural population politically conservative as long as their standard of living was maintained at subsistence levels. Land ownership was thus of little benefit for the development of independent or democratic political consciousness; but it was most useful for the creation of mass rural support for authoritarian rule and the creation of conditions for political stability.[10]

Rapid urbanization that was a concomitant of industrialization also drained off potential rural discontent. Large numbers of the fast-growing city populations were recent migrants from the villages. They represented a transitional class that was not fully integrated into city life and values; and they probably retained the conservative attitudes or political apathy of the countryside. This new class was potentially rebellious, but one recent study of the city of Taegu indicates that relatively rapid integration into urban society occurred with opportunities for upward mobility in terms of occupation and education.[11]

In other words, heavy investment in urban industry and relative neglect of the countryside did not adversely effect Park's political power. When by the end of the third republic it appeared that rural discontent might become a political factor (the opposition began to reflect rural discontent in its program), Park skillfully announced a change in direction in his economic planning, took over the opposition program, and began a propaganda barrage advertising his plans for balanced distribution of investment and income between city and countryside and the beginnings of a "New Village Movement" (*Saemaŭl undong*) to mobilize the rural population for the accomplishment of economic tasks. In response to political pressure, Park promised to satisfy all sectors of society even though such a policy may be impossible to achieve.

Growing tension with North Korea in the mid-1960s was also manipulated for political purposes in the third republic. South Korea committed itself to the dispatch of troops to South Vietnam in aid of the American war effort against the communist world, and North Korea changed its policy toward the south from clandestine infiltration to a more aggressive fomenting of revolution by the training of agents and commandos and by heavy investment in armaments and military hardware. The increasing level of hostility reached its culmination in the infiltration of commando groups, the thirty-one-man mission to assassinate Park, and the *Pueblo* incident in early 1968. As Baldwin has argued, the North Korean policy may have been taken in response to South Korean and American initiatives,[12] but in any case North Korea's new policy failed to stimulate a revolutionary reaction among the generally conservative rural populace in South Korea. Moreover, because Chinese and Russian support became less dependable in the late 1960s, the North Koreans decided to abandon their aggressive tactics in the south after 1968.

Nevertheless, the increasing tension had serious political effects in the south because it gave Park the license to act arbitrarily. It led to a wave of arrests of suspected spies and subversives and increased government pressure on the administration's critics in the press and among the students. It enabled Park to use the threat of invasion as a means of maintaining anxiety among the populace. He portrayed himself as the best, if not the only, leader who could maintain a strong defensive posture against the communist threat. In the presidential elections of 1971, opposition candidate Kim Dae-jung proposed a four-power guarantee of Korean independence in place of armed confrontation. Park, who had apparently been moving to a more conciliatory policy vis-à-vis the north, reversed positions prior to the election and raised the specter of North Korean invasion to cast doubt in the minds of the people about Kim's ability to prevent war or stave off invasion. That this was simply a political tactic was made clear by the speed with which Park again reversed his policy; within a year he was engaged in talks with North Korea over the problem of separated families.

Park was also skillful in his use of the reunification issue as a means of consolidating his political power. When he called for a national referendum in December 1972 to approve his amended "Restoration Constitution," he declared that he would interpret a negative vote on the constitution as a rejection of his reunification policy and his rapprochement with the north, and that he would abandon his current policy for a new one.[13] The issue was a phony one concocted only to ensure victory at the polls— if, indeed, persuasion of any kind was really necessary to win the referendum, since political activity had been outlawed and no freedom was allowed for the expression of opposition to the proposed constitutional amendments. Park thus used the reunification issue and generalized mass support for reunification as a means of legitimizing his leadership and creating a dictatorial political system. In the likelihood of clandestine opposition from militant anti-communists in the military and in the civilian population, Park may have needed something like a national referendum to provide him with a popular mandate against potential subversion. In any case, he was able to make a rapid change from anti-communist militancy to apparent rapprochement with

North Korea without suffering any major weakening of his political power mainly because of his skill in utilizing foreign policy issues to obtain popular support. Therefore, Park's use of economic development, anti-communism, and reunification as a means of cementing his hold on power has been highly effective.

A second significant trend in South Korean politics during the third republic was Park's change of attitude toward politics, political parties, and elections. The third republic began with a constitution that was aimed at eliminating minor parties, preventing schism and fractionation of existing parties, and creating a two-party system. Park seemed to be committed to the idea that stable politics depended on a two-party system, as illustrated by his concern for the early organization of the Democratic Republican party in 1962 during the period of military rule. The culmination of this effort at party-building was reached in the 1967 National Assembly elections, when the DRP obtained a two-thirds majority in the legislature, sufficient to enable it to pass constitutional amendments as well as ordinary legislation. Curiously, this victory probably marked a turning point in Park's attitude toward parties, for once he had his two-thirds majority, the Democratic Republican party itself no longer became so important to him because the legislature was now converted into a rubber stamp for executive policies. Even before 1967 Park had demonstrated his preference for a strong executive over a strong party or legislative system. Under his leadership the presidential secretariat, the CIA, the centralized police, and the Economic Planning Board, to name a few of the major executive institutions, had come to exercise tremendous control over the political and economic life of the nation. With the legislature reduced to impotence, the executive became even more consequential and conspicuous.

Park's loss of faith in party politics was also a result of the nature of the opposition, or at least his view of it. Many writers have commented on the inability of opposition politicians in South Korea to moderate their demands and work with the government in a spirit of compromise for the national good. Furthermore, the major opposition party, whatever its name at any given time, was usually split into several factions which coalesced only at election time to contest the government.

Opposition party weakness and unwillingness to compromise was not exclusively the fault of the opposition politicians. Undoubtedly the government did its best to infiltrate the opposition and foment division. Park's attitude toward the opposition was cavalier and disdainful in any case. When he did appeal to suprapartisan unity on national issues, he usually demanded capitulation on his own terms and was reluctant to compromise with an opposition that was unable to outvote him in the legislature. The opposition, on the other hand, undoubtedly disgruntled at the fact that they were underrepresented in the National Assembly in terms of the total popular vote they received at election time, and unwilling to submit docilely to the DRP majority, resorted to extra-legal or illegal tactics to block legislation. The opposition assemblymen boycotted the legislature and physically tried to prevent votes that would result in certain defeat, and they formed negotiating teams in an attempt to work out extraparliamentary compromises with Park. As long as Park felt that it was necessary to maintain the facade of democratic institutions, he was under some pressure to compromise with the opposition. This was most evident in the two years following the National Assembly elections of 1967, when the opposition boycott of the assembly in protest against corrupt election practices caused the suspension of normal legislative activity.

Park, however, was basically unwilling to tolerate opposition to his national leadership. He felt that the opposition parties and political competition were disruptive of national unity and subversive to the consolidation of his power, but he reluctantly went along with the system because he considered it necessary for legitimacy. After all, there was no basis for legitimacy in the South Korean political system other than the democratic structural and procedural system. Even in recent years when Park tried to base his claim to legitimacy on efficiency and achievement, he never fully abandoned the structure of a democratic system.

Park's intolerance for opposition was, of course, the fatal flaw in his policy to create stable two-party politics, for a two-party system presupposes a willingness to allow alternation and change of political leadership. Without the opportunity for an opposition to gain power there can be no two-party system;

there can only be a dominant-party system or, as Scalapino has called it, a one-and-one-half-party system.[14] Not only was Park unwilling to allow the opposition to gain power; he disliked the disruption caused by opposition protest and propaganda, for no matter how weak the legislature was, it at least provided a forum for opposition legislators. As Park's statements at the end of 1972 reveal, he regarded this situation as subversive to national interests.[15]

As added proof for the contention that Park undermined two-party politics because of his distaste for competitive politics rather than simply from fear of opposition victory, it should be noted that he abandoned the constitution of the third republic almost immediately after the split of the opposition New Democratic party (NDP) into two factions in 1972. Even though the NDP's candidate, Kim Dae-jung, had made a good showing in the 1971 presidential elections, he had failed to win his own party's election for party president. The party then broke apart as Yu Chin-san made a political comeback in 1972. In other words, the NDP had won enough seats in 1971 to destroy the government party's two-thirds majority, but it was still incapable of the unity essential for national leadership. Park therefore abandoned the third republic and two-party politics when the opposition was weak and divided, not strong and united.

The last reason for Park's shift away from an earlier commitment to party politics was probably a growing dissatisfaction with his own party. This interpretation is admittedly speculative, but it may be deduced from two facts: the existence of factionalism within the Democratic Republican party and the downgrading of the DRP's position in the government structure as a result of the "Restoration Constitution" of the Fourth Republic. Within the DRP the main lines of battle were drawn between the supporters of Kim Chong-p'il and their opponents. Kim apparently had hopes of succeeding to power as the party's presidential candidate in 1971, but these hopes were dashed in 1969 when Park decided to eliminate, by a constitutional amendment, the two-term restriction on the presidency. Kim's initial opposition to this amendment strained his relations with Park and weakened his position in the DRP. Park's subsequent appointment of Kim to the post of prime minister may have been partially motivated by an attempt to mollify Kim's supporters in the party. No matter what the facts of the situation, Park acted more and more like a transcendent national leader rather than a party chief. This attitude was revealed clearly by his downgrading of party politics in general in the "Restoration Constitution" of late 1972.

Under the terms of the "Restoration Constitution," all political parties are relegated to a minor position in the state. Park's new design for government calls for an enormously powerful president and executive, a National Council for Unification (NCU) composed exclusively of nonparty independents to pass on presidential proposals for unification, and a National Assembly, one-third of which is to be appointed by the president with the approval of the NCU. In case even this system challenges Park, the president also has the power to declare a national emergency or to present his measures directly to the people in a plebiscite.[16] Thus the downgrading of the National Assembly in the new constitution marks the reduction of party politics to insignificance. Park has thus abandoned the organization of politics in political parties for the creation of new institutions of central authority, mass participation in meaningless elections for the NCU and the National Assembly, and direct mass support by national referenda.

For that matter, elections had long since been transformed into a ritualistic exercise whereby the mass of the population was given a sense of participation in the political process. If election politics alone were the determining factors in the political process, the 1971 assembly elections should have been an important sign of growing maturity in the use of democratic institutions. The opposition New Democratic party increased its seats in the National Assembly to 89 (out of 204), making it more difficult for Park to manipulate the legislature. Park could tolerate the election process only as long as it did not threaten to interfere with his power. Partially for this reason, he revised the constitution in 1972 to make sure that the election process would remain a useful symbol of legitimation but could not actually challenge his authority. By the terms of the fourth republic's constitution, elections have been totally transformed into the political opiate of the masses, for their present function is exclusively to provide legitimacy for dictatorial rule and distract the public from violent forms of opposition.

The third major development of the third republic was the unremitting attack on the institutions and spirit of democracy and political freedom. The constitution was ignored when it suited the government's purpose and then amended in violation of legal procedure; the legislature was subverted by improper tactics; the mass media were suppressed; individual liberties and the right to due process of law were crushed under the heel of the state; and the students were eliminated as a meaningful force in politics.

Park's treatment of the constitution has been contradictory because he has continued to rely on it as a source of legitimacy at the same time that he has acted in contravention of its rules, thereby weakening public respect for it. The constitutional amendment for a third-term presidency in 1969 was conducted in an ostensibly legal way, since Park's party had a two-thirds majority in the National Assembly; but because the amendment was such an obvious device for the perpetuation of autocratic power, its passage constituted a violation of the spirit of the constitution itself.

The abandonment of the third republic and the creation of the "Restoration Constitution" in 1972, however, were carried out in a completely illegal manner. Park simply declared martial law and suspended the constitution, political activity, political parties, free speech, and the legislature. Then a new constitution was approved without debate by a national referendum. The constitution has been reduced to about the same position it occupies in communist regimes—a minor contribution to the legitimation of authority.

Park's treatment of the legislature was hardly better than his treatment of the constitution. In 1964–65 he rode roughshod over the National Assembly to gain approval of the treaty normalizing relations with Japan, and in 1967 he used the legislature to pass the presidential third-term amendment. Both measures were carried out in accordance with the legal provisions of the constitution, but not in the spirit of the constitution. In 1972 the legislature was suspended, and Park ruled through an Emergency Council of State that issued decrees that had the effect of law and were made "legal" with the creation of the fourth republic.[17] Under the fourth republic, the legislature has been reduced to impotence. The National Council for Unification will deal with all issues of reunification; Park appoints one-third of the members of the regular National Assembly (with the approval of the NCU). Park can sidestep the legislature altogether whenever he wishes simply by presenting proposals to a national referendum.[18]

During the third republic there were also repeated violations of civil liberties and political freedoms. After 1967 in particular, there were a number of spy incidents and trials. Korean students and intellectuals in West Germany and the United Kingdom were kidnapped and secretly repatriated to South Korea, where they were immediately put on trial for treasonous activities. Several Koreans from Japan who returned to South Korea were also arrested for spying. These trials were carried out, to be sure, in the midst of anxiety caused by increased tension with North Korea, so that the government's abandonment of legality in an attempt to eliminate subversives is understandable, though hardly laudable. Furthermore, it is beyond the purview of this paper to determine whether any or all of the individuals involved were innocent of the charges brought against them. But the method of arrest, use of torture, absence of clemency except under the greatest international pressure and protest, improper trial procedures, and severity of punishment all point to the increase of terror and abandonment of the guarantees for civil liberties on the part of the government.[19]

The government's treason trials also display a serious mistrust of intellectuals in general, particularly in the case of the men abducted from West Germany. This anti-intellectualism was made even more evident in the suppression of the press and students. Incidents of censorship and repression of the press are almost too numerous to recount in a short article. The imposition of "self-censorship" in 1965 was obviously not sufficient for the government's control of critical opinion. Later that year terrorists bombed the homes of journalists; in 1966 the *Kyŏnghyang sinmun* was forced out of business by a sudden recall of outstanding bank loans. In 1967 reporters of the *Kangwŏn ilbo* were attacked, and the CIA rounded up an editor and reporters of the *Chosŏn ilbo* on the grounds of violation of the anti-communist law. In subsequent years, writers—such as the poet Kim Chi-ha—and editors were frequently subjected to illegal arrest and detention for the publishing of relatively innocuous criticism. In 1970 the famous monthly magazine, *Sasanggye,* was finally forced out of business after two decades of government pressure. In 1971 members of the *Tari* magazine staff were arrested, and the editorial staff of the *Ch'angjo* journal was changed.[20] The fourth republic thus began its existence in 1973 with a press that has been hammered into submission. The editorials of the once independent daily, the *Tonga ilbo,* read like handouts from the Ministry of Information. A once outspoken press has been converted into the agent of state propaganda.

Park can also count the repression of the student movement as one of his main political accomplishments in the third republic. He was able to achieve this by learning from Rhee's mistakes and adopting more skillful tactics of repression. He scrupulously abandoned the use of overt force on the streets and began to devise new and more efficient tactics during the 1964–65 protests against the normalization treaty with Japan. At first mobile tactical squads of police were organized to prevent the students from reaching the downtown area. Then preventive moves were taken against the campuses by stationing armed troops with machine guns outside the campus gates to keep the students in. Spies and infiltrators were used in the classroom to maintain surveillance over students and professors. Martial law was declared, the campuses were invaded on occasion by armed troops, and student leaders were arrested. Professors and administrators were intimidated and forced to become agents of surveillance over their students.

The movement against the students culminated in the suppression of student protest against the ROTC system in 1971. Campus student organizations were disbanded, student publications were suspended, protesting leaders were summarily drafted, professors had to report on students who had missed ROTC classes, and in general administration and faculty were used to aid the government in obliterating campus protest.[21]

Korean students in the postwar period have become the scapegoats of oppressive regimes. They have been criticized by both

Korean and foreign writers for irresponsibility, violence, and disruptiveness. But because of their unique position in Korean society as young intellectual leaders as yet uncorrupted by pressures for livelihood and political ambition, they were the most important source of protest against corruption and repression. Their demise as a political factor will undoubtedly produce greater stability, at least for the present. Their exaggerated importance after 1960 was a product of a disorganized political system operating under democratic institutions and professed values; their removal from open politics was symptomatic of more developed authoritarianism.

Trends in voting statistics for the past twenty years have indicated growing support for opposition parties by an urban population that has increased by leaps and bounds, and in response to this Park turned against urban intellectuals in favor of the conservative rural population as a means of building popular support for his leadership. He has now promised the rural sector that the government will devote more attention to it; in the cities he is attempting to cater to the needs of the urban bourgeoisie and workers in economic rather than political terms. Park promises the bourgeoisie greater opportunities for affluence by a stable and growing economy; he promises the urban workers security and participation through stock ownership of business enterprises.[22] Building from a rural political base, Park is now trying to extend his political appeal into the cities without the use of political freedom, without the tactic of party organization, and at the expense of the liberal intellectuals. He appears to be gambling on the propositions that all classes of society value economic security more than political freedom and that controlled participation can be substituted for open and competitive politics.

5. THE FOURTH REPUBLIC

Many of the trends toward dictatorship and authoritarian rule in the third republic reached their culmination with the creation of the fourth republic in late 1972. Park's new constitution, ratified in a national referendum at the end of 1972, laid the groundwork for a strong autocratic government. The powers of the president have been increased enormously, and the authority of the legislature and the power of the political parties have virtually been destroyed. The president can dissolve political parties on vague grounds; he can dissolve the new National Assembly; he can declare national emergencies and martial law; he can issue presidential decrees that have the effect of law; he can abrogate civil liberties when he sees fit; he is elected for six-year terms by the NCU without debate (and without opposition, as he was in December 1972). The cabinet, but not the president, is responsible to the legislature. The president can appoint one-third of the members of the National Assembly. All power is now vested in the presidency with only minimal restriction from other institutions.[23]

The rights of the people have been weakened and their duties increased. Civil liberties are completely curbed. All citizens now have the duty (not the right) to work. Even private property is subject to state control. The citizenry can still participate in elections for members of the NCU and National Assembly, but both are now relatively weak institutions. Members of the NCU cannot be members of political parties, and local self-government is not to go into effect until the reunification of Korea.[24]

Park has justified the unconstitutional method of revising the constitution and the nature of the new constitution on the grounds of necessity. In his view the changing international situation has made South Korea's position more precarious; the country needs a structure more in keeping with Korean rather than Western circumstances, a structure that enables a strong executive to exert leadership to promote efficiency and economic growth, guarantee security, create national strength, and achieve reunification. Park stated that the old constitution would not permit substantial change of the state structure and might weaken South Korea by allowing debate and confusion over constitutional change and national policy. For this reason he took it upon himself to rewrite the constitution and seek direct approval from the people through a national referendum. He also insisted that he seeks to preserve democracy and "Koreanize" it as well, to build up national strength and efficiency.[25] In fact he has destroyed democracy, not Koreanized it.

6. THE FAILURE OF DEMOCRATIC INSTITUTIONS IN SOUTH KOREA

The failure of democratic institutions in South Korea can be ascribed to a number of causes. Probably the most significant one has been the absence of political leaders committed to democratic development. Both Rhee and Park have used democratic institutions primarily as a source of legitimacy at home and abroad. Whenever political forces created by democratic government threatened their power, they were suppressed. As the need for a democratic facade to obtain United States and other international support has decreased, the tendency to convert the political structure into a more accurate representation of authoritarian rule increased. The experience of the last quarter century has proved that democratic development was virtually impossible in the absence of political leaders strongly committed to democracy.

Although Rhee's and Park's leadership style has been dictatorial, they were not dictators who imposed their wills on a populace with democratic values. Although democratic ideas have been a part of the educational curriculum of the Republic of Korea, they have not taken root in the minds of the population. There has therefore been a lag between democratic political institutions and an authoritarian political culture in which respect for individual rights, civil liberties, competitive politics, and democratic process have been very weak.

Economic backwardness and demands for performance in economic development has led to a general impatience with delay. The political and economic elite, and probably the mass of the population, have therefore been willing to sacrifice political rights for material benefits.

Thus far the population in general has not benefited greatly from industrial growth, but this has not led to a revolutionary movement because the countryside has remained conservative, and the urban proletariat is as yet unorganized. Both these phenomena help to explain the weakness of democratic institutions in South Korea. On the one hand, the conservative class of petty landowners in the countryside has provided political support for Rhee and Park and has remained docile despite the growth of dictatorship and authoritarianism. On the other hand, the relatively large urban proletariat has remained disorganized because labor unions are still embryonic and political parties have mainly been organs of the conservative urban bourgeoisie and intellectuals.

Democracy has also failed to develop because political party organization has been weak. In part the weakness of political parties has been a product of government restrictions, but it is also a feature of the narrow class base of the parties themselves. The party politicians have still failed to identify the rural or urban masses as the true source of political strength, and this has been as much a product of their own class affiliation and outlook as of government restriction. Moreover, the general population has lacked the experience in self-government at the local level that would have been most important in inculcating respect for democratic process and institutions.

Democratic development has also been made difficult by the constant state of anxiety produced by military confrontation. This situation resulted in two phenomena: the growth of the military as a powerful political force, and the existence of an anxious public that can be cowed into docility whenever the specter of war is raised by the country's leaders.

Finally, democratic government has not flourished under a structure of political power based on autocratic rule backed up by an alliance of powerful elites in the bureaucracy, military, and industry. These elites control society and are the chief beneficiaries of economic progress; it is not in their economic or political interest to foster the growth of political pluralism or mass political power.

The Korean people in South Korea will continue to work out their own solutions to the problems of politics and political organization no matter what the character of their borrowed institutions. In the foreseeable future neither competitive democratic politics nor individual liberty will be important components of the political process in South Korea.

Notes

1. Coverage of the Rhee regime was based on the following sources: John Kie-chiang Oh, *Korea: Democracy on Trial* (Ithaca, N.Y., Cornell University Press, 1968), pp. 1–71; Gregory Henderson, *Korea, the Politics of the Vortex* (Cambridge, Mass., Harvard University Press, 1968), pp. 113–95; David C. Cole and Princeton N. Lyman, *Korean Development: The Interplay of Politics and Economics* (Cambridge, Mass., Harvard University Press, 1971), pp. 16–30; Richard C. Allen, *Korea's Syngman Rhee: An Unauthorized Portrait* (Tokyo and Rutland, Vt., Charles E. Tuttle Co., 1960); Lee Hahn-been, *Korea: Time, Change and Administration* (Honolulu, East-West Center Press, 1968), pp. 74–109; Robert T. Oliver, *Syngman Rhee: The Man Behind the Myth* (New York, Dodd, Mead and Company, 1954); W. D. Reeve, *The Republic of Korea: A Political and Economic Study* (London, Oxford University Press, 1963); Han Sung-joo, "Political Dissent in South Korea, 1948–61," in Kim Se-jin and Cho Chang-hyun, eds., *Government and Politics of Korea* (Silver Spring, Maryland, The Research Institute on Korean Affairs, 1972), pp. 43–69; C. I. Eugene Kim and Kim Ke-soo, "The April 1960 Student Movement," in C. I. Eugene Kim, ed., *A Pattern of Political Development: Korea* (Kalamazoo, Mich., Korea Research and Publications, 1964), pp. 48–60; Hong Sung-chick, "The Students' Values," in C. I. Eugene Kim, ed., *A Pattern of Political Development: Korea,* pp. 61–74; Princeton N. Lyman, "Students and Politics in Indonesia and Korea," in *Pacific Affairs,* Vol. 38, Nos. 3–4 (Fall-Winter 1965–66), pp. 282–94; William A. Douglas, "Korean Students and Politics," in *Asian Survey,* Vol. 3, No. 12 (December 1963), pp. 584–95.
2. For coverage of this period, see Henderson, *Korea,* pp. 176–82; Oh, *Korea: Democracy on Trial,* pp. 72–91; Cole and Lyman, *Korean Development,* pp. 31–33.
3. See note 2.
4. Cole and Lyman, *Korean Development,* p. 32; Henderson, *Korea,* p. 180.
5. Sources for this section are Oh, *Korea: Democracy on Trial,* pp. 73–163; Cole and Lyman, *Korean Development,* pp. 34–55; Henderson, *Korea,* pp. 182–90; Robert A. Scalapino, "Which Route for Korea?" in *Asian Survey,* Vol. 2, No. 7 (September 1962), pp.

1–13; Robert A. Scalapino, "Korea: The Politics of Change," in *Asian Survey*, Vol. 3, No. 1 (January 1963), pp. 31–40; Lee Chongsik, "Korea: In Search of Stability," in *Asian Survey*, Vol. 4, No. 1 (January 1964), pp. 656–65; C. I. Eugene Kim, "The South Korean Military Coup of 1961," in Jacques Van Doorn, ed., *Armed Forces and Society: Sociological Essays* (The Hague, Mouton, 1968), pp. 298–316.

6. It might also be noted that the evolution of Korean politics between 1963 and 1972 has been contrary to Huntington's prescription for the achievement of political stability in developing nations: to wit, the increase of political institutionalization by the development of strong parties as the means for the integration of increasing numbers of politically socialized people into the political system. In South Korea the trend toward autocracy has been accompanied by the weakening of political parties. See Samuel P. Huntington, *Political Order in Changing Societies* (New Haven, Conn., Yale University Press, 1968).

7. Sources for this section are Oh, *Korea: Democracy on Trial*, pp. 174–92; Cole and Lyman, *Korean Development*, pp. 56–118, 225–54; C. I. Eugene Kim, "Korea in the Year of *Ulsa*," in *Asian Survey*, Vol. 6, No. 1 (January 1966), pp. 34–42; Lee Chong-sik, "Korea: Troubles in a Divided State," in *Asian Survey*, Vol. 5, No. 1 (January 1965), pp. 25–32; Glenn D. Paige, "1966: Korea Creates the Future," in *Asian Survey*, Vol. 7, No. 1 (January 1967), pp. 21–30; Cho Soon-sung, "North and South Korea: Stepped-up Aggression and the Search for New Security," in *Asian Survey*, Vol. 9, No. 1 (January 1969), pp. 29–39; B. C. Koh, "The *Pueblo* Incident in Perspective," in *Asian Survey*, Vol. 9, No. 4 (April 1969), pp. 264–81; Joungwon Alexander Kim, "Divided Korea 1969: Consolidating for Transition," in *Asian Survey*, Vol. 10, No. 1 (January 1970), pp. 30–42; Joungwon A. Kim, "The Republic of Korea: A Quest for New Directions," in *Asian Survey*, Vol. 11, No. 1 (January 1971), pp. 92–103; Chae-Jin Lee, "South Korea: Political Competition and Government Adaptation," in *Asian Survey*, Vol. 12, No. 1 (January 1972), pp. 38–45; C. I. Eugene Kim, "The Meaning of the 1971 Korean Elections: A Pattern of Political Development," in *Asian Survey*, Vol. 12, No. 3 (March 1972), pp. 213–24; Kim Se-jin, *The Politics of Military Revolution in Korea* (Chapel Hill, The University of North Carolina Press, 1971); Kim and Cho, *Government and Politics of Korea;* Y. C. Han, "The 1969 Constitutional Revision and Party Politics in South Korea," in *Pacific Affairs*, Vol. 44, No. 2 (Summer 1971), pp. 242–58; Woo

Byung-kyu and Kim Chong-lim, "Intra-elite Cleavages in the Korean National Assembly," in *Asian Survey*, Vol. 11, No. 6 (June 1971), pp. 544–61; Kim Jae-on and B. C. Koh, "Electoral Behavior and Social Development in South Korea: An Aggregate Data Analysis of Presidential Elections," in *Journal of Politics*, Vol. 34, No. 3 (August 1972), pp. 825–59; Kim Kyŏng-wŏn, "Ideology and Political Development in South Korea," in *Pacific Affairs*, Vol. 38, No. 2 (Summer 1965), pp. 164–76; the June 1967 issue of *Korea Journal* with four articles on political parties and party politics in South Korea, see *Korea Journal*, Vol. 7, No. 6 (June 1967); Hahn Bae-ho and Kim Kyu-taik, "Korean Political Leaders (1952–62): Their Social Origins and Skills," in *Asian Survey*, Vol. 3, No. 7 (July 1963), pp. 305–23; Hahn Bae-ho, "Long Road to Democracy," in *Korea Journal*, Vol. 10, No. 8 (August 1970), pp. 20–24; Lee Young-ho, "The Korean People's Political Orientations: Multivariate Analysis (I)," in *Korean Quarterly*, Vol. 13, Nos. 1, 2 (Spring–Summer 1971), pp. 11–30; Y. C. Han, "Political Parties and Political Development in South Korea," in *Pacific Affairs*, Vol. 42, No. 4 (Winter 1969–70), pp. 446–64.

In preparing this article I made no attempt at an exhaustive coverage of materials in Korean or Japanese, but I did find the following items useful: Yi Ki-ha, *Han'guk chŏngdang paltalsa* [A history of the development of South Korean political parties] (Seoul, 1960); Ko Chun-sŏk, *Minami Chōsen seijishi* [A political history of South Korea] (Tokyo, 1970); Kim Kyŏng-su, "Han'guk chŏngdang chŏngch'i ŭi chemunje" [Problems in Korean party politics], *Sahoe kwahak*, 6 (1967), pp. 10–19; Yi Chŏng-sik, "Han'guk chŏngdang ŭi sajŏk chŏn'gae" [Historical development of Korean political parties], *Sahoe kwahak*, 6 (1967), pp. 20–47; Hwang Sŏn-p'il, "Sinmindang: onŭl ŭi kyebo" [The New Democratic party: today's factional genealogy], *Sindonga*, 8 (August 1972), pp. 184–201; Lee Young-ho, "Sa ich'il sŏn'gŏ ŭi chŏngch'i ŭisik" [Political consciousness in the April 27th elections], *Sindonga*, 6 (June 1971), pp. 80–96; Kim Yŏng-mo, "Sa-ich'il o-io sŏn'gŏ e taehan sahoehakchŏk koch'al" [A sociological investigation of the April 27 and May 25 elections], *Chŏnggyŏng yŏn'gu*, Vol. 7, No. 7 (July 1971), pp. 26–40; Ch'a In-sŏk, "Minjujuŭi ŭi t'och'akhwa munje" [Problems in the Koreanization of democracy], *Chŏnggyŏng yŏn'gu*, Vol. 7, No. 7 (July 1971), pp. 17–25.

8. The assembly also approved the measure to dispatch troops to Vietnam at the same time.

9. This point is stressed in Cole and Lyman, *Korean Development, passim.*

10. See Huntington, *Political Order in Changing Societies,* pp. 74–77, 209, 241–42, 374–96.

11. Herbert R. Barringer, "Migration and Social Structure," in Herbert Barringer and Man-gap Lee, eds., *A City in Transition: Urbanization in Taegu, Korea* (Seoul, 1971), pp. 287–334.

12. See Cho Soon-sung, "North and South Korea . . . ," B. C. Koh, "The *Pueblo* Incident in Perspective," and "Renewed Communist Threat to Korea: Infiltration of Communist Agents into Seoul," *Korea Journal,* Vol. 8, No. 5 (May 1968), pp. 16–29, and Frank Baldwin, "Patrolling the Empire: Reflections on the USS *Pueblo," Bulletin of Concerned Asian Scholars,* Vol. 4, No. 2 (Summer 1972), pp. 54–74.

13. *Tonga ilbo,* October 18, 1972.

14. Robert A. Scalapino and Masumi Junnosuke, *Parties and Politics in Contemporary Japan* (Berkeley and Los Angeles, University of California Press, 1962), p. 41.

15. Various announcements and statements beginning from October 18, 1972, in the *Tonga ilbo.*

16. My source is the complete text of the revised constitution in the *Tonga ilbo,* October 27, 1972, p. 6.

17. See article 7 of the Supplementary Articles to the Revised Constitution, *ibid.*

18. Article 49 of the Revised Constitution.

19. An excellent survey in English of the political persecutions and spy trials of the Park regime is in *Rōnin,* Vol. 1, Nos. 4, 5 (August 1972), and in Ko Chun-sŏk, *Minami Chōsen seijishi,* pp. 326 ff. The most egregious examples of government oppression occurred with the abduction of Korean intellectuals from West Germany in 1967, the 1969 arrest and subsequent execution of former assemblyman Kim Kyu-nam, the persecution of Paul Ryu (Yu Ki-jŏn), Law Professor at Seoul National University, for his outspoken stand in defense of due process of law, and the arrest of the Sŏ brothers and interference in the politics of *Mindan,* the pro-South Korean organization of Koreans in Japan.

20. See Lee Chong-sik, "Korea: Troubles in a Divided State," pp. 25–27; Cole and Lyman, *Korean Development,* pp. 73–75; Ko Chun-sŏk, *Minami Chōsen seijishi,* pp. 325, 335; *Rōnin,* Vol. 1, Nos. 4, 5. For a recent article on the Kim Chi-ha case, see Donald Kirk, "The Bold Words of Kim," in the *New York Times Magazine,* January 7, 1973, pp. 50–52.

21. *Tonga ilbo,* October 15–18, 1971.
22. See the article on "Efficient Distribution of the Profits of Enterprises," in *Tonga ilbo,* December 28, 1972.
23. See the section on the presidency in the revised constitution, Articles 43 through 62, in *Tonga ilbo,* October 27, 1972, p. 6.
24. Civil liberties are covered in Section 2 of the revised constitution, Articles 8 through 34, and the provision about local assemblies is in Article 10 of the Supplementary Articles, in *ibid.*
25. See Park's statement in *Tonga ilbo,* October 27, 1972.

Chronology

August 15, 1945	Japan surrenders and Korea is liberated from 35 years of colonial rule.
September 1945	U.S. forces land in southern Korea to accept Japanese surrender.
December 1945	Moscow Foreign Ministers' Conference decides on four-power trusteeship for Korea.
July 1947	Second U.S.–U.S.S.R. negotiations in Korea fail to reach agreement.
November 1947	United States takes the "Korean question" to the UN.
May 1948	Unilateral elections in southern Korea lead to the establishment of the Republic of Korea on August 15, 1948.
September 1948	Democratic People's Republic of Korea established in northern Korea.
June 25, 1950	Korean Civil War starts.
July 28, 1953	Truce agreement ending hostilities signed.
February 1954	Pres. Syngman Rhee offers South Korean troops to fight in Laos.
January 1958	United States places atomic weapons in South Korea.
April 1960	Syngman Rhee overthrown by student protests against rigged elections.
May 1961	Military coup ends civilian rule in South Korea.
June 1965	R.O.K.–Japan normalization treaty signed.
October 1965	R.O.K. expeditionary force, secretly financed by United States, arrives in Vietnam.
July 4, 1972	Joint declaration by North and South Korea.

October 1972	Martial law declared in South Korea.
January 1968	North Korean commandos attempt to assassinate Pres. Park Chung Hee, and U.S. intelligence ship *Pueblo* seized off Wŏnsan.

Notes on Contributors

Frank Baldwin took his Ph.D. at Columbia University, where he taught Korean history, language, and politics from 1968 to 1972. The recipient of a fellowship from the Foreign Area Fellowship Program and of a Fulbright program postdoctoral fellowship, he lived for several years in Japan and South Korea and traveled widely in Southeast Asia. He has contributed to *The New Republic, Ramparts, Christianity and Crisis,* the *Bulletin of Concerned Asia Scholars,* and the Grolier *Yearbook,* and is currently Executive Editor of *The Japan Interpreter,* a quarterly journal published in Tokyo.

Herbert P. Bix attended Harvard University, earning an M.A. in East Asian studies and a Ph.D. in history and Far Eastern languages. He is Assistant Professor of Japanese History at the University of Massachusetts at Boston. A member of the editorial board of the *Bulletin of Concerned Asia Scholars,* he has published articles in the *China Quarterly* and *The Japan Interpreter,* and was a contributor to *The Indochina Story* and *Remaking Asia: Essays on The American Uses of Power.*

Gerhard Breidenstein studied Protestant theology, German literature, and political science at the Universities of Frankfurt, Heidelberg, and Zurich. He took a doctorate in theology in Christian social ethics at Marburg University. He is the author of *Das Eigentum und seine Verteilung* (Property and Its Distribution). During his three-year tenure as an exchange professor at Yonsei University in Seoul, South Korea, he worked with the Student Christian Movement in South Korea and wrote *Students and Social Justice,* a student handbook published in Korean by the Christian Literature Society, Seoul, in 1971. He has since been engaged in research on North and

South Korea, and has been a contributor to *Internationales Asien-forum.*

Bruce Cumings is a Ph.D. candidate in political science at Columbia University and is writing his dissertation on Korean political movements and American policies in Korea from 1945 to 1947. He is the author of "Political Organization, Nationalism, and Self-Reliance in North Korea," published in *Problems of Communism* (March–April, 1974). He spent 1967 and 1968 in the Peace Corps in Seoul, Korea, and did research in Korea and Japan from 1971 to 1972. During the summer of 1973 he taught Korean politics and American foreign policy in Asia at the University of Washington, Seattle.

Jon Halliday is co-author (with Gavan McCormack) of *Japanese Imperialism Today.* He has written extensively on Korea, and his writings on the subject have been published in French in *Les Temps Modernes* and translated into several other languages. Mr. Halliday is a member of the editorial board of *New Left Review.* His *Political History of Japanese Capitalism* is scheduled for publication shortly in Pantheon's Asia Library.

James B. Palais took his Ph.D. at Harvard, and is an assistant professor in the Department of History and in the Institute for Comparative and Foreign Area Studies at the University of Washington, Seattle. He has recently completed a work tentatively titled *Politics and Policy in Traditional Korea,* and has published articles on Korean historiography in the *Journal of Asian Studies.*

Robert R. Simmons was a Peace Corps volunteer in Liberia from 1963 to 1965, and a lecturer in politics at the Chinese University of Hong Kong during 1969 and 1970. He has contributed to professional periodicals, notably the *Far Eastern Economic Review, Asian Survey,* and *The China Quarterly,* and is the author of *The Strained Alliance: Peking, P'yongyang, Moscow and the Korean Civil War.* He has done research in Hong Kong, Taiwan, South Korea, and Japan, and was awarded a National Defense Education Act fellowship in 1970. He received his doctorate from the University of California at Los Angeles, and is at present an assistant professor of political studies at the University of Guelph in Ontario, Canada.

Bernard Wideman worked as a copyboy for the *New York World-Telegram,* and spent six years in the navy as an officer. After doing graduate work in East Asian Studies at the University of Washington, he received his M.A. in 1969 and began work on a doctorate in history. He lived in South Korea from 1971 to 1973 as a Fulbright Fellow, researching the country's agricultural history. He remained in Seoul until July 1973, working as a stringer for the *Far Eastern Economic Review.* He is currently a free-lance journalist and an itinerant instructor for the University of Maryland in East Asia.

Index